W9-ABI-683

WITHDRAWN

Organization Theory

A Structural and
Behavioral Analysis

The Irwin Series in Management and
The Behavioral Sciences

Consulting Editors
L. L. CUMMINGS and E. KIRBY WARREN

Advisory Editor
JOHN F. MEE

Organization Theory

A Structural and Behavioral Analysis

WILLIAM G. SCOTT, D.B.A.

Professor of Management and Organization

and

TERENCE R. MITCHELL, Ph.D.

*Associate Professor of Management and Organization
and of Psychology*

Both of the University of Washington

LIBRARY
BRYAN COLLEGE
DAYTON, TN. 37321

 Third Edition 1976

RICHARD D. IRWIN, INC. Homewood, Illinois 60430
Irwin-Dorsey International Arundel, Sussex BN18 9AB
Irwin-Dorsey Limited Georgetown, Ontario L7G 4B3

56349

© RICHARD D. IRWIN, INC., 1967, 1972, and 1976

All rights reserved. No part of this publication may be
reproduced, stored in a retrieval system, or transmitted,
in any form or by any means, electronic, mechanical,
photocopying, recording, or otherwise, without the prior
written permission of the publisher.

Third Edition

First Printing, January 1976

ISBN 0-256-01788-3
Library of Congress Catalog Card No. 75–26101
Printed in the United States of America

Preface

Since 1962 four versions of this book have appeared. This present edition is a revision of *Organizaton Theory: A Structural and Behavioral Analysis for Management,* published in 1972. This revision was required by significant changes in the fields of organizational behavior and theory.

Changes have arisen from several sources. First, research in the behavioral sciences continues to produce new data. Textbooks must account for this information to reflect the current "state of the arts" in the field. Second, significant conceptual changes have occurred. For example, the contingency approach to management has grown into a major landmark in organization theory in the last four years. Thus, we felt that our book had to be revised so that these theoretical developments could be included. Third, important value changes appeared. Perhaps these changes are simply the rediscovery of old values, or perhaps they represent new directions. Nevertheless, we thought it necessary to assert unequivocally the rational motivation of management as the basic underlying attitude of management practice in organizing activities.

Therefore, the purposes of this revision are to extend and up-date the research base in this book; to incorporate major theoretical developments; and to suggest changing emphasis in values that have an impact on organizations.

These objectives are translated into concrete subjects in this volume. The first chapter stresses the importance of rationality as a management value, and proceeds to demonstrate this by a discussion of it as the historical foundation upon which present organization theory and organizing practice rests. Part I of the book covers the familiar territory of classical, neoclassical, and systems theory. However, modern organization theory has been "modernized" by including an analysis and critique of the contingency approach. Also, organization theory has to be cast into the context of "complex organizations." Such organizations are indeed the major arenas of contemporary management practice: recognition of this point is essential.

Part II treats the management of individuals and groups in organizations. Without doubt these behavioral areas concentrate most on the psychological and sociopsychological research that is pertinent to organization theory. Because of the vast amount of on-going research in these areas, they provide a fruitful source of scientific data used in this revision.

Various organization processes are discussed in Part III. Most of the chapters dealing with processes have been revised in light of current research data available. However, an important qualitative change has also been made. Recently more emphasis is being given to questions of effectiveness in organizational performance. The chapters on communication and technology both raise the effectiveness issue and consider the issue of *assessing* performance of various processes in organization. We believe, given the economic and energy problems that confront this nation, the momentum of issues that deal with appraising performance in organization will increase as a response to the rational imperative of organization itself.

The concepts and technologies of organizational change are the subjects of Part IV. Considered in this part are a number of current techniques for the modification and control of behavior, techniques that are usually stamped as the means for "changing organizations." Included are discussions of participation, MBO, goal setting, job enrichment, and organizational development. Attention is also given to the function of training.

Part V is a consolidation of material treated in the previous edition in three chapters. Organizational research is still the focus of this part of the book. Questions of theory construction, research design, and research implementation are discussed as are ethical considerations in experimentation.

The book concludes with a chapter on organizational governance in which alternative models are postulated.

Every effort was made in this edition to create a book that is at once an accurate, current reflection of the present status of organization theory and also a useful learning medium for the student.

In the process of revision we had one problem with language. It is that in English there is no pronoun that unambiguously refers to men and women together. At times we used the awkward locutions of "his or hers" and "he or she." Other times we used plural forms such as individuals or humans. In some situations we retained reference to the masculine pronoun to denote all people collectively. Such usage should not be interpreted as a sign of belittlement or ignorance of the important managerial roles played by women.

Our special thanks and appreciation go to the reviewers of our book: Robert L. Mathis, Western Kentucky University; David P. Gilfillan, Northwestern University; L. L. Cummings. University of Wisconsin; and E. Kirby Warren, Columbia University. Their assistance in the pre- and postrevision phases of this book contributed immeasurably to our efforts.

January 1976   WILLIAM G. SCOTT
                                                      TERENCE R. MITCHELL

Contents

Governance: *Substantive Due Process. Procedural Due Process.* Models of Organization Governance: *The Constitutional Model. The Autocratic Model. The Democratic Model. The Federal and Totalitarian Models.*

chapter 1

Managerial Rationality and Organization Theory

Two centuries of evolution were required to create modern organizations. These marvels of our industrial age are vast, complex, technologically advanced management systems. They are designed to use resources rationally in order to serve the material needs of society. The industrial revolution, beginning around 1790, brought a widening application of science through technology to industrial development. In its wake came enormous political, social, and economic changes in Europe and America and more recently in Asia and "Third World" countries. Mass production and mass consumption expanded affluence. Government became ever more concentrated and powerful. New forms of financing based upon sound central banking emerged. The search for energy and natural resources intensified. The rural peasantry gave way to the urban prolitariate. And a protected and institutionalized labor movement developed as a basic reality of labor-management relations.

In the midst of all this change, organization was the source of order and stability during turbulent times. However, industrialization and world power in the 20th century created special organizational puzzles. The solution of these puzzles was predicated upon a distinctive managerial world view which transcended nationality and organizational missions. *This world view is rationality.* Rationality is the common denominator of managerial behavior. It is a universal language that is understood across the boundaries of institutions and nations. Rationality is the fundamental imperative of management's organizing activities.

1

THE MANAGERIAL MODEL OF RATIONALITY

Organization theory cannot be understood apart from the concept of rationality. "The purpose of [organizational] design," as Carzo and Yanouzas point out, "is to provide conditions which facilitate optimal attainment of objectives."[1] Thus, rationality has guided those who think about, design, and manage organizations in their theories and actions. Rationality, therefore, must be the starting point for any treatment of organization theory.

Rationality has acquired a particular meaning in modern technological societies. It has specific *organizational* reference to the management of resources through the application of science, engineering, and economics. The kind of rationality that concerns us here is peculiar to Western industrial societies. As such it has characteristics that distinguish it from rational forms found in nonindustrialized civilizations.

Rationality applies to many situations. Whenever a human problem involves the minimization of means to accomplish an end, rationality is at service. However, the ends which people hope to realize will determine the *form* that a particular rational system will take. For example, a theological system will tell us the best route to go if we have salvation as an objective.

One of the chief goals of Western societies during this century, and substantially prior to it, has been to increase productivity. Therefore rationality applied to this goal had to rely upon the values of "practical" sciences such as engineering and economics because financial, material, and technological resources are required for the production of wealth. While they are vastly different, engineering and economics share one similar aim which is to minimize the resources used to accomplish an objective. In this sense, economics and engineering both seek *efficiency*.

The Ubiquity of Efficiency

The desire for efficiency is so widespread in industrial nations that it is virtually synonymous with rationality itself. Consequently managerial rationality is indistinguishable from efficiency, ratio of $E = O/I$. The aim of management, and the reason for being of organization theory, is to increase the value of E by adjusting the relative values of outputs

---

[1] Rocco Carzo, Jr. and John N. Yanouzas, *Formal Organization* (Homewood, Ill.: Irwin-Dorsey Press, 1967), p. 325.

over inputs. This requirement of theory and practice in organizing applies to every management level in every function.

While definitional refinements may be argued over, the major implications of the efficiency concept must be accepted otherwise there is no way to appraise what managers do in modern organizations. Managerial rationality within this framework is a form of *technical rationality* whose aim is clear cut. It is to find better and better techniques to improve organizational performance. This quest is universal among managers. Hospital administrators seek technical rationality as much as automobile manufacturers. Japanese industrialists are moved toward efficiency in similar ways as are their German counterparts. But technical rationality for its own sake is not sufficient. It is a means to an end.

The Goals of Technical Rationality[2]

The general purpose of technical rationality is to enlarge the production of wealth in terms of real goods and services. Nowhere has this been more evident than in traditional American values, rooted in the dream that "good" life was available to everyone. No small part of that dream has been the possibility of a relatively high degree of material well-being.

Out of this dream grew the belief that material *growth* was absolutely essential to the vitality of national life, and that the material *abundance* obtained from such growth was limitless. They were the necessary preconditions for the "good" life. Whatever else Americans sought could be found by them in the consumption of products and services. Material well-being was to an appreciable extent, the basis of *consensus* in the social order.

There has not been much difference between how Americans defined their individual aims and what managers tried to accomplish within organizations. Management practices generally have been consistent with the expectations of Americans at large. But as technology was carried by modern organization into nearly every corner of society, a new—and extremely important—premise was added to the American concept of the "good" life. This premise did not eradicate customary visions of individual happiness. Rather, it converted them to organizational terms.

---

[2] This section is drawn from William G. Scott, "Organization Theory: A Reassessment," *Academy of Management Journal*, June 1974, pp. 244–45, and David K. Hart and William G. Scott, "The Organizational Imperative," *Administration and Society*, November 1975.

The premise is that the dream of individual welfare could *only* be realized through modern organization and its managerial apparatus.

Traditional values survived, but their connotation changed. Thus, growth was a "good," but the most important growth was organizational. Abundance was a "good," but it was an organizationally produced abundance. Consensus was a "good," but the crucial consensus was among potentially conflicting interest groups within organizations. For the most part these organizationally derived "goods" did benefit individuals. By managing organizational resources efficiently, growth resulted in material abundance, that when distributed in a reasonably equitable way, promoted positive attitudes about the utility of organization, the legitimacy of management, and the general community of interest in expanding productivity. Thus, the values of growth, abundance, and consensus were the ends toward which the technical rationality of management was directed to achieve.

Thus we have seen a rise to preeminence of modern organizations as the chief social invention of our period. We have also seen a shift in traditional American values to suitable organizational terms. The values of growth, abundance, and consensus pursued by technically rational managers now supply the standards for acceptable social, economic, and technological policies. They define the nature of the problems to be solved by management theory and practice. They determine the kind of research that is conducted in management and allied fields. They influence the curricula studied in courses of learning in management. They shape the content of communication between managers of organizations and the people served by them. Finally they affect the expectations that people have of organizations and management. As such these values are the ruling forces of organization theory and management practice. Whether or not they will remain so is a matter for speculation.

But what is certain, is that organization theory has grown in power and complexity in order to serve the technical needs of management. However, despite the avalanche of research and theory about organization, its fundamentals are remarkably straightforeward. There is no better place to begin than with the rudimentary "idea" of organization.

THE "IDEA" OF ORGANIZATION

One of the popular books in 1970 was Toffler's *Future Shock*.[3] The wide appeal of this book rests on its dramatization of change, largely

---

[3] Alvin Toffler, *Future Shock* (New York: Random House, Inc., 1970).

those technological changes which appear to be unhinging our institutions and our psyches. Toffler's hypothesis is that change is upon us so fast that we are personally and organizationally unable to adapt to it or cope with it. So it seems to many, and particularly to those living on Manhattan Island, that all is coming unglued. Hence "future shock."

Toffler's theme is compelling. It may even be true. But Toffler is obsessed by discontinuity. His book is an endless recital of actual and potential disruptions to the order and pattern of society. Notably lacking in this work is the recognition by the author of continuities which stabilize, moderate, and give meaning to change.

An example in Toffler's book, which has direct bearing on our inquiry, is his discussion of organization. Chapter 7 is titled "Organization: The Coming Ad-Hocracy." In this chapter Toffler predicts a "brand new" way of organizing that presumably is consistent with an organization's need to adapt in a rapidly changing environment. His point is that organizations will no longer be predicated on permanence; but instead, they will be temporary structures that will come and go depending on the exigencies of the environment.

What is missing in Toffler's discussion is the recognition that the *idea* of organization persists even though the *form* of organization changes. This idea gives meaning and continuity to changes in organization design and theory. The idea of organization is simple enough. Two primary forces act in all formal organizations—the division of labor and the centralization of authority. Not only are these forces primary; they are also *opposing*. The division of labor fragments organizations. It splits organizations into smaller and smaller particles of specialization. Centralization of authority (which must be understood as coordination) coalesces. It combines the fragmented parts so that they move as a whole toward the achievement of organizational objectives.

One of the chief problems in organization theory is the balancing of these forces. As specialization increases, so improvement in the techniques of coordination must increase. The need for rationality in organizations imposes, almost as an "iron law," the imperative of preserving the balance between the division of labor and coordination. The result is an organizational design—a model of structure and behavior, if you wish—that is consistent with the necessity for technical rationality.

Weber noted this over 50 years ago when he identified the division of labor and the centralization of authority as the preeminent characteristics of his "ideal type" model of bureaucracy. Later, in the 1930s, two American scholars, Mooney and Reiley, in discussing the principles of organization, selected coordination as the "mother principle" but only because they understood that without it organizations could not function rationally in face of continuous specialization.[4] Finally, two contemporary authors, Lawrence and Lorsch, in their work *Organization and Environment: Managing Differentiation and Integration,* see integration and differentiation as the main elements needing reconciliation in organizations.[5] These elements reduce to coordination and specialization, respectively.

The idea of organization which we have sketched here provides the basis for conceptual continuity. The rationality in organizations sought by theoreticians and practitioners rests upon the interplay between the forces of specialization and coordination in organizations. And so while we see, historically, changes in organizational design, the search remains for better (more rational) combinations of techniques to reconcile these forces.

Thus the ways that managers organize has occupied the attention of numerous scholars in Europe and America during the last 75 years. A brief review of some of their major contributions illustrates the historical importance of rationality in organization theory.

THE DEVELOPMENT OF ORGANIZATION THEORY IN EUROPE

Technical rationality in organization theory received its first systematic treatment early in this century by Max Weber (1864–1920). He believed that rationality required the design and construction of an administrative system through the division of labor and the coordination of activities based on an exact study of kinds of human relationships necessitated for expanding productivity. To Weber, rationality was an organizational imperative brought about by man's technological genius. This imperative was satisfied, Weber thought, by bureaucracy.

Weber's Bureaucracy

Weber was sensitive to the changes in Europe at the turn of the century. He was convinced that the old organizational forms, that were

---

[4] James D. Mooney and Alan C. Reiley, *Onward Industry* (New York: Harper & Bros., 1931), chapters 1 through 5.

[5] P. R. Lawrence and J. W. Lorsch, *Organization and Environment: Managing Differentiation and Integration* (Boston: Division of Research, Harvard Business School, 1967).

appropriate for a feudal and agricultural society were outmoded. As these ancient forms declined, a new organizational system arose in their place. Weber called this system bureaucracy.[6] His analysis of it is a landmark contribution in organization theory.[7]

Although Weber studied mainly government agencies to discover the essential elements of his theory of organization, it became apparent that the principal characteristics of bureaucracy could be found in any organization, public or private, as long as they had the following features:

1. Large size as measured by the number of people employed.
2. The bulk of those employed were semiskilled and unskilled.
3. Relatively simple mass-production technology.
4. Relatively simple product or output.

Since most of the dominant organizations of Weber's time did share these features, bureaucracy, as a method of organizational analysis, seemed to be widely applicable.

Bureaucratic Characteristics. Weber saw such organizations as having five major qualities which set them apart from organizations in the past.

1. Division of Labor. This characteristic certainly was not new to organizations. But in application, bureaucratic organizations carried the division of labor to an intensive degree of refinement. Tasks were broken down into the most minute particles of specialization so that even the rawest industrial worker (or government employee) could master his or her task in the shortest time with a minimum of skill. One outcome of specialization was to make human labor interchangeable. Such interchangeability contributed greatly to organizational efficiency.

2. Centralization of Authority. Weber realized that the fragmentation of work compounded the problem of coordination. As he analyzed it, bureaucracies solve this problem through the centralization of authority. This is simply the progressive concentration of control over subordinate units in successively higher levels of authority in an organization's vertical command structure.

3. Rational Program of Personnel Administration. Employees of a bureaucracy are selected by comparing the objective standards set by

---

[6] Bureaucracy literally means government by bureau or agency.

[7] Max Weber, "The Essentials of Bureaucratic Organization: An Ideal-Type Construction," in Robert K. Merton et al., eds., *A Reader in Bureaucracy* (Glencoe, Ill.: The Free Press, 1952), pp. 18–27.

the officials of the organization for adequate performance of a job with the qualifications of the applicant for the job. Thus, a conscious effort is made to match the employee with the job. This characteristic differs significantly from past practices when often criteria for selection to organizations was based upon family or class. In principle, bureaucracies should not be influenced in their selection procedures by extraneous factors such as sex, race, ethnic origins, religion, or social class. The guiding criteria should be simply how well the potential employee is suited by way of education, training, knowledge, and skill to perform a function in an organization.

4. Rules and Regulations. Bureaucracies, according to Weber, have well-articulated policies which are impersonally and uniformly applied by officials both to employees within the organization and to the clients outside the organization.

5. Written Records. For the sake of organizational continuity and for the purpose of achieving uniformity of action bureaucracies maintain elaborate records which detail the transactions of the organization.

So these are the characteristics which the organizations studied by Weber exhibited. However, he had more in mind in the analysis of these organizations than to present merely a description of some of their major activities. Based upon these characteristics Weber proposed an analytical model of organizations.

Weber's Ideal Type Analysis

Weber's ideal type analysis is a methodological tool which can be used for assessing the performance of organizations.[8] It is a conceptual method by which the actual performance of an organization may be compared with an idealized model. The purpose of making such a comparison is to note variations between actual performance and the optimal performance set forth by the prescriptions of the model. Thus, the ideal type methodology provides an analytical method for studying organizations. Additionally such a method identifies activities which may need correction if the performance of the organization shows substantial deviation from the criteria of the ideal type.

For example, if an organization is having coordination problems, its policy makers should look at how the centralization of authority is being carried out. Or if the organization is experiencing difficulty with em-

---

[8] For an extensive discussion of ideal type analysis, see Rolf E. Rogers, *Max Weber's Ideal Type Theory* (New York: Philosophical Library, 1969).

ployee efficiency, administrators should examine its personnel program. Maybe people are not selected rationally, or perhaps they are being placed incorrectly.

So the ideal type is an analytical instrument to assist policy makers in adjusting their organizations to conform with rational standards. To Weber bureaucracy was the most rational system of organization available. Consequently managers who sought efficiency and optimal organization performance would be forced to use bureaucratic structures. While Weber clearly saw the dehumanizing potential of bureaucracy, he believed that it was an irresistible organizational wave. Just how correct Weber was in this opinion we will see later. For the present we turn to his French contemporary, Henri Fayol.

Fayol's Functionalism

Henri Fayol (1841–1925) was a mining engineer who rose above his highly specialized education to enjoy a distinguished career in French industry. In 1916 at the age of 75, he published his work, *Administration Industrielle et Générale,* in which he proposed a theory of management based upon his reflections about his years of active participation in business. This book was not widely known in America until an English version appeared in 1949 under the title *General and Industrial Administration.*[9]

Fayol's contribution is to a broad theory of management as the title of the book suggests. In fact, if Fayol is remembered it will be for his statement of the functional breakdown of administrative activities into the elements of planning, organizing, command, coordination, and control. There is hardly a modern "principles of management" textbook which does not rely upon this, or some minor variation of this system of classification.

We leave to others the job of explaining Fayol's ideas about general management theory. Our interest is with his explicit observations of organizational matters. Fayol did not have an organization theory in the sense that we attribute one to Weber. Fayol's statements about organizations are descriptive and fragmentary. His views are not integrated into a model for organizational analysis. Rather, Fayol is mostly concerned with giving advice about the best way to organize an enterprise.

Nevertheless Fayol identified the same elements of organizations as

---

[9] Henri Fayol, *General and Industrial Administration* (London: Sir Isaac Pitman & Sons, 1949).

did Weber. For example, his chapter 4, titled "The General Principles of Management," pertains almost exclusively to organization theory. Under such topics as the division of work, authority and responsibility, discipline, unity of command, and unity of direction, Fayol stresses the importance of specialization and coordination in much the same way Weber. did.

Fayol also emphasizes the rational selection of employees. One of the major subsections in his chapter on organizing is devoted to the need for scientific selection, placement, and training. This discussion is certainly one in spirit with Weber's concept of a rational program of personnel administration. Finally, the bureaucratic requirements of record keeping and uniformity in the application of policy is discussed by Fayol under the topic of control.

From a practitioner's standpoint, Fayol covers all the bureaucratic bases identified by Weber. These authors had essentially similar views of the nature of technical rationality in organization. These views were shared by Lyndall Urwick, and were published in 1937 in a truly remarkable book.

Urwick's Technique

The Institute of Public Administration at Columbia University published in 1937 a collection of articles on management under the title, *Papers in the Science of Administration.*[10] Urwick's papers in this volume were originally prepared in 1932 and 1933. They are "Organization as a Technical Problem," and "The Function of Administration."

By the time of Urwick's contributions the fundamentals of classic organization theory had been established on both sides of the Atlantic. While Urwick did not draw upon Weber for his analysis, he was influenced most certainly by Fayol and also by two Americans, Mooney and Reiley, whose book, *Onward Industry,* had just been published (1931).[11]

So firmly established was classical theory, that Urwick saw management's problem as the *application* of organization (bureaucratic) principles to operating situations in various enterprises. In short, he took the technical rationality of classic organization theory as given. The issue at his point in time was the development of *techniques* for application. Urwick's lead paragraph to his paper, "Organization as a Technical Problem" is especially revealing in this respect. He says:

---

[10] Luther Gulick and Lyndall Urwick, *Papers in the Science of Administration* (New York: Institute of Public Administration, 1937).

[11] Mooney and Reiley, *Onward Industry.*

It is the general thesis of this paper that there are principles which can be arrived at inductively from the study of human experience of organization, which should govern arrangements for human association of any kind. These principles can be studied as a technical question, irrespective of the purpose of the enterprise, the personnel composing it, or any constitutional, political or social theory underlying its creation. They are concerned with the method of subdividing and allocating to individuals all the various activities, duties and responsibilities essential to the purpose contemplated, the correlation of these activities and the continuous control of the work of individuals so as to secure the most economical and the most effective realization of purpose.[12]

In our opinion there is no clearer statement of the nature and aims of classic organization theory than this one. All the conceptual ingredients are contained in it. We find emphasis upon rationality and efficiency; we find the acknowledgement of the three essential elements of bureaucratic theory—specialization, coordination, and rational assignment of duties; and we find also the unequivocal position that the principles of classical organization theory are *universal*. Urwick's work represents, from the European side, the maturity classic theory had achieved by the early 1930s.

It is an anticlimax to note that Urwick dealt with the same organizational elements as Weber and Fayol. He identified coordination, hierarchy of authority, and specialization. He added to the analysis span of control, line-staff relationships, and functionalism. But the real message in Urwick's work is his call for improved techniques for the application of the rational principles of organization to ongoing enterprises. As Urwick said in 1933, "Rapid growth in scientific knowledge has placed unprecedented strain on man's powers of organization. The effects of that strain are just becoming apparent. Knowledge of an interest in the techniques of organization and in its basic principle of co-ordination, are as yet feeble."[13]

THE DEVELOPMENT OF ORGANIZATION THEORY IN AMERICA

Around 1900, a remarkable movement appeared in America, under the leadership of Frederick W. Taylor. Taylor was not an organization theorist. The ideas which he proposed reflected the need in America

---

[12] Lyndall Urwick, "Organization as a Technical Problem," in Gulick and Urwick, *Papers in the Science of Administration,* p. 49.

[13] Ibid., p. 88.

for a newly qualified manager who was capable of coping with emergent technological complexity and worker motivation. Taylor thought the answers lay in scientific management.

The Scientific Management Movement

The scientific management pioneers[14] sought to solve the riddle of a twofold problem. How does a society increase industrial productivity? How does the management of organizations within that society increase the level of worker motivation? The scientific management pioneers viewed the solutions to these problems much as a simultaneous equation. Taking care of one problem would automatically take care of the other. Scientific management's solution to the equation was keyed upon "mutuality of interests." If somehow workers' legitimate requirements for higher wages, and management's legitimate requirements for higher profits could be simultaneously achieved, many of the major difficulties besetting an industrializing nation would dissolve.

The goals that the scientific management pioneers hoped to achieve in management reform were truly global. Their vision of management in the new industrial society was very extensive. The aim of scientific management was in many respects utopian. The pioneers sought ultimately to create a society in which all who were employed in the industrial enterprise would find their private interests harmoniously allied in the *ceaseless quest for greater productivity*. This could not be accomplished without a deep commitment to the application of technical rationality to all aspects or industrial life, and this included organization.

Within the contents of this "grand idea," were the glimmerings of an organization theory. As early as 1895, Taylor wrote in a paper for the American Society of Mechanical Engineers[15] about the importance of separating planning from "doing." What Taylor hoped to form by this proposal was a distinction between "line" and "staff" work. He believed that for efficient performance, these functions had to be divided organizationally into separate specializations.

Also Taylor suggested functionalization as a system of organization.[16] This technique would, according to Taylor, make maximum use of the

---

[14] Frederick W. Taylor, Frank and Lillian Gilbreth, Morris L. Cooke, Henry L. Gantt, and Harrington Emerson.

[15] Frederick W. Taylor, "A Piece-Rate System," *Transactions* ASME, vol. 16 (1895), pp. 856–903.

[16] Frederick W. Taylor, *Shop Management* (New York: Harper & Bros. 1911), pp. 94–102.

specialized talents of individuals in the organization. Taylor applied the concept of functionalization to foremen. Since it violated the unity of command doctrine, functional foremanship never was widely accepted. However, this concept later became the foundation for the idea of functional staff authority which is a most important element in organization theory.

In addition to Taylor, one may certainly find in works of Henry Gantt and Lillian Gilbreth embryonic ideas about organization theory. One might say that these people, as well as the others who compose the company of scientific management pioneers, had a vision of organization not too dissimilar from that of Weber or of Fayol. In other words, if the scientific management pioneers had thought about it at all, it is likely that they would have been comfortable with the principal tenets of bureaucratic theory. However, being very practical types, and being concerned mainly with the development of techniques, the scientific management pioneers never actually gave themselves to the abstract exercise of theory building. Nevertheless their singleminded dedication to technical rationality and efficiency make them one in spirit with the great European contributors to organization theory.

"THE PRINCIPLES OF ORGANIZATION"

Under the title, *Onward Industry*,[17] Mooney and Reiley published in 1931 the first full-scale version of classical organization theory to appear in the United States. Framed as "principles," the theory that they proposed was very similar to Weber's theory of bureaucracy. But while Weber saw the division of labor as the primal moving force in organization, Mooney and Reiley identified coordination as the preeminent element of organizational design and theory building.

Thus, Mooney and Reiley wrote that coordination is the "mother principle," and that all the other principles of organization were in its service to achieve efficient performance of the specialized, but interdependent, organizational functions. With this as their initial premise, Mooney and Reiley went on logically and directly to show how the scalar principle, the functional principle, the principle of unity of command, and the line-and-staff principle related to the larger pattern of organization theory.

Later we discuss the details of Mooney's and Reiley's contributions.

---

[17] Mooney and Reiley, *Onward Industry*. Later revised by Mooney and published under the title *The Principles of Organization* (New York: Harper & Bros., 1947).

For now it is sufficient to say that their theory was entirely consistent with the norms of technical rationality which were evident in the works of Weber, Fayol, and Urwick. Indeed even in terms of the details of their analysis, the Mooney and Reiley approach differs slightly from that of their European counterparts. So it is correct to say that their work, accompanied by the work of the aforementioned Europeans, constitutes the body of doctrine commonly called classical organization theory.

However, the development of American theory did not rest simply with expansion of Mooney's and Reiley's initial analysis. While there has been considerable refinement of classical organization theory over the last 40 years, other theoretical developments have also been felt.

THE HUMAN RELATIONS AND ORGANIZATIONAL HUMANISM MOVEMENTS

The human relations movement began with research at the Hawthorne plant of Western Electric in 1927. Its principal investigators were F. J. Roethlisberger and William J. Dickson.[18] The primary contribution of this movement was to add new dimensions of theory, concepts, and research methodology to the study of organizations through the behavioral sciences.

The Human Relationists

The human relations movement brought to the study of organizations an orientation different than the one used by the classical theorists. These latter believe that rational economic assumptions about human motivation were sufficient to explain work behavior within organizations. Through the use of such behavioral sciences as sociology and psychology, the Hawthorne researchers demonstrated otherwise. They showed that human motivation was a complex affair that could only be understood by behaviorally slanted investigations. These researchers argued convincingly that the best designed organization, according to classical principles, may be confounded by small groups and by individuals who did not behave the way that the rational prescriptions of economic man said they should behave.

The human relationists did not have what could be legitimately called

---

[18] See F. J. Roethlisberger and William J. Dickson, *Management and the Worker* (Cambridge, Mass.: Harvard University Press, 1939).

through the application of the behavioral sciences appears in such areas as:

1. Organization structure.
2. Systems and contingency management.
3. Group dynamics.
4. Individual motivation.
5. Organizational processes.
6. Organizational change.
7. Research methodology.

Fittingly enough we begin our analysis where the classicists began—with an examination of formal structure. However, we end our book with a discussion of issues that they could not possibly have foreseen.

part I

Complex Organizations

omplex organizations are wonderful testimonies to human inventiveness. They are large, technologically based systems, with delicately balanced internal and external interrelationships, professionally managed within a control structure designed to achieve satisfactory performance of their technical, economic, and human components. Complex organizations are the answer to a complex social need. This need is for *systems of order* that respond rationally to the dynamics of the industrial age.

Technological Dynamics

The causes underlying American industrialization are many-faceted. Industrialization required new power sources, a program of mechanization, the growth of capital-good industries (machine tools and precision instruments), financial sources, and an innovative spirit behind the development of processes, materials, and methods. The economic history of the United States records how these factors and others combined to change America from a handicraft and rural economy to a major industrial nation geared to the economics of mass production.

In its initial stages of growth an emerging industrial nation is confronted by the major difficulty of developing technological expertise. Current American industrial might testifies to the effective use of science and engineering by management for the solution of technical problems. While in early stages of development, management drew primarily from the "nonhuman" sciences, presently the behavioral sciences are being called upon for improved utilization of people in organizations. So we discover historically, a continuous reliance upon applied science by management to supply techniques for more effective use of all resources.

Standardization and the division of labor are two key aspects of the application of technology to organization. Uniformity in performance is necessary for complex, large-scale enterprises. It applies to policy matters throughout the organization as well as to interchangeability of parts and equipment. Thus, standardization pertains to administrative activities as well as to the physical uniformity of parts and equipment required by mass-production techniques.

Closely allied to standardization is the division of labor. It is the breaking down of work into smaller elements or parts so that an employee may "specialize" in a simplified task rather than "generalize" in a fairly complicated job. The division of labor process has often been called the rationalization of work. No matter where the division of labor occurs—at the operative or administrative levels of the organization—all the subdivided functions are closely interrelated in terms of the total operation of the system. The result is that coordination of the parts is a paramount organizational need.

However, the growing effectiveness of mass production is only one side of the coin. The other side is the necessity for mass consumption which would not be possible without technological advances in distribution. Adam Smith observed that the division of labor was limited by the extent of the market; that is, the division of labor could be carried just as far as the available market for goods allowed. Market extension was of course created by the dramatic growth of transportation and communication networks. Technology was the chief element in the upward spiral of production and consumption.

Interrelational Dynamics

One important result of the technological dynamics that made industrialization possible was increased interdependency in complex organizations. It is popular to say that these organizations defy effective management. However such an assertion is more dramatic than true. Granted human and technical limitations prevent ideal performance in complex organizations. Nevertheless the primary objective of management research, science, and theory has been to augment management with technologies to enable it to cope with internal problems arising from organizational size and complexity. Once the boundaries of a system are defined, a formidable array of techniques are available to solve the puzzles within. Bureaucratic structure, specialized staff groups, management information systems, computerization, model building and simulation, behavioral modification and control are powerful tools to aid management in coping with internal problems of complexity.

However, there is another level of complexity, concerned with "interface" relationships, that stimulates little else than a great deal of rhetoric. These problems of complexity are no less real, but the difficulties they present defy rational, technical solutions. They stem from two sources: the magnitude of the systems involved and the inapplicability of current problem-solving techniques to the puzzles posed. These sources are so closely linked that we treat them as one.

As long as the boundaries of a system can be clearly defined, such as the logistics of supply in the U.S. Air Force, conventional technologies can solve technical problems within the structure of this enormously complex system. However conventional puzzle-solving techniques break down when the boundaries defining a system are relaxed and attention is given to relationships among interdependent organizations. Consider, for example, the highly interrelated system of food production, distribution, and consumption. It includes growers, processors, retail distributors, consumers, trade associations, and governmental regulatory agencies. Food is even an instrument of foreign diplomacy. The slightest disturbance in the system can set off shock waves far greater than its initial magnitude in terms of shortages, price increases, and generally uncivil behavior. Anyone who doubts this need only recall the threatened beef shortage during the summer of 1973.

We should not be misled. The techniques that are effective for managing internal organizational complexity are inadequate for managing interdependent relationships among autonomous organizations. While there are many reasons why this is true, one of the most important is that "interface" relationships involve political behavior that the current models of technical rationality do not comprehend.

Professional Management Dynamics

Professional managers are the human intermediaries responsible for moving technology and complex organizations toward objectives. Management, in this capacity, has to conform to three behavioral rules imposed by the organizational imperative.[1] These rules are rationality, stewardship, and pragmatism. We have already discussed rationality at length. But as a reminder the behavioral rule of rationality requires that management act in accordance with the principle of efficiency. The rule of stewardship is a by-product of rationality, and it is also a result of the separation of ownership from the control of organizations.

Clearly, one function of stewardship is to ensure that the resources and the wealth of an organization are conserved and increased. This tradition goes back to biblical times. It is currently believed that the best way to discharge this responsibility is by acting rationally. However, the development of the corporate system has given a new dimension to the concept of stewardship.

Corporate enterprise is a means for marshaling and distributing a business' resources. Among the many advantages of the corporate device, the most obvious is the opportunity it affords to amass large amounts of capital. The method of capitalization involves the relatively simple expedient of selling stock to private and institutional buyers.

The use of the corporation device is extensive. Not only have many businesses elected this method of financial organization but also the largest companies in America have assumed the corporate form. The private corporation is a characteristic landmark in American business.

The corporation is often stereotyped as a large organization engaged in a wide range of production and distribution operations. The modern corporation frequently is depicted as an ever-changing, complex apparatus serving the material needs of customers, owners, employees, and the public. These stereotypes are misleading because corporations are of many sizes, shapes, and types, each pursuing objectives with varying degrees of success.

All corporations possess the peculiar legal characteristic which admits the possibility for the *separation of ownership from control*. That is, the control over a property may be detached from the ownership of the property. The separation of business ownership from control and the numerical increase of people in managerial functions contributed to the management professionalization trend. A masterly analysis entitled, *The Modern Corporation and Private Property*, was like a manifesto for the professionalization of management.[2] It was the contention of its authors,

---

[1] David K. Hart and William G. Scott, "The Organizational Imperative," *Administration and Society*, November 1975.

[2] Adolf A. Berle, Jr. and Gardiner C. Means, *The Modern Corporation and Private Property* (New York: The Macmillan Co., 1932).

Berle and Means, that the modern corporation upset the traditional theory of property in which ownership and control of property were inseparable qualities. In many companies the stockholders, while legal owners, were for all practical purposes deprived of the privilege of control over their property.

This peculiar by-product of the corporation device placed management in a stewardship position. Stewardship can be visualized as management running a corporation to achieve the objectives of the owners. Basically, management acts as an intermediary between the corporation on one hand and the owners of the corporation on the other hand. This concept of stewardship resembles a "pure theory." The corporate structure allows management to operate fairly independently of the controls traditionally associated with the ownership of property. This situation often places management in a good position to exploit an organization's resources for ends not necessarily owner oriented.

It became apparent, as time passed, that the rule of stewardship was not confined to business corporations. This rule applied with equal force to all managers—in public agencies, labor unions, nonprofit organizations, and so on. The manager has to run the affairs of any organization in the interest of "others." It does not make a particle of difference who these "others" are: the public, stockholders of corporations, members of labor unions, students, participants in cooperatives, or patients, doctors, and nurses in hospitals.

Stewardship has had one important consequence for organization theory. It legitimizes the structure of authority. If management is to fulfill its obligations, those who are subordinate in a structure of authority (and this includes everyone except the chief executive) must be obedient to commands. Thus the managers are not only stewards of the interests of those outside the organization, they are also the stewards of the combined destinies of their subordinates.

Given the heavy obligations imposed by the rules of rationality and stewardship, how should a manager behave under this burden? The answer, which took years to evolve, and is now only partially understood, is that within complex organizations professional management must behave pragmatically. The rule of pragmatism requires no more than expedient behavior. Pragmatic behavior permits the organization flexibility in changing environments, since practical circumstances continually impose different contingencies on managers. Beyond this, the rule of pragmatism has no other moral content.

Control Structure Dynamics

Since the rule of pragmatism focuses on organizational problems of short duration, it is in some way incompatible with the managerial need for planning which is the anticipation of events yet unrealized. But the requirements of complex organizations have forced a reconciliation between the two. The future must be taken into account in order to set goals, map strategies, make budgets, establish policies, and allocate resources.

As more investment capital is committed to plant and equipment, as the time span between the beginning and the end of projects lengthens, as a more specialized work force is hired, and as the flexibility of an organization diminishes in relation to its fixed resources, planning activities expand dramatically. The problem is how to adjust the planning function to the rule of pragmatism. Certain practices have evolved to this end. First, guesswork must be eliminated. This necessitates the development and application of a technology of forecasting. As many external "variables" as possible must be controlled, since they influence the future direction of the organization in uncertain ways. Second, the possibility that the aberrant individual behavior will unpredictably alter the course of planned future events must be reduced. This practice has two subconditions. Behavior in the planning process itself must be controlled, by making it a collective activity. Group performance is more visible and predictable than individual performance. Then the implementation of plans must be controlled by means that are understandable to all involved. All of this places a premium on the design of organizational control systems.

Control, therefore, is the way that planning and pragmatism are reconciled. That control and planning are conceptual counterparts is a frequently cited, but little appreciated, management adage. However, it is certain that as planning grows, controlling also grows into structures of authority, power, and influence that are essential to the life of the complex organization.

Strategies for Coping with Complexity

Beyond any one other thing, coping with organizational complexity requires a managerial attitude or frame of mind that is consistent with the rule or rationality. Foremost is the necessity that management consider every problem of complexity as a technical puzzle to be solved.

Some such problems are directly accessible to management science.[3] For example, the development and marketing of the first commercial computer in the 1950s greatly accelerated technological advancement of the information processing field. From the computer emerged a large number of planning, controlling, and decision-making models that allowed management to solve certain organization puzzles of a size never experienced before; e.g., the use of PERT in the Polaris missile project.

The computer made similation of decision-making alternatives possible. It permitted the evolution of sophisticated accounting and reporting systems that gave management access to more information than ever before. Finally the computer, along with various kinds of "software" improved organizational communication creating more efficient flows of information to management decision-making centers. An entire field called "management information systems" developed from this application of computer technology.

As dramatic and powerful as management science techniques are, some aspects of complexity elude them. They fall into two general categories: problems of organization structure and problems of human behavior. Nevertheless, following the necessary attitude of rationality, both of these problem areas have to be defined by management as technical puzzles so that they can be solved with technical means.

This was no major obstacle in the instance of organization, since the precedent had been established by Max Weber. Bureaucracy is essentially a technical solution to organizational situations that require the coordination of masses of people, tasks, and resources. Albeit crude, the elementary notions of the division of labor and the hierarchy of authority are adequate enough to solve a wide range of organizational puzzles.

However, the important fact about this approach to organization is that it defined a basic management attitude which serves well in designing more elaborate structures. Organization is not mystical. The right to rule organizations does not come from God. Merit is determined by performance, not fidelity to a person. In short, organizations do not exceed the everyday experience of humans. Rather, organization is a technical puzzle capable of managerial manipulation in order to achieve objectives sought.

Human behavior is a different matter. There have been few prece-

---

[3] There are many management science techniques most of which are quantitative: included are operations systems analysis, operations research, industrial dynamics, PERT, PPBS, and linear programming.

dents, until recently, for treating behavior as a technical puzzle. In fact there are strong norms against it. The reduction of human behavior to a technical problem seems to some to violate human dignity, privacy, and freedom. Yet management has tenaciously sought technical solutions to human problems as we will see in Part II. Management's romance with the applied behavioral sciences cannot be interpreted in any other way. Management has hoped to find in science specific engineering-type techniques for the design and use of behavioral control programs. This is consistent with the rational mentality. If management allows behavior to be left outside the boundaries of technical puzzle solving, then there is no way it can cope effectively with this important element of organizational complexity.

This part is devoted to some of the important landmarks on the route of solving problems of organizational complexity. We examine organizational structure from the theoretical viewpoints of classical, neoclassical, systems, and contingency models. Following this is a general assessment of the status of organization theory.

chapter 2

Classical and Neoclassical Organization Theories

Bureaucracy, or the formal organization as it is also called, is the subject matter of classical and neoclassical theories. They are the first systematic attempts to deal analytically with the problems of organizational complexity. The classical theory is concerned mainly with structural relationships in organization, while neoclassical theory is devoted to the effects of human behavior in organizations as well as structure itself.

Organizing is one of the essential functions of management. Of all these functions it has received the most theoretical attention over the years with the possible exception of controlling. The reason, of course, is the emergence of complex organizations as dominant social institutions.

Traditionally, organization is viewed as a rational vehicle for accomplishing goals and objectives. While this view is probably true enough, it tends to obscure the inner workings and internal purposes of organization itself. For example, the automobile is a form of organization designed to accomplish transportation objectives, and so are trains and airplanes. This statement, however, tells nothing of their internal organizational arrangements. And further, it says nothing of the behavioral forms people adopt when riding in a car versus riding in a plane. This analogy can be applied to human organizations. Both the so-called formal and informal organizations are vehicles for accomplishing objectives. But their internal arrangements and purposes are different, and so the behavioral patterns of people in them are often different.

Another and more fruitful way of treating organization is as a mechanism having the ultimate purpose of offsetting those forces which undermine human collaboration. In this sense, the organization trend can be thought of as a product of an intensifying need for control. Organization tends to lessen the significance of individual behavior which deviates from values the organization has established as worthwhile. Further, organization increases stability in human relationships by reducing uncertainty regarding the nature of the system's structure and the human roles inherent in it. As a corollary to this point, organization enhances the predictability of human action because it limits the number of behavioral alternatives available to an individual. As Presthus points out, "Organization is defined as a system of structural interpersonal relations . . . individuals are differentiated in terms of authority, status, and role with the result that personal interaction is prescribed. . . . Anticipated reactions tend to occur, while ambiguity and spontaneity are decreased."[1]

In addition, organization has built-in safeguards. Besides prescribing acceptable behavior forms for those who elect to submit to it, organization is also able to offset the influence of human action which transcends its established patterns.

Few segments of society have engaged in organizing more actively than business. The reason is clear. Business depends on what organization offers. Business needs a system of rational relationships among functions; it needs stability and predictability in terms of the internal and external activities in which it engages. Business also needs harmonious relationships among the people and processes which make it up. Put another way, a business organization has to be relatively free from the destructive tendencies that may result from divergent internal interests.

However, the domain of organization has not stayed the exclusive province of business. The needs for effective organizing exist in other large-scale enterprises like government, the military, labor unions, hospitals, and universities. They present organizational puzzles to solve which have certain common denominators in spite of institutional differences. Various theories of organization have been, and are being, developed to solve these puzzles. This chapter and the next take up three theories of organization which have had considerable influence on management thought and practice. They are the classical, neoclassical, and

---

[1] Robert V. Presthus, "Toward a Theory of Organizational Behavior," *Administrative Science Quarterly*, June 1958, p. 50. Regulation and predictability of human behavior are matters of degree varying with different types of organizations in something of a continuum. At one extreme are bureaucratic-type organizations with tight bonds of regulation. At the other extreme are informal organizations, with relatively loose bonds of regulation.

modern. Each of these theories is fairly distinct, but at the same time they are not unrelated. They share a common devotion to rational norms.

THE CLASSICAL THEORY

The classical theory of organization deals almost exclusively with the *anatomy* of the formal organization. It has a rich heritage that includes—as we mentioned in Chapter 1—such famous scholars as Weber, Fayol, Mooney and Reiley, Gulick and Urwick. Today, just about every textbook in management, on the introductory level, contains a treatment of organization following the lead set by these people and others who pioneered the development of formal theory.

Defining the Formal Organization

Finding a definition of the formal organization is not a difficult job. Four elements of a definition reappear consistently in management literature. Briefly explained, they are:

1. A System of Coordinated Activities. This element underscores the fact that all organizations are composed of parts and relationships. The "parts" of the organization refer to activities or functions performed. The formal system appears when these activities are geared into a logical relationship.

2. A Group of People. Although an organization can be charted on paper it needs people to bring it to life. Personnel are required to implement the activities.

3. Cooperation toward a Goal. Cooperation is strictly a human phenomenon. In normal behavior cooperation is always purposeful. Therefore, organizations must have objectives to lend purpose to the actions of people performing functions.

4. Authority and Leadership. Organizations are structured on superior-subordinate relationships. As a result, authority is a universal element in all formal organizations. Leadership, however, is a personal quality which prompts willing collaborative effort toward a goal.

A comprehensive operational definition is obtained by combining these elements. *A formal organization is a system of coordinated activities of a group of people working cooperatively toward a common goal under authority and leadership.*

A definition does little to illuminate the rationale of formal organizations. For this reason we examine the classical foundations and pillars of the theory.

The Foundations of Classic Theory

While points of emphasis may differ among classical theorists, they agree upon the elements that compose the foundations of theory. Few writers have articulated these elements as clearly as Mooney and Reiley. Therefore, we base our discussion of the foundations upon their analysis.[2]

We have previously noted the importance of coordination to Mooney's and Reiley's theory of organization. Indeed, coordination, in their eyes, constitutes the essence of organization. They say that "Coordination . . . is the orderly arrangement of group effort, to provide unity of action in the pursuit of a common purpose."[3]

Coordination, and hence organization, rests upon four conditions that must exist before any "unity of action" is possible. These conditions are:

1. *Authority*—either democratically or autocratically derived—may be viewed as the supreme source of government for any particular organization. Examples of such coordinating bodies are boards of directors in business, the joint chiefs of staff in the military, executive officers of national labor unions, the boards of regents of universities, and so on.

2. *Mutual service* constitutes the social legitimacy of the organization. Every organization exists because it serves a social purpose; that is, the organization is recognized by public policy or informal public agreement as having a useful function to perform in a society. Thus organizations exist because they are viewed by society as providing it with net positive utilities.

3. *Doctrine*, in simplest terms, is the definition of the organization's objectives. Such objectives set out the basis of an organization's legitimacy; and they provide as well the source of various actions which are used to secure internal organizational coordination. Hence, the policies, procedures, rules, and regulations of organizations are based upon statements of doctrine.

4. *Discipline* is behavioral regulation imposed either by command or self-restraint. Discipline is necessary to coordination to ensure organizationally predictable, reliable, and supportive behavior from the people participating in it. Discipline is derived negatively from coercion, or positively from willing personal commitment to organizational objectives.

---

[2] James D. Mooney, *The Principles of Organization* (New York: Harper & Bros., 1947), chapter 2. This edition, upon which we base our references, brought out under the sole authorship of Mooney, is identical in all major respects to the 1931 edition, called *Onward Industry,* that Reiley coauthored.

[3] Ibid., p. 5.

These foundations are broad enough to apply to any organization regardless of structural design and form. However, the classicists had in mind a particular application. They believed that there is "one best way" of achieving organizational coordination. So upon these foundations they built the pillars of classical theory. *The pillars of formal theory are the classical prescriptions of techniques for the rational structuring of organizations.*

Pillars of the Formal Organization Theory

1. *Division of labor* is without doubt the most important of the four pillars of classical organization theory. Division of labor has been mentioned as the chief reason for coordination.

As a human organization grows work must be divided, otherwise one job would be so inclusive that its performance would be impossible. So work is broken down, usually along lines as natural as possible, to provide clear areas of specialization. The reason for dividing work is to improve the technical performance of the organization.

Division of labor, or specialization, is not restricted to production-line jobs but extends to all the functions at the highest levels in the organization. Figure 2–1 illustrates the growth of managerial specialization in a business organization.

Stage I in this figure represents a one-person operation in which the owner is performing all three organic business functions—creation, distribution, and finance. As business gets better the boss hires another employee to perform the function of production, as shown in Stage II. Stage III represents a phase in growth where all three organic business functions are performed by specialists, with the boss acting as coordinator. Finally, Stage IV demonstrates a further division of labor within the organic functions themselves.

This demonstration of organizational growth is a classical treatment, showing how a business will expand by specializing the organic business functions. This approach to the division of labor in classical organization theory is frequently treated under such topical headings as departmentation, or functional evolution and devolution.

The division of labor is so basic to classic organization theory and coordination that the other three pillars derive from it as corollaries. For example, vertical and horizontal growth, through the scalar and functional processes, requires specialization and departmentalization of functions. Structure is dependent on the direction which specialization

FIGURE 2–1
The Growth of Managerial Specialization

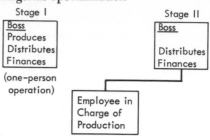

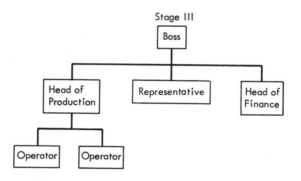

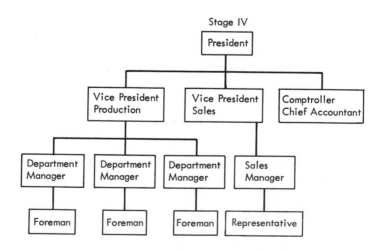

of activities travels during organization development. Finally, span of control problems results from the number of specialized functions, and specialists, under the jurisdiction of a manager.

2. The *scalar and functional processes* deal with the organization's vertical and horizontal growth, respectively. The scalar process refers to the growth of the chain of command which results in levels added to the organizational structure. The scalar process is accomplished through the dynamics of the *delegation* of authority and responsibility. Figure 2–2 demonstrates this process.

FIGURE 2–2
The Scalar Process

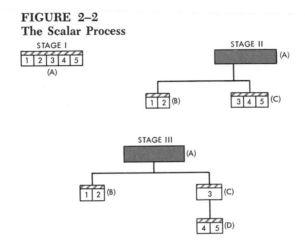

Assume that "A" starts out with specific job responsibilities 1, 2, 3, 4, and 5 in Stage I. In Stage II, "A" delegates to "B" responsibilities 1 and 2, and to "C" responsibilities 3, 4, and 5. "C" in Stage III delegates to "D" job responsibilities 4 and 5. The shaded areas indicate ultimate authority and responsibility which cannot be delegated. Thus, while at Stages II and III, "A" does not have the *specific* job responsibilities had formerly, he or she still is accountable to a higher authority for the performance of those to whom these tasks have been delegated. Through the scalar process, then, the organization has grown vertically from one to three levels.

The functional process is the method by which the organization grows horizontally. The dynamics of the functional process is the *division of labor*. This process is illustrated in Figure 2–3.

In Stage I, "A" is supervising "B" who has job responsibilities 1, 2, 3, and 4. On the authority of "A" in Stage II, three of the jobs formerly

FIGURE 2–3
The Functional Process

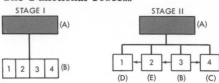

performed by "B" are split off into separate functional jurisdictions *on the same level* under "C," "D," and "E." Thus, the second level in this diagram has moved from one position in Stage I to four positions in Stage II via the division of labor along functional lines.

The basic processes of organizational growth described here are applicable to the line as well as to the emergence of the staff functions in an organization.

3. *Structure* is a term which is applied to the relationships that exist among the various activities performed in an organization. The purpose of structure is to provide an orderly arrangement among functions so that the objectives of the organization can be accomplished effectively. Structure implies system and pattern.

Classical organization theory usually works with two basic structures: the line and the staff. The line organization refers to the primary chain of command which devolves directly from organic functions—creation, finance, and distribution of a good or service. The staff organization is frequently treated as advisory and facilitative functions for the line. Also, such activities as committees and liaison functions fall quite readily into the purview of structural considerations.

The functional structure also falls within the scope of our deliberations. It certainly is "classical" since Frederick W. Taylor introduced the concept about 60 years ago. However, we postpone considering it until later in the chapter because of the special problem of analysis it poses.

4. The *span of control* concept relates to the number of subordinates a manager can effectively supervise. Graicunas has been credited with first making the point that there are numerical limitations to the subordinates one person can control.[4] In a more recent statement on this subject, Brech points out that "span" refers to ". . . the number of persons, themselves carrying managerial and supervisory responsibilities, for

---

[4] V. A. Graicunas, "Relationships in Organization," *Papers on the Science of Administration* (New York: Columbia University, 1937).

whom the senior manager retains his over-embracing responsibility of direction and planning, co-ordination, motivation and control."[5]

Regardless of interpretation, the span concept directs attention to the complexity of human and functional interrelationships in an organization. The number of interrelationships among individuals grows at a rapid pace when people are added to a department. Further, span of control has significance also in terms of the shape of the organization that evolves through growth. Wide span yields a flat structure; short span results in a tall structure, Figure 2–4.

FIGURE 2–4
Span of Control and Organizational Structure

TALL STRUCTURE	FLAT STRUCTURE
X	X
X X	X X X X X X X X X X
X X X X	
XX XX XX XX	
Levels....4	Levels....2
Span 2	Span 10

The Classical Principles of Organization

The pillars of classical organization theory have certain logical counterparts that may be expressed as principles. More accurately, these "principles" might be described as biases in the classical model. But, in any event, the principles most often cited are (*a*) the scalar principle, (*b*) the functional principle, and (*c*) the line-staff principle. These principles, however, are subordinated to the overriding coordinative principle which identifies *unity of action* as the proper rational goal of formal organization structure. Thus by following the specifications of the subordinate principles, the fulfillment of the rational imperatives of coordination are most effectively accomplished.

---

[5] E. F. L. Brech, *Organization* (London: Longmans Green and Co., 1957), p. 78. Udy talks of the span of control in terms of the relation of technological processes to formal organization structure. He suggests that size alone does not explain span. Span is related to technological process and the span of attention. Span of attention is equal to the total number of tasks, plus the maximum number of specialized operations ever performed at once, plus a factor "C" which is 1 or 0 depending on whether combined effort is ever present (1) or always absent (0) in the entire process. If the span of attention is greater than five then any technological process will tend to be performed on three or more levels of authority. If the span of attention is equal to or less than five then technological processes will tend to be performed on fewer than three levels. Stanley H. Udy, Jr., "The Structure of Authority in Non-Industrial Production Organizations," *American Journal of Sociology*, May 1959, pp. 582–84.

The first of the subordinate principles, the scalar principle, prescribes that the following conditions be met by organizations as they grow vertically.

1.   Unity of command.
2.   A determinate hierarchy.

Coordination is facilitated in the view of the classical model if a person is accountable to one and only one superior in a hierarchical system where positional authority is unambiguously defined.

The scalar principle is fully revealed in the functional principle. Through the division of work, the number of specialized activities increases in an organization. The effects of growth are felt in the form of an enlarged number of functions in an organization's line structure and in the emergence of staff activities. The span of control concept is addressed to the former event and the line-staff principle is addressed to the latter event.

Although never stated in the form of a "principle" the span of control is expressed in classic theory as a *bias toward close supervision*. The classicists believed that coordination would be most effectively accomplished when a superior is responsible for a restricted number of subordinates (usually four to six on managerial levels). Such a circumstance presupposes that delegation of authority is kept to a minimum, such that the amount of discretion exercised by subordinates is greatly limited. As we said above, the consequence of short spans are tall organization structures; that is, organizations with many levels of supervision.

Another outcome of the functional process is the emergence of staff in the organization structure. The staff actually represents the specialization process carried to a high degree of refinement. The staff causes particular problems for classical organization theory. Since staff groups concentrate people with considerable expertise (like cost accountants or quality control experts) in narrow areas of specialization, they pose the real possibility of violating the unity of command principle. Because of their considerable knowledge within their area of specialization they can potentially exercise command authority over the line. Such a situation could put the line executive, usually a foreman, in the position of dual accountability: accountable to the immediate superior in the line, and to the staff specialist as well.

The classicists believed that this relationship is detrimental to achieving coordination, and hence, unity of action. Therefore, the line-staff principle stated by Mooney and Reiley specified that the staff should function in just an advisory and facilitative capacity, but without command authority over the line.

Many criticisms of classical theory have been made, and we will discuss some of them later. However, March's and Simon's indictments of classical theory are useful to mention as a bridge to our discussion of neoclassical theory. They say: "First, in general there is a tendency to view the employee as an inert instrument performing the tasks assigned. Second, there is a tendency to view personnel as a given rather than as a variable in the system."[6] Because of its focus on the anatomy of organization, the classical school overlooks the significance of human behavior on the formal structure. In summary, the classical theory has a *mechanistic* approach to organizations.

It would not be fair to say that the classical school is unaware of the human problems which affect organization. They simply do not treat in any systematic way the interplay of individual personality, small groups, intraorganizational conflict, and the decision process in their conception of the formal structure. Additionally, the classical school has failed to incorporate in its theory the contributions of the behavioral sciences as part of a comprehensive explanation of human behavior in the organization. Neoclassical theory evolved from efforts to overcome these deficiencies.

THE NEOCLASSICAL CRITIQUE

The neoclassical school has been associated in the past with the human relations movement. Recently, it has identified more broadly with those who recognize and attempt to compensate for shortcomings in classical doctrine. An excellent example of this approach is Pfiffner's and Sherwood's concept of *organizational overlays*.[7] Building upon the anatomical structure of classical formal theory, Pfiffner and Sherwood add the various modifications which result from such behavioral overlays as small (informal) groups, decision and power systems not synonymous with formal authority systems, informal communication channels circumventing prescribed channels, and so on.

The neoclassicist school does not have a theory as do the classicists. Rather, the neoclassical school includes all those who protest against

---

[6] James G. March and Herbert A. Simon, *Organizations* (New York: John Wiley & Sons, Inc., 1958), p. 29.

[7] John M. Pfiffner and Frank P. Sherwood, *Administrative Organization* (Englewood Cliffs, N.J.: Prentice-Hall, Inc., 1960).

the inadequacies of the classical model of organizational behavior, but are not willing to divorce themselves completely from it. Thus an analysis of this movement must treat the neoclassical critique of the pillars of classical theory.

The Division of Labor

Since the division of labor is basic to organization, it is not surprising to find that it has elicited a vast amount of comment. Around the turn of the century Émile Durkheim had this to say about the division of labor in industrial organizations:

> The division of labor presumes that the worker, far from being hemmed in by his task, does not lose sight of his collaborators, that he acts upon them, and reacts to them. He is, then, not a machine who repeats his movements without knowing their meaning, but he knows that they tend, in some way, towards an end that he conceives more or less distinctly. He feels he is serving something. For that, he need not embrace vast portions of the social horizon; it is sufficient that he perceive enough of it to understand that his actions have an aim beyond themselves.[8]

This is a strange statement of support for the division of labor. It comes from a man whose work on suicide produced the concept of *anomie.*

Anomie is a French word meaning "lack of rules." However, its implications go far beyond this literal translation. *Anomie* means a lack of self-discipline resulting from an individual's inability to identify with the rule-laden activities. *Anomie* also means an "aloneness among many." While the division of labor causes great functional interdependency among work activities, it also depersonalizes these activities so that the individual finds little meaning in them, much less meaning in the complex organizational system which supports advanced forms of specialization.

While Durkheim did not see *anomie* applying to the division of labor, others have, and it has provided an endless source of research and speculation. Long before organization theory absorbed the interest of behavioral scientists, early studies were made of accidents, fatigue, monotony, and boredom which were caused by specialization.[9] Later, the research emphasis shifted from the physiological consequences of

---

[8] Émile Durkheim, *The Division of Labor in Society* (New York: The Free Press of Glencoe, 1947), p. 373.

[9] Hugo Munsterberg, *Psychology and Industrial Efficiency* (Boston: Houghton Mifflin Co., 1913).

the division of labor to the problems of alienation which resulted from workers' inability to find satisfaction in their jobs. Thus, one dimension of neoclassical criticism has been directed against the depersonalization of work *at the operative level.*

Another dimension of neoclassical comment on the division of labor concerns the problems of interdependency. The division of labor intensifies employee interdependency. Each segment of a production line is intimately connected by the functions which come before and after it. Similarly, executives at high levels in an organization are dependent on the activities and decisions of other executives.

The conditions of interdependency caused by the division of labor create strains and tensions. Whyte, in his study, *Human Relations in the Restaurant Business,* describes the stresses which result from the interrelations of cooks, countermen, waitresses, and kitchen runners.[10] Nor are these tensions restricted to operative-level employees. The division of labor which results in the emergence of staff organizations creates its own special frictions with the line executives.

Because the division of labor gives rise to many different, and often quite narrow, areas of specialization, the need for managerial coordination becomes paramount. Coordination requires a higher order of motivational ability to get people to work cooperatively. This is not particularly easy. At the operative level, for example, it is extremely difficult to convince assembly-line workers that their function contributes significantly to the final product. The routine and boring nature of the job stifles enthusiasm and inhibits any latent desire these employees might have to see "the big picture" and the relation of their job to it.

Specialization breeds a somewhat different problem at executive levels. The division of labor tends to segment the organization into enclaves of authority and influence. Often executives regard them as their own special empires which have first call on their attention and abilities. Efforts to weld areas of executive specialization into a consistent, synchronized part of the overall organization are frequently resisted by managers as an undue infringement on their jurisdictions. Thus, specialization brings about jealously guarded functional segments in the organization.

These few comments about the effects of the division of labor should be contrasted with the classical idea that the reason for specialization is efficiency. It cannot be doubted that mass-production techniques have brought about a high order of industrial output. But at the same time,

---

[10] William F. Whyte, *Human Relations in the Restaurant Business* (New York: McGraw-Hill Book Company, 1948).

the ultimate of efficiency hoped for from the division of labor has been denied because of the human problems it has created.

In order to overcome these problems, a number of recommendations have been made by the neoclassical school. For example, participation in the decision-making process has been offered to get the operative employee "involved" in the job and interested in the company. Participation allows employees to have some say in their destiny in an often all-too-impersonal environment.

Job enlargement is another approach which has gained currency as an offset to the ill effects of the division of labor. Job enlargement proposes to reverse the specialization pattern. Organizations, particularly manufacturing companies, are advised to reintegrate highly specialized tasks into larger job blocks requiring greater skills of the employees and presumably providing them with greater satisfactions.

For the younger executive, bottom-up management, or the establishment of junior boards, is another management device. Bottom-up management gives the junior executive a chance to participate in top-management decisions. This allows the younger person to see the company from a top-level perspective and acts as a counterbalance to specialization in one activity.[11] These and other techniques for offsetting the human disadvantages of the division of labor are discussed throughout this book.

The Scalar and Functional Processes

This pillar causes problems associated with the delegation of authority and responsibility. The implicit assumption of classical theory about the delegation process is that the *capacity* (ability) of the individual is equated to the *authority* (command and task) of the function. This "ideal" is not altogether as unrealistic as it seems at first. The classic theory has a "classic" solution for cases where individual capacities are greater than their authority and less than their authority.

Case 1. Capacity Exceeds Authority. The obvious solution is promotion or transfer to functions with responsibilities commensurate with the ability of the individual.

Case 2. Capacity Less Than Authority. There are several alternatives in this case which include demotion, or discharge in extreme circum-

---

[11] For further discussion of this subject, see William B. Given, *Bottom-Up Management* (New York: Harper & Bros., 1949).

stances. Also, in some situations deficiencies in individual capacities may be overcome by training.

Thus, classic theory assumes that authority *tends* to equal the capacity of people actually performing organizational functions. The catalyst of this tendency is the *rational program of personnel administration,* which stems directly from bureaucratic theory.

Neoclassicists reject the classical position on delegation on two levels. First, they feel it is not instrumentally possible to gain a *real* feel for individual capacity so that an adequate match can be made between individual ability and lines of organizational career opportunities. Beyond this, neoclassicists would severely criticize the state of personnel appraisal methods which often determine the degree of success a person will achieve in an organization.

The classicist counters these points by arguing that while the present "state of the arts" is crude, managers are improving selection, placement, promotion, and planning techniques. In other words, there is nothing *in principle* which prevents establishing and maintaining long-run equalized relationships between capacity-authority. If the issue is merely one of technique, it can be improved to whatever arbitrary level of perfection management chooses.

This brings us to the second level of criticism. The neoclassicists maintain that it is not possible in principle to establish the sought for relations between capacity and authority. This is because the logic of formal relationships is not the only logic prevailing in human organizations.

Systems of power, influence, and decision are present in organizations which operate according to a logic of their own and thereby do not correspond to those systems prescribed by the formal structure. They may be capable, therefore, of perpetuating imbalances between capacity and authority. This is an example of what Pfiffner and Sherwood are talking about when they analyze the organizational modifications resulting from power and decision overlays. Capacity and authority imbalances cannot be accounted for within the logic of formal organization theory.

Structure

Structure provides endless opportunities for neoclassical criticism. The general theme is that human behavior disrupts the best laid organizational plans and thwarts the cleanness of the logical relationships founded in the classical structure. The neoclassical analysis of structure centers on frictions which appear internal to the organization among people performing different functions.

Line and staff relations constitute a problem much discussed in this respect. Many organizations have difficulty keeping the line and staff working together harmoniously. Line-staff frictions have numerous causes. Dalton, in an early study of line-staff relationships, isolated five which he feels are most important.[12]

First, the basic differences in duties carried on by line and staff executives can be a cause for friction among them. The staff executive usually lives in a technical world and speaks a technical language. The line executive is more of a "generalist," having specific job duties to perform but also occupied by problems of leadership and motivation.

Second, Dalton found marked distinctions between the line and the staff executives on the counts of age and education. Overall the staff executive was younger and, as might be expected, better educated than the line executive.

Third, as a matter of attitude, staff personnel constantly felt they had to justify their existence.

Fourth, the line executives felt the staff was trying to undermine their authority by expansion into areas thought by line managers to be properly in their jurisdiction.

And fifth, the staff had a feeling it was "under the thumb" of the line organization in the sense that promotion could come only through the approval of influential line managers.

Dalton does not wish to generalize these findings to all industrial situations. However, they certainly contain some universal ingredients of conflict. In many ways staff executives are not prepared for what they meet in day-to-day organizational operations. They are trained to enter a world of logical relationships and to carry out precise functions. Instead, their freedom to act logically is limited by the people with whom they must work. It appears that the most successful staff executives are those who enlist the support of powerful line officers.

Further, traditional management thinking points out clear-cut divisions in line and staff roles. Theoretically, line work ends in a finished product or service which is distributed to consumers. Staff work ends in paper; i.e., reports. In some organizations, however, it is difficult to see a black-and-white distinction between line and staff work. Under

---

[12] Melville Dalton, "Conflicts between Staff and Line Managerial Officers," *American Sociological Review*, June 1950, 342–51.

such circumstances, members of a staff organization feel their contribution is an integral part of the finished product. Indeed, this may be the case, particularly in large, technologically complex organizations.

Also, it seems that the logic of structure is against the staff executive. Typically, the staff organization is a flat type of structure while the line is tall. Reflection on this point inevitably leads staff executives to conclude that no matter how good they are there are fewer places for them to be promoted in the staff as compared to the line. The plusher, lucrative jobs are more plentiful in the tall-type line organization. But, again, the emphasis for line management is weighted toward administrative, generalist skills rather than technical specialties. This perhaps is a partial explanation for the rather large numbers of engineers, accountants, and the like, who, after taking their first degree in a specialty, are back in graduate school working for an M.B.A. in "management." They found they could progress just so far in their specialty. Advancement, as many of them see it, rests on their ability to assume broader administrative responsibilities.

The structural difficulties of line-staff relationships raises other problems discussed by Pfiffner and Sherwood under the functional overlay. We observed earlier that the concept of the functional organization was introduced by Frederick W. Taylor. He proposed it as a way of making better use of foreman specialization.

Taylor noted that many foremen had abilities and specialties which were not used to their fullest extent. His solution to this waste of supervisory talent was to employ the foreman as overseer of those who were working in his area of specialty as well as overseer of those who fell within the administrative scope of his department. Thus, under functional foremanship the foreman would have dual responsibilities. He had functional responsibility for a certain specialized activity of operatives in another department; and he had general administrative responsibility for all the operatives in his own department regardless of the specialized jobs they performed.

To illustrate, let us imagine a furniture manufacturing company making four lines—traditional, modern, French provincial, and colonial. Let us suppose that in producing each line four activities (similar in each line) are performed—cutting, shaping, assembling, and finishing. Lastly, assume that the supervisor in charge of the traditional line is a cutting specialist; the supervisor over modern is a shaping expert; the French provincial supervisor is an assembly expert; and the colonial supervisor is a specialist in finishing. To meet the objectives of the func-

FIGURE 2–5
The Functional Organization

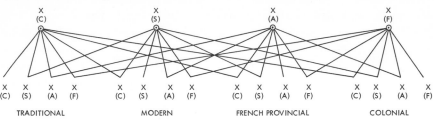

tional organization, a system of relationships as shown in Figure 2–5 is required.

This cumbersome arrangement was not accepted by industry in the form Taylor recommended.[13] But functional foremanship was the genesis of the concept of *functional staff authority*. A technical staff organization is delegated functional authority within a limited area of jurisdiction over a specialized area of line operations. For example, the foreman must be concerned with quality. However, in order to ensure the maintenance of quality many manufacturers establish quality control staff departments with authority over this functional area. In a very real sense the staff can exercise line authority over the foreman to guarantee that the department is run in conformity to the quality standards the staff sets up and administers. The example of the quality control staff applies equally well to other technical staff jurisdictions in a large manufacturing company.

The obvious difficulty created by the functional concept is that it violates one of the most sacred classic principles—the unity of command. But no amount of rationalization on the part of classicists regarding the line origins of functional authority ever will circumvent the fact that where it exists a set of behavioral transactions are introduced among managers which are not encompassed in the classical model.

Span of Control

Neoclassicists react in two directions against classic span of control presuppositions. The first line of criticism is aimed at the notion that there is a *determinate* supervisory-subordinate ratio which can be gener-

---

[13] Frederick W. Taylor, *Shop Management* (New York: Harper & Bros., 1911), pp. 94–102.

alized to most administrative situations. Thus, we read about such "ideal" ratios, although less frequently now, as 15 to 25 subordinates for first-level supervision and 5 to 8 subordinates in executive spans.

Critics are quick to point out that merely the mathematically possible relationships among people are the least significant determinate of span. Rather, more importantly, the effectiveness of supervision is determined by four other factors which in combination situationally create "satisfactory or unsatisfactory" spans of control.[14]

1. Individual differences in managerial ability.
2. Effectiveness of organizational communication.
3. Effectiveness of formal control exercised over operations.
4. Organizational philosophy on centralization versus decentralization of authority.

The second direction of neoclassical criticism is more telling than the first. It is against the "close supervision bias" in classic theory. Most classic statements of "ideal" spans imply close supervisory control of subordinates. Four to six executive subordinates is ideal because it enables their superior to supervise them closely. The same can be said about the ratios recommended for first-level supervision.

As we have shown in Figure 2–4, the extent of span determines the shape of the organization. A wide span with a significant delegation of authority generates a flat organization. A narrow span with authority retained centrally results in a tall structure. Now in line with current thinking, backed by a considerable amount of research on the differential effectiveness of leadership styles, neoclassicists stress that ideal spans are those which reduce tight control through delegation of authority creating a decentralized structure. Their argument is for a general or democratic leadership climate reflected by a wide span of control. It has been demonstrated, they claim, that this approach, which permits more individual discretion on the job, produces greater human satisfaction and more efficient accomplishment of organizational goals. So as the classic bias is toward close supervision, the neoclassicists favor loose supervision.

---

[14] These four factors were drawn from the following sources: John M. Pfiffner, "The 'Third Dimension' of Organization," *Personnel*, March 1952, pp. 391–99; Waino W. Suojonen, "The Span of Control—Fact or Fable?" *Advanced Management*, November 1955; and Walter B. Schaffir, "Current Trends in Organization," *Management Review*, March 1954, pp. 145–46. For discussion of an attempt to establish a rational basis for span of control, see Harold Stieglitz, "Optimizing Span of Control," *Management Record*, September 1962, pp. 25–29.

The Trouble with Classical Theory and Neoclassical Criticism

The ultimate test of a good theory is whether or not it works in practice more often than not. Does it serve as a useful guide to action? When this test is applied to classical theory we get ambiguous answers. Sometimes it works; sometimes it does not work. There are two sets of reasons for this confusion. First, classical theory has built-in, logical contradictions. For example, rules are given in formal organizations in order to control behavior. However, as the neoclassicists point out, people frequently seek to get around rules. Therefore, management makes more rules to control "deviant" behavior. This cycle goes on over and over again, resulting in a *rule laden* bureaucracy that is counterproductive to organizational efficiency. As a result of what Mouzelis calls "the dialectic of bureaucracy," the classical model breaks down under the strain of its internal inconsistencies.[15] In practice this means that classical theory is unable to deliver on its promises to management for an altogether rational system of organization. But as they say, "It's good enough for government work." In other words, despite its limitations, classical theory is often applied usefully to solve many organizational problems.

Second, the most important criticism of classical theory is that it is unable to cope with problems of complexity beyond a certain level. This objection must be examined in greater detail. Classical theory is limited in dealing with problems of complexity mainly because of its insistence that coordination is best achieved by being imposed from above. Why is classical theory dominated by this fixation on hierarchical control?

To answer this question, we have to appreciate the character of organization which provided the "foot in reality" for the classical model. In general terms, this organization was big, but not gigantic; it had considerable interrelatedness among functions due to specialization, but it was not enormously complex as a consequence of advanced technology and products; finally, the bulk of the people employed needed a low order of skills, and comparatively few highly trained specialists, engineers, and scientists were necessary.

It is fair to say that these characteristics were evident in the organizations with which the greats of the classical school had direct experience. James Mooney was a vice president of General Motors prior to its post-

---

[15] Nicos P. Mouzelis, *Organization and Bureaucracy* (Chicago: Aldine Publishing Co., 1968), pp. 59–62.

war expansion. Max Weber's orientation was toward the German governmental bureaucracy. And Urwick was an industrial consultant in England. When the works of Henri Fayol became generally available, it was found that he too observed similar formal organizations much alike in size and character as those which provided the reality orientation for the mainstream of German-English-American theory.

The significance of this is that the assumptions of classical theory have to be suspended for the sake of coordination if, empirically, a particular organization falls outside the conceptual limits of the classical model. That is, an organization may be tiny and simple or gigantic and complex. There are numerous examples of how giantism and technological advancement have in concrete circumstances made a mockery of unity of command, idealized line-staff relationships, and close supervision.

Within the limits of the classical model, unity of command, separation of line and staff activities, and close supervision might make some sense, especially since classic orientation was toward work which required a relatively low order of skills. But to impose the same conceptual constraints upon organizations which do not have these characteristics, or are at least not dominated by them, involves costs in coordination breakdown which are not compensated for by the values which unity of command, separation of line and staff work, and close supervision might yield.

The neoclassicists tried to compensate for the limitations of classical theory, modifying it with insights from the behavioral sciences. But always, in their early days and through the 1950s, they worked within the ground rules laid down by classical theory. The human relationists were not attempting to change theory so much as they were trying to make it fit the "realities," as they saw them, of human behavior in organization. It was a heroic effort, but it fell short. One cause was the inadequacy of human relations research for identifying and correcting the weaknesses in classical theory. A second cause stems from the limitations in techniques in applying behavioral programs in organizations. The applied aspects of the behavioral sciences were simply not capable of meeting the demand made upon them by management. Thus, management became disenchanted with the movement, and by 1959 it had largely vanished from the management scene.

However, the difficults of the neoclassicists went beyond merely the shortcomings of their techniques. They had conceptual troubles as well. Being hung up on classical theory, the human relationists were particularly interested in making hierarchy work better. Much of their energy went into using the behavioral sciences to improve superior-subordinate relationships. This accounts for one of the old criticisms that human relations programs were manipulatory. Actually, they were, but in the sense that the people who used them were trapped by their perceptions of the real world as molded by classical theory.

So in general, the neoclassicists wanted to modify organization theory, not transform it revolutionarily. However, by 1960, changes in organization and technology could no longer be ignored. These changes required a reformulation of theory into a new statement that we will discuss in the next chapter.

chapter 3

Modern Organization Theory

Modern organization theory has two basic models that are treated in this chapter—the systems model and the contingency model. The systems model appeared around 1960, and since then it has grown to a dominant position in management thought and practice. Presently, systems models provide the field of management with concepts which affect or may affect major breakthroughs in management practice. These include work being undertaken in: (1) organizational development, (2) organizational behavior, (3) sociotechnical systems, (4) industrial dynamics, (5) operations research, (6) management information systems, and (7) human resource systems. Even the venerable fields of business policy, personnel management, marketing management, and management principles are seeking the scope provided by the systems approach to managing. The contingency model is a relatively recent arrival, but it is a logical extension of the systems approach to complex organizations and adds a dimension missing in early efforts to apply systems thinking.

The distinctive qualities of modern organization theory emerge from its foundations in the biological sciences, its reliance on empirical research data, its interest in interdependencies of all kinds, and its orientation toward environmental interchanges which makes the contingency model essential to its structure of thought. Modern organization theory accepts the systems model as its starting point for the theories, concepts, and methods of analysis necessary for the management of complex orga-

49

nizations.[1] It asks a number of related questions which were considered by the classical and neoclassical theories of organization but not effectively integrated into practical models of complex organizations. The systems model provides an opportunity for integrating answers to the following questions raised by thoughtful managers, namely:

1. What are the strategic parts of the system?
2. What is the nature of their interdependency?
3. What are the main processes in the system that link its parts and permit their adjustment to each other?
4. What are the goals sought by the system?
5. What are the conditions of organizational "health" that should concern management?
6. How do systems interchange with their environments?

Modern organization theory is not a homogeneous body of thought. Each writer and researcher has his special emphasis when he considers the system. One unifying strand in modern organization theory is the effort made to look at human systems in their totality. Wolf stressed, some time ago, the need to view organization as a "system of causality, which determines an organization's character."[2] He emphasized the need to study organizations as a whole and not just parts of the organization in isolation.

Wolf's position is similar to that of other writers currently discussing system theory. For example, Kast and Rosenzweig take this position in their article "General Systems Theory: Applications for Organization and Management."[3] Somewhat more technical, with an emphasis on application is Hare's, *Systems Analysis: A Diagnostic Approach.*[4] Buckley's useful anthology stresses the role of system theory in the behavioral sciences.[5]

---

[1] A distinction has to be made between systems theory and systems analysis. Systems analysis provides a mathematical, computer-based technology that like a taxicab can take you almost anywhere. Systems theory, however, is heavily value oriented and, consequently, concerned with ends. Our concern is with systems theory in this chapter, not systems analysis.

[2] William B. Wolf, "Organizational Constructs: An Approach to Understanding Organization," *Journal of the Academy of Management,* April 1959, p. 7.

[3] Fremont E. Kast and James E. Rosenzweig, "General Systems Theory: Applications for Organization and Management," *Academy of Management Journal,* December 1972, pp. 447–65.

[4] Van Court Hare, Jr., *Systems Analysis: A Diagnostic Approach* (New York: Harcourt, Brace and World, 1967).

[5] Walter Buckley, ed., *Modern Systems Research for the Behavioral Scientist* (Chicago: Aldine Publishing Company, 1968).

The work in modern organization theory is pioneering—which makes its appraisal difficult and its direction obscure. While its future is not clear, one thing is certain. The questions being asked about complex organizations cannot be adequately answered by classical and neoclassical doctrine. Understanding human organization requires a creative synthesis of massive amounts of empirical data, a high order of deductive reasoning, and an appreciation of individual and social values. Accomplishing these objectives and including them in a framework useful to management practice appears to be the goal of modern organization theory.

THE SYSTEMS MODEL

If they did nothing else, the Hawthorne studies emphasized the importance of systems as a means for understanding complex organizations. Lawrence J. Henderson, who was associated with the Hawthorne research group in its early days pointed out, "The interdependence of the variables in a system is one of the widest inductions from experience that we possess; or we may alternatively regard it as the definition of a system."[6] System and the interdependency of parts are interchangeable ideas. It is really quite impossible to understand individual behavior or the activities of small groups apart from the social system in which they interact. A complex organization is a social system; the various discrete segments and functions in it do not behave as isolated elements. All parts affect all other parts. Every action has repercussions throughout the organization because all of its elements are linked.

Henderson has a diagram, shown in Figure 3–1, which by analogy explains the concept of the interdependence of variables in a system. He says, in explanation of this diagram:

> The four rigid bodies A, B, C, and D are fastened to a framework a, b, c, d by the elastic bands 1, 2, 3, 4, and 5. A, B, C, and D are joined one to another by the elastic bands 6, 7, 8, 9, and 10. Here the conditions of statical equilibrium can be worked out mathematically, or determined empirically by introducing spring-balances into the bonds 1, 2, . . . 10, and reading the balances.
>
> Now imagine the point of attachment of 5 on the frame to be moving toward b, all other points of attachment remaining unchanged. What will happen? Consider A. There will be action on A by the path 5,

---

[6] Lawrence J. Henderson, *Pareto's General Sociology* (Cambridge, Mass.: Harvard University Press, 1935), p. 86.

FIGURE 3–1
The Interdependence of Parts in a System

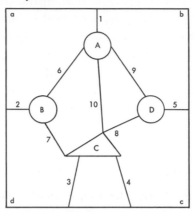

Source: Lawrence J. Henderson, *Pareto's General Sociology* (Cambridge, Mass.: Harvard University Press, 1935), p. 14. Used with permission.

9, by the path 5, 8, 10, and by the path 5, 8, 7, 6. But in each case these actions do not cease at A, just as they do not previously cease at D. The first, for example, continues along the path 10, 8, and so back to 5. If we try to think of all this as cause and effect we must inevitably reach a state of confusion.[7]

The extent of interdependence is multiplied in social systems. Complex organizations have so many puzzles, both human and nonhuman, that the most advanced engineering technologies cannot solve them all. But despite this, management must cope organizationally with problems of complexity. Faced with this critical task the question is, where to begin? Practicing managers typically begin at the level of "systems analysis" because its techniques are useful for solving immediate problems. Theorists and researchers usually start at a more general level and work down to specific cases of application. This is how we shall begin our examination of the systems model and move from abstractions about general theory to the more analytical issues faced by the practitioner.

General System Theory

Science attempts to find order in the complexity of nature. But to deal with such complexity science must first segment and establish boun-

---

[7] Ibid., pp. 13–14.

daries. Thus, there are physical, biological, and behavioral sciences, each trying to understand the organization, and hence the pattern of the events they observe. Ludwig von Bertalanffy noting this about science pursued it to its logical conclusion. He observed that if science is indeed concerned primarily with problems of organization, then it is only reasonable that the most general science of all ought to be a science of organization itself. This was the core idea that eventually became general system theory.[8]

General system theory is devoted to discovering organizational universals. Its aim is the creation of a science of organizational universals—or, a universal science using the elements and processes common to all systems as a starting point. There are several segments or levels of systems which eventually should be integrated as the general system theorist speculates about an inclusive theory of organization. Boulding presents a classification of such levels.[9]

1. The static structure—level of framework, the anatomy of a system.
2. The simple dynamic system—level of clockworks that involve necessary predetermined motions.
3. The cybernetic system—level of the thermostat, simple feedback and control circuit designed to enable a system to maintain a given equilibrium.
4. The open system—level of self-maintaining systems that exhibit the ability of rejuvenation, growth, and reproduction. This level moves toward and includes living organisms.
5. The genetic-societal system—level of cell society, characterized by a division of labor among cells.
6. Animal systems—level of mobility, evidence of goal-directed behavior.
7. Human systems—level of symbol interpretation and idea communication.
8. Social system—level of human organization.
9. Transcendental systems—level of ultimates and absolutes that exhibit systematic structures but are unknowable in essence.

By finding universals common to all levels of organization, this approach to the study of systems has intriguing possibilities for management. A good deal of light could be thrown on social systems if struc-

[8] Ludwig von Bertalanffy, "The History and Status of General Systems Theory," *Academy of Management Journal*, December 1972, pp. 407–26.

[9] Kenneth E. Boulding, "'General System Theory—The Skeleton of a Science," *Management Science*, April 1956, pp. 202–5.

turally analogous elements could be found in simpler systems. It is usually easier to study the less complex and generalize to the more complex. Cybernetic systems, as a case in point, have characteristics which seem to be similar to the feedback, regulation, and control phenomena in human organizations. Thus certain facets of cybernetic models may be generalized to human organizations.

Considerable danger, however, lies in poorly founded analogies. Superficial similarities between the simpler systems and social systems are apparent everywhere. But instinctually based ant societies, for example, do not yield particularly valuable information for understanding rationally conceived human organizations. Care should be taken that analogies used to bridge system levels are not mere devices for literary enrichment. For systems to be analogous, *they must exhibit inherent structural similarities or implicitly identical operational principles.*[10]

Since modern organization theory has its roots in general system theory, it owes it debts for much more than titillating analogies. One such debt is to the biologists who contributed to general system theory.[11] The idea of interpreting human organization as an *organic* system came from them. That social organizations are living systems is a central concept in modern organization theory.[12] This debt is widely recognized in management thought. However, the other debt is less so acknowledged. Early conservationists were among the first system thinkers.[13] These forerunners of the modern ecology movement point out that in nature everything is related to everything else, and that a change in a single element in a natural system will disturb the order of all relationships in that system. The intellectual debt of modern organization theory

---

[10] Roderick Seidenberg, *Post-Historic Man* (Boston: Beacon Press, 1951), p. 136. The fruitful use of the type of analogies spoken of by Seidenberg is evident in the application of thermodynamic principles, particularly the entropy concept, to communication theory. See Claude E. Shannon and Warren Weaver, *The Mathematical Theory of Communication* (Urbana: The University of Illinois Press, 1949). Additionally, the existence of a complete analogy between the operational behavior of thermodynamic systems, electrical communication systems, and biological systems has been noted by U. S. Touloukian, *The Concept of Entropy in Communication, Living Organisms, and Thermodynamics* (Purdue Engineering Experiment Station, Research Bulletin 130 n.d.).

[11] Ludwig von Bertalanffy, *Problems of Life* (London: Watts and Co., 1952).

[12] The contrast between system theory and classical organization theory should be noted in this regard. Classical theory owed its intellectual debt to Newtonian physics for its *mechanistic* perception of organization. The difference of viewing organization as giant "clockworks," compared to viewing it as a living entity, is dramatic.

[13] For example, see Roosevelt's discussion of game parks in Africa. Theodore Roosevelt, *African Game Trails* (New York: Charles Scribner's Sons, 1910), pp. 13–16.

to the ecologists is for the idea of *interdependency* among the living and nonliving parts of a system.

Thus, modern organization theory is founded upon the notions of organic interdependency in social systems. This point should be kept in mind throughout this chapter. But it is especially important for the discussion of organization change treated in a later chapter. However, the way organization theory has been incorporated into a systems framework has to be discussed next.

The System Framework of Modern Organization Theory

Modern organization theory's use of system concepts is far less abstract than what is encountered in general system theory. Henderson's illustration, Figure 3–1, is a convenient place to begin because it can be easily converted to show the basic ideas behind modern organization theory. Figure 3–2 represents a framework for thinking about organization in system terms, using the Henderson model. The large box repre-

FIGURE 3–2
The Framework of System Analysis

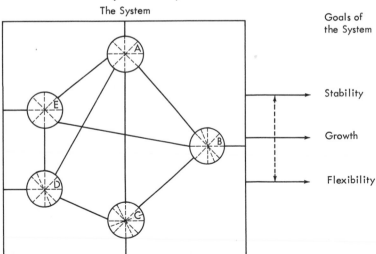

Key:
   1. Circles represent parts of the system.
   2. Broken lines represent intrapart interactions, i.e., individuals with other individuals.
   3. Solid lines represent interpart interaction.
   4. Both the solid and broken lines are the processes which tie the parts of the system together.

sents the total system or, if you will, the organization. The circles stand for the parts in the system, keyed as follows.

A. Individuals.
B. The formal organization.
C. Small groups.
D. The structure of status and role-expectancy systems.
E. The physical environment of the work situation.

The lines both broken and solid indicate linking processes. The key linking processes are:

1. Communication.
2. Balance.
3. Decisions.

The broken lines simply signify intrapart links—that is, linking individuals to individuals, jobs to jobs within the formal organization, and so on.

The solid lines represent interpart links—that is, individuals to the small groups, the formal organization to the systems of status and roles, and so on.

Finally, the system as a whole strives to achieve certain goals. They are:

1. Stability.
2. Growth.
3. Flexibility.

The system can seek any one of these goals, or any combination of them. With this framework in mind, a discussion of the system's respective parts and processes follows.

The Parts of the System. The first basic part of the system is the *individual's* personality structure brought to the organization. Elementary to an individual's personality are the motives and attitudes which condition the range of the personal expectancies hoped to be satisfied by participating in the system.

The second part is the formal arrangement of functions, usually called the *formal organization.* The formal organization is an interrelated pattern of jobs which provides the structure for the economic and efficiency pursuits of the organization.

The third part is the small group. The nature of this organization is explained in a subsequent chapter.

The fourth part is the *status and role* arrangements which exist in the organization. It is obvious that in any formal organization, statuses and roles are internally linked by hierarchical ordering. At the same time, there are also informal orderings of statuses and roles in terms of prestige groups and occupations. Status and role are connected closely to power, influence, authority, and leadership.

The fifth part is the *physical setting* in which the job is performed, plus the technical-engineering-efficiency considerations which link the various jobs together.

1. Intrapart Interactions. Within each of these parts, interactions exist among the units which compose them. Obviously individuals interact with individuals, and small groups with other small groups; status systems and roles by their relative nature are dependent on each other for meaning, different jobs are interdependent on other jobs for the satisfactory performance of the total organization, and so on.

The fundamental cause for intrapart interactions is the division of labor. Dependency of units within the parts of the system arises from specialization. Now, since the parts are internally interdependent, they have to be bound together by processes. As mentioned before, these processes are communication, balance, and decisions.

2. Interpart Interactions. Just as the units in the parts of the system have interactional patterns, so also do the parts interact with each other. The individual has expectancies regarding the job he or she is to perform; and, conversely, the job makes demands (or has expectancies) relating to the performance of the individual. Considerable attention has been given by writers in modern organization theory to incongruencies resulting from the interaction of organizational and individual demands. Argyris, for example, sees a conflict resulting from the demands made by the job and the nature of the normal, mature personality. The formal structure of the job does not meet the demands of the mature individual, hence the person is forced to find outlets in activities that are frequently not sanctioned by the formal organization.[14]

The interactions which exist between the small groups and the individual can be conveniently discussed as the mutual modification of expectancies. The small group has demands which it makes on members in terms of anticipated forms of behavior, and individuals have expectancies of satisfaction they hope to derive from association with people

---

[14] Chris Argyris, *Personality and Organization* (New York: Harper & Bros., 1957), especially chapters 2, 3, 7.

on the job.[15] Both sets of expectancies interact, resulting in people modifying their behavior to accord with the demands of the group, and the group—perhaps—modifying what it expects from individuals because of the impact of personalities on group norms.[16]

In the physical surroundings of work, interactions are present in complex man-machine systems. The human "engineer" cannot approach the problems posed by such interrelationships in a purely technical fashion. As Haire says, these problems are in the domain of the social theorists.[17] Attention must be centered on the human responses stemming from a technologically ordered production function. From this standpoint, work cannot be effectively organized unless the psychological, social, and physiological characteristics of people participating in the work environment are considered. Machines and processes should be designed to fit certain generally observed psychological, physiological, and social properties of humans, rather than workers being hired to fit machines and technical processes.

The interactional pattern among jobs, the informal organization, and the individual may be considered within the framework of E. Wight Bakke's *fusion process*.[18] The fusion process is largely concerned with the modification of role expectancies relative to both role demands made by the formal and informal organizations and role perceptions peculiar to the individual. Organizational expectancies and individual perception of the expectancies modify each other. This process is basic to the continuity and stability of the organization.

Let us summarize what has been said so far about systems. First, systems are made up of parts which are interdependent. Additionally, the parts themselves are composed of units which also are interdependent, and the various intra- and interdependencies have been discussed. The parts are woven into a configuration called the organizational system. The processes which link the parts together contributing to the maintenance of the configuration are taken up next.

---

[15] Conditions determining whether or not individual expectancies are satisfied are discussed by Alvin Zander, "Group Membership and Individual Security," *Human Relations*, 11 (1958), 99–111.

[16] For a larger treatment of modification of expectancies, see George C. Homans, *The Human Group* (New York: Harcourt, Brace and Co., 1950), chapter 5.

[17] Mason Haire, "Psychology and the Study of Business: Joint Behavioral Sciences," in *Social Science Research on Business: Product and Potential* (New York: Columbia University Press, 1959), pp. 53–59. See also George F. Weinwurm, "Computer Management Control Systems through the Looking Glass," Management Science, July 1961, pp. 411–19.

[18] E. Wight Bakke, *Bonds of Organization* (New York: Harper & Bros., 1950).

The Linking Processes. We consider processes such as communication, decision making, and balance in subsequent chapters. It is through them that basic interactions are carried out which sustain the life of the organization. As Deutsch points out, communication allows the parts of the organization to "talk" with each other; it brings in information from the outside world, and it provides the means for storing and retrieving information within the system.[19]

Communication and decision function within a structure of networks. These networks bear little semblance to the idealized formal structure of organizations. Indeed, communication may travel along routes to decision centers which bypass or override formally established communication channels. Decisions may be made at centers in the organization which have small relation to the formal authority "officially" designated to the holder of a specific position in a center. Keyed to this complex system of transactions and network interrelationships is the process of balance, the chief purpose of which is to maintain stability among the parts of the organization.

To view the linking processes in networks is not to admit anarchy or to introduce chaos to organizations. It merely acknowledges that large organizations have many more dimensions than those recognized by classic theory. From these dimensions, these organizational overlays, come the dynamics of organizations. If communication *had* to follow formally established channels at all times, little of organizational importance would get done. If decisions were always made by the people who had the authority to make them, then we would have to deny the existence of power systems which correspond to nothing else but the formal structure of authority. Yet power systems do exist in organizations, superimposed on the prescribed system of formal authority. It is through these links, formally specified or not, that the parts of the system are vitalized and moved toward the accomplishment of goals.

The Goals of the System. The parts, interactions, and processes of an organizational system do not exist for themselves, although there may be some argument on this point.[20] They are focused on more general system goals, which in turn, are essential for accomplishing more specific missions of complex organizations. The general goals of systems are

---

[19] Karl W. Deutsch, "On Communication Models in the Social Sciences," *Public Opinion Quarterly*, 16 (1952), 356–80.

[20] For example, some might argue, as we see in the chapter on group dynamics, that *the* purpose of the *small* group is to provide a medium for interaction from which people get intrinsic satisfaction. However, given the mission orientation of complex organizations, there is no reason to suppose that interaction is their sole justification.

stability, growth, and flexibility. These goals are fundamental to the organic models of modern organization theory; they are derived from the heritage of system theory in the biological sciences; and most importantly, they are the criteria for appraising organizational "health."

Organizational "health" at one time meant the way by which managers went about processing organizational inputs—such that the use of inputs were minimized relative to outputs. The level of success in this activity was called efficiency, and the object of management was to increase it. We have written already about rationality, and why it is important needs little additional comment. Higher efficiency means lower costs, lower prices, higher profits, better competitive status, and so on. In other words, the continuous improvement of efficiency meant that everyone—management, customers, employees, and ultimately all of society— would be better off. Therefore, organizational well-being or "health" was judged by the degree of efficiency its management was able to achieve.

At the time when efficiency (or rationality) was the most popular, and indeed the only official standard for judging managerial performance, the use of the word "health" was seldom found in connection with organization. It appeared recently, within the last 15 or 20 years, when the concept of the organization as a "living system" became widely accepted. The notion of an organization as an organic entity assumes that like all living things, it must show three conditions if it is to be judged "healthy." First, it has to be stable in the sense that its parts have to be harmoniously integrated. Stability is the essense of orderliness, and the opposite of chaos, anarchy, or disintegration. Second, the system should be growing or mature. Of the two growth is preferable since it indicates youth and vigor. Growth, consequently, is a sign of development, promise, and opportunity, all valued commodities in our society.[21] The "Pepsi generation" has its counterpart in organization theory! Third, the system must be adaptable, because healthy, complex organisms can adjust to a large number of environmental contingencies. Further, adaptability (flexibility) is evidence of survival potential, and of course this has to be highly regarded in times of rapid change.

Thus to the old-fashioned notion of efficiency, growth, stability, and flexibility have been added as criteria for judging the health of complex organizations. The sum of these four criteria is expressed by a new

---

[21] There are signs that the value of growth is being reconsidered in terms of nongrowth and stability. William G. Scott, "Organization Theory: A Reassessment," *Academy of Management Journal*, June 1974, pp. 242–54.

ideal for management to seek—*organizational effectiveness.* At present, no one is sure what precisely organizational effectiveness is, let alone how to measure it. But the words have a nice ring, and there is, in fact, a consensus that stability, growth, adaptability, and efficiency in varying combinations are the stuff out of which organizational survival is made and organizational missions are accomplished. Therefore managers must be sure that what they do contributes to these goals, otherwise the missions of making cars, canning peas, or distributing social security benefits is likely to be undermined.

Some Applications of Modern Organization Theory

Our discussion of the system model has moved from a high level of abstraction (general system theory) to an intermediate level (the framework of modern organization theory). Now we go down another step in abstraction to consider certain applications of system theory to complex organizations. *Cybernetics* is concerned primarily with problems of control, the *matrix organization* with problems of structure, and *lateral relationships* with problems of behavior.

Cybernetics. Cybernetics is related to both communication and control. But cybernetics is a crucial aspect of systems theory, and so the essential details of this concept are presented here.

Cybernetics is a fruitful idea because it integrates the linking processes and generalizes them to a wide variety of systems. Decisions, information (communication), and control (balance or regulation) are indispensable elements of complex systems. This is true regardless of whether we are speaking of human, mechanical, or electrical systems. The flip-flop of an electronic relay acting upon the information fed it through a communication channel in a computer is as much a decision center as an iron-maned marketing executive pondering alternative promotion programs for a new product. Stafford Beer notes that ". . . decisions are the events that go on in the network, and they are describable . . . in terms of the information in the system, and the structuring of communication."[22]

In this sense, then, decisions and information cannot be understood apart from the system's communication pattern, and this pattern in turn is a reflection of the decisions required and the information necessary upon which to base them. Now, balance, the third linking process, is

---

[22] Stafford Beer, *Cybernetics and Management* (New York: John Wiley & Sons, Inc., 1959), p. 11.

introduced in the form of control or regulation.[23] Here we come to the heart of cybernetic processes. *Regulation of the system network by the feedback of information produced in it is the core of cybernetics.*

The important phrase in the above sentence is regulation ". . . by the feedback of information produced . . ." in the system. This means that some of the energy (output, information) created by a system is tapped to provide a means of control. There is no need to go over the *mechanics* of feedback. We need to note, however, that *one* of the requirements of a cybernetic system is self-regulation. There are many systems which exhibit stability, like the solar system, but not self-regulation. A self-regulated system is one which utilizes some of its internal energy to preserve its level of behavior around some preestablished norm. A room thermostat is a common example; statistical quality control in a factory is another.

While self-regulation is a necessary condition for a cybernetic system, it is not a sufficient condition. A steam engine with a governor is self-regulating but not cybernetic Nor are other more complex systems exhibiting self-regulatory properties of equal interest to cyberneticians. An advanced computer capable of reading out or adjusting for input errors is not properly a cybernetic system. Beer presents an interesting method of classifying systems to pinpoint cybernetic areas. Figure 3–3 shows his approach.

Deterministic systems do what they are told to do. For all practical purposes their outcomes are predictable even though their internal workings may be complicated. They offer no variety in outcomes other than what their "programs" allow and these outcomes are uniquely forecastable for each system.

Probabilistic systems do not have uniquely determined outcomes. They have varying degrees of variety which for prediction purposes may be described in chance terms. As we move from simple systems, through complex, to exceedingly complex, we find that our application of statistical probability techniques becomes less productive of meaningful predictions about the behavior of the system. In the extremely complex category, systems are capable of such a wide variety of behavior that probability analysis is of little value for forecasting. According to Beer, it is precisely at this level that cybernetics focuses.

Cyberneticians are interested in problems of regulation and control in exceedingly complex, probabilistic, self-maintaining (open) systems.

---

[23] The basic reference on cybernetics and its wider implications is Norbert Wiener, *The Human Use of Human Beings*, rev. ed. (New York: Doubleday Anchor Books, 1950; 1954). See also Richard F. Ericson, "Visions of Cybernetic Organizations," *Academy of Management Journal*, December 1972, pp. 427–43.

FIGURE 3–3
Classification of Systems

Degree of Complexity	Type of System	
	Deterministic	*Probabilistic*
Simple	Adding machine Shotgun Machine-shop layout	Coin tossing Jellyfish movements Statistical quality control
Complex	Electronic digital computer Radar-controlled antiaircraft battery Automated factory	Stock market speculation Conditioned reflexes Allocation of sales promotion dollars in a multiproduct company
Exceedingly complex	None	The economic system The human brain The human organization

Source: Stafford Beer, *Cybernetics and Management* (New York: John Wiley & Sons, Inc., 1959), p. 18. Used with permission. The classification method is shown as presented by the author. Minor changes in the system examples are made.

The economy, the human brain, and human organization are systems which fit the description. Because of the insensitivity of these systems to conventional forms of analysis, cybernetics is necessarily interdisciplinary. That is cyberneticians, must look for answers in many fields like biology, physics, information theory, semantics, highly imaginative mathematics as that involved in game theory. It is from synthesis of data and generalizations from these areas that analytic resources will come for investigation of control problems.

The language of cybernetics has become a part of managerial vocabulary. Such words as feedback and self-regulation imply both management strategies and behavioral norms for improving the effectiveness of organizations. While words are important, because they influence attitudes and behavior, cybernetics has made a more important contribution. Since it emphasizes regulation in exceeding complex systems, it has become a model for thinking in regard to the application of advanced information technology to the control of complex organizations. For example, industrial dynamics models are replete with feedback loops designed to regulate highly complex human systems. It is indeed difficult to find a case of complex organization using sophisticated management information technology which has not adopted cybernetic models as an integral part of its mode of operation.

The Project and Matrix Structures. The project and matrix forms of organization structure are an extension of Frederick W. Taylor's idea of "functional foremanship" which we discussed in a previous chapter. They are designed to make maximum advantage of managerial specialization, but they are applied to organizational situations of much greater complexity than Taylor had visualized. These structures also depart from the traditional line-staff structure in a number of significant ways that Cleland summarizes in Figure 3–4.

FIGURE 3–4
A Comparison of Traditional and Project Viewpoints

Phenomenon	Project Viewpoint	Traditional Viewpoint
Line-staff organizational dichotomy	Vestiges of the hierarchal model remain, but line functions are placed in a support position. A web of authority and responsibility relationships exists.	Line functions have direct responsibility for accomplishing the objectives; the line commands, staff advises.
Scalar principle	Elements of the vertical chain exist, but prime emphasis is placed on horizontal and diagonal work flow. Important business is conducted as the legitimacy of the task requires.	The chain of authority relationships is from superior to subordinate throughout the organization. Central, crucial, and important business is conducted up and down the vertical hierarchy.
Superior-subordinate relationship	Peer to peer, manager to technical expert, associate to associate relationships are used to conduct much of the salient business	This is the most important relationship; if kept healthy, success will follow. All important business is conducted through a pyramiding structure of superiors-subordinates.
Organizational objectives	Management of a project becomes a joint venture of many relatively independent organizations. Thus, the objective becomes multilateral.	Organizational objectives are sought by the parent unit (as assembly of suborganizations) working within its environment. The objective is unilateral.
Unity of direction	The project manager manages across functional and organizational lines to accomplish a common interorganizational objective.	The general manager acts as the head for a group of activities having the same plan.
Parity of authority and responsibility	Considerable opportunity exists for the project manager's responsibility to exceed his authority. Support people are often responsible to other managers (functional) for pay, performance reports, promotions, and so forth.	Consistent with functional management; the integrity of the superior-subordinate relationship is maintained through functional authority and advisory staff services.
Time duration	The project (and hence the organization) is finite in duration.	Tends to perpetuate itself to provide continuing facilitative support.

Source: David I. Cleland, "Understanding Project Authority," *Business Horizons,* Spring 1967, pp. 63–70. Reprinted with permission.

As Cleland's analysis shows, the premises upon which the project organization is based are quite different from those usually assumed by traditional structures. For example, the project organization is a *temporary* organization, whereas the traditional organization is formed on the premise that it will last indefinitely. Further, the unity of command principle is violated by the project organization, while in the traditional organization this principle is assumed to be one of the chief means of securing coordination. Also, the project organization violates the scalar principle because of the absence of a determinate hierarchy, at least in one part of the overall organization structure. That is, project managers, while functionally distinct, do not stand in a scalar relationship. Neither do they stand in a sort of relationship which can be spoken of meaningfully as line-staff.

In a structural sense there is little that distinguishes between a project and a matrix organization. Figure 3–5 shows the form these types of organizations often assume.

Note that the left side of the chart shows the production, marketing,

FIGURE 3–5
A Project (Matrix) Organization

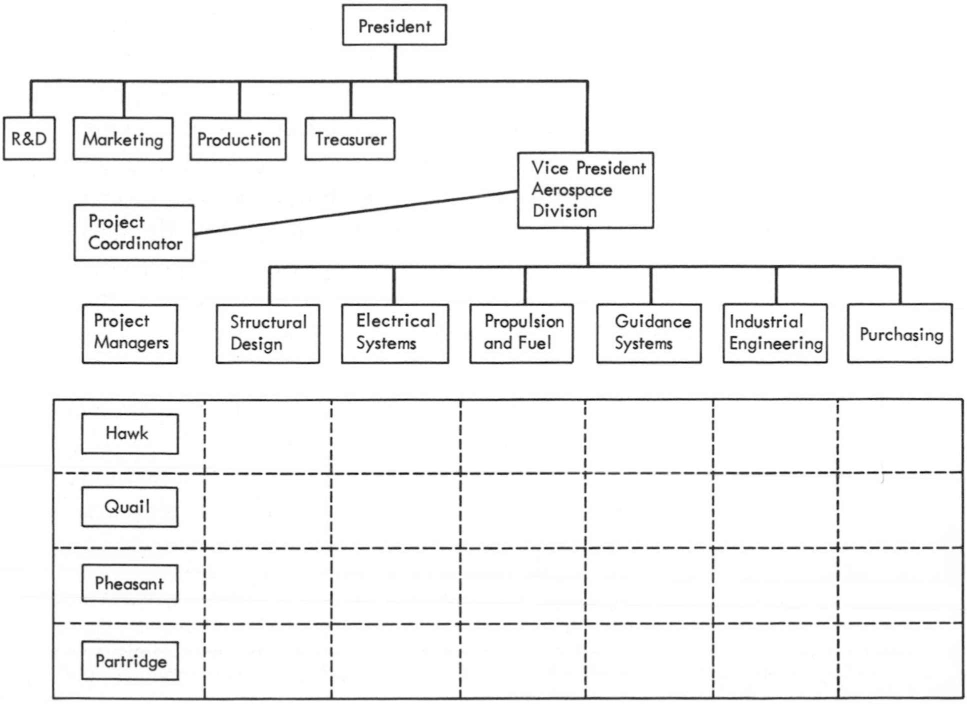

and support divisions involved in the conventional aircraft business. This segment of the company follows a typical line-staff structure. The right side of the chart depicts the organization of the Aero-Space division. Horizontally shown are the line departments where engineers, scientists, and technicians are "housed" for administrative purposes. Thus we see a structural design department, an electrical systems department, and so on.

To the left of these departments, vertically arranged, are the missile projects for which the company currently has contracts, i.e., Hawk, Quail, and so on. Supervising each of these projects is a project manager. The personnel he needs to operationalize his project are drawn from specialists out of their respective administrative departments. Upon completion of a project these people may return to their administrative "pool" for reassignment.[24]

Time is the factor that makes the difference between project and matrix structures. In the project structure, when a specific project is completed, the system that supported it is terminated, whereas the various system components in the matrix organization are assumed to have indefinite life-spans. Consequently the amount of turbulence is greater in the project organization. This distinction is more than "academic" since it implies differences in rates of technological change, unceasing quests for new projects, rapid movement of personnel, and higher levels of uncertainty for all involved. In other words, the relative stability of the matrix organization environment compared to the environment of the project organization results in different management problems to solve. It is not by accident, therefore, that the tranquility of university life permits some schools to operate a matrix structure, while the hustle of the aero-space industries requires a project approach to organization. However, one would not be able to appreciate the dynamics in these two situations by merely looking at the charts of these respective organizations.

Lateral Relationships.   The most important contrast between project-matrix-type structures and traditional line-staff structures is behavioral. The former encourages, indeed requires, lateral and diagonal interactions among managers while the latter discourages them. This is an important

---

[24] Of course, there are other reasons for reassignment. A project might be discontinued, or it might be running ahead of schedule so that some of its personnel can be transferred to other projects. Then, too, individuals might be promoted or request transfer from one activity to another. One important function of the administrative department head is to keep track of these changes as well as to anticipate the personnel requirements of the project managers.

point since it says that in some circumstances coordination may be more effectively achieved through the *minimization* of hierarchial authority. This is, of course, a clear departure from the traditions of classical organization theory. However, we must be careful. Reducing the influence of command authority does not mean that it is eliminated altogether. The matrix does not represent the total organization; rather it is a *segment* of an organization subordinated to higher decision levels. Further, when command authority is reduced in some parts of an organization, it has to be replaced by something else. What arises to fill the void are behavioral transactions that can be classified as political.

Observers of the complex organizational scene, like Leonard Sayles, report that trading, bargaining, negotiation, conflict, and compromise are typical forms of behavior among managers engaged in working out their lateral relationships.[25] Through these political activities managers attempt to achieve coordination among themselves, a function that was formerly thought to be the prerogative of hierarchy. This behavior is outside the scope of the classical model of organization. Unfortunately its implications are barely understood in modern organization theory. However, there are two ways to approach this problem. One is the contingency approach which we take up next; the other way is to visualize the organization as a political system which we defer to a later chapter.

THE CONTINGENCY APPROACH

Between the years 1973 and 1975, over roughly an 18-month period, 3 books of readings were published claiming to present a contingency approach to management. This event was of some considerable significance because it established a new feature on the landscape of organizational theory. While 45 of the 98 articles selected by the editors of these books appeared in their original form before 1970, the contingency view of things seems to be something more than putting "old wine in new bottles."

The relationship of the contingency approach to system theory is parallel to the relationship of the neoclassical approach to the classical model of organization theory. As we pointed out, the neoclassicists tried to extend classical theory by adding insights from the behavioral sciences

---

[25] See Leonard Sayles, *Managerial Behavior* (New York: McGraw-Hill Book Company, 1964). Sayles does not restrict his analysis to lateral relations in project organizations. Rather, he sees these relations appearing in many large complex organizations, regardless of whether they are recognized or not by official policy.

to it. By doing so they hoped to make this model more useful in everyday, practical management affairs. However, the neoclassicists never actually turned their backs on the premises of classic organization theory. They just tried to modify these premises in order to account for the "realities" of human behavior in organization.

Those who endorse the contingency approach take much the same stand relative to system theory. They accept system theory's premises about interdependency and the organic nature of organization. They accept the open adaptive character of such organizations as well as the need to preserve flexibility in the face of change. But, as they correctly note, system theory is very abstract and difficult to apply in practical managerial situations. The exponents of the contingency model claim, not without certain pride, that it offers a means for the unifying of theory with practice in a systems framework.

The Nature of the Contingency Model

Although there is shading of emphasis, a considerable agreement exists among authors about the nature of the contingency model. Tosi and Hamner rely heavily of B. F. Skinner's behaviorist theory. They say, "When a subsystem in an organization 'behaves' in response to another system or subsystem, we say that the response was 'contingent' on the environment. . . . Hence, a 'contingency' approach is an approach where the behavior of one subunit is dependent on its environmental relationship to other units or subunits that have some control over the consequences . . . desired by that subunit."[26]

Consequences, therefore, are always contingent upon behavior within the environment. This is fairly unadulterated Skinnerean behaviorism, because if a manager wants to change behavior he must alter the environmental contingencies to bring forth different consequences. From Tosi's and Hamner's point of view, the debt that the contingency approach owes to Skinnerean psychology is considerable. As they observe, "The form of an organizational system is not simply a matter of managerial choice. . . . Organizational form is largely a function of, or contingent upon, the external environment."[27]

This is not the place to criticize the Skinnerean model other than to say that emphasis upon strict behavioral determinism (the complete

---

[26] Henry L. Tosi and W. Clay Hamner, *Organizational Behavior and Management: A Contingency Approach* (Chicago: St. Clair Press, 1974), p. 1.

[27] Ibid., p. 5.

dependence of behavior upon environment) may be unduly rigid, restricting its managerial applications to very simple situations such as packing containers.[28] Alternatively, Kast and Rosenzweig offer a somewhat broader view of the contingency approach. They note:

> The contingency view seeks to understand the interrelationships within and among subsystems as well as between the organization and its environment and to define patterns of relationships or configurations of variables. It emphasizes the multivariate nature of organizations and attempts to understand how organizations operate under varying conditions and in specific circumstances. Contingency views are ultimately directed toward suggesting organizational designs and managerial actions most appropriate for specific situations.[29]

Despite varying degrees of emphasis, which seem to hinge upon how closely Skinner is followed, contingency model builders show a surprising amount of consensus on common themes. First, they are unanimous in their rejection of universal principles of management. They clearly state that there is no one best way to manage or organize. What managers do depends upon the circumstances and the environment. Thus, management practice is entirely *situational*. Second, since management practice is situational, it follows that management has to sharpen its diagnostic skills, so it will know the right thing to do at the right time. The contingency approach supplies management with diagnostic concepts, tools, methods, and techniques which are helpful in analyzing and solving situational problems. Third, the contingency approach is applicable to a number of managerial tasks, particularly those with heavy behavioral components. Kast and Rosenzweig see contingency models useful in strategy formulation, organizational design and redesign, information decision systems, influence systems and leadership, and organizational improvement.[30] In short, wherever there is a need to define or to redefine organizational relationships a contingency model may be of service.

It is easy enough to put the contingency approach down for its paucity of content. How many different ways can you say, it all depends? After all management theory has been saying this for years—the situational

---

[28] The most frequently cited example of the use of Skinnerean techniques in industry is the case of Emery Air Freight. We discuss the idea of positive reenforcement as a motivational device in Chapters 6 and 15 pertaining to motivation and to job design.

[29] Fremont E. Kast and James E. Rosenzweig, *Contingency Views of Organization and Management* (Chicago: Science Research Associates, 1973), p. 313.

[30] Ibid., pp. 329–44.

approach to leadership has been around for a long time. However, we will reserve our critical remarks on contingency models for the next chapter.

The real significance of the contingency approach to modern organization theory lies in the fact that it represents the first serious attempt to answer the question, How do systems interchange with their environment? As you recall, the questions we raised at the beginning of this chapter, pertaining to parts, interdependency, processes, adustments, and goals, fell within the analytical framework of systems theory. The phenomenon of organizational environmental exchange constituted a considerable theoretical void. The contingency approach is an attempt to provide something more useful to practicing managers in complex organizations. Also to the extent that politics is the "art of the possible" the contingency approach may be helpful in understanding and dealing with the political behavior inherent in modern organization structures. This point is considered at greater length in Chapter 20 which deals with the subject of organizational governance.

chapter 4

An Assessment of Organization Theory

The previous chapters presented a review of the development of organization theory, stressing its objectives, content, and structure. Our aim was to summarize the "paradigm" of the field as accurately as possible without the undue embellishment of personal opinions. However, organization theory and management practice is by nature value laden. Consequently any appraisal of the present status of the field is bound to carry with it certain judgments by the authors that may not be shared by others who are either studying organizations or running them. This is a risk that must be accepted.

Although organization theory is not truly scientific, it does share with science in general certain qualities that are useful to examine as a beginning of our assessment of the field. Most fields of science, such as chemistry, genetics, or astronomy, have a unifying vision of natural phenomenon to which they apply their specialized knowledge and methods. This vision combined with techniques of investigation results in an explanation (prediction and control) of the events which occur within the boundaries of the phenomenon studied by a science. As a science matures its theorems about the shape of its universe change. The direction of change in three sciences—physics, economics, and sociology—are discussed as a basis of comparison to organization theory.

The first comprehensive, and empirically verifiable, outlook of the physical universe was presented by Isaac Newton in his *Principia*. Classical physics, founded on the work of Newton, constituted a grand scheme in which a wide range of physical phenomena could be organized and predicted.

Newtonian physics may rightfully be regarded as "macro" in nature because its system of organization was concerned largely with gross events, of which the movement of celestial bodies is an example. For years classical physics was supreme. But as it became applied to smaller and smaller classes of phenomena in the physical universe physics eventually adopted the view that everything in its realm could be discovered simply by subdividing problems. At that point physics had moved into the "micro" order. In the 19th century, however, a revolution took place in physics largely because events in the physical universe were being noted which could not be explained adequately by the analytical equipment supplied by the classical school. The consequences of this revolution are described by Eddington:

> From the point of view of philosophy of science the conception associated with entropy must I think be ranked as the great contribution of the nineteenth century to scientific thought. It marked a reaction from the view that everything to which science need pay attention is discovered by microscopic dissection of objects. It provided an alternative standpoint in which the centre of interest is shifted from the entities reached by the customary analysis (atoms, electric potentials, etc.) to qualities possessed by the system as a whole, which cannot be split up and located—a little bit here, and a little bit there. . . .
>
> We often think that when we have completed our study of *one* we know all about *two*, because "two" is "one and one." We forget that we have still to make a study of "and." Secondary physics is the study of "and"—that is to say, of organization.[1]

Although modern physics deals in minute quantities and oscillations the conception of the physicist is on the "macro" scale. He is concerned with the "and"—that is, the organization of the world in which the events occur. This does not invalidate the usefulness of classical physics in explaining a certain range of phenomena. But classical physics is no longer the undisputed law of the universe. It is instead a special case.

Early economic theory—and Adam Smith's *Wealth of Nations* comes to mind—examined economic problems in the macro order. Fundamentally, *Wealth of Nations* is concerned with matters of national income and welfare. Later, the economics of the firm, "microeconomics," dominated the theoretical scene in this science. And, finally, with Keynes's

---

[1] Sir Arthur Eddington, *The Nature of the Physical World* (Ann Arbor: The University of Michigan Press, 1958), pp. 103–4.

The General Theory of Employment, Interest and Money, a systematic view of the economic universe was reintroduced on the macro level.

The first era of the developing science of sociology was occupied by the great social "system builders." Comte, the so-called father of sociology, had the macro view of society in that his chief works are devoted to social reorganization. Comte was concerned with the interrelationships among social, political, religious, and educational institutions. But as sociology progressed the science of society compressed. Emphasis shifted from the macro approach of the pioneers to detailed, empirical study of small social units. The compression of sociological analysis was accompanied by study of social pathology, or disorganization.

In general, physics, economics, and sociology appeared to have two things in common. First, they offered a macro point of view as their initial systematic comprehension of their areas of study. Second, as the science developed, attention fragmented into study of the parts of organization rather than the system as a whole. This is the "micro" phase. In this anomolies appeared that could not be explained in terms of the old general theory.

In physics and economics, discontent was evidenced by some scientists at continual atomization of the universe. The reaction of the micro approach was a new theory or theories dealing with the total system on the macro level again. In this new macro phase a reconstruction of general theory was sought that would explain (account for) the anomolies uncovered in the previous micro period. The reason for this "macro-micro-macro" order of scientific progress lies in the hypothesis that usually the things which strike people first are of great magnitude. The scientist attempts to discover order in the vastness. But after "macro" laws or models of systems are postulated, variations appear which demand analysis, not so much in terms of the entire system but rather in the specific parts which make it up.

Intense study of the microcosm may result in new general laws replacing the old models of organization. In any event, microscosmic studies appear to be part of a cycle in science which leads to a reformulation of principles on higher levels of generality than had previously existed in the earlier macro phase.

Change in Organization Theory

The macro-micro-macro cycle is one way of describing scientific change. Some argue, as does Eddington, that as a science moves through these phases it become progressively more powerful in its ability to explain events that fall within its boundaries. Whether this is true or not, and it seems to be less the case in the "social" sciences, we will not attempt to explore here.[2]

The point is that *there has yet to be a paradigmatic revolution in organization theory.* In the 75 years of its existence, organization theory has stayed true to its heritage. This is not to say that organization theory is static. Actually, it is a very lively, interesting, and progressive field of study, research, and practice. Nevertheless, most changes which have occurred are conservative meaning that progress of the field has been through the evolution and extension of core concepts, especially that of rationality.

Organization theory has not changed radically, that is paradigmatically; and if the main exponents of the field have their way it never will. The defenders of the paradigm, the conservative theorists, researchers, and practitioners, will defend the barricades against any and all threats of radical change to established values and practices which define the essense of the field. What is important to these guardians of the faith is the continued rational solution of the endless number of puzzles posed by complex organizations. The paramount rule is that puzzles are attacked according to the prescriptions of the paradigm so that the unique requirements of organization theory and management practice are served.

Thus the ends of organization theory have remained unchanged through the years, whereas the means used to achieve the ends have changed rapidly. The ends, as we have stated in Chapter 1 are organizationally created growth, abundance, and consensus obtained with the greatest dispatch by rational management performance.

Everything else pertaining to organization are means, and this includes the various theories of organization that we have discussed. To the extent that these theories, and the techniques of management derived from them contribute to the health of the organization, they are useful. When they fail to make such contributions they are discarded. Since no organizational magic has been found yet, the experimentation with new means for puzzle solving occupies the attention of literally thousands of managers, technicians, researchers, and scholars. It is little wonder that the field is so dynamic—complex organizations absorb the talents of a large segment of the "best and the brightest" in our society.

---

[2] See Thomas S. Kuhn, *The Structure of Scientific Revolutions* (Chicago: The University of Chicago Press, 1962).

The attention given to means has had an interesting and subtle consequence. The clarity of ends tends to fade, and we often are trapped by the fallacy, as a result, of believing that when we are debating the relative merits of means, we are debating the ends. Actually we are doing no such thing. To illustrate, Frederick W. Taylor knew exactly what he was trying to accomplish in organizations. He wanted to help management run them more efficiently and scientific management was, in his mind, the means to do it. Although his approach was primitive, there was no confusion of means with ends in his thinking. Much the same can be said for other early contributors to classical organization theory.

With neoclassical theory, some of the distinction between ends and means began to dissolve. As an effort to "save" classical theory behavioral science techniques and concepts were the means employed. Rationality remained the basic end in the theoretical paradigm, but it was an *implicit* goal. Neoclassical theory marked the beginning of the muddle of ends and means which was exacerbated in modern organization theory by the humanists.

A good deal of the means-ends jumble in modern organization theory resulted from the humanistic application of the behavioral sciences. During their heydays of the late 1960s, the exponents of sensitivity training technologies would shudder at the suggestion that their practices have the primary organizational purpose of helping management make more rational use of human resources. Rather they preferred that their techniques be used for more uplifting purposes like self-actualization of the individual or improvement of the work climate of the organization. Efficiency, if it was ever acknowledged as a goal by the humanists, was very low priority.

Yet it is hard to believe that management can buy the programs of oragnizational humanism simply out of an attitude of "human kindness" toward employees. Somewhere in the recesses of the minds of practicing managers and their humanist consultants lurked the expectation that such programs would satisfy in some measure the requirements of technical rationality in complex organizations. But little of this was ever stated explicitly, until the organization development movement made some hesitating steps in this direction just recently. In too many instances behavioral science techniques were treated as ends in themselves, justified as being "good for people and organizations" in their own right. However, during the late 1960s and early 1970s murmurings could be heard about the way humanistic programs contributed to the "viability" of the system, promoting its "health," and enhancing its "openness" to environment inputs.

Mostly this was rhetoric, caused in part by the extraordinarily vague notions of organization imposed by the macro-orientation of system theory, but also caused by the influence of organizational humanism in the 1960s. The humanistic values and programs were emotionally appealing since they aspired to raising peoples' awareness. But they were also within management's financial grasp given the affluence of the previous decade. As America advanced into the 1970s, confronted by the realization of limited resources and by perilous economic conditions, it grew evident that the luxurious hocus-pocus of the organizational humanists could not be afforded. Some reassessment of where organization theory and management practice stands at this time is absolutely essential.

A return to the simplicity of classical theory is impossible. Organization complexity and technology has limited the usefulness of this alternative. In spite of the excesses of the humanists it is clearly desirable and necessary to maintain system theory and extend the behavioral sciences. Both have the potential to contribute to the process of organizing. What is obviously needed at this point is a reorientation of theory that does two basic things. First, a reorientation must address the problems of complex organization with whatever advanced technological means that are at hand or can be developed. Second, it must be prepared to confront the imperative need that organizations have at this time for increased rational performance. In other words the present demands on theory require the restatement of the established paradigm in the strongest possible terms. This is the mission of the contingency approach in modern organization theory.

The New Microphase of Contingency Management

The contingency approach is a return to a paradigmatic basics. It reasserts the obligation of organization theory to dwell upon the practical, day-to-day, situational puzzle-solving jobs that confront all managers trying to run organizations rationally. Contingency models draw upon the methods and findings of the behavioral sciences against the conceptual backdrop of system theory to meet this obligation. But these elements of modernism are entirely within the traditions of the field, which has always held that whatever is potentially useful in theory and technology should be seriously considered by management for possible application.

The proposition that the contingency approach is a new microphase in the theoretical cycle can be supported two ways. First, a statement made by Kast and Rosenzweig is revealing. They say that "Once we have more complete understanding of what *is* and what *happens,* we can begin to consider normative propositions of what managers *ought to do or seek.*"[3] Obviously the quest for what is and what happens in organization implies the tireless application of behavioral science methods to research questions *of modest dimensions.* We know so little presently about behavior, that we must be content with discovering tiny particles of reliable data before we can begin to grasp the larger realities of system processes. Given the mission of the contingency approach this dedication makes sense. However, it must be appreciated that behavioral science research, focusing on microproblems, is reductionist in nature. Such is inconsistent in spirit to the aim of system theory. Inconsistencies, like this one, in the conceptual framework of organization theory will simply have to be taken in stride.

Second, the unabashed pragmatisim of the contingency approach is further evidence of its micro-orientation. Pragmatism imposes no moral imperative on management other than to correctly diagnose situations in order to react with rational expediency. The attention of the contingency approach is on the here and now necessity of solving puzzles and putting out fires. The point is that concern for the situation at hand will effectively stiffle any motivation that theoreticians or practitioners might have for the broader effects of their ideas and decisions. This brings to light a fundamental discrepancy in the above quotation of Kast and Rosenzweig, although in fairness this discrepancy is present in most examples of contingency thinking.

It is simply that "finding out what is and what happens" in organization is an enormously consuming task in itself. Contingency types are likely to be so occupied with the pressing problems of the moment, with each solution to these problems creating other pressing problems, that they never will get around to addressing the basic moral question of "what ought to be." The microcosmic world of pragmatism is not a place where philosophy flourishes. But then again the paradigm of organization has not been particularly hospitable to philosophy. So its ab-

---

[3] Fremont E. Kast and James E. Rosenzweig, *Contingency Views of Organization and Management* (Chicago: Science Research Associates, 1973), p. 346.

sence in the contingency approach will probably not be missed by those people who are intimately involved in management affairs.

This discussion of the contingency approach might lead one to the conclusion that its analysis procedes against a value-neutral background, rather of the sort attributed to scientific research. Belief in this kind of normlessness is actually encouraged by writers in the field. Their insistence that there are no right or wrong ways of managing or organizing, that "principles" of management should be discarded, and that situational diagnosis is everything seems to support the claim for such value neutrality.

However, nothing can be farther from the truth. The contingency approach is not normless. Instead, it is intensely conservative in that it relies upon and pursues established values. Contingency thinking is supposed to help managers achieve rationality, efficiency, growth, abundance, consensus, effectiveness, and whatever else managers require to increase the performance of their organizations.

The committment of contingency thinking can be stated by paraphrasing Kast and Rosenzweig, "What managers *ought to do* is to seek what *is*." This is not just a normative proposition; it is a practical and precise statement of what managers have to do in order to stay managers.

In some ways the contingency approach is a refreshing breeze in management, that will help clear away some of the humanist and general system theory fog. It does, however, create almost as many problems as it solves. These problems are largely in the metaphysical domain and cannot be effectively treated in a book like this. As Kuhn says, the purpose of a textbook is to expound the paradigm of a field. Philosophy and moralistic speculation that exceeds the boundaries of the paradigm must be expressed in another form.

This concludes our discussion and critical assessment of the main structural components of organization theory in which a number of themes were emphasized. While all the schemes of organizing are imperfect, they are held together by the common thread of rationality. Although rationality became indistinct and undervalued in the last decade of organization theory, the problems of the 1970s are likely to force its reassertion. A technological society cannot survive continuous assaults upon its foundations of efficiency and its source of energy. Management in organizing will have to stress both the imperative of efficiency and conservation if the world's investment in technological progress is to be sustained. Given the many demands made on modern management by a variety of interest groups, such a mission will be difficult to accomplish. Management clearly needs the general support of employees and citizens of a technological society.

Truly the problems of organizing in a structural sense are less imposing in this context compared with the problems of modifying and controlling behavior. But such is the stuff of which management's legitimacy and political support is derived. Consequently we examine in the next part some of what we know about organizational behavior, since the influence of individuals and groups is essential to the effective management of organizations.

part *II*

Individual and Group
Behavior

The first part of the book described the historical and theoretical foundations for analyzing the total organization and its structures, processes, and interdependences. But one must also investigate the behavior of the individual organizational participants. In the last ten years a whole new approach to a key ingredient in organization theory has developed to study the behavior of individuals working alone and in groups, in the organizational setting. In order to build a more comprehensive theory of how organizations worked it was necessary to understand how the individual components worked. That is, why do people in organizations do the things they do? Part II addresses itself to this question.

We begin with an analysis of some of the characteristics that the individual brings to the work setting. More specifically, Chapter 5 covers the rather general human processes of perception and personality development. Issues of what people perceive, why, and how and when they perceive it, and how it impacts on their behavior are discussed. The nature of personality, its development, stability and importance are also described. Both processes help us to understand how people behave in an organization.

The following chapter on motivation is both general and specific in its coverage. We discuss the basic motivational process and review the principles which have broad acceptance. Our focus then switches to the application of these principles to the work setting. Theories dealing with needs, expectations, equity, and goals are reviewed. Skinner's operant techniques are also discussed. A review of the empirical findings is used to evaluate these different approaches.

Chapter 7 on attitudes deals with a pervasive question that is of great importance to administrators: What aspects of the job are likely to lead to satisfied employees? We discuss the definition, measurement, and change of attitudes and the types of organizational aspects which are related to job attitudes. Some of the social psychological theories of attitude change (e.g., cognitive dissonance) are reviewed in terms of their utility for understanding organizational behavior.

The final chapter in this section deals with the individual in the group setting. We briefly review some of the research that shows what people do differently in groups when compared to how they behave alone. The small group is described and the processes that occur within it are explored. Research on social influence, interpersonal attraction, and communication is reviewed. The conclusions of this chapter lead us rather directly to the next part of the book which deals with broad organizational processes.

chapter 5

Perception and
Personality Dynamics

In our observations of others it is clear that responses to a given situation are different for different people. Our explanation of the phenomena might be that "they didn't see it that way" or "they wanted different things." Or we might explain the differences by saying "He does that because he's aggressive or naturally bright." People do indeed differ in their responses to the same situation and the explanations given frequently refer to some underlying processes which are related to individual differences. Two such processes are *perception* and *personality development*. The rest of this chapter will define and discuss these processes in light of their relationship to organizational behavior.

PERCEPTION

Individuals are being constantly bombarded by sensory stimulation. There are noises, sights, smells, tastes, and tactile sensations. Yet somehow we manage to process this information without confusion. This process is known as perception and may be defined as "the experience people have as the proximate result of the sensory inputs. The process is one of selection and organization of sensations to provide the meaningful entity we experience."[1]

---

[1] Blair J. Kolasa, *Introduction to Behavioral Science for Business* (New York: John Wiley & Sons, Inc., 1969), p. 211.

83

Factors Influencing Perception

There are two basic components of this definition. First, perception is a system of *selection* or screening. Some information is processed, some is not. Think of the times, for example, that you were disturbed by the ticking of a clock just before you went to sleep. The noise made by the clock is not typically selected. That is, you notice it only for a brief time and only occasionally. The noise, itself, however, is constant. This screening helps us to avoid processing irrelevant or disruptive information.

The second component is *organization*. The information that is processed must be ordered and categorized in some fashion that allows us to ascribe meaning to the stimulus information. The stimulus provides certain cues as to its nature. An orange has color, texture, shape, and size, all of which help in the categorization process. These categories may be more or less elaborate but their central function is the reduction of complex information into simpler categories. However, to say that perception is a process of selection and categorization begs the question. How exactly does one choose to select what one does and categorize this information in their own unique fashion?

There are numerous general factors which are related to what one perceives. The first factor is called response disposition: People tend to perceive familiar stimuli more quickly than unfamiliar ones. Research has shown, for example that when words are flashed on a screen at high speeds, subjects tend to recognize words that are frequently used more readily than ones that have infrequent usage.[2]

A second factor is one's feelings toward the objects in question. There is considerable evidence that those things for which we hold strong feelings are also recognized more quickly than neutral stimuli.[3] In general it appears that we select things about which we hold positive feelings but in some cases we recognize negative stimuli, especially where recognition would lead to the avoidance of a highly negative situation. It should be pointed out that frequency and evaluation are not independent of one another. It appears that the more frequently one is exposed to something the greater the likelihood that it will be positively evaluated. Those in advertising would recognize the "repetition is recognition" principle here. The current debates over the presentation of violence and sex in the mass media are also tied to this relationship.

---

[2] R. C. Johnson, C. W. Thomson, and G. Frincke. "Word Values, Word Frequency, and Visual Duration Thresholds," *Psychological Review*, 67 (1960), 332–42.

[3] See the review by Paul F. Secord and Carl W. Backman, *Social Psychology* (New York: McGraw-Hill Book Company, 1964), pp. 22–24.

Another factor of importance is called response salience. Secord and Backman define salience in the following manner. "Certain *contemporary* conditions predispose the organism to make certain responses. Given several responses which have been equally practiced, a particular one may be elicited by experimental instructions, by an immediately preceding sequence of behavior, by the presence of a motivated state, or by some aspect of the immediately present stimulus situation."[4] Frightened people would perceive fearful objects; hungry people would perceive food objects, and so on. So, both historical variables such as exposure and evaluation and contemporary factors such as needs and expectations influence what one perceives.

Besides these more "internal" factors there are some external conditions which increase the likelihood that something will be perceived. One obvious condition is the intensity of the stimulus. We will tend to notice bright lights, pungent odors, and loud noises. Many advertisements utilize this idea by presenting their product in attention getting ways. They use bright distinctive colors and frequently advertisements on radio and television are slightly louder than the program being interrupted. In examining our own personal behavior we can probably remember times when we raised our voice in a discussion to gain someone else's attention. This happens in the workplace as well. For example, bright danger signs may be placed where they will be noticed, or loud buzzers or bells may be used to signify the beginning or end of work or rest periods.

Another factor that frequently prompts attention is motion. Thus, moving objects tend to be more readily perceived than stationary objects. Again in advertising we can notice the utilization of this principle. Lights on signs come on sequentially or intermittantly to give the appearance of motion. Store displays frequently have moving parts. Many of the studies in engineering psychology concentrate on the optimal man-machine match and therefore attempt to design display panels such that distracting motions are reduced while important motions are accentuated.

A third external factor is simply the size of the object. Large obtrusive objects tend to be perceived more easily than small ones. This may result in differential treatment for people or for physical objects such as machines. Both Bill Russell and Wilt Chamberlain have been the constant recipients of rather inept jokes about their size—and, of course, it's rather hard for them to hide in a crowd. But there is also research which suggests that size is related to attention and goodness. That is,

---

[4] Ibid., p. 16.

we tend to pay attention to larger things and somehow bigness has a goodness quality to it.

A final set of variables are those that represent that physical environment. Research by Segall, Campbell, and Herskovits has shown that ones surrounding environment is related to his perceptions.[5] They present evidence that people living in situations or cultures called "carpentered" (numerous structures with right angles) tend to have different perceptions of two-dimensional representations of three-dimensional objects than those who live in noncarpentered environments. More specifically, they are able to look at a picture (which is two dimensional) and respond to it as if it were three dimensional. The authors also present data supporting the idea that people who live on plains have different perceptions about the representation of vertical lines than do people living in environments where views of distant territory are absent. In summary, what one perceives is a function of both his past experiences and his immediate environment. To some extent the specific content of these experiences and environments are determined by one's culture, but the underlying processes or major contributing factors are the same. The next section discusses how these factors are related to our perceptions of people.

Person Perception

Almost everyone spends part of each day interacting with other people and in general, this interaction progresses rather smoothly. Most of our relationships are harmonious and pleasant. Yet to maintain these relationships requires a knowledge of social behavior which we seldom verbalize. That is, we are constantly making judgments about other people's needs, emotions, and thoughts and we do this rather automatically. Research has shown that there are three sets of characteristics which influence these perceptions and it is these variables which we will now discuss.

The Person Perceived. In an interpersonal situation one's evaluation and behavior toward the other is partly influenced by the characteristics of the individual with whom he is interacting. These characteristics fall under four headings: physical, social, historical, and personal.

Some of the more important *physical* ones are gestures, posture, facial expressions, and pigmentation. An example of the first one might be

---

[5] M. H. Segall, D. T. Campbell and J. J. Herskovits, *The Influence of Culture on Visual Perception* (Indianapolis, Ind.: The Bobbs-Merrill Co., Inc., 1966).

the characteristics that one attributed to Tiny Tim the first time they viewed him walking across a stage. Even though the "feminine" personality traits attributed to him were probably false the fact remains that people do indeed make this sort of judgment. One's posture also is important. One often attributes laziness or lack of motivation to someone who slouches. Also, in many foreign countries one's importance is tied to how tall he or she stands in relation to others. For example, a Thai who is interacting with a countryman of higher status will try not to have his head be higher than that of his companion even when this companion is physically shorter. Facial expressions and features may influence our feelings about others as well. Smiling is related to positive attitudes, for example, and people with eyes that are small and close together are often judged to be shifty or dishonest.[6] Finally, and perhaps most important is the fact that in many cultures darker skin pigmentation is associated with negative attributes. Research has shown that darkness is related to hostility, dishonesty, unfriendliness, slyness and other variables which one might classify as negative.[7] Studies of American heroes and villains shows that blondness and light skin is most frequently associated with heroes and darkness and swarthiness with villains.[8]

The *social* characteristics which appear to be important are voice qualities and appearance. In many cases one's education, place of residence and status can be tied to his manner of speech. It is also clear that one's clothes and grooming are used by others in their evaluation. It is currently the fashion to call anyone with long hair and casual attire a "hippie," which implies judgments about his political, social, and moral values.

Certain *historical* factors or attributes have a large effect on our evaluations of others. One's sex, age, occupation, religion and, most importantly, race, contribute to others' evaluation of that person. A study by Triandis and Triandis showed that the racial characteristic is twice as important as occupation, religion, or nationality in determining whether another individual will be accepted into an American's social group (called social distance).[9] People from other countries tended to weight

---

[6] See Paul F. Secord, "The Role of Facial Features in Interpersonal Perception," in R. Tagiuri and L. Petrullo, eds., *Person Perception and Interpersonal Behavior* (Stanford, Calif.: Stanford University Press, 1958) pp. 300–315.

[7] Paul F. Secord, W. Bevan, and B. Katz. "The Negro Stereotype and Perceptual Accentuation," *Journal of Abnormal and Social Psychology*, 53 (1956), 78–83.

[8] See Secord and Backman, *Social Psychology*, pp. 49–74.

[9] Harry C. Triandis and Leigh M. Triandis, "Some Studies of Social Distance," in I. Steiner and M. Fishbein, eds., *Current Studies in Social Psychology* (New York: Holt, Rinehart and Winston, Inc., 1965), pp. 207–16.

characteristics such as religion (Greeks) or occupation (Germans) as most important.

Finally, there is the vast array of personality traits or characteristics attributed to others which influences one's evaluation of them. The data on this topic seems to indicate that people are attracted to others whom they perceive to be similar to themselves. We will return to this point in our discussion of interpersonal attraction in Chapter 8. In summary, it appears as if a wide variety of cues given off by another person help in our evaluation of them. Some of these cues may give us accurate information and some may be inaccurate. The particular way in which these cues are used is partially dependent upon one's culture and values; that is, the characteristics of the perceiver are also important.

The Perceiver. In general there appear to be two sets of variables about the perceiver that are important in understanding one's perceptions of others. First, one's own social and personality characteristics make a difference. In the Triandis and Triandis study mentioned above people who were more secure, more independent, and had a high tolerance for ambiguity were more accepting of others who were different from themselves. People who were high on a scale reflecting the social sophistication or breadth of perspective of the subject were more accepting than those who had low scores on this scale. The implications for selection in multiracial or national organizations that desire an accepting attitude is clear.

It also appears as if the complexity of one's perceptions about other people is important. People differ in ways that they describe others. Some use physical characteristics such as tall, dark, and handsome, to describe someone, while others might use a central trait: sly, tricky, and ruthless. A third level of complexity would include a wide variety of traits such as friendly, aggressive, and honest while a fourth description might include both favorable and unfavorable characteristics: sly, honest, passive, and charming. This latter constellation of traits is a more complex mode of perceiving than that which uses traits which are all very similar, or physical characteristics. Fiedler's research in the area of leadership has shown that the leader's complexity of perceiving his or her co-workers is significantly related to the group's performance, depending upon the situation in which they are working.[10]

The Situation. The final set of circumstances which are related to

---

[10] Fred E. Fiedler, *A Theory of Leadership Effectiveness* (New York: McGraw-Hill Book Company, 1967).

one's perceptions of others is the situation in which one finds himself. If you are traveling in another country you may find that your evaluation and interaction with a fellow American is very different from how you would have behaved if you had met at home. The familiarity of the situation is important as are the norms or expectations that influence one's behavior. A professor's evaluation of a student who slapped him on the back and said, "Hi, Prof" might differ depending upon whether the professor was in the middle of a lecture to 200 people or at a graduation party. People judge other's behavior as indicants of their personality and these judgments are partially related to the appropriateness of the behavior vis-à-vis the situation.

Perception, then, of both people and objects is dependent upon some historical factors, some current factors and some situational factors. Our past experience, culture, and learning influence these judgments as do our current needs and feelings along with the physical and social environment. These relationships are important in understanding why people behave the way they do. They are also important for areas of organizational behavior such as leadership, selection, and training.

Implications for Organizational Participants

The perceptual world obviously intrudes on much of our behavior. It shapes what we see, how we evaluate it and the ways we behave toward it. This is true for both our observations of objects and people. There are, however, a number of systematic errors that people are inclined to make because of the perceptual process. You will recall that perception entails a simplified categorization process and that our past experience, present needs, and aspects of the environment all tend to shape this sorting and labeling activity. Described below are a number or ways that this process generates inaccurate or unrepresentative information.

Stereotyping. We are frequently confronted with situations where we know very little about a person except some prominent characteristic such as age, race, or occupation. Given just this one bit of information we tend to make a classification which attributes a whole set of characteristics to the person. This categorization process is called stereotyping and it serves the function of reducing the complexity of the interpersonal world. Instead of dealing with people in terms of their unique individuality we frequently deal with them as representatives of a class or category.

In some cases this process may be helpful. Stereotyping reduces ambiguity and enables one to classify people quickly and easily. In other situations it may provide too simplistic an evaluation and lead to errors of judgment. A number of studies have helped to clarify our understanding of the stereotyping process.

The interesting fact is that there is some consensus among people as to what attributes are most descriptive of a given group. Research by Karlins, Coffman, and Walters asked 100 Princeton students to indicate which attributes from a list of 84 were most applicable to 10 ethnic groups.[11] If traits were assigned at random one would expect about 6 percent of the students to pick any given characteristic for any given group. However, for almost every ethnic group at least three traits were selected by over 20 percent of the students and at least one attribute by over 50 percent of the students. For example, Americans were seen as materialistic (67 percent), English as conservative (53 percent), and Germans as industrious (59 percent). Thus, there appears to be some agreement about the attributes that belong with a given classification.

Triandis argues that the reason for this consensus is that there may be a kernel of truth in the attribution process.[12] He suggests that people make judgments of other groups compared to their own group. If Germans on the average are seen as slightly more industrious than Americans then that characteristic will be part of the stereotype even though the average difference may be very small.

One obvious area in organizations which suffers from sterotyping is the selection interview. In most cases the prospective employee spends a short time with the interviewer and yet decisions about hiring are frequently made on this basis. Dress, race, age, sex, and past occupational experience all serve as dimensions for which people have stereotypes. It is for these reasons that many industrial psychologists are increasing the emphasis on objective tests and work simulations as predictive devices for selection. In any case, stereotyping is prevalent in most interpersonal exchanges. The task of the organization is to remove ways in which stereotyping is dysfunction and in many cases illegal.

Halo Effects. Another bias in evaluating others is the halo effect. Here we are referring to the process where one's impression (either favorable or unfavorable) of a person in one area tends to influence

---

[11] M. Karlins, T. L. Coffman, and G. Walters, "On the Fading of Social Stereotypes: Studies in Three Generations of College Students," *Journal of Personality and Social Psychology*, 13 (1969), 1–16.

[12] H. C. Triandis, *Attiude and Attitude Change* (New York: John Wiley & Sons, Inc., 1971).

his or her judgment about other areas. The early research by Asch on impression formation described such misperceptions.[13] Subjects who were told an individual was skillful, industrious, intelligent, practical, determined, and warm also attributed the characteristics wise, humorous, popular, and imaginative. However, when cold was substituted for warm, there was a marked tendency to attribute negative traits to the person.

In organizations halo effects may appear in performance ratings. In most cases a supervisor only observes a small sample of an employee's actual behavior. If for some reason or another the supervisor samples an area where the employee does well (e.g., in meetings or on an interpersonal skill level), the supervisor may judge the individual's performance to be excellent in other areas about which he has little information. The obverse is obvious—a well-known principle of CYA ("cover your ass") exists in many organizations. Thus, employees may be more concerned with not making a noticeable mistake than with excellent performance.

One area of research that is directly related to stereotyping and halo effects has been conducted by Fiedler.[14] His measure of leadership style asks a manager to rate his "least preferred co-worker" (LPC) on a number of attributes. Those people who tend to have halo effects in that they see their LPC as bad on every dimension tend to be more directing and structuring in their approach to leadership. Managers who say that their LPC can be good in some areas (perhaps unrelated to work) tend to be more interpersonal and flexible in their leadership style.

In terms of interpersonal behavior and halo effects we often find that supervisors tend to rate subordinates higher that have similar values or personality characteristics. Senger reported on 28 managers and 151 subordinates engaged in grocery retailing and as expected the closer the match between the values of the manager and the subordinate the more competent the subordinate was rated.[15] Clearly, then, these halo effects have an important impact on various areas of organizational behavior.

Projection. This term has assumed a number of different meanings. Its original usage suggested that people relieve feelings of guilt about

---

[13] S. E. Asch, "Forming Impressions of Personalities," *Journal of Abnormal and Social Psychology,* 1946, 258–90.

[14] Fiedler, *A Theory of Leadership Effectiveness.*

[15] J. Senger, "Managers' Perceptions of Subordinates Competence as a Function of Personal Value Orientations," *Journal of the Academy of Management,* 14 (1971), 415–24.

themselves by projecting the blame onto someone else. More recently the term has come to mean any situation where one attributes to others the same feelings that he or she is having. There is also evidence that people will attribute to others those characteristics which one feels represent negative aspects of his or her own personality. Some research shows that people high on traits such as stinginess, obstinancy or disorderliness see others in a similar light.

This process serves an important role in maintaining a positive self-concept. We can justify our own aggressiveness, pettiness, or greed by saying that others are worse. However, these types of misperceptions are critical for a number of organizational situations. What frequently occurs is that we may make inferences about the causes of people's behavior based on what we would do in the same situation. If we want a raise, we think others want the same thing; if we constantly butter up the boss, we are suspicious of the motives of subordinates. Obviously a number of interpersonal and technical decision areas could be effected.

Selective Perception. A final perceptual process which leads to inaccuracies is called selective perception. We've already discussed the fact that our current needs and past experience partly determine what we attend to and what we perceive. It is also true that the more ambiguous the external situation, the more we rely on these internal cues.

A good research example of selective perception was provided by Dearborn and Simon.[16] They had 23 executives read a long (10,000 words) and factual case study about a steel company. Each of the executives was placed in one of four groups depending upon their departmental affiliation. There were six from sales, five from production, four from accounting and eight miscellaneous (R&D, PR, etc.).

Each of these executives were asked to list what they thought was the major problem that a new president of the steel company should deal with first. Table 5–1 presents these data.

It is clear that people tended to see problems in those areas of major interest to themselves. Accountants and sales executives were concerned with financial sales problems. Production people were anxious about classifying various production issues. Two executives in public relations and industrial relations saw human relations as the problem. These executives attended to those aspects of the situation which were directly relevant to their own goals and concerns.

At a somewhat broader level selective perception has a major impact

---

[16] D. C. Dearborn and H. A. Simon, "Selective Perception: A Note on the Departmental Identifications of Executives," *Sociometry,* 21 (1958), 140–44.

TABLE 5-1
Selective Perception of Managers

| | | Number Who Mentioned | | |
| | | --- | --- | --- |
Department	Total Number of Executives	Sales	"Clarify Organization"	Human Relations
Sales	6	5	1	0
Production.	5	1	4	0
Accounting	4	3	0	0
Miscellaneous	8	1	3	3
Totals	23	10	8	3

Source: D. C. Dearborn and H. A. Simon, "Selective Perception: A Note on the Departmental Indentifications of Executives," *Sociometry,* 21 (1958), 143.

on the communication and decision processes. We hear what we want to hear and screen out other information. We overestimate the importance of past trends or circumstances. We simplify rather complex relations to fit an already determined pattern.

In summary, we make a lot of perceptual mistakes. To overcome these problems we must consciously develop a number of "checking" mechanisms to aid us in situations where stereotyping is most dangerous. We must attempt to use only accurate, observable, reliable information about others. We should become better aware of our own biases and learn to truly take the "role of the other." Finally, in many organizations people are depending upon technological aids. Computers can store, record, and generate data on a variety of issues. Hopefully all of these processes can reduce inaccuracies and in many cases inequities that occur because of perceptual errors.

The aggregate of all our perceptual biases and experiences is part of what makes us unique. This uniqueness is typically described as one's personality. We turn now to an analysis of this concept.

PERSONALITY

The Matter of Uniqueness

That the individual possesses bodily sensations, perceptions, drives, attitudes, motives, values, and goals is undeniable. In fact, these elements which comprise human behavior have been widely studied. So in one sense we know a great deal about behavior. Nevertheless something is lacking in this superabundance of scientific research on behavior.

There is a deficiency in our understanding of the process which integrates into an acting whole the many facets, both physiological and psychological, which comprise the individual. This integrating process has been called by some the self, by others personality. But in any case it is conceived of as an organizing element beyond the parts which in total compose the individual. Because of the almost limitless possibilities for variety and combination of these parts uniqueness, as a product of personality organizing, is a commonplace observation.

The notions of personality and uniqueness pose difficulties for science in general and psychology in particular. On the one hand, science seeks generality. The particularization which the study of personality forces on science is hard to reconcile. Indeed, because of this difficulty some psychologists claim that it is impossible to study personality scientifically. They say if we are to know anything about this process we will learn through art or literature which involves purely subjective insights.

On the other hand, certain psychologists (e.g., some behaviorists) have denied that such a thing as personality exists at all. Behavior, they say, can be explained according to stimulus-response and conditioning principles. They would go further noting that the admission of an intrinsic organizing force which produces uniqueness in humans is not only unscientific, but borders on the unpardonable crime of a metaphysical interpretation of behavior.

Be this as it may, Allport observes that in recent years, after decades of obscurity, the concept of self or some similar label, has been resurrected and given currency as an integrating, organizing process in human personality.[17] The fact that this can and has been done without trespassing on the mystical regions of metaphysics is necessary to recognize. This change in attitude is important to administration and its use of the behavioral sciences. Those theories of behavior which have found some acceptance in administration, such as Maslow's hierarchy of needs and Argyris's notion of psychological development, have rested largely on a holistic interpretation of personality.[18] A policy framework for executive action in motivation and organizational design requires an integrated conceptualization of personality.

Administrators need more than facts on such discrete subjects as perception, learning, and drives. A *program* of motivation requires the as-

---

[17] Gordon W. Allport, *Becoming* (New Haven, Conn.: Yale University Press, 1955), p. 55.

[18] See A. H. Maslow, *Motivation and Personality* (New York: Harper & Bros., 1954), chapter 3 and Chris Argyris, *Personality and Organization* (New York: Harper & Bros., 1957), chapter 2.

sumption that it is "whole man" who seeks satisfaction in the organizational setting. Dissecting people in terms of IQ or attitudinal profiles might serve limited personnel objectives for selection, placement, or promotion. But it may not be useful when it comes to modifying the organizational climate in order to secure higher levels of motivation and satisfaction. It is only by:

1. Recognizing the uniqueness of personality (the principle of individual differences),
2. But appreciating that there are certain uniformities in personality which can be studied scientifically, and
3. Knowing that each personality is anchored in a social matrix that a meaningful program of change in the environmental milieu can be evolved.

What Is Personality?

Personality while often regarded by the lay person as a description of a fixed self, is rather a process of change. More specifically it is the description of human psychological growth and development. Within the context of change and development, Bonner gives six propositions intended to clarify the nature of personality.[19] It is useful to review these propositions and to show their relevance to administrative practice.

1. Human Behavior Consists of Acts. In any complex behavioral form such as play or participation in an organization the whole individual acts. In seeking goals the individual acts totally. While such discrete processes as learning, perception, or cognition may be important aspects of acts they are merely a part of it. Hence a view of personality must focus on the pattern of the total act rather than isolated psychological or physiological aspects of it. One might say that personality itself is the equivalent of this conceptualization of the total act. This proposition is the most generalized and it ties in with what we said in the previous section about the need in administrative theory and practice for a unified conception of behavior.

2. Personality Conceived as a Whole Actualizes Itself in a Specific Environment. This proposition indicates that the individual cannot be understood apart from his or her environment. In fact, the person environment forms a syndrome, two or more mutually dependent interacting

---

[19] Hubert Bonner, *Psychology of Personality* (New York: Ronald Press Co., 1961), pp. 38–40.

parts, creating a fairly stable structure of relationships which possesses an inherent potential of predictability, as long as one is sufficiently sensitized to it.

The importance of this proposition has not been lost on students of administration. The interactional nature of the individual, the small group, and the formal work situation have been a source of emphasis since the Hawthorne experiments. Recently, as a result of changes in the applied behavioral sciences, efforts have been made through training to sensitize executives to the interactional climate so that they can act in it and on it with greater effectiveness. More is said about this in Chapter 16 on management development.

3. *Personality Is Characterized by Self-Consistency.* The normal personality is in a state of dynamic equilibrium. It preserves its identity, yet is able to change. It is flexible, but it maintains a consistent character. This proposition and the next one are closely related.

4. *Personality Is Goal-Directed Behavior.* In a real sense it is the choice among goals that distinguishes one personality from another. The individual, through his personality strives for more than self-consistency. He tries to obtain ends. Granted those ends he seeks and those he avoids are in part determined by their contribution to the maintenance of self-stability. But at the same time, the power to select and strive for goals imparts a dynamic quality to personality as well as lending unity to it.

A great deal of the literature draws management's attention to the unity and individuality of each personality on the one hand, coupled with a person's striving for the satisfaction of motive on the other. Motives and goal-directed behavior have been discussed already but it should be noted that of all the qualities of personality, these have the most extensive treatment in the literature of administration.

5. *Personality Is a Time-Integrating Structure.* Personality embodies the past and anticipates the future. From the standpoint of explaining behavior, the behaviorists and the psychoanalytic schools emphasize the past. Humans are a product of conditioned responses, habits learned in the past; or people in adulthood reenact in new styles the archaic solutions to conflicts which they faced in childhood. While much is true in these explanations of behavior they are inadequate. They do not work out well in terms of man's anticipation of the future.

People are also future oriented. Nowhere is this more evident than in administration which counts planning first among the executive functions. It is just recently in the area of decision theory and motivation that any serious attention has been given to the forward-looking quality of personality which plays a key role in policy, production, and participation decisions throughout the organization.

6. Personality Is a Process of Becoming. Bonner states this last proposition in these terms ". . . personality is an organization of potentialities striving to actualize themselves."[20] One might use this statement as a rallying slogan for the value system of industrial humanism. Indeed, the organizational changes and modifications suggested by those movements claiming allegiance to the social ethics in American management thought have foremost in mind an environment which will allow for the actualization of the individual's personality.

Determinants of Personality

The interplay of three major determinants affect the formation and development of personality. They are the individual's physiological inheritance, the groups with which one is affiliated, and the culture in which one participates.

Physiological Determinants. Heredity supplies the individual with the basic equipment for survival and growth. This includes such constitutional factors as body type, muscular and nervous systems, and the glandular apparatus. Also heredity equips the person with a basic intellectual capacity. But the ways in which intelligence manifests itself in later life are more a function of environment.

Other physiological determinants of personality include reduction of organic drives such as hunger, thirst, and sex. These drives and others like them, while basic to the species, may be satisfied in many ways which are determined more by the culture than by the primitive urge itself.

The Group. The family and the school are the most influential institutions in shaping the emerging personality. Later in life so-called anchorage groups or primary affiliations at work or in social or recreational activities mold the personality. These associations are labeled anchorage or reference groups because they give the individual points of reference; they define the role played by the individual along with his or her position in a social matrix.

The Culture. This determinant is closely associated with the anchorage groups above. The individual is a participant in a generalized or prevailing culture which defines social roles and sanctions their perfor-

---

[20] Ibid., p. 40.

mance. Certain broad cultural expectations with respect to major roles, like that of parent, husband, wife, minister, or teacher act on the individual. Also, being a member of many anchorage groups within a society, the individual participates in a number of subcultures which modify behavior.

Measurement of Personality

There appear to be four major methods of measuring personality characteristics.[21] In some cases, experimental procedures are established which help in the assessment of some characteristic. The military, for example, has certain simulations through which they purport to measure leadership skills. A second method uses rating scales. In this situations peers or friends make judgments about an individual's traits. These types of ratings are frequently used in recommendation forms. A third approach requires the subject to fill out a questionnaire. These questionnaires typically present a set of structured questions to the individual and he or she responds by checking the correct answer or with a true-false or choice response. The Minnesota Multiphasic Personality Inventory is perhaps the most well-known and frequently used test of this variety.[22] The test employs over 400 questions and provides information about a variety of personality characteristics. A final approach to the measurement problem utilizes projective tests. These tests have the subject respond to a picture, an ink blot, or an uncompleted sentence by writing a story about the stimulus information. The responses are then scored on a set of dimensions supposedly related to personality traits.

In all four methods there are strong and weak points and excellent and poor tests. It is suggested that the reliability and validity of the test be thoroughly checked before instituting such a device. Recent Supreme Court decisions and congressional hearings have also stressed limitations with which the personnel director should be acquainted.

Use of Personality Tests

Almost all organizations use some kind of selection devices to gain information about possible employees. In Chapters 6 and 8 we will discuss the empirical findings that relate personality characteristics to organizational behavior and performance. In general it appears as if these

---

[21] For a full discussion, see Norman R. F. Maier, *Psychology in Industry* (Boston: Houghton Mifflin, 1965), pp. 302–32.

[22] *Minnesota Multiphasic Personality Inventory* (New York: Psychological Corporation, 1945).

techniques have been incorrectly used in many cases. Even in cases where they have been applied with extreme caution the results are not terribly impressive. Both the uniqueness of the individual and the complexity of the situation have forced us to realize that there are no simple formulas for selecting people for organizational positions. In the following section we discuss some specific personality measures and their relationship to important aspects of the organizational environment.

PERSONALITY AND BEHAVIOR

The utility of personality measure depends upon their accuracy in predicting those behaviors that may be important for organization effectiveness or adjustment to organizational life. Jobs are different in so many ways that often the best we can do is simply to examine the relationship between some personality characteristic and a broad occupational category or status level. Since much of the research emphasizes the use of personality inventories within a specific firm the literature is filled with studies that report, let's say, the correlation between nine different factors of a specific inventory and one's position or job type in a specific company. So, an initial question would simply ask whether personality measures are in general related to occupational status.

A review of a series of studies by Ghiselli and Barthol showed a number of differences.[23] Their data suggest that in fact certain personality measures do show rather consistent relationships for certain occupational groups. The strength of the relationships, however, is weak. Most of these results make sense in terms of our general beliefs of what certain groups are like. Sales clerks, for example, tend to be high in measures of empathy which taps an individual's ability to put oneself in another's position. If we believe that people generally seek out jobs in which they will feel comfortable then we would expect at least some relationship between their personality and type of occupation chosen.

But besides the general question of occupational differences one might want to know how well personality measures predicted specific behavior or performance within an organizational setting. In this instance personality measures serve as selection devices. We've already mentioned that the indiscriminate use of these tests typically provides at best moderate predictions for later success. For example Harrell followed up the success of three Stanford MBS classes.[24] After 5 years he divided the groups

---

[23] E. E. Ghiselli, and R. P. Barthol, "Role Perceptions of Successful and Unsuccessful Supervisors," *Journal of Applied Psychology*, 40 (1956), 241–44.

[24] T. W. Harrell, "The Personality of High Earning MBA's in Big Business," *Personnel Psychology*, 22 (1969), 457–63.

into thirds according to their income and compared the top third with the bottom third on 55 personality measures gathered when the MBS's were still at Stanford. Only 13 of the 55 measures showed reliable differences and these traits were as we would expect. High earners tended to have a lot of energy, self-confidence, boldness, and less apprehension about making decisions. These findings are fairly typical in terms of the effectiveness of personality inventories in predicting later success.

A much more frequent research strategy is to examine a small set of personality measures for given groups or situations in attempts to predict specific behaviors. Thus, our theoretical development has become more refined. And when one examines the research findings of this type some consistency appears. Some of these relationships are described below.[25]

Interpersonal Style and Group Behavior. Some personality measures attempt to assess the particular ways in which people respond to others and this general interpersonal style is reflected in their social behavior. Fiedler, for example, has found that socially distant leaders tend to be more directive in their behavioral style and tend to be most effective in situations calling for such a style.[26] A prominent personality measure that fits in this category is an individual's "authoritarian" orientation.[27] People who score high on this scale believe it is correct that there should be status and power differences among people and that the use of power and hierarchical decision making is proper in organizational settings. In general the research shows that these types of people use directive behavior, are more inclined to conform to rules and regulations and tend to emerge as leaders in situations requiring a more autocratic and demanding style. Another set of interpersonal style measures assess the general tendency to like or trust other people or to avoid and distrust them. People high on the trust dimensions like group situations, contribute positively to group cohesiveness, enhance social interaction and avoid competitiveness.

Social Sensitivity. A second set of traits can be described as those dealing with the individual's sensitivity to other people. There are a number of tests available that measure empathy, sociability, and insight. As one would expect people high on these dimensions tend to do well in social settings, are warmly accepted in the group and interact more with others.

---

[25] Fiedler, *A Theory of Leadership Effectiveness.*

[26] See M. E. Shaw, *Group Dynamics* (New York: McGraw-Hill Book Company, 1971) for a review.

[27] T. W. Adorno, E. Frenkel-Brunswick, D. J. Levinson, and R. N. Sanford, *The Authoritarian Personality* (New York: Harper & Bros., 1950).

Ascendant Tendencies. One would expect that individuals differ in their attempts and desires to be prominent and dominating in organizational settings. Numerous tests attempt to measure such traits as assertiveness, dominance, or prominence. Recently Christie has developed a popular scale called the Mach IV which supposedly taps the degree to which the individual is high on Machiavellianism; that is, the degree to which one uses people to gain their ends.[28]

The results using these types of tests are somewhat mixed. It is fairly well accepted that these types of individuals are more assertive in their behavior and make more leadership attempts. They also seem to have a substantial impact on group decisions. The data are unclear, however, as to whether such people actually make good leaders or are accepted and well liked. In most cases it seems as if this type of style is accepted only where the group is highly task oriented or under stress.

Dependability and Social Stability. People who are consistent, responsible and generally predictable seem to behave in some consistent ways that are important for group effectiveness. People who are seen as dependable and stable will probably be desirable as group members. Unconventional or unexpected behavior is likely to be disruptive.

The research on these traits supports these predictions. Unconventional people are frequently disliked and rejected by the group. People who are anxious or show emotional instability are likely to be found in groups that are low in cohesiveness or morale. The anxious individual is frequently unable to pursue the group task, tends to vacillate on important judgments, and has lower aspirations for the group.

Locus of Control. There are also a number of personality measures that tap an individual's cognitive style. These traits are related to the ways in which the individual processes information and the judgments he or she makes based on these observations. Locus of control (as well as the next three traits discussed) refers to such a characteristic.

People who see what happens to them in the world as being caused by their own behavior are classified as having an internal locus of control. Those who believe that what happens to them occurs because of luck or chance are said to have an external locus of control. A recent paper by Mitchell, Smyser, and Weed summarizes most of the results found for organizational participants.[29]

In general, internals tend to be more satisfied with their work and are more satisfied on the job when they are working under a participative

[28] R. Christie, et al., *"Machiavellianism,"* (unpublished manuscript, Department of Social Psychology, Columbia University, 1968).

[29] T. R. Mitchell, C. M. Smyser, and S. E. Weed, "Locus of Control: Supervision and Work Satisfaction," *Academy of Management Journal* 18 (1975) 623–30.

management system. Externals on the other hand appear to prefer a directive style more than internals do. It was also found that internals were more likely to hold managerial positions than lower level jobs. This implies that internals either are more likely to rise to managerial positions or that people become more internal as they increase in status.

In examining the power bases and behaviors used by internal and external managers we find a fairly consistent picture. The internal manager tends to use more considerate behavior and relies on expertise, rewards, and attractiveness as sources of influence. Externals emphasize more coercive power bases and use more structuring behaviors. This trait may be of potential importance for predicting individual effectiveness in the more open and flexible organizational settings that are being forecast for the future.

Risk Taking. There has recently been a major research effort aimed at assessing an individual's propensity to take risks either individually or within the group setting.[30] There is some agreement that there are individual differences on this dimension and that this characteristic can be systematically related to various aspects of the group interaction and decision process.

In general, high risk takers seem to spend less time making decisions and use less information making these decisions. A recent study by Taylor and Dunnette substantiated these findings with 79 line managers of a large manufacturing firm.[31] These managers worked on some simulated personnel decisions involving the choice of which individual to hire. High risk takers took a shorter time to make their choice and used fewer bits of information than did low risk takers. The decision accuracy however was the same for both groups.

Dogmatism. A cognitive style that refers to people being closed minded and inflexible is frequently described as dogmatic. A scale developed by Rokeach purports to measure this trait and has been used in a number of studies investigating leadership, group process, and interpersonal adjustment.[32]

In decision-making tasks we find that these types of individuals take little time to make their decisions but are highly confident of their ac-

---

[30] N. Kogan, and M. A. Wallach, *Risk Taking: A Study in Cognition and Personality* (New York: Holt, Rinehart and Winston Co., Inc., 1964).

[31] R. N. Taylor, and M. D. Dunnette, "Influence of Dogmatism, Risk-Taking Propensity, and Intelligence on Decision-Making Strategies for a Sample of Industrial Managers," *Journal of Applied Psychology,* 59 (1974), 420–23.

[32] M. Rokeach, *The Open and Closed Mind* (New York: Basic Books, Inc., Publishers, 1960).

curacy. There are also results that suggest that dogmatism is associated with limited search for information as well.[33] A recent study by Espositio and Richards found that high dogmatics perceived a large discrepancy between how they would ideally spend their time on the job and how they actually spent their time.[34]

There is also some evidence on the proper match between a leader's behavioral style and the degree to which subordinates are dogmatic types. Weed and Mitchell found that a structuring leadership style was preferred by subordinates high on the dogmatism dimension while a considerate style was preferred by people low on the dimension.[35] Across four different types of tasks it was found that performance was highest when low dogmatic subjects worked with a leader who was high on both considerate and structuring behavioral dimensions.

Cognitive Complexity. One final cognitive dimension refers to the individual's ability to differentiate and integrate various aspects of a cognitive domain. That is, to what extent is the individual able to break, let's say, a task down into its component parts, see the underlying similarities and differences with other tasks and generally view the situation in a complex fashion. There are currently numerous tests that tap cognitive complexity and reviews of this research are available.[36]

Two major areas of research are relevant for organizational settings. First, there are a number of well-documented findings in the decision-making area. People who are high in complexity process more information, search for more information, entertain more alternative solutions, and use more complex decision strategies than people who are low in complexity. Data from numerous laboratory and field settings substantiate these general findings.[37]

A second area of research has tied complexity to leadership style and effectiveness. There is some evidence that highly complex leaders are more interpersonal in their behavioral style and that they tend to

---

[33] B. H. Long, and R. C. Ziller, "Dogmatism and Pre-decisional Information Search," *Journal of Applied Psychology*, 49 (1965), 376–78.

[34] J. P. Espositio, and H. C. Richards, "Dogmatism and the Congruence between Self-Reported Job Preference and Performance among School Supervisors," *Journal of Applied Psychology*, 59 (1974), 389–91.

[35] S. E. Weed, and T. R. Mitchell, "Leadership Style, Subordinate Personality and Task Type as Predictors of Performance and Satisfaction with Supervision," *Journal of Applied Psychology* (in press.)

[36] S. C. Streufert, *Cognitive Complexity: A Review* (Lafayette, Ind.: Purdue University, Technical Report No. 2, October 1972).

[37] R. J. Ebert, and T. R. Mitchell, *Organizational Decision Processes: Concept and Analysis* (New York: Crane, Russak & Company, 1975).

use more resources in problem solving.[38] There is also some support for the idea that situations high in variability of the environment are handled better by leaders high in cognitive complexity.

In summary, then, we can see how personality measures may have an important impact on how people behave in a group or organizational context. Obviously the job of the organization is to try to match an employee's personality with his job and the people with whom he works. As we suggested earlier, using one test or one inventory has historically turned out to generate poor predictions of long-run success. However, a more recent approach being used by many companies is the assessment center. In this type of situation the prospective employees take a series of personality, cognitive, and ability tests and also engage in a number of simulations that reflect the work setting for which they may be selected. The emphasis is on the use of multiple predictors for rather specific situations and jobs. Thus, the particular emphasis on any given trait may differ from job to job.

The data supporting assessment centers is moderate but better than what preceded it.[39] At least we no longer expect one trait or inventory to predict success for all the positions in an organization. Our small group research also reflects a more sophisticated outlook. Most current theories of individual or group effectiveness see personality as only a small part of the personality-behavior-situation interaction used to predict effectiveness. As our theories become better substantiated hopefully more results can be translated into practice.

An overall assessment of this chapter suggests a number of conclusions. First, people bring certain perceptual and personal tendencies to the workplace and these tendencies influence their behavior in some predictable ways. Second, the organization has some control over these tendencies. The job environment can create certain perceptions rather than others. Selection tests can be used to assess the types of people entering the organization. Finally, some attempt at matching perceptual and personal skills with a particular job can be made. Individual effectiveness should be enhanced through such a matching process.

---

[38] T. R. Mitchell, "Cognitive Complexity and Leadership Style," *Journal of Personality and Social Psychology*, 16 (1970), 166–74.

[39] A. Howard, "An Assessment of Assessment Centers," *Academy of Management Journal*, 17 (1974), 115–34.

chapter 6

Motivation

As we observe people at work we are frequently struck by their different styles or work habits. Some people are always on time, put in a good day's work and stay late. Others are less punctual and tend to get through the day with a minimal amount of effort. Some investigators have estimated that the best worker may be two to three times as productive as the worst worker. Some of this difference may stem from styles, some from skills and some from attitudes the worker brings to the task. The tendency however is to attribute the differences between these two extremes to skill. That is, we say that the worker with poor performance just doesn't have the ability. But there is something more than that. There also seems to be a willfulness about the difference. The worker with excellent performance seems to want to do well while performance may seem irrelevant to the marginal employee. In this instance, we usually refer to motivation. We suggest that one individual is more motivated or driven than the other person.[1]

In some general sense, motivation implies a wanting or volitional action by an individual. Motivation, in a more traditional sense among management writers, means a process of stimulating people to action to accomplish desired goals. Although many words are substituted for motivation (such as actuating and directing), the meaning of the process is reasonably clear. Traditionally, motivation is seen as something imposed on a worker. It is viewed as a function which a manager performs in order to get subordinates to achieve job objectives.

---

[1] E. E. Lawler, III, *Motivation in Work Organizations* (Monterey, Calif.: Brooks/Cole Publishing Company, 1973), p. 6–7.

There is another side to this definition. It is profitable to look at the motivated state of the individual. We need to be concerned with those inner forces which energize and move the individual into avenues of behavior directed toward accomplishing goals. Admittedly, these inner forces may be triggered by outside events such as a managers' behavior or the actions of a co-worker. But it is how these outside forces impact on the individuals beliefs, values, and intentions that helps us to understand motivation.

Traditionally, an examination of these forces involves two questions. The first is simply why does the organism do anything at all. That is, Why do we bother to get up in the morning? Why do we initiate any action? All of these questions concern our arousal. The second issue centers around our choices. Given that we are aroused and active why do we choose one line of action rather than another? We will find that most theories of motivation center on one of these two questions.

Historical Perspective

One of the earliest ideas about what motivates people can be found in Greek writings and later in the ideas of the British philosophers John Stuart Mill and Jeremy Bentham. The underlying idea, called hedonism, was that an organism behaves in a fashion that will maximize its pleasure. We do what we do because we believe that what we do will give us more pleasure than anything else we might do. However, since these authors never attempted to assess just what people anticipated to be the consequences of their acts the theory was of little use empirically. That is, it did little to further our understanding of how these choices came to be more or less favorable.

Further developments in the area began to shed some light on the answers to these two basic questions. First, it was argued by Thorndike, that of several responses that an organism makes to a situation those which result in satisfying or pleasurable consequences are strengthened. Those that lead to uncomfortable or unpleasant outcomes are weakened. Those that are strengthened become more probable, those that are weakened become less probable in response to the same situation.[2] Our present choices were explained in terms of past consequences. However, this "law of effect" as it was called still did little to explain why the consequences were pleasurable or not pleasurable.

---

[2] E. L. Thorndike, *Animal Intelligence* (New York: The Macmillan Co., 1911).

The explanation of why the organism behaves at all and consequently why responses are more or less pleasurable was tied to the idea of physiological needs. The organism was seen as having hunger, thirst, and other drives and pleasure resulted from reduction of these drives. At this point the "law of effect" or reinforcement would become important. A baby's behavior just prior to being fed, for example, would be strengthened. Most psychological theories are based upon the ideas of drives and reinforcement. Those theories that attempt to specify and codify the drives that motivate people are concerned with content. Those that try to describe their choice behavior will be designated as process theories. Although this distinction is not clear for every theory it points out quite nicely the distinctions we have stressed so far.

Psychological Theories: Process and Content

Perhaps the most well-known classical theory of the process type mentioned above was developed by C. L. Hull.[3] This theory suggests that behavior can be predicted from two major classes of variables: *drive* and *habit strength*. Drive is seen as those variables representing the amount of deprivation of some need while habit strength refers to the frequency of previous stimulus-response connections in similar circumstances. Drive was originally concerned with just physiological needs but was later broadened to include the reduction of any strong internal stimulus. Specifying these needs falls into the area of content theories.

Theories dealing with human needs have produced an extensive list of items that motivate an individual. The idea is that an unsatisfied need produces tension (sometimes called motives) and that tension reduction is satisfying. Categorizing produces three general categories of needs.

Basic Drives. The biological drive, already mentioned, requires the satisfaction of those basic needs essential to maintain physiological integrity—organic survival. The nature of satisfaction for this drive is specifiable. The need for food, water, rest, air, and elimination is necessary for the survival of the human organism, even though the level of satisfaction of these biological requirements differs from person to person.

Primary Motives. There are two primary motives—psychological and social. The psychological motive results in a quest by an individual to maintain mental integrity or balance. The social motive stems from

---

[3] C. L. Hull, *Principles of Behavior* (New York: Appleton-Century-Crofts, 1943).

the natural gregariousness of people, and their need to associate with others.

Derived Motives. This last category provides the richest source of motives underlying human behavior. These motives are derived from the basic social and psychological motives. Examples might include the individuals need for security or recognition or power. It is these motives which are highly variable in the sense that they change in their importance both between and within individuals. An example of such a theory is presented by H. A. Murray. Throughout his career he postulated about 20 different needs that he believed humans attempted to satisfy and this list included needs from all three of the categories above.[4]

Motivation in Organizations

Most of us spend a good portion of our waking hours either working in organizations or dealing with organizational participants. More than 80 percent of our population works in some sort of organization during their lifetime. This setting is therefore a natural place to study the causes and consequences of motivation.

A second important reason for viewing motivation in the organizational context is that our standard of living as well as our "quality of life" is dependent upon the effectiveness and efficiency of these institutions. We are a highly interdependent society and the impact of one organization (e.g., General Motors) or group (e.g., truck drivers) on the rest of society may be enormous.

One problem with any investigation of organizational life is that, just like people, organizations come in many different forms and sizes. They vary in terms of the kinds of skills needed, the clients they serve and the product they produce. However, there are some common elements which we can emphasize. In general, we have sets of people banded together over time with similar goals. As Lawler points out these factors lead to the following major characteristics.

1. *Money plays an important role.* It plays a role because to attract and retain people, work organizations have to pay people. Further, to survive, work organizations have to be financially viable. Thus, in all work organizations the obtaining, allocating, and spending

---

[4] See H. A. Murray, *Explorations in Personality* (New York: Oxford University Press, 1938).

of money is a crucial issue. Since it is important to many people, money obviously can influence motivation. Thus, any discussion of motivation in work organization must consider how the way an organization handles its money influences the motivation of its employees.

2. *Some type of hierarchy exists.* The structures of most work organizations are characterized by superior/subordinate relationships. The reason for this is simple: As organizations grow they develop coordination problems and someone or something is needed to see that the activities of the employees represent a coordinated effort toward whatever the goals of the organization are. Organizations try to solve this problem by making some people responsible for coordinating the work of others and by creating information and control systems to monitor the work of employees. Admittedly, at times it is hard to believe that the extensive hierarchies that are developed (some organizations have as many as 20 levels) actually contribute to coordination. There is no doubt that in our society the superior/subordinate relationship—the hierarchy itself—is crucial in terms of motivation. The essence of supervision is in influencing the behavior of those being supervised—for example, by influencing motivation. The hierarchial structure of organizations also means that some people have more status and power than others. Because of this, the possibility of promotion within the structure is often important to people and thus exerts a significant influence on motivation.

3. *People are given assigned tasks to perform.* Taken together, all the tasks a person does are called his job. Large organizations have literally thousands of different jobs. The reason for this division of labor is simple: no one person can perform all the functions that are necessary to do such things as manufacture and sell a car. Thus, people are given responsibility for different parts of the manufacturing and sales process. Recent research has shown that how tasks are grouped to form jobs has a crucial influence on motivation. This connection should not be surprising. The person who works on an assembly line and does the same task over and over again every 15 seconds is obviously in a different environment from that of the person who does a less repetitious task, just as a salesman is in a different position from that of a corporation president.[5]

Thus, we are frequently concerned with the role of compensation systems, leadership, technology, and the work environment in the study

[5] Lawler, *Motivation in Work Organizations,* pp. 5–6.

of motivation. But before proceeding to an analysis of specific motivations we should examine the concept of motivators more thoroughly.

Motivation and Performance

We mentioned earlier that we often attribute differences in performance to ability and motivation. Psychologists have distinguished between these factors for many years. The study of ability has led to the development of numerous aptitude and skill-related tests that assess individual differences on important work-related dimensions. Our study of motivation or the volitional part of performance has been less successful.

We have been faced with a number of problems. First, we have little understanding of how this motivation component combines with ability. Vroom has suggested the following formula:[6]

$$\text{Performance} = f(\text{Ability} \times \text{Motivation})$$

The postulated relationship is multiplicative which implies that both ability *and* motivation must be high for good performance. If either component is low or zero then performance will be low.

At the present time, however, our assessment skill of ability factors has outdistanced our understanding of the motivational factor. In a recent paper entitled "Performance Equals Ability and What" Marvin Dunnette has concluded that "ability differences still are empirically the most important determiners of differences in job performance."[7] Thus, we have yet to ascertain how motivation combines with ability to produce different performance levels.

But an equally compelling problem is to accurately describe the motivational process. Before we can start investigating how ability and motivation combine we must agree upon what we mean by motivation and how it is measured. There are three main theoretical approaches that have been tried. The first strategy is an attempt to specify individual motives that are related to organizational performance. The second set of theories describes *sets* of needs or motives and their interrelationships. Both of these first two orientations are concerned with our arousal or

---

[6] V. H. Vroom, *Work and Motivation* (New York: John Wiley & Sons, Inc., 1964).

[7] M. D. Dunnette, *Performance Equals Ability and What,* Center for the Study of Organizational Performance and Human Effectiveness, University of Minnesota, Technical Report No. 4009 (Minneapolis, 1973), p. 22.

energizing question about motivation. The final approach emphasizes the process which prompts individuals (once they are aroused) to behave in specific ways.

Organization Theories: Individual Motives

Competence and Curiosity. A now classic paper by Robert W. White stated the evidence for what he called a need for competence.[8] Animals and humans show a desire to master their environment and this mastery is pleasurable independent of outside rewards. White argues that all organisms must learn to interact successfully with their environment and that this behavior is a combination of both instinctual and learned drives. This motive is supposedly aroused when we are faced by new challenging situations and dissipates after repeated mastery of the task. The obvious implications for job design are that challenging jobs are motivating in themselves and that if enough variability is present the competence motive may be maintained.

A highly related set of motives are described as curiosity, or activity motives. Early animal research discovered that organisms seemed to enjoy activity and exploration for their own sake. Rats will prefer places filled with objects to an empty box and monkeys will persist in solving puzzles for many days without any contingent rewards. Children when given control of what can be shown on a television will choose complex stimuli over simple ones.[9]

Research on adults show similar findings. One well-known study had college students placed in a darkened room which was partially sound-deadened. They wore opaque goggles and gloves to reduce other sensations. They were provided with a cot; food was also available. Almost none of the subjects could endure the lack of stimulation more than two days, and numerous examples of hallucinations were reported.[10]

In studies in organizational settings similar findings are available. People develop negative attitudes toward highly repetitive tasks and

[8] R. W. White, "Motivation Reconsidered: The Concept of Competence," *Psychological Review*, 66 (1959), 297–333.

[9] H. F. Harlow, "Mice, Monkeys, Men and Motives," *Psychological Review*, 60 (1953), 23–32; C. B. Smock, and B. G. Holt, "Childrens' Reactions to Novelty: An Experimental Study of Curiosity Motivation," *Child Development*, 33 (1962), 631–42; and R. C. Miles, "Learning in Kittens with Manipulatory, Exploratory, and Food Incentives," *Journal of Comparative and Physiological Psychology*, 51 (1958), 39–42.

[10] W. H. Bexton, W. Heron, and T. H. Scott, "Effects of Decreased Variation in the Sensory Environment," *Canadian Journal of Psychology*, 8 (1954), 70–76.

report experiencing fatigue and boredom. They increase their work breaks and attempt to vary their environment.[11]

Theoretical explanations are available for these kinds of motives. Berlyne has argued that we become adapted to certain levels of stimulation.[12] Slight discrepancies from this level appear to be pleasurable but large deviations are noxious and prompt the person to reduce the discrepancy. Given this type of rationale we would expect people to differ in terms of their adaptation levels and, therefore, in the attractiveness of stimulus variability on the job. In fact, research by Bills many years ago suggests that this may be the case. Highly complex jobs were pleasant for bright people but caused high rates of turnover for people who were less intelligent. The reverse was true for highly repetitive jobs.[13] If one believes that intelligence is partly related to one's preference for complex stimuli then Bills's evidence is supportive of the adaptation idea.

The Achievement Motive.   Perhaps the most thoroughly researched individual motive is the achievement motive. David McClelland is most closely connected with this work and has developed a rather comprehensive theory around the need for achievement (nAch). He suggests, first of all, that people differ in their need for achievement and that this need is illustrated in their writing and behavior. His technique for assessing nAch is the Thematic Apperception Test (TAT) which presents the subject with an ambiguous picture and asks for his interpretation of what is happening in the picture. Achievement-related themes are counted and the subject's score supposedly reflects the individual's desire for high achievement.[14]

The behavioral characteristics of high achievers has also been investigated. First of all, they tend to prefer moderate risks to situations where there is no risk or where the risk is very high. Situations where outcomes are left to chance such as gambling are avoided. A second major characteristic of high achievers is that they like immediate feedback. They desire to know how they are doing and will tend to gravitate to jobs where there is frequent assessment on fairly specific performance criteria

[11] W. E. Scott, "The Behavioral Consequences of Repetitive Task Design: Research and Theory," in L. L. Cummings and W. E. Scott, eds., *Readings in Organizational Behavior and Human Performance* (Homewood, Ill.: Richard D. Irwin, Inc., 1969).

[12] D. E. Berlyne, "Arousal and Reinforcement," in D. Levine, ed., *Nebraska Symposium on Motivation* (Lincoln, Neb.: University of Nebraska Press, 1967).

[13] M. Bills, "Relation of Mental Alertness Test Scores to Positions and Permanency in Company," *Journal of Applied Psychology,* 7 (1923), 154–56.

[14] D. C. McClelland *Achieving Society* (Princeton, N.J.: D. Van Nostrand Co., 1961).

(e.g., sales or certain management positions). Finally, high achievers seem to enjoy doing a task just for the sake of accomplishment. Task completion provides intrinsic rewards and money is desired only as a measure of excellence not as a provider of material wealth. Because of this interest in accomplishment the high achiever is frequently involved with the task and may be seen as "task oriented."

An obvious question is how does one become a high achiever? McClelland suggests that child-rearing practices are most important. Children who are fairly independent but have parents who provide clear expectations and feedback (preferably physical rewards such as hugging) developed into high achievers. But McClelland also believes that adults are changeable and can acquire greater nAch. He has developed a comprehensive training program designed to increase achievement motivation and has tested it in numerous settings.

The theory has been developed on a broader scope than individual behavior. McClelland feels that the productivity of whole cultures and societies can be predicted from the degree to which the population illustrates a need for achievement. He cites historical examples of analyzing the major written works of a culture for nAch. He reports that societies that exhibit high nAch will later experience economic growth and prosperity. Countries low on nAch will face economic decline.

Thus, we have two major propositions: first, the productivity of a firm or country can be tied to the nAch of its members and, second, that people can increase their nAch through training. The empirical support for these hypotheses is fairly convincing. Warner and Rubin report that company growth rates of a number of technically based firms in the Boston area were predictable from nAch scores and Hundal reports the same thing for small firms in India.[15]

In a series of studies McClelland and his colleagues attempted to increase nAch through various training procedures. They report that in a number of cases those who were trained experienced subsequent entrepreneurial success and were more active in stimulating business growth and in new economic ventures.

Affiliation Motive. In contrast to nAch not much research has been conducted on the motive to affiliate with others. Harlow's research with monkeys suggested that we have some sort of innate need for contact.[16] He provided two surrogate mothers one of wire and the other of cloth.

---

[15] H. A. Warner, and I. W. Rubin, "Motivation of Research and Development Entrepreneurs," *Journal of Applied Psychology,* 53 (1969), 178–84.

[16] H. F. Harlow, "The Nature of Love," *American Psychologist,* 13 (1958), 673–85.

Even though half of the monkeys were fed from the wire mother (by means of a bottle inserted in the wire) almost all of the monkeys preferred to cling to the terry cloth mother. If we believe in physiological drive reduction as the explanation of behavior then either mother should have been equally attractive. However it appears from Harlow's research that monkeys develop attachment to their mother based partly on contact comfort.

Another well-known study which illustrates the affiliation motive was conducted by Schachter.[17] Undergraduate women were subjects in the experiment and were introduced to a rather sinister looking Dr. Zilstein who stood in front of machines that were littered with wires, knobs, and switches. The women were told that they were going to participate in an experiment on the effects of electric shock and there would be a short delay while they set up the equipment. Each subject had the opportunity to wait by themselves or with another subject (who was a stranger). The results showed overwhelmingly that they preferred someone elses company.

A more refined version of the study gave women the same initial story but then divided the subjects into two groups. One group was given the same choice as above. They could wait alone or with someone else who was a participant in the experiment. The second group was given a choice of being alone or with someone else who was just waiting out in the hall to talk to an adviser. In the latter case, most of the women preferred to be alone. Thus people may prefer to affiliate with others, but the affiliation is more desirable when the people are similar in some important ways.

The more general implications are interesting. There is some sociological literature about how people tend to congregate together during a crisis. Reports from combat situations indicate that soldiers frequently bunch up during a battle which may be exactly what the enemy wants. There are also a number of organizational case studies which discuss similar problems. The classic example is the systems expert who rearranges all the desks in the office in such a way that productivity should be greatly increased. However, in the process the employees' ability to communicate with each other is also severely restricted. And rather than increases, decreases in productivity are observed.

To date, however, very little research has been specifically conducted on this motive. McClelland has a measure of need for affiliation but

---

[17] S. Schachter, *The Psychology of Affiliation* (Stanford, Calif.: Stanford University Press, 1959).

the nAch results are far more substantial. Part of the problem is that affiliation is so complex and it is hard to separate out the factors. We are not sure if someone seeks out the comfort of another for stimulation, status, love, or just to be with someone else. Thus, while it is obviously important it is hard to isolate.

Other Motives. A number of other social motives have been investigated. For example, Adler in 1911 suggested that one of a person's dominant drives was for power and others have suggested that security is a major motivating factor.[18] In this latter instance people supposedly attempt to protect themselves from unknown contingencies. It is primarily fear and avoidance oriented. Finally, a number of ethologists have recently argued that humans have an innate need for status. We will discuss this issue more thoroughly in Chapter 12 on status but the principal idea is that all animal social groups have a status hierarchy and that there is an innate drive to establish and maintain such hierarchies.

Organization Theories: Motive Classification Systems

There are three major theories in the area of organizational behavior that attempt to classify human needs into an orderly overall system.

Maslow's Theory. The familiarity of the hierarchial concept of human needs must be attributed to the excellent interpretation given it by Maslow.[19] His well-known approach is based on the idea of *prepotency* of needs.[20] Maslow scales human needs; the most prepotent are lowest on the scale. The physiological needs are first (lowest), then safety needs, love, esteem, and finally the needs for self-actualization. Once the more specific physiological needs are satisfied, *they cease to be motivators of behavior.* The individual then turns to the satisfaction of successively higher levels of needs which are, in order of prepotency:

1. *Safety.* Freedom from fear of external threats such as criminal assaults and climatic extremes.

2. *Love.* The desire for affectionate relationships among family and friends. It is the need to belong to warm supportive associations of other people.

---

[18] A. Adler, "Individual Psychology," in Carl Murchison, ed., *Psychologies of 1930,* trans. Susanne Langer (Worcester, Mass: Clark University Press, 1930), pp. 398–99.

[19] A. H. Maslow, *Motivation and Personality* (New York: Harper & Bros., 1954).

[20] Prepotency means urgency of satisfaction. A thirsty man will devote all his energies to finding water. Once the need is satisfied, needs at the next level will be activated and the cycle of satisfaction begun again.

3. *Esteem.* The wish for a high valuation of one's personal worth by oneself and the need for the esteem of others. This need manifests itself in two ways. First, a person requires self-knowledge of competence and mastery in some aspect of the world's endeavors. Second, a person needs the recognition of these achievements by others.

4. *Self-Actualization.* The need to actualize one's intrinsic potentials. The satisfaction of the preceding needs does not produce contentment in individuals. Rather they will be restless unless they can find fulfillment in doing what they are fitted to do. As Maslow puts it, "this need might be phrased as the desire to become more and more what one is, to become everything that one is capable of becoming."[21]

There are several refinements of Maslow's theory which must be made explicit. First, this hierarchy refers to the motivational scale of normal, healthy people living in a relatively highly developed society. That is, a society which provides with reasonable reliability for the satisfacton of physiological and safety needs. Second, if we are interested in what actually motivates behavior, not in what has or will motivate it, we have to say that a satisfied need is not a motivator. Third, for most normal adults the physiological and safety needs are not motivators. It is only for certain people in our society, those abnormally deprived by one circumstance or another, that these lower needs dominate behavior. It is true among those who have not experienced warm affiliative relationships, or even the esteem of others, that these needs become dominant motivators. The withdrawal of satisfaction of these needs from those who have experienced such satisfactions in the past does not cause these people to begin immediately to search for reaffirmation of love and recognition.

Therefore, and this is crucial from the standpoint of policy conclusions, the theory predicts that it is probably only the quest for higher order needs that is the motivating force, organizing and directing the behavior, of a normal adult person.

A recent paper by Wahba and Bridwell reviewed all the empirical research up to 1972 that tested all or parts of Maslow's propositions.[22] Their findings are rather discouraging. In reviewing the classification system they found some evidence that one can distinguish between broad categories of higher and lower needs. Managers, for example, tend to value esteem, autonomy, and achievement rather than security or social

---

[21] Maslow, *Motivation and Personality*, p. 82.

[22] M. A. Wahba, and L. G. Bridwell, "Maslow Reconsidered: A Review of Research on the Need Hierarchy Theory," *Proceedings of the Academy of Management*, 1973, 514–20.

relationships. This pattern of differences seems to be similar for managers at different organizational levels, for managers versus nonmanagers, and for good versus poor managers. There is very little evidence however that the specific five category system and its internal ordering have much validity.

A second set of criticisms center around the motivational dynamic of the theory. There is very little empirical support for the idea that deprivation of a need leads to domination of that need. That is, the higher the deprivation or deficiency of a given need, the higher its importance or desirability. Numerous investigations now show that need deficiency is not strongly related to need importance. A related idea which Maslow suggests is that as one need is gratified the need next highest in the order becomes activated and serves as a motivator. There is little empirical support for this hypothesis from either longitudinal or cross-sectional studies.

So, what is the overall evaluation as of today? Well, Maslow's approach to motivation has helped to emphasize that most managers are concerned about higher order needs. The empirical research seems to support this contention. The major problems with the theory are twofold. First, to the degree that managers are indeed motivated by only one or two needs such as achievement or self-actualization, the theory tells one very little about how to activate that motivation. These concepts mean different things to different people and therefore the theory provides us with very little practical information about how to proceed.

The second problem is that the theory attempts to specify the motivational hierarchy for everyone. It is clear that not everyone follows exactly the pattern suggested by Maslow. A starving artist, for example, may forego social and physical needs in an attempt to "do his thing." Thus, the specific internal dynamics of the theory are questionable. However, the emphasis on higher order needs has been an important contribution to the understanding of managerial motivation.

Aldefer's Theory. Based upon the above criticisms and some other modifications, Aldefer has suggested a similar but improved classification system.[23] Figure 6–1 presents an illustration of how Maslow's and Aldefer's theories are comparable. The more simplified version has only three need categories: existence, relatedness, and growth. Existence needs combine the maintenance of material existence, survival needs, and safety. Motivators for these needs would include pay, fringe benefits, and working conditions in the organizational setting. Aldefer's second

[23] C. P. Aldefer, *Existence, Relatedness and Growth: Human Needs in Organizational Settings* (New York: The Free Press, 1972).

FIGURE 6–1
Aldefer's Modification of Maslow's Hierarchy of Needs

level—relatedness—includes Maslow's social and esteem levels. Thus, relationships with people at work such as co-workers, subordinates, and superiors are important at this level. The growth category corresponds to the upper level ego and self-actualization needs described by Maslow.

But while the categorization system has many similarities to Maslow, the dynamics of motivation suggested by Aldefer are distinctly different. There is no built-in assumption about deprivation/domination or deficiency/activation. Aldefer suggests that when people have not satisfied their higher order needs that lower order needs may become important. Thus the importance of any need as a motivator depends upon the satisfaction of both those above it and below it. He also assumes that all needs can be active at the same time and therefore prepotency of needs is not an integral part of Aldefer's theory.

The empirical findings on the specifics of Aldefer's theory are too few and, therefore, insufficient for any sort of overall judgment of the propositions. There is support, however, for the general ideas and the theory certainly fits the data better than Maslow's system.

Herzberg's Theory. Another classification system suggested by Frederick Herzberg attempts to classify those organizational outcomes which motivate people.[24] Two sets of motivators are suggested and they are listed below.

Extrinsic Factors	*Intrinsic Factors*
1. Pay, or salary increases.	1. Achievement, or completing an important task successfully.
2. Technical supervision, or having a competent superior.	2. Recognition; being singled out for praise.
3. The human relations quality of supervision.	3. Responsibility for one's own or other's work.
4. Company policy and administration.	4. Advancement, or changing status through a promotion.
5. Working conditions; the physical surrounding.	
6. Security of the job.	

[24] F. Herzberg, *Work and the Nature of Man* (Cleveland, Ohio: World Publishing Co., 1966).

The theory, known as the "two-factor theory" or the "motivation-hygiene" theory describes a set of factors called intrinsic or motivators and a set of factors called extrinsic or hygienes which supposedly influence behavior on the job. Herzberg argues that the extrinsic factors are related to job dissatisfaction and the intrinsic factors to satisfaction. When the extinsic factors fall below some acceptable level the individual would become dissatisfied. Increments above this acceptable level are not hypothesized to lead to increments in satisfaction. On the other hand, increments in the intrinsic factors are related to satisfaction and supposedly motivation as well. Absence of these factors would not necessarily lead to job dissatisfaction. Satisfaction and dissatisfaction are described as two different concepts derived from different antecedents and therefore they should have no particular relationship to each other graphically these relationships are as follows:

Dissatisfied ——— hygienes ——→ Neutral

Neutral ——— motivators ——→ Satisfied

The controversy over the support for Herzberg's ideas is less noticeable today in the current literature. The theory has been extensively tested and reviews of the research are available.[25] In general, the evidence against the theory seems to be greater than the evidence for it. The theory suffers, first of all, from its assumptions that the motivator and hygiene factors operate in the same fashion for everyone. This statement is just not true. The second area of skepticism is about the methods used to gather the data. Herzberg originally used the "critical incident" technique to generate his theory. This technique requires employees to indicate specific incidents which they felt were related to their satisfaction or dissatisfaction with their job. Validation studies using this technique have generally supported the theory while other techniques have not. The theory, therefore, appears somewhat method bound.

In spite of these criticisms Herzberg's theory was responsible for some major contributions to our understanding of motivation. First, the theory took some of Maslows' ideas and attempted to apply them to the work setting. His emphasis on the role of job content factors had been neglected by other theorists. His applications of job enrichment principles are perhaps too simplistic, but they have had a major impact on man-

---

[25] R. J. House, and L. A. Wigdor, "Herzberg's Dual Factor Theory of Job Satisfaction and Motivation," *Personnel Psychology*, 20 (1967), 369–90.

agerial practices. Overall, then, his additional refinements have considerably improved our knowledge of the conditions most likely to lead to job satisfaction.

In summary, the hierarchical concept has played an important role in theory and practice. Its appeal is obvious. If true, it would suggest what sorts of organizational rewards will be the most efficient motivators for employees at different levels and how this will change throughout one's professional career. While it came up short of providing all that was originally suggested it has helped us to understand why different people are motivated by different rewards and the content of these rewards.

Organization Theories: The Choice Process

Given that we have a good idea of what prompts someone to seek need gratification we must learn how this prompting is translated into action. This requires an analysis of the process of motivated choice: Why do we do one action rather than another? Three main theories are discussed.

Exchange Theories. There is a growing body of literature that describes a person's behavior as an exchange process. Dissonance theory, exchange theory, equity theory, and social comparison theory all emphasize the same idea: that discrepancies between what individuals do, want, or expect and what they get motivate them to reduce the discrepancy.[26] The four major concepts involved are reward, cost, outcome, and comparison level.

> The term *reward* is a familiar one. The review of other theories has taken note of rather important rewards that are achieved in interaction. For example, consensual validation about the world as well as about oneself is a kind of reward that theories such as Newcomb's suggest people exchange in interaction. Any activity on the part of one person that contributes to the gratification of another person's needs can be considered a reward from the standpoint of the latter person. The term *cost* is similarly a very broad concept. The costs of engaging

---

[26] See the following four works: G. C. Homans, "Social Behavior as Exchange," *American Journal of Sociology*, 63 (1958), pp. 597–606. J. S. Adams, "Inequity in Social Exchange," in L. Berkowitz, ed., *Advances in Experimental Social Psychology*, vol. 2 (New York: Academic Press, 1965), pp. 267–99. L. Festinger, *A Theory of Cognitive Dissonance* (New York: Harper & Row, Inc., 1957). K. E. Weick, "The Concept of Equity in the Perception of Pay," *Administrative Science Quarterly*, 11 (1966), pp. 414–39.

in any activity not only include "punishment" incurred in carrying out that activity, such as fatigue or anxiety, but also, as Homans argues, include the value of rewards foregone by engaging in this activity rather than alternative activities. The term *outcome* refers to rewards less costs. If the outcome of an interaction is positive, it may be said to yield a *profit;* if it is negative, a *loss.* Because a person profits from an interaction with another, however, does not necessarily mean that he likes that person. For attraction to occur, the outcome must be above some minimum level of expectation or desserts, called the *comparison level.* This level is influenced by his past experiences in this relation, his past experiences in comparable relations, his judgment of what outcomes others like himself are receiving, and his perceptions of outcomes available to him in alternative relations.[27]

Although the concepts are defined above in terms of interpersonal behavior the central ideas are generalizable to other situations. Adams and Weick, for example, have applied these general ideas to motivation in organizations under the heading of equity theory.[28] According to Adams, employees develop certain ideas about how much they put into a job (inputs) and what they get out of it (outcomes). Internally, there is some standard against which this input/output ratio is compared. This standard is developed through observations of others or by knowledge of similar jobs or from past work experience. When a state of equity exists, supposedly the individuals are comfortable with their situation and no change should occur.

However, when inputs are seen as too great in comparison with outcomes and this internal standard then a state of *underreward* inequity is experienced. Obviously the employee can (a) reduce inputs, (b) increase outcomes, or (c) change the internal standard. If outcomes are too great when compared to inputs a state of *overreward* inequity exists and one can reduce this tension by (a) increasing inputs (e.g., working harder), (b) decreasing outcomes (e.g., accept less pay) or (c) change the internal standard.

A look at the empirical research shows that:

> Laboratory experiments using students as subjects have considered the effects of overpayment and underpayment as compared with those of equitable payment. Different effects are observed for hourly versus

---

[27] Paul F. Secord and Carl W. Backman, *Social Psychology* (New York: McGraw-Hill Book Co., 1964), p. 253.

[28] Adams, "Inequity in Social Exchange," pp. 267–99, and Weick, "The Concept of Equity," pp. 414–39.

incentive payment and for manipulation of inputs (perceived qualifications) versus manipulation of ouputs (pay level). In general, underpayment results in decreased output, and overpayment in increased output, except under the incentive payment condition, where changes in output would produce even more inequity. With overpayment via incentives the usual result has been an increase in quality rather than quantity. The above results have been less clear-cut when outputs have been manipulated rather than inputs. Predictions from equity theory are made very difficult by the complexity of the variables making up the input-output package and the multitude of ways in which inequity can be resolved. However, the theory presents a clear warning to organizations that they must learn a great deal more about the nature of the input-output comparisons and the way they develop and change.[29]

Part of the general problem with the theory has been to define clearly what is meant by inputs, outcomes and comparison levels. Weick has pointed out numerous ambiguities with these definitions. For example, if a comparison person talks a lot to friends, is this an indication of low inputs (spends less time working) or an outcome (has friends at work)? Or is coming late to work a low input (works less) or a favorable outcome (has more time at home)? Also, there has been difficulty in pinning down who represents a comparison person. It appears as if this standard may change from time to time and place to place.

A summary of the research findings would suggest that the predictions with regard to underpayment have better support then the hypothesis about overpayment. Somehow people have a greater tolerance for being overrewarded than underrrewarded. There are two major issues to which the theory should be addressed. First, most of the data has been generated from laboratory studies with student subjects or in simulations of organizational settings. Further research is needed in organizations to determine the generalizability of these findings.

The second issue is concerned with the mode of inequity reduction. More specifically, in any situation of inequity there are numerous ways a given subject may behave. He can change his own costs or outcomes or he may attempt to change the costs or outcomes of his comparison person. Very little is known about these modes of resolution in terms of their relationship to specific situations or types of people. Again, more research is needed.

---

[29] John P. Campbell, Marvin D. Dunnette, Edward E. Lawler III, and Karl E. Weick, *Managerial Behavior, Performance, and Effectiveness* (New York: McGraw-Hill Book Company, 1970) p. 347.

Instrumentality or Expectancy Theory. Research in a number of different areas of psychology has suggested that behavior is a joint function of the degree to which the behavior is perceived as instrumental for the attainment of some outcomes and the evaluation of the outcomes. In general these theories demand that the evaluation of each outcome be multiplied by the instrumentality of the act for reaching the outcome and then summed across outcomes. The individual will choose the behavior which has the highest anticipated payoff; that is, the behavior which is perceived as most directly leading to things the individual wants.[30] This basic idea also appears in our discussions of theories of attitudes and decision making.

A more complete statement of instrumentality theory in industrial psychology was presented by Vroom. His statement of the theory has been the basis for most of the subsequent work in this area. Vroom's book, *Work and Motivation*, presents two models; the first for the prediction of the valences of outcomes, and the second for the prediction of force toward behavior.[31] An outcome is simply anything an individual might want to attain. The valence of an outcome for a person is defined conceptually as the strength of his or her positive or negative affective orientation toward it. Valence refers to the anticipated satisfaction associated with an outcome, and is distinguished from the value of the outcome—the actual satisfaction resulting from attainment of the outcome.

The valence model states that the "valence of an outcome to a person is a monotonically increasing function of the algebraic sum of the products of the valences of all other outcomes and his conceptions of its instrumentality for the attainment of these other outcomes."[32] Symbolically,

$$V_j = f_j \left[\sum_{k=1}^{n} (V_K I_{jK}) \right]$$

where

V_j = The valence of outcome j.
I_{jK} = The cognized instrumentality of outcome j.
         for the attainment of outcome K.
V_K = The valence of outcome K.
n = The number of outcomes.

---

[30] For a review, see Terence R. Mitchell and Anthony Biglan, "Instrumentality Theories: Current Uses in Psychology," *Psychological Bulletin*, 76 (1971), 432–54.

[31] Vroom, *Work and Motivation*.

[32] Ibid., p. 17.

Cognized or perceived instrumentality is defined conceptually by Vroom as the degree to which the person sees the outcome in question as leading to the attainment of other outcomes. Instrumentality varies from minus one (meaning that the outcome in question is perceived as always leading to *not* attaining the second outcome), to plus one (meaning that the outcome is perceived as *always* leading to the attainment of the second outcome).

Although this model is general to the prediction of the valence of any outcome, it has been applied most frequently to the prediction of job satisfaction. In essence the satisfaction of the worker with his job is seen as a function of the instrumentality of the job for attaining other outcomes and the valence of those outcomes. We will refer to this model as the *job satisfaction model.*

The force toward behavior is predicted in the second model. "The force on a person to perform an act is a monotonically increasing function of the algebraic sum of the products of the valences of all outcomes and the strength of his expectancies that the act will be followed by the attainment of these outcomes."[33] Symbolically,

$$F_i = \sum_{j=1}^{n} (E_{ij}V_j) \qquad (i = n = 1, \ldots, m)$$

where,

F_i = The force to perform act i.
E_{ij} = The strength of the expectancy that act i will be
     followed by outcome j.
V_j = The valence of outcome j.
n = The number of outcomes.

The individual's expectancy is defined by Vroom as his belief concerning the probability that the behavior in question will be followed by the outcome of interest. An expectancy is a perceived probability, and therefore ranges from zero to plus one. It is distinguished from instrumentality in that it is an action-outcome association, while instrumentality is an outcome-outcome association which ranges from -1.00 to $+1.00$. While expectancies are perceived possibilities, instrumentalities are perceived correlations.

Vroom suggests that this second model can be used to predict choice of occupation, remaining on the job, and effort. In practice, it has been

---

[33] Ibid., p. 18.

tested with respect to job performance; and we will, therefore, refer to it as the *job performance model*. Specifically, Vroom states that the force on the individual to exert a given amount of effort is a function of the algebraic sum of the products of the valence of each level of performance and the person's expectation that each level of performance will be attained by that amount of effort. Note that the amount of effort, not performance, is predicted by Vroom. Effort is considered to be a behavior, while performance is an outcome.

Representations of both the job satisfaction model and the job performance model are presented in Figures 6–2A and 6–2B. A more elaborate

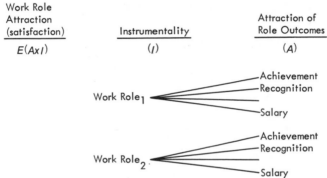

FIGURE 6–2A

Job Satisfaction Model*

Work Role Attraction (satisfaction)	Instrumentality	Attraction of Role Outcomes
$E(Ax I)$	(I)	(A)

Work Role$_1$ —Achievement / Recognition / Salary

Work Role$_2$ —Achievement / Recognition / Salary

FIGURE 6–2B

Job Performance Model

Probability of the Act	Act	Expectancy		Attraction of Work Role
$E(Ax I) E$				

Person

Superior Effort E_1 / E_2 — Attainment of Effective Performance — $-- E(Ax I)$ / Nonattainment of Effective Performance — $-- E(Ax I)$

Standard Effort E_1 / E_2 — Attainment of Standard Performance — $-- E(Ax I)$ / Nonattainment of Standard Performance — $-- E(Ax I)$

* This figure is a slight modification of the models presented by G. Graen.
Source: G. Graen "Instrumentality Theory of Work Motivation: Some Experimental Results and Suggested Modifications," *Journal of Applied Psychology Monograph,* vol. 53, no. 2, part 2 (April 1969).

model is presented in Figure 6–3. This hybrid model was developed by Campbell, Dunnette, Lawler, and Weick in an attempt to incorporate modifications deemed necessary through the process of empirical verifica-

FIGURE 6–3

Hybrid Model

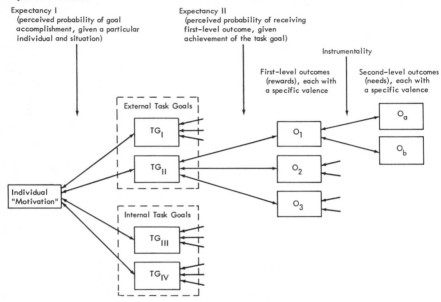

A schematic representation of a hybrid expectancy model of work motivation outlining the determinants of the direction, amplitude, and persistence of individual effort.

tion.[34] The major addition of these authors is to make a clear distinction between task goals, first-level outcomes, and second-level outcomes. Task goals might be things such as quotas, time limits, standards or the expression of loyalty or positive attitudes for the firm. First-level outcomes refer to incentives such as salary, promotion, and responsibility, while second-level outcomes refer to more basic needs such as food, housing or freedom from anxiety.

In terms of the two theoretical components, outcomes and expectancies, there are some empirical results.

> A small amount of information is available concerning the expressed preferences of managers for various types of pay plans (first level outcomes). In general, managers tend to prefer their compensation in

---

[34] Campbell et al., *Managerial Behavior.*

straight salary rather than in various types of fringe benefits. However, this generalization is based on rather limited information, and there may be a substantial discontinuity in preferences as salary increases. At the lower salary levels there might be a greater preference for fringe benefits and other rewards instrumental for satisfying the need for security, while at higher levels money could take on greater instrumentality for status and achievement needs. Salary level has not been controlled in previous research.

An even smaller fund of knowledge concerns the degree to which rewards are in fact contingent on behavior in organizations. Correlational data from Haire, et al. (1967) suggest that they are not.[35] In our own survey of 33 firms we found very little evidence that money was actually being used as an incentive linked to performance.

Some research attention has been given to the perceived contingencies between behavior and rewards (expectancy II) that managers have. The picture is not encouraging. Even if it is there, the link is seldom perceived. If basic experimental psychology has demonstrated anything, it is that contingent rewards have more predictable effects than noncontingent rewards. Much more needs to be learned about how individual perceptions of type II expectancies develop and what influences them.[36]

Reconceptualizations of Vroom's theory have become more and more elaborate, and as a consequence few investigators have fully tested the theory. In general, the theory has been supported by most of the studies that have tested it.[37] The relationships reported (correlation coefficients) between predicted effort or satisfaction and actual effort or satisfaction have been on the order of .20 to .50 which still leaves a lot of the variance of effort or satisfaction unexplained.

The major strong point of the theory is that individual differences are built into the prediction of motivated behavior. Different people may have different ideas about the instrumentalities that exist or different feelings about outcomes. The motivation process that prompts their behavior, however, is the same. The implications for managers, are (1) to find out the valued outcomes of employees and (2) to be consistent with the use of these outcomes as rewards or punishments.

The major problem with the theory in terms of its utility also seems

---

[35] M. Haire, E. E. Ghiselli, and M. E. Gordon, "A Psychological Study of Pay," *Journal of Applied Psychology Monograph,* 51 (4, Whole No. 636) (1967).

[36] Campbell et al., *Managerial Behavior,* p. 347.

[37] See Mitchell and Biglan, "Instrumentality Theories," and T. R. Mitchell, "Expectancy Model of Job Satisfaction, Occupational Preference and Effort: A Theoretical, Methodological and Empirical Appraisal," *Psychological Bulletin,* 82 (1974), 1053–77.

to be its detailed level of specificity. To the degree that instrumentalities or valences change over time, information on these variables becomes quickly dated. The theory, therefore, may be an accurate description of the motivation process but would be of little practical help for motivating employees.

Goal Setting. Our final approach which investigates the underlying cognitive process for motivation is termed goal setting. The initial statement of the theory was presented by Edwin Locke.[38] Conscious goals, incentives and intentions are related to job performance and in general goals, the goal-setting process, and their role in determining intentions are seen as the main antecedents to motivated behavior.

The key terms and a summary of the theory are as follows.[39]

Intentions or Conscious Goals. The terms *intentions* and *conscious goals* are synonymous; they are defined as "what the individual is consciously trying to do."

Task Goal. A task goal is a performance standard. Locke does not make a sharp distinction between a conscious goal and a task goal. The former results when an individual accepts the latter and redefines the task in terms of the goal. The performance standards in Locke's studies usually have been defined in quantitative terms, and little attention has been paid to qualitative performance standards.

Goal Acceptance. Locke makes a distinction between goal acceptance and goal commitment. Goal acceptance refers to whether or not an individual assumes or takes up a task goal or performance standard. Goal commitment refers to how long a person expends effort in attempting to achieve a task goal. Goal commitment, then, is similar to the persistence of behavior.

Incentive. An incentive is defined by Locke *"as an event or object external to the individual which can incite action."*[40] This is a broad definition and Locke, has, therefore, assigned several functions to it. One of these functions is to suggest specific performance standards.

Task. Locke does not explicitly define task, nor does he systematically vary the nature of the tasks used in his laboratory studies. Although he maintains that his results hold up over a wide variety of tasks, most

[38] E. A. Locke, "Toward a Theory of Task Motivation and Incentives," *Organizational Behavior and Human Performance*, 3 (1968), 157–189.

[39] Modified from T. W. Dobmeyer, "A Critique of Edwin Locke's Theory of Task Motivation and Incentives," in H. L. Tosi, R. J. House, and M. D. Dunnette, eds., *Managerial Motivation and Compensation* (East Lansing, Mich.: Michigan State University Business Studies, 1971), p. 244–59.

[40] Locke, "Toward a Theory of Task Motivation," p. 161.

of those used have been of a relatively rote variety requiring little complex ability.

Locke's major theoretical proposition is that conscious goals or intentions influence task performance. Conscious goals also mediate the influence of incentives on behavior. That is, incentives may lead an individual to set goals or to accept performance standards assigned by someone else.

The theoretical generalizations have suggested that hard goals are better than easy ones as long as they are accepted. One would also expect that participation in the goal-setting process would be more effective than assigning goals. Participation should increase commitment and acceptance. It appears as if individual goal setting is more powerful than group goals. It is the impact of the goals on individual intentions that are important. Finally, the more specific and well defined the goal the greater the impact on incentive. Supposedly, a general goal such as "do your best" is ineffective.

A recent review of the empirical studies carried out in organizational settings is fairly supportive of these propositions.[41] Latham and his colleagues have carried out a number of field applications of goal setting with Weyerhaeuser employees.[42] For example, Latham and Kinne report that a group of pulpwood producers and their logging crews, after engaging in a training program on goal setting, produced significantly more cords of wood than a control group. Also, Latham and Baldes found that logging truck drivers increased their productivity 50 percent (resulting in a savings of hundreds of thousands of dollars) when specific hard goals were set and accepted.

The major problem with the theory is that a number of theoretical components are relatively unrefined. Variables such as goal acceptance, commitment, and goal difficulty are mediators of the goal effort cognitive process and need further clarification. In many practical cases goals may not be specific enough to be clearly defined. Also, strong managerial support and involvement is necessary. Finally, we often observe that an individual's job behavior is dependent on the behavior of others. Individual goal setting seems less applicable in these interdependent situations.

[41] G. P. Latham, and G. A. Yukl, "A Review of Research on the Application of Goal Setting in Organizations," *Academy of Management Journal* (in press).

[42] See G. P. Latham, and S. B. Kinne, "Improving Job Performance through Training in Goal Setting," *Journal of Applied Psychology*, 59 (1974), 187–191. Also G. P. Latham, and J. J. Baldes, "The Practical Significance of Locke's Theory of Goal Setting," *Journal of Applied Psychology*, 60 (1975), 122–24.

In summary these cognitive approaches to understanding the motivational process have some marked communalities. All of them emphasize what the individual sees as the consequences of his or her job behavior and the attractiveness of these outcomes. They all suggest that the conscious intentions of the individual cause behavior and that this intention is modified by what one expects to get, what others are seen as getting, and the personal goals that are set. Future research efforts may be able to provide a meaningful integration of these conceptualizations.

Skinner's Operant Conditioning

Many of us in the organizational area have never considered Skinner's work as really applicable to organizational settings. Somehow our area was too complex to be handled by what was viewed as a rather simple mechanistic approach to human behavior built on data generated in the laboratory from animals. However, in *Beyond Freedom and Dignity*, Skinner describes and advocates the utilization of Skinnerian principles for the social design of our institutions and our culture.[43] This work is not to be taken lightly. Numerous researchers in our own field are now writing on this topic. A number of studies have set up reinforcement schedules in work organizations and have found supportive results. Symposia at the 1974 Academy of Management and the American Psychological Association meetings were devoted to the application of Skinner's ideas to the work setting.

What, in fact, does Skinner have to say that is important for understanding work behavior? Well, there are two major components of the theory that are important: environmental determinism and reinforcement. Two types of behavior are attributed to the human organism, respondents and operants. The former type of behavior is assumed to occur as a function of direct stimulation. An example, given by Skinner occurs when a person sneezes. These behaviors are attributed to their survival value and have played only a minor role in Skinner's research.

The operant behavior, which is emitted in the absence of any *apparent* external stimulation, has been the major unit of investigation. When this type "of behavior is followed by a certain kind of consequence, it is more likely to occur again, and a consequence having this effect is called a reinforcer. Food, for example, is a reinforcer to a hungry organism; anything the organism does that is followed by the receipt

---

[43] B. F. Skinner, *Beyond Freedom and Dignity* (New York: Alfred A. Knopf, Inc., 1971).

of food is more likely to be done again whenever the organism is hungry. Some stimuli are called negative reinforcers; any response which reduces the intensity of such a stimulus—or ends it—is more likely to be emitted when the stimulus recurs. Thus, if a person escapes from a hot sun when he moves under cover, he is more likely to move under cover when the sun is again hot. The reduction in temperature reinforces the behavior it is 'contingent upon'—that is, the behavior it follows."[44]

The central and most important characteristic of this approach is the complete omission of any reference to the consciousness of the organism. A reinforcer is a stimulus which *increases or decreases the probability of a response*. A reinforcer does not "feel good" or "bad" but it is defined simply in terms of its effects on observable behavior. Using this approach Skinner has developed what he calls schedules of reinforcement in which the frequency and timing of rewards are specified. In general, positive reinforcement works better than negative reinforcement and reinforcers should occur immediately after the behavior. Thus, through schedules of reward and punishment we can "shape" our employees to behave in a fashion deemed desirable.

The application of these ideas to motivation would require a number of steps. First the desired behaviors would need to be specified. Is motivation the number of hours worked? The amount of energy expended? While a problem of agreement exists here it also exists for our other theoretical approaches. Second, we must determine what is positively and negatively reinforcing for individual employees as well as their current rate of motivation. Third, we would apply a selected reinforcement schedule. According to the theory, motivated behavior would increase.

Fred Luthans has provided a detailed description of how such a process should be implemented. Figure 6–4 shows these steps and the critical terms for behavioral contingency management (BCM) are defined.

> *1. Identify.* The first step of B.C.M. is to identify a performance-related behavior problem. B.C.M. only deals with observable, measurable behaviors. Attitudes, desires, motives and other "inner" states are not dealt with. Also, only behaviors related to performance are targeted for change. There are a myriad of behaviors occuring in any work situation, some of them are related to performance and some of them are not. For example, complaining is often targeted as a behavior problem but may have nothing to do with performance. If the behavior has

---

[44] Ibid., p. 27.

FIGURE 6–4

Behavioral Contingency Management

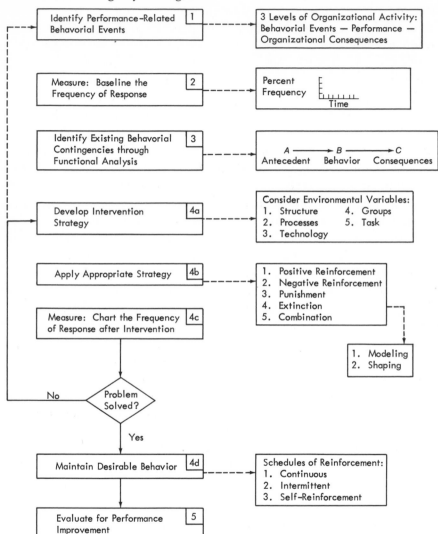

nothing to do with performance, then it is not appropriate for B.C.M. The same is true of performance problems. If there is a performance problem because of machinery or knowledge (technology) difficulties or a lack of training or ability, then this is not suitable for the B.C.M. technique. Only performance problems that are traced to behavior are appropriate for B.C.M. Typical examples in an industrial setting would include productivity, quality, tardiness, absenteeism, and safety.

2. *Measure.* After the performance-related behavior problem has been identified, a baseline frequency must be obtained. A tailor-made tally is designed to measure how often the targeted behavior is occurring under current conditions. This tally, which permits objective measurement usually on a yes-no basis, is then transferred to a graph. The vertical axis represents frequency and the horizontal dimension is time. The resulting baseline is often very revealing in and of itself. Sometimes the baseline reveals that the behavior is occurring much more than expected and sometimes much less.

3. *Analyze.* The third step of B.C.M. is to functionally analyze the antecedents and the consequences of the targeted behavior. Called A (antecedent) → B (behavior) → C (consequence) contingency analysis, this is an extremely important step in successfully changing the targeted behavior. The A → B → C contingency reveals what are the antecedent cues which set the occasion for the behavior to be emitted and what are the contingent consequences that are currently maintaining the behavior. For example, one targeted behavioral problem that often comes up is the taking of unscheduled breaks by a machine operator on a production line. An A → B → C analysis in one case revealed that the antecedent cue was the clock. At almost exactly half-way between start-up and the first scheduled break of the morning, between the scheduled mid-morning break and lunch, between lunch and the first mid-afternoon break and between the mid-afternoon break and quitting time, the operators in this shop were going to the rest-room. Importantly, the clock was not causing the unscheduled break behavior; it was merely serving as a cue for the behavior to be emitted. The reinforcing contingent consequences in this case were social gatherings at the rest room. To change the behavior, the environmental contingencies must be changed. This is the goal of the next step.

4. *Intervene.* This is the first action step of B.C.M. Based on the functional analysis, an appropriate intervention strategy is developed. Positive reinforcement is without question the most effective strategy. Desirable behaviors are accelerated through the use of positive reinforcement. Natural as opposed to contrived reinforcers are mainly used in B.C.M. A natural reinforcer is one that exists within the existing environmental setting. Social (attention, recognition, praise, and affection) and Premack (arranging existing policies and procedures, such as scheduling, so that the more desirable response follows the less desirable response) are the two most common types of natural reinforcers. The use of natural reinforcers generally involves no cost to the organization and are generally very powerful. Contrived reinforcers, on the other hand, are brought into the existing environment, are usually costly, are difficult to administer contingently, and the individual becomes satiated very quickly. Extra

money and gifts such as watches and green stamps would be examples of contrived reinforcers. A negative reinforcement strategy can be used to accelerate desired behavior but is difficult to use effectively. Punishment can be used to decelerate undesired behaviors absolutely necessary. Extinction is a much more desirable strategy to decelerate behaviors but has the disadvantage of taking more time. Both punishment and extinction should always be used in combination with positive reinforcement. For example, if unsafe behavior is punished, the incompatible safe behavioral responses should be positively reinforced. More sophisticated modeling and shaping procedures can also be employed as intervention strategies in B.C.M. After an intervention is made, frequency data is collected and charted to see if the intended results are in fact occurring. If not, another intervention is attempted. Continued charting of responses gets away from subjective rewards and punishers that managers "think" are reinforcing and punishing but often turn out to have the opposite effects. The intervention is always made contingent upon the targeted behavior and is maintained through appropriate schedules of reinforcement. At first a continuous schedule is used, then an intermittent, and finally the goal is to attain a self-reinforcing participant in the pursuit of organizational objectives.

5. *Evaluate.* The purpose of B.C.M. is performance improvement. The goal is not behavioral change for behavioral change's sake. "Bottom-line" performance results is the goal. In an industrial organization, improved productivity, quality, tardiness, absenteeism, or safety is the goal. In a hospital, it may be better patient care and in a welfare agency more effective client service. B.C.M. conducts rigorous evaluations to insure that such improvements are in fact taking place.[45]

Luthans reports that this approach has been successfully taught to first-line supervisors in manufacturing firms. Yukl reports that the process has worked well with tree planters and Nord has been successful in decreasing absenteeism by using operant conditioning techniques.[46]

A number of criticisms have been leveled at the operant technique. First, many people argue that just because behaviorists only look at the relationship between environmental contingencies and behavior there

---

[45] F. Luthans, "An Organizational Behavior Modification (O.B.MOD.) Approach to O.D." (Paper presented at the Thirty-Fourth Annual Meeting of the Academy of Management, Seattle, Washington, 1974), pp. 3–5. Also, see F. Luthans and R. Kreitner, "Behavioral Contingency Management," *Personnel,* July 1974, for a slightly different view.

[46] G. A. Yukl, "Effects of Reinforcement Schedule and Incentive Magnitude on Employee Performance: A Preliminary Report" (Paper presented at the Thirty-Fourth Annual Meeting of the Academy of Management, Seattle, Washington, 1974). Also see W. Nord, "Improving Attendance through Rewards," *Personnel Administration,* 1970, 37–41.

is no convincing evidence that these environmental events are necessarily the cause of that behavior. One's cognitive assessment of the environment, for example, expectancies of receiving a reward, and evaluation of the reward, may also be the cause. Many cognitive theorists would certainly see reinforcement as a powerful determinant of cognitions and behavior. But they would argue that environmental events are not all that cause behavior.

There are also some who fear the application of operant ideas as a technology.[47] They argue that individual consent (e.g., goal acceptance) is an integral part of the motivational process and any attempt to omit it smacks of manipulation and control. To the degree that the theory is based on the underlying principle of environmental determinism there may be room for concern. Clearly, under operant techniques there is no reason why personal inputs are necessary. If you can manipulate the contingencies you can change the behavior.

Some attempts at integration have been made.[48] Most motivational theorists would agree that rewards should follow behavior immediately and that the value of the reward is important. An individual motivational process is central to the major theories and all of the approaches discussed except goal setting postulate a sort of maximization idea: The individual will choose to behave in a fashion that will bring the largest payoff. Thus, the important components for understanding the motivational process are one's past rewards, one's expected rewards, the value of organizational rewards, the goals set by the individual, the process in which rewards are administered (timing, frequency) and one's underlying needs. We will point out throughout the text how these ideas have been incorporated into managerial practice in terms of training programs, incentive conditions, bonus plans, job design, and organizational change.

---

[47] T. R. Mitchell, "Cognitions and Skinner: Some Questions about Behavioral Determinism" (Paper presented at the Thirty-Fourth Annual Meeting of the Academy of Management, Seattle, Washington, 1974). Also see J. D. Nolan, "Freedom and Dignity: A 'Functional' Analysis," *American Psychologist*, 29 (1974), 157–60.

[48] T. R. Mitchell, "Motivation Theory: An Attempt at Integration" (Paper presented at a conference on Work Design in York, England, August 1974). Also see S. F. Jablonsky, and D. L. Devries, "Operant Conditioning Principles Extrapolated to the Theory of Management," *Organizational Behavior and Human Performance*, 7 (1972), 340–58.

chapter 7

Attitudes

I n a 1935 article which reviewed the research on attitudes, Gordon Allport stated that "The concept of attitude is probably the most distinctive and indispensable concept in contemporary American social psychology."[1] In the organizational setting, attitudes are thought to be tied to
one's personality and motivation. An employee is said to have a good
"attitude" about work, or we seek out our supervisor's opinion or attitude
about some topic. The purpose of this chapter is to clarify what we mean
by the word "attitude" and discover how it can be useful in understanding organizational behavior.

Definition

Although Allport uncovered over 100 different definitions in his review, he also found some consistencies. Social scientists from a variety
of fields seemed to agree that attitude could be seen as a *predisposition
to respond in a favorable or unfavorable way* to objects, persons, concepts, or whatever. Underlying this dimension are some important
assumptions. First, *attitude is related to behavior.* Based upon one's attitude toward something an individual is predisposed to behave in a particular way. One could argue that one's attitude about the job is related
to the attendance record. Second, *attitude is an unidimensional variable*
and that dimension is tied to one's feelings about an object. The particu-

---

[1] Gordon W. Allport, "Attitudes," in M. Fishbein, ed., *Readings in Attitude Theory
and Measurement* (New York: John Wiley & Sons, Inc., 1967), p. 3.

lar feeling is one of favorability or affect or attraction—i.e., the degree to which something is liked (a pleasant feeling) or disliked (an unpleasant feeling). Third, *attitude is a hypothetical construct.* It is something which one carries around inside of him. Its consequences may be observed, but the attitude itself cannot.

This definition means that attitude is different from both beliefs and values. Beliefs are typically concerned with the relationships between objects, people, and events. We will find that most attitude techniques use beliefs as a method for inferring attitudes but they are not the same thing. Values, on the other hand, are frequently defined as ideas about how everyone should feel or behave. They have a quality of "oughtness" about them.

These assumptions have been challenged in various ways over the years and we will touch upon these controversies in our discussions of how attitudes are measured and changed. At this point, however, we will discuss how attitudes are formed; that is, how attitudes are acquired.

Formation

In Chapter 6 on "Motivation" the question of why the individual does anything at all was discussed. Answers to this question were related to early childhood behavior. A child has a variety of physiological drives which are satisfied in various ways. The satisfaction of these drives becomes linked to the circumstances that surrounded the satisfaction. If the child finds food satisfying he or she will begin to associate that good feeling with the surrounding circumstances (mother, a time of day). After a while very complex patterns of behavior may become associated with need satisfaction and just how specific attitudes are formed will be determined by an individual's personal history.

The central idea running through the process of attitude formation is that these feelings are *learned.* An individual acquires these feelings through experience with the world around him or her. An implication of this idea is that *all objects acquire an attitude.* One has feelings that may run from positive to negative about everything. Perhaps the most striking support for this idea has been provided by Osgood's research.[2] He and his co-workers were interested in the underlying dimensions of meaning; that is, what dimensions do all people use in

[2] C. E. Osgood, G. J. Suci, and P. H. Tannenbaum, *The Measurement of Meaning* (Urbana: University of Illinois, 1957).

their descriptions of things around them. Hundreds of concepts, objects, or people (for example, freedom, house, mother) were rated on hundreds of bipolar adjective scales. An example is presented below.

Freedom

Good	–	–	–	–	–	–	–	*Bad*
	+3	+2	+1	0	–1	–2	–3	
Open	–	–	–	–	–	–	–	Closed
Strong	–	–	–	–	–	–	–	Weak
Pleasant	–	–	–	–	–	–	–	Unpleasant

Using a mathematical process known as factor analysis, Osgood was able to determine what scales seemed to have similar response patterns. These scales seemed to fall in three main groups: One that reflected evaluation (good-bad, pleasant-unpleasant); one that reflected activity (active-passive, fast-slow); and one that reflected potency (strong-weak, heavy-light). Osgood was able to show that this evaluation or attitude factor not only appeared for different stimulus objects but also for different samples of people. Other cultures also use this dimension in their ascription of meaning to objects and Osgood has summarized much of this research by stating that "human beings the world over, no matter what their language or culture, do share a common meaning system, do organize experience along similar symbolic dimensions."[3]

Another important implication is that people ascribe attitudes to things or objects based upon what the things or objects are related to. Food is related to a feeling of satisfaction, mother is related to food, and so on. One's attitudes about an object, are formed through the relationship of that object to other things or objects. If those related objects are liked, so is the new object; if they are disliked, the reverse would be true. One's attitude is formed by the degree to which the attitude object is associated with other pleasant or unpleasant objects.[4] We may like a supervisor because he or she is friendly, sincere, and honest or we might dislike our job because it was boring or tiring. In either case, the evaluations are formed according to the association between the attitude object and other related states, concepts, or objects.

---

[3] Charles E. Osgood, "Cross-Cultural Comparability in Attitude Measurement via Multilingual Semantic Differentials," in Fishbein, *Readings in Attitude Theory*, p. 112.

[4] See Milton J. Rosenberg, "Cognitive Structure and Attitudinal Affect," as well as M. Fishbein and B. H. Raven, "The AB Scales: An Operational Definition of Belief and Attitude," in Fishbein, *Readings in Attitude Theory*, pp. 325–32 and pp. 183–90. Also note the similarity of these ideas with the "expectancy theory" of motivation presented in Chapter 6.

Most attitude measurement techniques reflect this idea in the way that they estimate one's attitude.

ATTITUDE MEASUREMENT

Techniques for measuring attitudes vary in a number of ways. Some are direct, some indirect. Some are more structured than others and certain techniques require verbal responses while others may use a paper and pencil. We will describe a few of the most frequently used techniques in detail and also provide a brief description of alternative devices which are available.

Direct, Structured, Paper and Pencil Tests

Perhaps the first attitude questionnaire for which there was an underlying theoretical rationale was developed by L. L. Thurstone, in the late 1920s.[5] A large set of statements about the attitude object is generated by the investigator and then rated by judges as to their favorability in terms of that object. If one were interested in people's attitudes about the war in Vietnam he or she might generate the following five sentences (along with many others).

The War

a. is preserving freedom.
b. is expensive.
c. is in the best interests of the United States.
d. is immoral.
e. is limiting social welfare expenditures.

Judges are then asked to place the statements in one of 11 categories according to their belief about the favorability of the statement with respect to the attitude object. The accompanying scale shows how one judge might rate the statements above.

	A		C			E	B		D	
1	2	3	4	5	6	7	8	9	10	11
Favorable				Neutral				Unfavorable		

Many judges perform this task and statements for which there is agreement (i.e., most of the judges place it in the same category) are

---

[5] L. L. Thurstone, "Attitudes Can Be Measured," *American Journal of Sociology,* 33 (1928), 529–54.

selected for the scale. These sentences are presented to the subject who checks those that believe to be true. The subject's attitude is computed by averaging the scale scores of those items checked. For example, a subject who believed statements *a* and *c* would have an attitude score of 3 (2 plus 4 divided by the number of statements) which would indicate a favorable attitude about the war. A subject who checked *b* and *d* would have a score of 9 which would indicate an unfavorable attitude about the war.

There are a number of important aspects of this approach.[6] When judges are making their ratings of the sentences, what are they really doing? They are rating the degree to which they feel a related object is a good or a bad thing. More specifically, the reason that statement *d* receives a 10 is because being *immoral* is bad and sentence *d* links the war with immorality. *Preserving freedom* is a good thing for most people so if one believes that the war is linked to that concept then he would have a favorable attitude. One's attitude is determined therefore, by the degree to which the attitude object is seen as linked to good or bad things.

The limitations of this technique should be pointed out. Judges are needed and that is expensive. Different questionnaires must be formed for different attitude objects and that too is expensive. It should also be noted that controversial statements may not wind up on the questionnaire. For example, some judges might think that limiting welfare expenditures was a good thing while others might believe the opposite. When there is disagreement the sentence is discarded which means that perhaps some of the most important statements about a topic would never be on the scale that was eventually given to subjects. Finally, just because the judges agree on the favorableness of a certain sentence does not guarantee that the subjects will feel the same way. Some subjects may feel that preserving freedom is a bad thing and *for them* that sentence, if checked, would reflect a negative attitude about the war.

Since the development of the Thurstone scale, numerous other direct, structured, paper and pencil tests have been developed in an attempt to remedy some of the problems described above. Osgood, for example, has suggested the use of four or five bipolar adjective scales from the evaluative dimension described earlier. If one wished to measure attitudes about the war in Vietnam with an Osgood scale (called the Semantic Differential) the following scales might be used.

---

[6] Many of these ideas were obtained through personal communication with Martin Fishbein.

War in Vietnam

	+3	+2	+1	0	−1	−2	−3	
Pleasant	—	—	—	—	—	—	—	Unpleasant
Friendly	—	—	—	—	—	—	—	Unfriendly
Good	—	—	—	—	—	—	—	Bad
Kind	—	—	—	—	—	—	—	Cruel
Beneficial	—	—	—	—	—	—	—	Harmful

An average over all scales is the subjects attitude score. Note again that the subject is indicating the degree to which the attitude object is related to favorable or unfavorable adjectives. This technique correlates highly (in the 80s) with more traditional techniques such as a Thurstone scale. The good points about this approach are that the judges do not have to be used and the same scales can be used for different attitude objects.[7] Two other techniques developed by Rosenberg and Fishbein actually attempt to measure the degree to which the subject feels the attitude object is related to other objects. Both of these authors report high correlations between their techniques and other measures of attitude. Again, almost all of these techniques emphasize that attitudes are formed according to their relationships with other objects and the evaluation of the objects.

Other Paper and Pencil Techniques

Numerous other attitude measurement techniques have been developed.[8] Some are indirect and unstructured such as sentence completion techniques or the use of the Thermatic Apperception Test (TAT). The former technique would present a partially completed sentence such as: racial intermarriage _____ , and the subject completes the sentence. Numerous sentences are used and the material is scored by judges in an attempt to evaluate the favorability of the content about the attitude object. The latter technique (TAT) has the subject write a story about a picture and judges again rate the content of the written product.

Other devices, although indirect, are also structured. One test asks the subject to fill out an attitude scale as his best friend would. The idea is that we like the same things that our friends like and therefore, the subjects responses should be a fairly good indication of his own feelings. Another technique asks subjects to do the same task as judges

---

[7] Osgood does report that some caution should be taken with widely different concepts due to a scale-concept interaction. See Osgood et al., *The Measurement of Meaning.*

[8] Donald T. Campbell, "The Indirect Assessment of Social Attitudes," *Psychological Bulletin*, 47 (1950), 15–38.

for a Thurstone scale (i.e., categorize sentences as to favorability) but they make as many categories as they wish.[9] The number of categories and the number of items in each category are used as indicants of the subject's attitude. The fewer the categories, the greater the involvement and the subject usually places the least number of sentences in the category which represents his own feelings.

The major argument for using indirect tests is that direct tests demand "socially desirable" responses from the subject or that they contain demand characteristics. However, the reliability and validity coefficients for most indirect tests are lower than those for direct tests. It has yet to be shown that they are better than the more standard techniques such as those developed by Thurstone, Likert, or Osgood.

Physiological Measures

Researchers in the attitude area have also attempted to develop physiological measures of affect or favorable feelings. It is argued that a physiological measure of attitude would avoid the problems of social desirability or demand characteristics which might occur in paper and pencil tests. Such a measure would also be more direct.

One method which was believed to be promising was the Galvanic Skin Response. The GSR is a measure of the electrical resistance of one's skin and this resistance is sensitive to emotional changes that take place in the human body. These changes cause an individual to sweat, which changes this electrical resistance. The results with this tool are not very reliable and seem to be most effective only when dealing with negative stimuli. The reactions to positive stimuli are less pronounced.[10]

A recent technique developed by Hess suggests that one's pupil dilation is a good indicant of his attitude.[11] According to Hess, an individual's pupils dilate when he sees something he likes and constrict when presented with a negative stimulus. To obtain this measure Hess uses a box with an elaborate set of mirrors and cameras. The stimulus object is presented on a screen and the pupil opening is photographed and then measured. Although very little research has of yet been conducted

---

[9] Muzafer Sherif and Carolyn Wood Sherif, "The Own Category Procedure in Attitude Research," in Fishbein, *Readings in Attitude Theory*, pp. 190–98.

[10] See Joseph B. Cooper and David Pollock, "The Identification of Prejudicial Attitudes by the Galvanic Skin Response," in Fishbein, *Readings in Attitude Theory*, pp. 180–83.

[11] E. H. Hess and J. M. Polt, "Pupil Size as Related to Interest Value of Visual Stimuli," *Science*, 132 (1960), 349–50.

with this technique it may turn out to be an effective, unobstructed measure of one's attitude.

Job Attitudes: Measurement of Morale

There are numerous attitudes related to job activity which have interested social scientists. There is a large body of literature dealing with interpersonal attraction (our attitudes toward other people, for example). The most frequently researched attitudes, however, are those dealing with one's overall feeling toward his or her job. This attitude is typically called morale or job satisfaction and specific methods have been developed to measure it.

The technique which is most well known is the Job Description Index (JDI) developed by Pat Smith and her co-workers.[12] This scale presents the worker with a series of adjectives as possible descriptions of five aspects of the job (work conditions, pay, promotions, supervision, co-workers). The employee places a Y, an N, or a ?, for a "yes," "no," or "don't know" response, next to each adjective. A copy of this scale is presented in Figure 7–1.

The favorable points about the JDI are worth mentioning. First, the technique generates a satisfaction score for five job areas as well as an overall score. This information helps the investigator in using the tool as a diagnostic device. He or she can determine with what areas people are more or less satisfied. Another strong point is the scale's ease of administration. It is not necessary to develop a new scale for each job. There is also extensive normative data available for the JDI. Thousands of employees have filled out this scale in many different types of organizations across the country. It is possible, therefore, to not only make comparisons between job aspects in the same organization but in some cases one might compare different organizations on the same job aspect. For example, if data has been gathered in a similar organization then one could compare the satisfaction with pay at the other firm.

A second technique which is frequently used was developed and used by Porter and Lawler.[13] Their method also gathers information about different job aspects. The employee is asked to what degree he thinks a certain job characteristic exists in this present position and how

---

[12] Patricia Cain Smith, Lorne M. Kendall, and Charles L. Hulin, *The Measurement of Satisfaction in Work and Retirement* (Chicago: Rand McNally and Co., 1969).

[13] Lyman W. Porter and Edward E. Lawler III, *Managerial Attitudes and Performance* (Homewood, Ill.: Richard D. Irwin, Inc., 1968).

FIGURE 7–1

Items in Final Version of JDI°

Each of the five scales was presented on a separate page.

The instructions for each scale asked the subject to put "Y" beside an item if the item described the particular aspect of his/her job (e.g., work, pay, etc.), "N" if the item did not describe that aspect, or "?" if he/she could not decide.

The response shown beside each item is the one scored in the "satisfied" direction for each scale.

Work	*Supervision*	*People*
Y Fascinating	Y Asks my advice	Y Stimulating
N Routine	N Hard to please	N Boring
Y Satisfying	N Impolite	N Slow
N Boring	Y Praises good work	Y Ambitious
Y Good	Y Tactful	N Stupid
Y Creative	Y Influential	Y Responsible
Y Respected	Y Up-to-date	Y Fast
N Hot	N Doesn't supervise enough	Y Intelligent
Y Pleasant	N Quick-tempered	N Easy to make enemies
Y Useful	Y Tells me where I stand	N Talk too much
N Tiresome	N Annoying	Y Smart
Y Healthful	N Stubborn	N Lazy
Y Challenging	Y Knows job well	N Unpleasant
N On your feet	N Bad	N No privacy
N Frustrating	Y Intelligent	Y Active
N Simple	Y Leaves me on my own	N Narrow interests
N Endless	Y Around when needed	Y Loyal
Gives sense of	N Lazy	N Hard to meet
Y accomplishment		

Pay	*Promotions*
Y Income adequate for normal expenses	Y Good opportunity for advancement
Y Satisfactory profit sharing	N Opportunity somewhat limited
N Barely live on income	Y Promotion on ability
N Bad	N Dead-end job
Y Income provides luxuries	Y Good chance for promotion
N Insecure	N Unfair promotion policy
N Less than I deserve	N Infrequent promotions
Y Highly paid	Y Regular promotions
N Underpaid	Y Fairly good chance for promotion

* Researchers wishing to use these scales in their own work are asked to inform the senior author of their intentions and to request permission for use. [See p. 82, ¶ 3.]

Source: Patricia Cain Smith, Lorne M. Kendall, and Charles L. Hulin, *The Measurement of Satisfaction in Work and Retirement* (Chicago: Rand McNally and Co., 1969).

much he would like for there to be. He then rates the importance of that characteristic. Three such questions are presented below.

Job Security

1. How much is there now?

very much — — — — — — — — — — very little

2. How much should there be?

very much — — — — — — — — — — very little

3. How important is it to me?

very important — — — — — — — — — — very unimportant

A difference score between what there is now and what there should be is weighted by the importance score. Two or three questions may be included for each job aspect which again provides an overall score as well as a score for each aspect.

There are other similar techniques available but the two described above are perhaps the most frequently used and the most reliable. Note that both methods assess one's attitude about the job by measuring the degree to which the job is linked to other favorable or unfavorable objects. This assumption underlies almost all of the theorizing on attitude measurement and theory.

ATTITUDE ORGANIZATION AND DYNAMICS

Given that one has developed attitudes about most of the things around him how is this information organized? How do we come to like other people on our job? All of these questions are tied to the ideas of attitude organization and dynamics.

Firtz Heider was one of the first investigators to suggest a general theory of attitude organization (called balance theory).[14] His specific interests were in the area of interpersonal attraction and he suggested that we like people who like the same things we do. When this situation does not exist (e.g., we perceive that a friend likes something we dislike) we feel uncomfortable and are motivated to change one of our attitudes.

The theory is presented in the form of the POX model. P stands for the perceiver or person, O for the other or another person, and X for a concept, object, or thing. Now, the link between these three parts can be either positive or negative. That is, P either likes or dislikes the object and the other person and has a perception or belief about the other's feelings toward the object in question. All possible combinations are presented in Figure 7–2. A plus stands for a positive feeling, a minus for a negative one.

Each triad represents a cognitive state: The state is positive (balanced) if by multiplying the three signs you generate a plus (triads 1, 5, 6, 7) and negative (unbalanced) if a minus sign is generated (triads 2, 3, 4, 8). For example, if you (P) like your supervisor (O) and you believe that both of you dislike the idea of close supervision (X), then you would have a balanced state (triad 6). On the other hand, if you believed your supervisor liked the idea of close supervision,

---

[14] Fritz Heider, "Attitudes and Cognitive Organization," *Journal of Psychology*, 21 (1946), 107–12.

FIGURE 7–2

situation 2 would exist—you perceive that someone you like is attracted to something you dislike. In this situation it is predicted that the individual will feel uncomfortable and will be motivated to change one of his attitudes in order to return to a state of cognitive balance.

Further theoretical modifications of this model were presented by Newcomb (called symmetry) and Osgood (called congruity).[15] The former approach attempted to make a distinction between relationships formed out of physical or legal necessity and those out of interpersonal attraction. In some situations (e.g., at work) one may be forced to interact with another person and this type of relationship is different from, let's say, a marriage bond. These different types of bonds have implications for which link in the triad is most likely to change. Newcomb also attempted to assess how O actually felt about X instead of relying on P's perceptions of O's feelings.

Osgood's theory of congruity took the idea one step further by quantifying the links. He assessed the *amount* of favorability involved and presented a model which predicted what links would change and how much. These predictions are based both on the degree of favorability and the strength of that feeling. The empirical results have supported his ideas fairly well.

One of the major criticisms of these models was related to their simplicity. People have more than just one concept or object about which they may agree or disagree with a friend. It was also argued that these approaches did not tie together the relationship between attitudes and

―――――――
[15] See Theodore M. Newcomb, "An Approach to the Study of Communicative Acts," *Psychological Review*, 60 (1953), 393–404; and Charles E. Osgood and Percy H. Tannenbaum, "The Principle of Congruity in the Prediction of Attitude Change," *Psychological Review*, 62 (1955), 42–55.

behavior. In an attempt to overcome these problems Leon Festinger developed the theory of Cognitive Dissonance.[16]

Dissonance theory attempted to include both multiple objects or concepts as well as behavioral links while still using the underlying principle of balance or cognitive consistency. The theory has prompted more research than perhaps any other theory in social psychology partly because of some of its counterintuitive predictions.

One set of these predictions comes from the model of forced compliance, presented in Figure 7–3. This model attempts to predict an indi-

FIGURE 7–3
The Forced Compliance Model

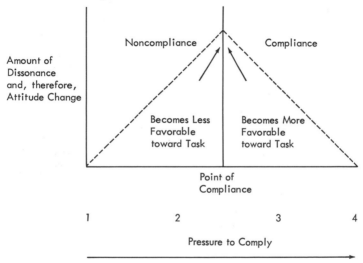

vidual's attitude when pressured to do something against his or her wishes. If, for example, one wished to have a subordinate do an unpleasant job (some routine task), the theory predicts that just enough pressure to induce him to comply should be used (position 3). At this point he has done something that he finds unpleasant and should be experiencing dissonance. That is, his behavior is not consistent with his attitude. He should therefore become more favorable toward the act he has just done in order to reduce the dissonance and justify his behavior. If too much pressure is administered (a threat of dismissal perhaps), the employee would probably comply with his supervisor's wishes but

---

[16] Leon Festinger, *The Theory of Cognitive Dissonance* (New York: Harper & Row, Publisher, 1957).

still detest the task (position 4). He has little trouble justifying his behavior. If too little pressure is applied the employee may refuse to do the job and become even more unfavorable toward this type of work (position 2). This prediction is made because the individual has said no to his supervisor and must justify his behavior in order to avoid feeling uncomfortable. He, therefore, becomes even more negative about the job involved.[17] Clearly, in position 1 there is little need for change: The employee says no to a passing suggestion to do some unpleasant task. His behavior is consistent with his attitude and he has not been made to feel uncomfortable in his refusal (as is the case for position 2).

Festinger and his co-workers have presented data to support this model in a variety of studies.[18] In some cases these studies have not been as methodologically sound as one would like but in general, the theory has increased our understanding of the ways in which attitudes are organized and changed. One of the most important implications has been a reanalysis of the attitude-behavior relationship. More specifically, Festinger argues that in some cases (e.g., forced compliance) it is our behavior that causes our attitudes rather than the reverse. This idea has been carried forward in more detail by the work of Daryl Bem and his colleagues.[19]

Attitudes and Behavior.   From 1930 to 1932, Richard La Piere and a Chinese couple traveled around the United States by car. Of the 251 establishments which they approached for services, food, or lodging only one refused their service. La Piere later sent out a questionnaire to these establishments to discover their attitudes toward Orientals and their willingness to serve them. Of the returned questionnaires 95 percent of the people said *they would refuse service to Chinese.* Clearly there is a discrepancy between reported attitude and actual behavior.[20]

La Piere's research was not the only study that failed to find that behavior could be predicted from attitudes. Two general approaches have been taken in response to the problem. The first emphasizes a multidimensional definition of attitude. This argument suggests that if the one affective dimension (evaluation) does not predict behavior then more information is needed. Attitude is defined as having three dimen-

---

[17] See L. Festinger and J. M. Carlsmith, "Cognitive Consequences of Forced Compliance," *Journal of Abnormal and Social Psychology,* 58 (1959), 203–10.

[18] Festinger, *The Theory of Cognitive Dissonance.*

[19] Daryl J. Bem, "Self-Perception Theory," in L. Berkowitz, ed., *Advances in Experimental Social Psychology,* 6 (1972), 6, 1–62.

[20] Richard T. La Piere, "Attitudes versus Action," *Social Forces,* 13 (1934), 230–37.

sions: affect, cognitions, and behavioral intentions. This new conceptualization of attitude prompted investigators to develop new measurement techniques to assess these additional dimensions.[21] However, it appears that those new methods suffer from the same shortcomings as the original ones. The second response to the problem suggests why this is the case.

Most attitude measurement procedures assess feeling toward a rather general stimulus (e.g., Chinese). They generate this estimate by obtaining information about a number of objects to which the attitude object is tied. Fishbein and others have pointed out that perhaps we should be measuring more specific attitudes rather than general stimulus objects. If one wants to know whether a proprietor will serve a Chinese couple that is well dressed, speaks excellent English, and arrives in an automobile, then one should measure attitudes about that sort of couple rather than Chinese people in general. Measuring feelings toward a general stimulus provides one with little information about an individual's behavior in particular circumstances. Fishbein has reported correlations in the .50s and .60s between attitude and behavior using this approach.[22] With respect to attitudes about the job we have already noted how a more detailed breakdown of job attitudes is currently being emphasized.

ATTITUDE CHANGE

Given that certain attitudes exist, how does one change them? Based upon earlier discussions it seems clear: The attitude object should be linked to other objects which are pleasant or unpleasant, depending upon the desired change. We will discuss four general areas of research dealing with strategies to produce these changes.

Presentation Format. One implication of the above conceptualization is that relationships between the attitude object and other objects should be made clear and explicit. Numerous researchers have studied how to present information in a format which will most likely facilitate change. One strategy that has been studied suggests that both sides of an argument should be presented so that the individual is aware of both the favorable and unfavorable consequences of changing his attitude. Secord and Backman summarize the experimental results this way:

---

[21] For a multidimensional approach, see Harry C. Triandis, *Attitude and Attitude Change* (New York: John Wiley & Sons, Inc., 1971), pp. 7–25.

[22] Fishbein and Raven, "The AB Scales," pp. 183–90.

One-sided communications are more effective for people who already agree with the communicator, but people who disagree with the communicator do not change their opinions in response to one-sided communications. Just the reverse is true for two-sided communications. Moreover, a two-sided communication is more effective than a one-sided communication in innoculating the audience against countercommunications. Whether the communicator draws the conclusion implied by his message or leaves it up to the audience does not seem to make a distinct difference in the audience's acceptance of it.[23]

Another issue subjected to study deals with whether one should come first or second in a two-sided debate. In general these findings suggest that the first person has the greatest impact especially when the audience is unbiased and hears the counterproposal immediately.

Information Source.   A second technique employed in attitude change studies is to link the product, message, or idea with an attractive credible source. Bob Richards (past Olympic pole vault champion) advertises the Breakfast of Champions (*Wheaties*) while Ed McMahon advertises Budweiser Beer (a product with which he is reputed to be familiar). Heider's balance principle is operating here. We are attracted to the product because we are attracted to the source. Both the credibility and the attractiveness of the communicator are related to attitude change.[24] It has also been suggested that the link must be maintained. When the individual forgets the source his favorable attitude toward the product may dissipate. We should, therefore, keep the communication linked to the communicator if change is to be permanent.[25]

Fear Arousal.   An alternative strategy which has been suggested is to link an undesirable attitude or behavior with frightening consequences in an attempt to change the attitude. Research in this area suggests that this technique is only useful when the recipient of the information can immediately do something to relieve his anxiety or fear. Otherwise, it is argued, the individual will actively avoid thinking about the whole issue due to the dissonance or unpleasant feelings that occur when the information is recalled. In situations where immediate relief is not available mild fear arousal is more effective.[26]

---

[23] Paul F. Secord and Carl W. Backman, *Social Psychology* (New York: McGraw-Hill Book Company, 1964), p. 163.

[24] K. Giffin, "The Contribution of Studies of Source Credibility to a Theory of Interpersonal Trust in the Communication Process," *Psychological Bulletin,* 6 (1967), 104–220.

[25] C. I. Hovland and W. Weiss, "The Influence of Source Credibility on Communication Effectiveness," *Public Opinion Quarterly,* 15 (1952), 635–50.

[26] C. I. Hovland, I. L. Janis, and H. H. Kelly, *Communication and Persuasion,* (New Haven, Conn.: Yale University Press, 1953).

Position Discrepancy. Another area of the literature deals with the amount of change advocated. The degree to which the communicator's position differs from that of the target person influences the amount of change that takes place. In general, for issues where the target is not highly involved, the greater the discrepancy, the greater the change. That is, the more extreme the position advocated the more the individual will change his attitude in the advocated direction. However, for issues of high involvement it appears that a moderate discrepancy produces the most change.[27] When the communicator takes a position which is at the opposite end of the continuum for some important issue, the recipient is likely to reject the communicator and the communication. The message is seen as "biased" and the communicator as an "extremist." Since most people are highly involved with their feelings about religion, politics, sex, and work it is not surprising that great shifts are infrequent on these issues, despite the continuing advocates of radical change.

In summary, attitudes were defined as the positive or negative feelings about the contents of our physical and cognitive environment. They are formed through their links with other objects and they are changed through changes in these same links. They help to determine one's feelings about his job and his behavior while on the job. Their importance in other areas of organizational behavior is well documented and will be discussed next.

ATTITUDES AND THE WORLD OF WORK

When we consider our attitudes toward work we are involved in a complex, ever-changing phenomena. Most work is done in large industrial settings where policy is set by infrequently seen professionals. Most people work directly in some capacity with machines and production and profits are of central importance. Most of this activity is carried out during set hours and in urban settings. Work also serves many different purposes for people. It is obviously a source of economic security: a way in which needed goods and services can be provided and obtained. It is a source of social interaction. Most people's social lives center around people they know from work. Finally work is a source of self-esteem. We evaluate ourselves partially according to our work performance. However, for any one of these descriptive dimensions or functions there is great personal variety. Thus, we have some difficulty in finding a commonality of meaning for the term work.

---

[27] See Sherif and Sherif, "The Own Category Procedure," pp. 466–93.

Whatever the task, however, people have evaluative feelings about it. They like or dislike certain aspects of their work and they have an overall assessment of favorability for what they do. Attitudes are good reflections of these feelings and they have been an important aspect of organizational research for 50 years.

The Hawthorne studies first highlighted the importance of worker attitudes. As a result of the attention given to small groups of employees who were being observed, the workers reported a freer attitude about what they did on the job. They felt the organization was interested in them and they liked it. Their social and work activities changed and performance increased as well. These initial studies prompted the researchers to investigate further the attitudes of all the employees and an extensive program of interviewing was commenced. From these data management gained an insight into the employees' attitudes about work conditions, rate-busters, supervisors and many other issues which affected their behavior on the job.

The Situation Today

After 50 years of investigating job attitudes many authors feel we are facing a crisis of major proportions. A special task force of HEW recently published a review of current trends and suggested that significant numbers of American workers are dissatsified with the quality of their working lives. Dull, repetitive, seemingly meaningless tasks, offering little challenge or autonomy, are causing discontent among workers at all occupational levels."[28]

This same report lists the following signs of problems in the workplace.

The growth in the number of communes.
Numerous adolescents panhandling in such meccas as Georgetown, North
    Beach, and the Sunset Strip.
Various enterprises shifting to four-day workweeks.
Welfare caseloads increasing.
Retirement occurring at ever earlier ages.

There are reported increases in absenteeism, sabotage, and turnover in many industries. Productivity may be decreasing and there is a great increases in the days per year lost from work through strikes.

---

[28] *Work in America: Report of a Special Task Force to the Secretary of HEW* (Cambridge, Mass.: The M.I.T. Press, 1973), p. 11.

An economist or technologist viewing these symptoms may point out the numerous favorable changes that have occurred in the workplace. Working conditions are generally better. Industrial safety is important, and the possibility of severe injuries has decreased. Women and children are seldom engaged in back-breaking labor and generally arbitrary dismissals and pay cuts are rare.

The economic conditions are better for most employees. Real income, standard of living, health status, and life expectancy are all greater. Pensions, while still far from perfect, are available for many employees. The *Work in America* report presents us with a paradox: Things seem better by almost any standard yet people are not satisfied with their jobs.

The response to this paradox has been twofold. First, many writers point out that the needs of employees has shifted. Instead of placing their major emphasis on the economic aspects of the job they are concerned with the meaning of the job in some broader context. A recent survey conducted by the Survey Research Center at the University of Michigan with a representative sample of 1,533 workers from all occupational levels found the following ranking of job aspects in terms of their importance.

1. Interesting work.
2. Enough help and equipment to get the job done.
3. Enough information to get the job done.
4. Enough authority to get the job done.
5. Good pay.
6. Opportunity to develop special abilities.
7. Job security.
8. Seeing the results of one's work.

Thus, while working conditions have become better, employees' expectations about organizational life have changed as well.[29]

A second suggestion that explains the paradox argues that researchers have been investigating the wrong types of job attitudes all these years. Louis Davis argues that we have focused too much attention on jobs themselves.[30] From the time of Frederick Taylor's scientific management we have seen jobs as activities to be done and attended to what makes

---

[29] Ibid., p. 13.

[30] L. E. Davis, "Job Satisfaction Research: The Post-Industrial View," *Industrial Relations*, 10 (1971), 176–93.

these activities easier to accomplish. Even the interpersonal concerns have maintained this focus.

Our central concern with the job has omitted a larger focus: the structure and content of jobs in a broader social, political, and organizational setting. Rather than treating the individual as the operating unit we should move to a more global analysis. Rather than seeing the individual as being primarily motivated by comfort and money, we should stress a more involved and personal accomplishment frame of reference. Finally, rather than seeing employees as a labor commodity we must view them as integral members of the organization. What Davis is suggesting is that we are moving into a postindustrial era and that people want different things from organizational life. Our new interest in attitudes about autonomy, involvement and actualization influence our concepts of effectiveness, utilization of personnel, and the definition of work roles. Organizational strategies for analysis and change should reflect these movements.

The Research Results

The empirical findings on job satisfaction in general and on specific aspects of the job that lead to satisfaction seems to reflect some of these concerns. A recent monograph on Job Satisfaction was prepared for the Manpower Administration by the Survey Research Center (SRC) at the University of Michigan.[31] These researchers review a large number of national surveys on job satisfaction carried out by Gallup and by SRC since 1958. A summary of the SRC survey data is presented below because the Gallup data is very similar. One can see that anywhere from 8 percent to 19 percent of the people surveyed reported they were dissatisfied with their job. It is likely that unemployed people are also dissatisfied with their opportunities to attain a meaningful job. Thus, up to one quarter of the people seeking work or current employees may have negative attitudes about the workplace. A number of interesting findings were discussed in more detail in the SRC report. First, there seems to have been very little change in the last ten years. According to their report things have been at the same level of satisfaction (or dissatisfaction) for the last 15 years. Second, as we would expect the most dissatisfied people are young, poorly educated, members of minorities, or in low status occupations.

---

[31] *Job Satisfaction: Is There a Trend?* Manpower Research Monograph No. 30 (U.S. Department of Labor, 1974).

FIGURE 7–4

Percentage of "Satisfied" Workers, 1958–1973, Based on Seven National Surveys

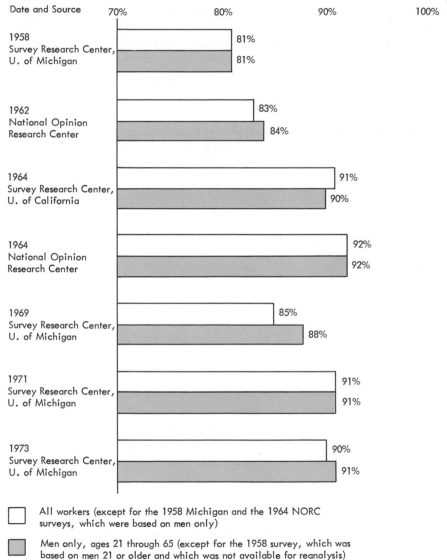

Date and Source		
1958 Survey Research Center, U. of Michigan	81%	81%
1962 National Opinion Research Center	83%	84%
1964 Survey Research Center, U. of California	91%	90%
1964 National Opinion Research Center	92%	92%
1969 Survey Research Center, U. of Michigan	85%	88%
1971 Survey Research Center, U. of Michigan	91%	91%
1973 Survey Research Center, U. of Michigan	90%	91%

☐ All workers (except for the 1958 Michigan and the 1964 NORC surveys, which were based on men only)

▨ Men only, ages 21 through 65 (except for the 1958 survey, which was based on men 21 or older and which was not available for reanalysis)

Source: *Job Satisfaction: Is There a Trend?* Manpower Research Monograph No. 30 (U.S. Department of Labor, 1974).

These data present an additional reason for our general feeling that people are dissatisfied with their work in the face of greater economic and physical security. It is only in the last ten years that we have systematically attempted to listen to minorities, the young, and the worker in marginal jobs. Thus, while these people have probably had low job morale for many years it is only recently that we are attending to their concerns.

Antecedents of Favorable Job Attitudes

There is a considerable body of literature dealing with both the antecedents and consequences of having high morale. For many organizations this has become a legitimate goal by itself. Due to historical factors and the human relations movement, some organizations have tried to create a climate where people are happy to work *regardless* of whether or not it leads to high productivity. We will briefly summarize the literature relating job satisfaction to organizational characteristics and the effects of this satisfaction on behavior.

Supervision. In general, considerate supervisory behavior seems to correlate positively with job satisfaction.[32] A number of studies show first that changes in supervision lead to changes in satisfaction, and second, that a considerate style of behavior is also positively related to satisfaction. Two precautionary comments are worth making. First, most of the evidence for the above relationships and for many that follow is correlational and therefore does not imply causal relationships. It is just as plausible that having satisfied workers causes a supervisor to be considerate than the reverse. Second, since the relationships are generally moderate (correlations of .20 to .40), there are numerous cases where the reverse may be true; that is, there are most certainly situations where close supervision is appreciated. There just happen to be more cases where it does not (at least for the situations that have been empirically investigated).

Another important aspect of supervision is the degree to which subordinates may participate in decisions that effect their work. In general, it appears that some participation is related to positive feelings about the job. However, there are some limiting conditions. The decisions should be about topics with which the employees are familiar and have some expertise (for example, the work pace). The participation should

---

[32] For a review, see Victor Vroom, *Work and Motivation* (New York: John Wiley & Sons, Inc., 1964), chapter 5.

be real—that is, the information offered by the employees should actually be part of the decision process. And finally, too much participation may be related to negative attitudes. To some extent employees want to be supervised, or at least they don't want to be inundated with all of the organization's problems.

Job Content. Both the standardization and specialization of work tasks have tremendously increased productivity throughout the world. The relationship with satisfaction appears to be curvilinear. A moderate amount of these variables appears to be most highly related to morale. Figure 7–5 shows this relationship.

FIGURE 7–5

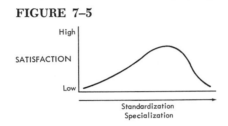

When the job is neither specialized nor standardized, an employee would have difficulty knowing what or how to do the job. At the other extreme are situations which are highly repetitive and boring. Although these points may differ for different types of people or jobs, it is clear that the extreme ends of these continuums are related to low morale.

Two possible corrections for the problems of too much specialization are job rotation and job enlargement programs. The employees are able to either expand the number of tasks they are doing or to rotate to different tasks. The important point to make is that one must first ascertain the current location of his employees on the curve.

Traditional Incentives. Promotional opportunities and wages have traditionally been cited as variables which are related to job satisfaction. In the case of promotions it does appear that employees are more satisfied with situations where this opportunity is likely than when it is not. The relationship is weak, however, and this is probably due to the fact that promotions are a relatively infrequent experience. There are numerous other things that happen every day (supervision, the job content, and so on) that are more highly related to morale.

The research on the effect of wages on morale and productivity is vast and no attempt will be made here to immerse ourselves in this morass. It does appear that people are more satisfied with high wages than low wages. The strength of the relationship is questionable as is the causality question. An important factor seems to be one's reference group. People seem to be satisfied when their wages are higher than those received by others who are doing a similar job. When one compares favorably he or she is satisfied and the reverse seems to be true when the comparison is unfavorable. Satisfaction related to wages, therefore, seems to be a joint function of the absolute amount and a comparison with others. Just what this function looks like is as yet unknown.

Consequences of Favorable Job Attitudes

The question here is simply, "In what ways do satisfied employees behave differently from dissatisfied ones?" Four main topics will be reviewed: turnover, absences, accidents, and productivity.

Turnover.   One would expect the relationship between job satisfaction and turnover to be negative. The greater the satisfaction the lower the turnover. In general the results support this hypothesis with correlations from $-.13$ to $-.42$ reported in the literature.[33] It appears that the strength of this relationship is partly dependent on the degree of full employment that exists. There are always going to be some people who leave because of dissatisfaction and some who leave because they have to (the individual moves, a family crisis, and so on). In times of full employment when numerous job opportunities are available we would expect the percentage of those who leave because of low satisfaction to be greater than when times are hard. Accordingly, the relationship between turnover and satisfaction should be stronger during full employment and indeed this is what is reported in the literature.[34]

Absences.   The relationship between absenteeism and satisfaction is also predicted to be negative. The higher the satisfaction the fewer the absences. Although generally supportive, the results are far from conclusive (correlations from $-.14$ to $-.38$).[35] Again, the issue is clearer if one considers a third variable. Many long-term periods of absence are experienced by old faithful members of the organization and these people are probably not dissatisfied. A study by Kerr, Koppelmeier, and Sullivan in a metal fabrication factory pointed out this problem.[36] Job satisfaction was correlated .51 with total absenteeism for 29 depart-

---

[33] Ibid., pp. 175–78.

[34] Ibid., p. 178.

[35] Ibid., pp. 178–80.

[36] W. A. Kerr, G. Koppelmeier, and J. J. Sullivan, "Absenteeism Turnover, and Morale in a Metals Fabrication Factory," *Occupational Psychology*, 25 (1951), 50–55.

ments but —.44 with unexcused absences. As we would expect, people who choose to stay at home and lose their pay are less satisfied than those who have good attendance. Also, Porter and Steers recent review of over 60 studies in the last 15 years provided substantial support for the relationship between dissatisfaction and turnover and absenteeism.[37]

Accidents. Some authors have suggested that dissatisfied employees are more likely to have accidents. There is very little evidence to support this conjecture. It is hard to think of an individual saying "I'm unhappy here so I'll stick my arm in this press." It is true that workers *who have had accidents* may be more unhappy than those who have not but it is not clear that unhappiness caused the accidents. The most important factor that is related to accidents seems to be related to attentiveness. The more attention the employee pays to the job the less likely he or she is to have an accident.

Productivity. For many years it was assumed that a happy ship was a productive ship. The way to obtain higher levels of efficiency was through morale. A number of thorough and rather devastating reviews have shown little support for this hypothesis. In Figure 7–6 a review of 20 studies is presented. The median correlation between job satisfaction and productivity is .14. If the studies are divided according to their type of criterion (ratings versus "hard" criteria) or according to the level of analysis (group or individual), the median is about the same. Some authors have even argued that what little relationship does exist could be attributed to the reverse relationship: productivity causes satisfaction.

When one considers the models of motivation and attitudes which we have discussed this relationship is no longer so puzzling. If attitudes or behavior are related to the degree to which they are tied to favorable or unfavorable related objects, then there is no reason to believe that liking the job will prompt one to high levels of effort. People are attracted to jobs for various reasons (the work conditions, the friendships, the supervision, and so on). They may find that all of these things can be obtained without extra effort and indeed, this is the case in many organizations. It is true that some rewards may be lost such as a bonus or a promotion but in many cases these incentives are not of utmost importance. The other incentives are typically not related to effort and it should not be surprising therefore, that overall job satisfaction is only slightly related to output.

[37] L. W. Porter, and R. M. Steers, "Organizational Work, and Personal Factors in Employee Turnover and Absenteeism," *Psychological Bulletin,* 80 (1973), 151–76.

FIGURE 7-6

Correlational Studies—Job Satisfaction and Job Performance

Author(s) and Date	Type of Analysis*	Population	Corre-lation	Type of Criterion of Productivity	N
Baxter cited in Brayfield & Crockett (1955)	Ind.	Insurance agents	.23 .26	Ratings Objective	233
Bellows cited in Brayfield & Crockett (1955)	Ind.	Air force control tower operators	.005	Ratings	109
Bernberg (1952)	Ind.	Hourly paid workers	.05	Ratings	890
Brayfield cited in Brayfield & Crockett (1955)	Ind.	Female office employees	.14	Ratings	231
Brayfield & Mangelsdorf cited in Brayfield & Crockett (1955)	Ind.	Plumber's apprentices	.203	Ratings	55
Brayfield & Marsh cited in Brayfield & Crockett (1955)	Ind.	Farmers	.115	Ratings	50
Brody (1945)	Ind.	Production employees on piece work	.68	Objective	40
Fleishman, Harris & Burtt (1955)	Gr.	Work groups in an equipment mfg. plant	−.31	Ratings	58
Gadel & Kriedt (1952)	Ind.	IBM Operators	.08	Ratings	193
Giese & Ruter (1949)	Gr.	Departments in mail-order company	.19	Objective	25
Hamid (1953)	Ind.	Insurance agents	.22	Objective	552
Heron (1954)	Ind.	Bus drivers	.308	Objective	144
Lawshe & Nagle (1953)	Gr.	Departments in an office	.86	Ratings	14
Lopez (1962)	Ind.	Administrative-technical personnel	.12	Ratings	124
Mann, Indik & Vroom (1963)	Gr.	Truck drivers—large work groups	.14 −.21	Ratings Objective	28
Mann, Indik & Vroom (1963)	Gr.	Positioners—small work groups	.18 .02	Ratings Objective	24
Mossin (1949)	Ind.	Female sales clerks	−.03	Ratings	94
Sirota (1958)	Ind.	Employees in an electronics firm	.11	Ratings	377
Sirota (1958)	Ind.	Supervisors in an electronics firm	.13	Ratings	145
Vroom (1960a)	Ind.	Supervisors in a package delivery co.	.21	Ratings	96

* Ind. = individual; Gr. = group.

Source: Victor Vroom, *Work and Motivation* (New York: John Wiley & Sons, Inc., 1964), chapter 5.

Because high morale does not necessarily lead to greater output does not mean that organizations should no longer attend to the satisfaction of its employees. We have already discussed how satisfaction is partially tied to turnover and absenteeism which do, of course, cost the firm money. There is also evidence that the interaction patterns of satisfied workers is different and we will discuss these findings in Chapter 8 on "Group Dynamics." But most important is the fact that many people believe that satisfaction is a legitimate goal in and of itself. Since almost everyone is employed at one time or another and most of us for long periods of time, arguments to make the work setting pleasant seem not only justified but necessary.

Obviously, where physical discomforts are at issue they can be removed or where misperceptions seem the problem more accurate or detailed information can be provided. Participation and involvement in meaningful decisions seems to increase satisfaction and various group exercises can facilitate this working arrangement. Job previews also seem to clarify expectations and facilitate adjustment to new jobs. Other techniques involve role playing where employees attempt to see organizational life from the point of view of someone else (e.g., their supervisor, an upper level manager). Many types of job redesign have been shown to change attitudes. But these topics carry us beyond the central concern of this chapter and will be dealt with later. Attitudes clearly impact on our feelings about organizational life and our job-related behavior.

chapter 8
Group Dynamics

Although organizations vary widely in their size, many of the sub-units or divisions are composed of small groups. The small group is composed of a restricted number of people, usually fewer than seven, who enjoy personal interaction over a fairly long span of time. People in this relationship show a degree of commonality of interest often expressed as a goal upon which there is mutual agreement. To facilitate the actual process of goal accomplishment, a differentiation of role and function usually exists in the small group. Additionally, the group itself has some amount of self-sufficiency to enable it to adapt to changing conditions in its environment. The emphasis, therefore, on groups in organizations is primarily caused by the division of labor. Large tasks are subdivided into smaller ones and groups form according to their function.

INDIVIDUALS AND GROUPS

An initial area of inquiry was to determine the ways in which groups differed from individuals working alone or independently. Organization theorists were particularly interested in whether groups were more effec-tive than individuals working by themselves. The results of this research produced generalizations which highlighted how the processes were different rather than concluding which was best. Which process was most effective seemed to depend on a number of situational factors.

One finding was that people are aroused by the group context. Just sitting in a room with other people changed the individual's behavior from when he or she was working alone. This phenomenon is known as social facilitation.[1] One's motivation appears to be heightened in the group context and more dominant (well-practiced) behavior tends to appear. One's attention may be raised but so may one's tendency for distraction. The appropriateness of the behavior is dependent on both one's past experience and present situational demands.

A second finding concerned the interaction process in groups. The research showed that the weighting process is different in groups. If five people are working alone and we aggregate their work effort then each person should be contributing about 20 percent of the final product. In groups, however, the contribution is more highly differentiated. Thus, some people contribute substantially more than others.

A related idea was termed brainstorming. It was thought that one benefit of the group process was that someone else's ideas would trigger off new ideas for other group members. If this were true, more ideas could be generated in the group than if people were working alone—an important plus for group functioning and effectiveness. However, the experimental results did not seem to support this contention. In many cases people working alone produced more and higher quality ideas than those who worked in a group.[2] When one adds the fact that more work hours are spent in the group context to generate the same number of ideas as people working alone it appears as if brainstorming as a rationale for group effectiveness is inadequate.

A final difference which seemed to be substantiated was the idea of the risky shift. Kogan and Wallach found that people tend to be more risky in groups than when they are solving a problem alone.[3] There are a number of competing explanations for this phenomena. Some researchers believe that since the weighting process is different, more confident people will dominate and be willing to take risks. Others believe that there is a cultural norm supporting risk which people feel obliged to support in front of others. Finally, some authors suggest that more relevant and risky arguments are brought out by the group process. While there is still disagreement about why this riskiness occurs

[1] R. R. Zăjonc, and S. M. Sales, "Social Facilitation of Dominant and Subordinate Response," *Journal of Experimental Social Psychology*, 2 (1966), 160–68.

[2] M. D. Dunnette, J. Campbell, and K. Jaasted, "The Effect of Group Participation on Brainstorming Effectiveness for Two Industrial Samples," *Journal of Applied Psychology*, 47 (1963), 30–37; and T. J. Bouchard, and M. Hare, "Size, Performance and Potential in Brainstorming Groups," *Journal of Applied Psychology*, 54 (1970), 51–55.

[3] N. Kogan, and M. A. Wallach, *Risk Taking: A Study in Cognition and Personality* (New York: Holt, Rinehart and Winston, Inc., 1964).

the fact that it does occur obviously has important implications for organizational decision making.

In summary, groups are distinctly different from individuals working alone. People are aroused in groups, they contribute different things to the final product and they seem to be more willing to take risks. Thus the study of groups and their interaction process has been a major focus of many social psychologists and organizational researchers.

AN OVERVIEW OF GROUP VARIABLES

A frame of reference for the study of the small group is presented in Figure 8–1. The variables presented in the diagram do not represent all of the possible dimensions that are operating in small groups. The figure merely lists most of the major variables which have been studied extensively by social scientists. There are two aspects of this diagram on which we should elaborate. First, it presents rather dramatically the complexity of the situation. For many years social scientists have been studying the relationships between two or perhaps three variables. So, for example, an industrial psychologist might examine the correlation between the leader's intelligence and group performance. Given that there are so many factors influencing performance it is not surprising that the results generated have produced few consistently high relationships.

A second characteristic of the diagram is that it may be viewed as an input-process-output system. There are people working together who have abilities, traits, attitudes, and other individual characteristics. These people are interrelated in various ways according to the structure of the group and the situational constraints. These three sets of variables (group composition, group structure, and task and environment) might be viewed as inputs. The group process covers who says what to whom and deals mainly with the actual behavior that occurs in the group. The final three sets of dimensions cover the major outputs or consequences of the group's behavior: changes in the group (group development), changes in the environment or task (task performance) and changes in the people (effects on group members). These outputs in turn become inputs.

The purpose of this chapter is to review the empirical findings that relate input characteristics to group process or output. We will not attempt to cover all of the possible relationships that could be generated from the figure. Certain findings are presented elsewhere in the book

FIGURE 8–1

Frame of Reference for Analysis of Groups

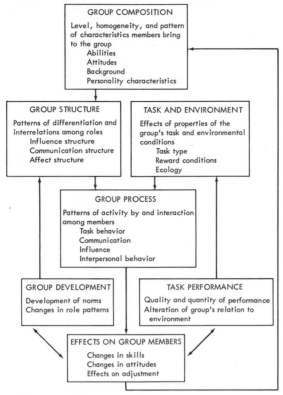

Source: Modification of a figure presented by J. McGrath in *Social Psychology: A Brief Introduction* (New York: Holt, Rinehart and Winston, Inc., 1964), p. 114.

(for example, the relationships between job attitudes and performance) and others have been infrequently examined. The results reported, therefore, represent what we consider to be the most important and most reliable findings generated to date on small group dynamics.

GROUP COMPOSITION

We have already described a number of individual characteristics such as attitudes or motivation and their relationship to job behavior and performance. There are also numerous studies that relate personality characteristics or personal interests to measures of satisfaction, turnover, and effectiveness. These results seem applicable to groups of all sizes and will therefore be briefly covered at this point.

Personality Characteristics

In general, the search for personality characteristics that are useful for predicting effectiveness on the job has not been fruitful. A review of the validity of these measures by Guion and Gottier in 1965 found that the best techniques were those that seemed to measure specific characteristics known to be necessary for the job in question. They summarized their findings as follows:

> In brief, it is difficult in the face of this summary to advocate, with a clear conscience, the use of personality measures in most situations as a basis for making employment decisions about people. It seems clear that the only acceptable reason for using personality measures as instruments of decisions is found only after doing considerable research with the measure in the specific situation and for the specific purpose for which it is to be used. Sometimes, unvalidated personality measures are used as instruments of decision because of "clinical insight" or of gullibility or superstition or of evidence accumulated in some other setting. All of these may be equally condemned unless specific situational data can be gathered that the insight, superstition, or borrowed validity is in fact predictive.[4]

More recent reviews by Schuh (personality measures and turnover) and Campbell et al. (personality characteristics and effectiveness) have not been quite so pessimistic, partly because of the inclusions of interest measures in their reviews and partly because more recent studies have been better controlled.[5]

Vocational Interests

Perhaps the three most well-known tests of personal interests are the Kuder Preference Record, the Strong Vocational Interest Blank and the Allport-Vernon Study of Values, with the first two being the most fre-

---

[4] R. M. Guion and R. F. Gottier, "Validity of Personality Measures in Personnel Selection," *Personnel Psychology*, 18 (1965), 160.

[5] A. J. Schuh, "The Predictability of Employee Turnover: A Review of the Literature," *Personnel Psychology*, 20 (1967), 133–52. Also, see John P. Campbell, Marvin D. Dunnette, Edward E. Lawler, III, and Karl T. Weick, Jr., *Managerial Behavior, Performance and Effectiveness* (New York: McGraw-Hill Book Company, 1970), pp. 164–233.

quently used. A summary of the literature relating interest blanks to various output measures (for example, ratings, performance records, turnover) by Allan Nash was relatively favorable. He reports that all three of the measures mentioned above "seem to have been found useful as predictors of potential" and he lists four factors which have been generally related to managerial effectiveness.[6]

1. Social service, humanitarian, people-oriented interests.
2. Persuasive, verbal literary interests.
3. Rejection of scientific, technical, and skilled trade interests.
4. Interests in business, business contact, and closely related occupations.

The review by Campbell et al. covered the relationships between both personality and interest measures and the effectiveness of middle and higher level managers. Their review also looked at the differences between clinical judgments and objective or actuarial judgments of the individual characteristics. They report that in most cases, actuarial measures are better predictors and that perhaps a third or more of the variability "of overall general managerial effectiveness can be expressed in terms of personal qualities claimed by managers taking part in the investigations."[7]

In summary, specific tests seem better than general ones. Interest blanks seem better than personality tests. And finally, objective tests seem to do a better job than clinical predictions. However, even with extensive measures of individual characteristics, it is clear that a large percentage of the variability in performance is left unexplained.

TASK AND ENVIRONMENT

Some of the characteristics that affect the group's behavior and output can be fairly well controlled by the organization. That is, there are certain conditions under which the group works that are given for the group members. For example, the type of task, the size of the group, and the conditions of reward are all part of the "work environment." As shown in Figure 8–1, these variables may be related to both the group structure and to the group process and output measures. Their

---

[6] A. N. Nash, "Vocational Interests of Effective Managers: A Review of the Literature," *Personnel Psychology*, 18 (1965), 30.

[7] Campbell et al., *Managerial Behavior*, p. 197.

relationships to structural properties of the group will be discussed in the next section.

The Task

Review of the literature in the small group area reveals an uneven distribution of scientific effort in several substantive and methodological areas. One area which has received insufficient attention is the area of environmental influences on group behavior and performance. In particular, not enough attention has been given to the group task. What generally happens is that more often than not, a researcher, interested in testing certain "choice" predictions from his "pet" theory, designs a neat study and devises a clever task, or finds groups that are working on such a task, which is uniquely suited for the particular subject population, variables, and conditions under investigation. Furthermore, not only do different investigators use different tasks, but the same investigator quite often will use different tasks for different studies in the same research program.

Two major problems occur because of this lack of comparability. First, to the degree that the type of task influences group interaction and output, the use of incomparable tasks will result in systematic variation across studies due to noncomparable tasks. Deutsch for example, found more interaction resulted from discussion of "human relations" problems than mathematical problems.[8] Generalizability of results is therefore limited.

The second problem is that different success criteria are used as assessments of group performance. Typical measures are correctness of the solution, how much time it took, quantity, creativity, and so on. These are not the same thing and to the degree that they differ it is again difficult to generalize. The overall problem, then, is that small group researchers have often used tasks to study groups but not groups to study tasks.

The major thrust of research trying to solve these problems has concentrated on the development of a description of the components of different tasks. Two such approaches will be described briefly below. Since these techniques are relatively recent developments there are few generalizations which can be inferred from the results.

---

[8] Morton Deutsch, "The Effects of Cooperation and Competition upon Group Process," in D. Cartwright and A. Zander, eds., *Group Dynamics* (New York: Harper & Row, 1968), pp. 461–84.

Dimensional Approach. In 1963, Marvin Shaw developed a set of ten dimensions on which he attempted to scale various tasks.[9] These dimensions reflected the clarity of the goal, the variety of ways to reach the goal, the degree to which one could verify the correctness of the solution, and so on. These dimensions have been used by various researchers to generate agreed-upon measures of such things as task difficulty or task structuredness or task type. Shaw and Blum, for example, present results that show directive leaders were more effective in a structured task (group size = 5), while nondirective leaders had higher performance scores in unstructured tasks.[10] Fiedler has also used these dimensions in the development of his "contingency model" of leadership effectiveness where he also finds that certain leadership styles are more or less effective depending upon the degree of structure in the task.[11]

An extensive study conducted by Hackman used dimensions similar to Shaw's to divide tasks into three levels of difficulty and three types of tasks (production, discussion, and problem solving). The interaction of each group was recorded and each behavior was categorized into 16 different categories (e.g., clarification, structure answer, and so on). Each task was also rated on six different measures of output or productivity. The three-by-three design allowed the investigators to examine the effects of task type and task difficulty on group process and output.[12]

The author reports that different tasks produced significant differences in 10 out of the 16 behavior categories and all of the 6 output ratings. For example, more structuring of the problem occurred in discussion tasks than in problem-solving tasks or production tasks. The task difficulty dimensions produced significant differences in 4 of the 16 behavioral categories and 5 of the 6 output dimensions. Although, at this point it is rather premature to generalize these findings it is clear that the type of task and its difficulty greatly influence the behavior and output of the group and that based upon the above findings the task-type dimension produces greater effects.

Structural Role Theory. Another recent development in the study of tasks has been presented by authors interested in the structural char-

---

[9] M. E. Shaw, *Scaling Group Tasks: A Method for Dimensional Analysis* (Gainesville, Fla.: University of Florida, 1963).

[10] M. E. Shaw and J. M. Blum, "Effects of Leadership Style upon Group Performance as a Function of Task Structure," *Journal of Abnormal and Social Psychology,* 55 (1957), 213–17.

[11] Fred E. Fiedler, *A Theory of Leadership Effectiveness* (New York: McGraw-Hill Book Co., 1967).

[12] J. R. Hackman, *Effects of Task Characteristics on Group Products* (Urbana, Ill.: University of Illinois, Department of Psychology, 1966).

acteristics of the organization. One such approach was developed by Oeser and Harary called Structural Role Theory (SRT).[13] This theory looks at the people, positions and tasks that exist in a group (or organization for that matter) and graphically represents the relationships that exist between these elements. Figure 8–2 presents a diagram of possible

FIGURE 8–2

Informal Relationships

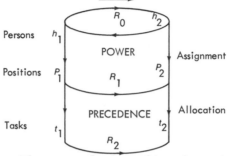

Elements and relationships of organizational structure. h_1 and h_2 are persons; p_1 and p_2 are positions; and t_1 and t_2 are tasks. Informal relationships (R_0) such as liking and communication connect persons. Positions are connected by power relationships (R_1). Tasks are connected by precedence relationships. (R_2), which are relationships that define the order in which subtasks must be completed.

Source: Adapted from O. A. Oeser and F. Harary, "A Mathematical Model for Structural Role Theory I," *Human Relations,* 15 (1962), 89–109.

relationships. Various indices have been developed that assess, for example, the degree to which various tasks require collaboration (two people working together on a variety of subtasks) or coordination (one individual finishes a subtask and passes it on to a co-worker). A study by Ilgen and O'Brien has shown that these indices are significantly related to the amount of interaction: the greater the collaboration the more interaction.[14] However, in the study reported, this interaction was

---

[13] O. A. Oeser and F. Harary, "A Mathematical Model for Structural Role Theory I," *Human Relations,* 15 (1962), 89–109.

[14] D. R. Ilgen and G. O'Brien, *The Effects of Task Organization and Member Compatibility on Leader-Member Relations in Small Groups* (Urbana, Ill.: University of Illinois, 1968).

more argumentative in pure collaborative groups and productivity was lower in this condition than when subjects had both collaboration and coordination built into the task setting. These findings suggest that even when the task is the same, the way in which people work together on the task or divide it up affects both the behavior and the output of the group. Other researchers have also found that the physical spacing affects interaction and we will discuss this research in our review of the literature on interpersonal attraction.

In general, both of the approaches show that the task and the ways in which people complete it are related to behavior patterns and output. The next step will require an integration of these strategies and hopefully the development of general principles that reflect these relationships.

Group Size

Managers are often faced with the task of setting up a group to carry out some function. Some decision about the size of the group must be made. Numerous researchers have studied the impact of group size on group interaction, satisfaction, and productivity.

Size and Interaction. Perhaps the most well-known research on small group interaction processes has been done by Bales. His Interaction Process Analysis is one of the best known and most reliable observation systems that have been developed. Observations are made about who says what to whom and each act is placed in 1 of 12 categories (e.g., gives information or shows tension). A study by Bales and Borgatta investigated the interaction of groups ranging in size from two to seven.[15] The experiment was carried out in a laboratory with subjects working on a "human relations" case problem.

The findings reported by Bales and Borgatta and replicated by others seem to indicate that very small groups show more tension, agreement, and asking for opinion whereas larger groups show more tension release, and giving of suggestions and information. The authors argue that in very small groups it is more important that everyone gets along well together and people have more time to develop their ideas and arguments. In larger groups one can be more direct because of the greater number of people and also because any given individual's talking time is reduced.

It is also reported that groups with an even number of members

---

[15] R. F. Bales and E. F. Borgatta, "Size of Group as a Factor in the Interaction Profile," in A. P. Hare, E. F. Borgatta, and R. F. Bales, eds., *Small Groups* (New York: Alfred A. Knopf, Inc., 19), pp. 396–413.

behave differently from groups with an odd number of members. Bales and Borgatta suggest that the even-numbered groups have a greater difficulty in obtaining a majority and therefore there is more tension and less antagonism or disagreement.

Size and Satisfaction. A study by Slater replicated the above findings and extended the research to cover the area of member satisfaction.[16] Subjects were placed in groups of sizes two to seven and worked on a human relations case. Their interaction was recorded and afterward the participants filled out a questionnaire which included questions about the subjects' feelings toward the size of the group and the reasons for these feelings.

Besides replicating the Bales and Borgatta results, Slater also found interesting relationships between group size and satisfaction. For this type of task it appeared that participants were most satisfied when working in a group of size five. This result is probably task specific and one should be careful in the generalizations of the findings. The reasons that subjects gave for choosing size five do seem to be more general. Slater reports that smaller groups were tense and nondirect and larger groups failed to provide enough time for everyone. He summarizes the results by implying that small groups provide physical freedom with psychological restrictions and large groups are physically restricting but psychologically less tense.

Size and Productivity. The relationship between group size and output seems to depend mostly upon the type of task upon which people are working. An excellent paper by Steiner and Rajaratnam states very explicitly why this is the case.[17] They suggest that productivity is a function of the maximum fit between people and jobs (called potential productivity) and certain decrements due to coordination and motivation:

Actual Productivity = Potential Productivity − (Coordination Decrements and Motivation Decrements)

As size increases so do motivation and coordination decrements. The relationship between potential productivity and size depends upon the task. In a straight "additive" task each new worker can produce the same extra amount (certain piece-rate jobs might fit here). Clearly, the greater the number of employees, the greater the output. Other

---

[16] P. E. Slater, "Contrasting Correlates of Group Size," *Sociometry,* 21 (1958), 129–39.

[17] I. Steiner and N. Rajaratnam, "A Model for the Comparison of Individual and Group Performance Scores," *Behavioral Science,* 6 (1961), 142–48.

types of tasks are dependent upon the most competent or least competent group member. In the former case an increase in size increases the probability of getting a competent individual. In the latter case, increases in size would increase the chances of getting someone who was incompetent and would, therefore, hinder productivity. Finally, on tasks where individuals complement each other in skills, increases in size are helpful up to a point of diminishing returns. More specifically, past a certain point taking a new member may decrease motivation and coordination more than he or she adds to groups skills. These findings suggest that very large groups would have a lower output than a somewhat smaller group for "complementary" and "best member" tasks. For "additive" tasks increasing size probably continues to increase productivity although coordination and motivation decrements also increase. For "worst member" tasks increments in size lead to decrements in output.

Research in organizational settings on group size has typically investigated groups ranging from size four or five and up. Since very small units (two or three members) are typically not part of the analyses we would expect a negative relationship between size and satisfaction. Also, because output increases with the group size for additive tasks, stays about the same for complementary and "best member" tasks, and decreases for "worst member" tasks, one would not expect great differences in output as a function of group size when task type was not taken into account. Porter and Lawler in reviewing over 20 studies dealing with this topic state that: "The literature on subunit size shows that when blue-collar workers are considered, small-size subunits are characterized by higher job satisfaction, lower absence rates, lower turnover rates, and fewer labor disputes. The evidence does not show, however, a consistent relationship for blue-collar workers between accident rates and subunit size, or between productivity and subunit size."[18] These empirical findings in organizations seem to support the small group data discussed above.

Reward Structure

The purpose of this section is not to discuss the relationship between amounts of reward and satisfaction or productivity (see Chapters 6 and 7 for this information) but rather to look at the way in which the rewards are distributed. In some organizations one's reward is tied

---

[18] L. W. Porter and E. E. Lawler, III, "Properties of Organization Structure in Relation to Job Attitudes and Job Behavior," *Psychological Bulletin*, 64 (1965), 40.

explicitly to the output (piece-rate systems for example) while in others salaries or bonuses may be partially tied to group efforts (athletic teams). Still other organizations establish systems where a fixed amount of money must be divided up among employees so that what one person stands to gain another may lose (academic salaries and raises are often from a fixed pot). These different reward structures have frequently been classified along a cooperation-competition dimension and it is this literature with which we will now deal.

The best summary to date on the literature covering this area was presented by Miller and Hamblin.[19] These authors reviewed 24 studies that compared cooperative with competitive groups and found that 14 of the research projects supported the contention that competitive groups were more productive while 10 projects found the reverse—hardly conclusive support for either hypothesis.

In rethinking the concepts of cooperation and competition, these authors suggested that these two concepts were not pure types anchoring down the opposite ends of a single dimension. They pointed out that these concepts could be most usefully broken down on two dimensions rather than one and the dimensions they suggested were: (1) interdependence, and (2) differential reward. By interdependence they meant the degree to which the group members need each other to complete the task. By differential reward they meant the degree to which individual effort received compensation. A high differential reward situation would be one where, perhaps, the most efficient member received twice as much as the least effective member from a somewhat fixed amount of resources. A low differential reward situation would be one where everyone in the group received the same compensation. Dividing these variables into highs and lows one can produce the accompanying two-by-

		INTERDEPENDENCE	
		High	Low
DIFFERENTIAL REWARD	High	1	3
	Low	2	4

two table with four possible situations. Miller and Hamblin believed that productivity would be lower in situations 1 and 4 than in 2 and 3. In situation 1 people are highly dependent on each other and yet, to the extent that one person does well, another group member stands

[19] L. Miller and R. Hamblin, "Interdependence, Differential Rewarding, and Productivity," *American Sociological Review*, 28 (1963), 768–78.

to lose. In situation 4 group members do not need each other to complete the job yet everyone receives the same compensation. In both cases, there appears to be a mismatch between how success is achieved and how the rewards are distributed. Situations 2 and 3 on the other hand show a consistent relationship between effort and reward. In situation 2 where everyone is highly interdependent rewards are distributed equally. In situation 3 where people work independently rewards are given based upon one's individual contribution.

This theoretical conceptualization was tested by Miller and Hamblin and was generally supported. Also, in a reanalysis of the 24 studies on the topic they found that the results of 23 of them could be predicted from their formulation.

Although no such summary has been done for the effects of cooperation and competition on satisfaction of interaction patterns it does appear that Miller's and Hamblin's findings for productivity are relevant for these variables as well. A study by Myers indicated that situation 2 has greater satisfaction than situation 1.[20] Also, the study by Ilgen and O'Brien indicated that greater communication took place in collaborative tasks than tasks where individuals were not interdependent.

The implications of these findings are important. Organizations should be careful to match their reward structure with the degree of interdependence inherent in the task. To introduce what is traditionally called a competitive system (high differential reward) when employees are dependent upon each other may very well decrease performance instead of increasing it. To make sure that every one gets the same compensation on a task where employees work and contribute independently may hinder effectiveness. These variables are also important for determining certain structural characteristics of the group which we will discuss next.

GROUP STRUCTURE

Another important determinant of group behavior concerns how the individuals relate to one another and to their environment. These relationships specify which people should influence, communicate with, and be attracted to, others in the group. Through a variety of procedures the organization can partly determine how these patterns will form. In the following section we will review some of the literature which

---

[20] A. E. Myers, "Team Competition, Success, and the Adjustment of Group Members," *Journal of Abnormal and Social Psychology*, 65 (1962), 325–32.

discusses ways to develop more or less communication, influence, attraction, and the effects of these developments on group process, and output.

Communication

In general, communication has to do with conveying information from one individual or set of individuals to another. This information may be verbal, physical, or written and it may convey feelings, ideas, or factual material. Finally, the process may flow in one direction or back and forth. Since this topic is discussed in detail in Chapter 9 we will be concerned here with only the experimental research on small group communication patterns.

Communication Level. Very little research has been carried out on exactly how specific patterns of communication develop although the consequences of specific patterns have been extensively studied. In general, the question asked has dealt with how to produce more or less communication and how these levels of communication are distributed among group members.

It appears that in most small groups where discussion is not artificially restricted there is usually one person who does about 40 percent of the communicating.[21] The amount of communication by the other participants is sharply reduced with these differences partly determined by the number of group members. In reviewing these studies Freedman, Carlsmith, and Sears state that "This type of pattern seems to hold in all sorts of groups—whether they are highly structured or unstructured, new or old, or are composed of friends or strangers, young or old persons."[22]

The two variables which are controlled by the organization that seem to be strongly related to the *amount* of communication in a group are the task demands and the physical location of the participants. Numerous empirical studies have shown that the way in which people are supposed to work together according to the organization chart influences their communication. We cited earlier, for example, a study by Ilgen and O'Brien which showed that more communication took place in groups that were collaborating than those that were coordinating their efforts

[21] R. F. Bales, *Interaction Process Analysis* (Reading, Mass.: Addison-Wesley, 1950).

[22] J. L. Freedman, J. M. Carlsmith, and D. O. Sears, *Social Psychology* (Englewood Cliffs, N.J.: Prentice-Hall, Inc., 1970), p. 136.

or working independently.[23] The organization may also facilitate communication simply by placing people physically close to one another. Studies in academic settings, housing projects, and business firms have supported the idea that people communicate more with people that are readily accessible than with those who are more remote.[24]

Two other variables that are related to communication are under somewhat less control of the organization. It appears that the greater the cohesiveness or attractiveness of the group members the more communication. The direction of causality here seems to be both ways. That is, we communicate with people we like and we come to like people with whom we communicate.[25] We will describe ways that this cohesiveness can be produced in the discussion on interpersonal attraction.

The final antecedents seem to be related to the flow of communication. More specifically, it has been found that in most organizations the flow of information is downward from supervisor to subordinate. The variable underlying this phenomena seems to be status. The more status the individuals have in the organization the more likely they are to be spending more time sending communications to those below them in rank or position than to those above. Reed has provided some evidence that this flow may be reversed in cases where subordinates both trust their supervisor and feel that he or she is important for the attainment of their own personal goals.[26] This suggests that when the organization can select or choose individuals who are trustworthy, they will facilitate this type of communication flow.

Communication Nets. Numerous experiments have tested the behavioral and performance outcomes of various small group communication patterns. Perhaps the best known are those conducted by Bavelas whose findings have generally been supported in subsequent studies by other researchers.[27] Four types of networks were used by Bavelas: the circle, chain, "Y," and wheel (see Figure 8–3). Communication between individ-

---

[23] Ilgen and O'Brien, *The Effects of Task Organization.*

[24] L. Festinger, "Informal Social Communication," *Psychological Review,* 57 (1950), 271–82.

[25] See A. J. Lott and B. E. Lott, "Group Cohesiveness as Interpersonal Attraction: A Review of Relationships with Antecedent and Consequent Variables," *Psychological Bulletin,* 14 (1965), 259–309.

[26] W. Reed, "Upward Communication in Industrial Hierarchies," *Human Relations,* 15 (1962), 3–15.

[27] Alex Bavelas, "Communication Patterns in Task Oriented Groups," *Journal of the Acoustical Society of America,* 22 (1951), 725–30.

FIGURE 8–3

Small Group Communication Nets

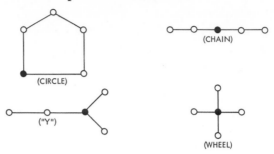

uals was permitted just along those channels prescribed by the pattern. The communicators were experimentally "insulated" from cross talk.

Four experimental results with respect to these networks need comment.[28]

1.   Centrality of position in sending and receiving messages produces group leaders. The leaders, identified in the networks by a black dot, are strategically positioned to relay the information to other group members which is necessary for task performance.

2.   From the standpoint of efficiency in *organizing* for task performance, the wheel is the fastest, followed by the "Y," the chain, and the circle. The reader should observe that this is a descending order of centrality. In the wheel, the leader may communicate with each other member with equal facility. Communication becomes increasingly difficult for the leader in each of the other networks.

3.   The researchers found a differential effect in solving problems. For simple problems which require a minimum of interaction the wheel is the fastest. Group members are content to send all information to the central source to be acted upon and coordinated. For more difficult problems requiring interaction, the circle is fastest. In another set of experiments, Shaw found an all-channel network with free communication to be the fastest among all other types in handling complex problems.[29]

4.   Satisfaction with the product seems to be highest in the circle network where everyone participates in the decision-making process. Morale also seems to be related to the degree of participation, with the member occupying the central position being the most satisfied in

---

[28] See M. Shaw, "Communication Networks," in L. Berkowitz, ed., *Advances in Experimental Social Psychology,* vol. 1 (New York: Academic Press, 1964).
[29] Ibid.

most cases (except where he is overloaded).[30] So it does appear that satisfaction and performance are related to how much and to whom one communicates although the specific patterns and the difficulty of the tasks seem to produce differential effects on these outcomes.

Social Influence and Conformity

There appear to be two major ways that the organization can affect the degree to which people will do what they are asked to do. One way is to assign to various positions in the organization the rights to use powerful rewards and punishments. These rights or sanctions and their usage are discussed in Chapters 13 and 14 under the topics of power and leadership, respectively, so we will not elaborate on them here.

However, a second method of getting people to comply with one's wishes is through the process of social influence. This process is concerned with the ways in which the situation, and especially the group norms or expectations of one's peers, are related to the patterns and amounts of influence that exist in the group. We will discuss various ways that one can increase this conformity through changes in the task, the setting, and the participants. A brief discussion of the consequences of conformity will also be included.

Conformity Induction. Perhaps the most well-known research in this area was first conducted by Solomon Asch.[31] In a series of classical experiments, Asch demonstrated the profound effect group pressure has on individual judgement. Asch rigged an experimental situation in which a group was preinstructed to state wrong judgments publicly when asked to match the length of a given line with one of three unequal lines (see Figure 8–4). In a substantial number of cases (33 percent), an

FIGURE 8–4
Stimulus Objects Used in
Asch Experiment

Key: Confederates say that
line C is most like line x.

---

[30] Ibid.

[31] S. E. Asch, "Studies of Independence and Conformity: A Minority of One against a Unanimous Majority," *Psychological Monographs,* 70 (1955), 9 (Whole No. 416).

uninstructed subject who perceived the correct relationship between the lines denied the evidence of his senses when subjected to group pressure. The independent subject did not know he was being plotted against. Furthermore he was so placed in the group that he was the last to state his judgment. The research using this setting has been extensive and is included in the following discussion.

The major contributors of social influence can be broken down into four categories: task demands, group characteristics, individual characteristics, and combinations of these three.

Task Demands. The first variable of interest is the degree of ambiguity of the answer and whether there is an answer at all. In situations which are ambiguous and for which there is no answer there appears to be more conformity than where either of these two conditions do not hold. That is, there is less conformity when the situation is not ambiguous and has no answer (opinions about politics, for example) or where it is not ambiguous and there is an answer (Asch's study). The more that people are unsure about handling the task correctly the more they will use the information given to them from others.

A second dimension of task demands has to do with the conditions under which one must respond to the pressures or influence attempt. It has been found, for example, that the earlier in time one commits himself to an issue the more difficult it is for him to change later. Coupled with this is the idea of public commitment. Individuals who declare their position on an issue publicly are more likely to conform to group pressure than those who can make a private declaration.

The reward structure of the task has also been studied. In conditions where the group is interdependent there seems to be greater conformity. It appears that if the individual feels that both he and others stand to suffer as a consequence of his behavior that he will deviate less from what the group thinks is the correct thing to do than if only he would suffer.[32]

Characteristics of the Group. One result found in studies by both Asch and Hardy indicated that the unanimity of group pressure was strongly related to how frequently an individual conformed to the group.[33] More specifically, individuals tend to conform less to the group consensus when this consensus is not held by all the members.

---

[32] H. Gerard, "Deviation, Conformity and Commitment," in I. Steiner and M. Fishbein, eds.; *Current Studies in Social Psychology* (New York: Holt, Rinehart and Winston, Inc., 1965), pp. 263–77.

[33] See K. R. Hardy, "Determinants of Conformity and Attitude Change," *Journal of Abnormal and Social Psychology*, 54 (1957), 289–94.

The number of people in the group also effects conformity. Asch presented results showing that the effects of unanimous pressure on conformity changes very little after the group reaches four or five members. In the experimental setting described earlier where the naïve subject responds after hearing the responses of a number of confederates, Asch found that the amount of conformity ceases to increase by utilizing more than four confederates. Apparently, additional members do not add additional pressure.

Finally, studies by Milgram have indicated that the closeness of supervision affects the conformity.[34] In situations where the group can use surveillance (close to the idea of public commitment) to check the responses of the pressured individual there is more conformity. It is probably important to point out that the investigations cited here deal with behavioral conformity, not necessarily attitude change. In many of these cases the individual may do what is required of him but not really believe what he has said or done. The usefulness of this type of conformity depends upon the goals of the organization.

Personality Characteristics. The research on the kinds of people who are likely to conform is limited. One study by Crutchfield correlated a variety of personality test scores with the amount of conformity displayed in an Asch-type experimental setting.[35] He reports negative correlations between intelligence, tolerance, and ego strength scores and conformity. Brighter, more tolerant people with a strong self-concept or ego tend to conform less than those who are low on these dimensions. He also reports a positive relationship between a measure of authoritarianism or rigidity and conformity. He failed, however, to find consistent relationships between conformity and a set of other personal or physical characteristics.

Combinations of the Task, the Group, and the People. There appears to be ample evidence that people who work together and like each other have greater influence over each other than when this attraction is absent. The study by Lott and Lott cited earlier found that highly cohesive groups had both more communication and more influence with group members than groups that were low in cohesiveness.

Also, the degree to which one can deviate from group norms appears to be tied to his or her past record of performance and conformity.

---

[34] S. Milgram, "Some Conditions of Obedience and Disobedience to Authority," *Human Relations*, 18 (1965), 57–76.

[35] R. S. Crutchfield, "Conformity and Character," *American Psychologist*, 10 (1955), 191–98.

Hollander provides evidence that shows that individuals who have displayed competence in the past and have conformed to group norms can deviate from these norms in order to initiate change or move the group in a new direction.[36] He argues that the competent, conforming individual builds up "idiosyncrasy credits" with his fellow group members when they come to trust his judgments and believe that he has the groups' interests at heart. When this situation is reached the individual may initiate change without great fear of rejection or refusal.

In summary, there appear to be a number of strategies available to the organization that would facilitate conformity. They may choose certain types of people, encourage discussions of important issues, initiate reward systems that demand interdependence, keep a close watch on what is done, and so forth. Whether the outcomes are beneficial or not depends upon the organization's goals.

Conformity Outcomes. Very little research has studied the differences in performance or satisfaction as a function of the degree of conformity present in the group. Some inferences, however, do seem to be justified. To start with, the relationship between conformity and effectiveness should be moderated by the task and the motivational inclinations of the employees. For tasks where diversity of opinion is needed, a group with everyone conforming to one opinion would probably have a detrimental effect on performance. Also, the employees may not be motivated to use their influence to further productivity. There are, in fact, cases where group pressure has been used to hinder effectiveness. The "binging" of rate-busters by group members (rate-busters were hit on the arm) in the Hawthorne studies is a good example.

Lastly, it would appear that an individual's satisfaction or morale vis-à-vis the group's ability to pressure one to conform would depend on the similarity of the opinions of the individual and the group. For those who concur with the group this pressure might increase morale. For those who disagree it should be a very unpleasant situation in which to work.

Interpersonal Attraction

The third structural characteristic of groups is the pattern and the amounts of attraction that exist among group participants. We will proceed with the same format by describing the variables that lead to

---

[36] E. P. Hollander, "Competence and Conformity in the Acceptance of Influence," *Journal of Abnormal and Social Psychology*, 61 (1960), 365–69.

attraction and then turn to the relationship between attraction and various organizational outcomes.[37]

Antecedents of Attraction. Once again, the trilogy of the task, group, and individual is an excellent frame of reference for studying the variables that contribute to interpersonal attraction. The one aspect of the task which has been frequently studied is the physical closeness of the participants. Investigations in numerous organizational settings have shown that the closer people are the more likely it is that they will become friends. People who live or work next to one another are likely to communicate with each other and are more likely to form friendships than they are with people who are more remote.[38]

A second finding related to the task is that groups that have a successful history with a task seem to like each other more than if they have been unsuccessful. In attempts to discover the causal nature of this relationship it appears that success does cause attraction (we will discuss the reverse relationship later). When success is manipulated in experimental settings, the groups with high success have greater liking for their fellow members than do the members of unsuccessful groups.[39]

One of the group characteristics to which we have already alluded is cooperation. Deutsch's classical study in 1951 of cooperation and competition found that groups working together for common goals had a higher level of attraction than those groups in which there was competition. Similar findings imply that a participative supervisory style also increases intermember attraction.[40] Groups in which the individuals can participate in the decision-making process are apt to be composed of people who like one another.

The greatest contributions to interpersonal attraction, however, appear to come from the personal characteristics of the participants. In our elaboration of attitude theories one of the ideas that frequently reappeared was that people like people who like the same things they do; that is, people are attracted to those who are similar to them. Empirical results supporting this contention have been summarized elsewhere but in general it appears that similarities in race, background, education, attitudes, and values all lead to attraction.[41] Other studies have seemed

---

[37] See Lott and Lott, "Group Cohesiveness as Interpersonal Attraction."

[38] Festinger, "Informal Social Communication," pp. 271–82; R. White and R. Lippitt, *Autocracy and Democracy* (New York: Harper, 1960), chapters 3 and 5.

[39] See Lott and Lott "Group Cohesiveness as Interpersonal Attraction," for a review.

[40] Deutsch in Cartwright and Zander, *Group Dynamics*, pp. 461–84.

[41] Lott and Lott, "Group Cohesiveness as Interpersonal Attraction."

to show that people who are similar in personality characteristics *before* they meet have a better probability of becoming good friends than those who have different personalities. The "opposites attract" theory has minimal empirical support.

Consequences of Attraction. Two of the effects of high attraction on group behavior have been discussed. People who like each other tend to communicate with one another and can influence one another. Other research results show that groups of people who like each other will be freer in their expressions of hostility and aggression toward an outside disruptive person or group.[42] Since the definition of job satisfaction as measured by most investigators includes questions about an employee's feelings toward co-workers it is also a foregone conclusion that groups with members attracted to one another will be more satisfied than those who have negative feelings for their co-workers.

However, the major output of interest—performance—has not been positively related to the level of attraction. In some cases it was helpful; in others this was not the case. A brief summary of what has been covered so far should explain why this has occurred. Given that group members are highly attracted to one another it follows that they will have influence over one another, that they probably think and believe similar things and that they will frequently communicate these feelings. All of these tendencies should lead to greater productivity only when the employees are motivated to work hard. When this motivation is lacking, these characteristics should lead to the lowest level of output. An experimental study by Schachter, Ellertson, McBride, and Gregory tested these assumptions.[43] Groups of three were set up to perform an assembly-line type of task and the attraction and motivation of the participants was manipulated. Half of the groups were told that they were similar and would like one another, while half were told the opposite. (This has been shown to be a fairly good way to manipulate attraction.) During the task the participants were allowed to communicate with one another by notes. These messages were controlled by the experimenter and half the subjects received notes urging them to work hard (high motivation) and half received messages suggesting that they slow down or "take it easy." These manipulations produced four types of groups which are shown in Figure 8–5. Groups that had high attraction and high motiva-

---

[42] A. Pepitone and G. Reichling, "Group Cohesiveness and the Expression of Hostility," *Human Relations*, 8 (1955), 327–38.

[43] S. Schachter, N. Ellertson, D. McBride, and P. Gregory, "An Experimental Study of Cohesiveness and Productivity," *Human Relations*, 4 (1951), 229–38.

FIGURE 8–5

Attraction and Performance
Motivation

MOTIVATION

		High	Low
ATTRACTION	High	1	4
	Low	2	3

tion (cell 1) had the highest productivity, whereas groups that had
high attraction with low motivation had the lowest productivity (cell
4). These results support the idea that attraction can increase or decrease
output depending upon employee motivation.

OVERALL PERSPECTIVE

The purpose of this chapter as stated earlier was to acquaint the
reader with the research conducted in the area of group dynamics. A
systems framework was used and a review of the various inputs and their
effects on organizational behavior and outputs was presented. By now,
the complexity of the area is surely appreciated. Figure 8–6 shows this
complexity. As can be seen in Figure 8–6, there are numerous dimensions
of the people, their jobs, and the structure of their groups, which are
related to how they behave toward one another, how much they like
one another, and how much they produce.

In a recent review of this area Hackman and Morris suggest a number
of ways that organizations can change or modify these inputs in order
to improve performance and effectiveness. For example they suggest
that norms can be clarified and changed through various diagnostic
or feedback procedures such as working with an outside consultant or
by training. Task redesign may also change group norms. The employee's
efforts can be modified through various motivational interventions. Hackman and Morris feel that "whether a group develops a norm of high
or low effort depends substantially on the quality of the experiences
members have as they work on the task—and that these experiences
in turn are largely determined by the task itself."[44] In general people
will be more motivated on jobs which have some variety, closure, impor-

---

[44] J. R. Hackman and C. G. Morris, *Group Tasks, Group Interaction Process, and
Group Performance Effectiveness: A Review and Proposed Integration* (New Haven,
Conn.: Yale University, Technical Report no. 7, August 1974), p. 41.

FIGURE 8–6

Framework Showing the Relations among the Focal Input Variables, Group Interaction Process, and the Three Summary Variables in Affecting Group Performance Effectiveness

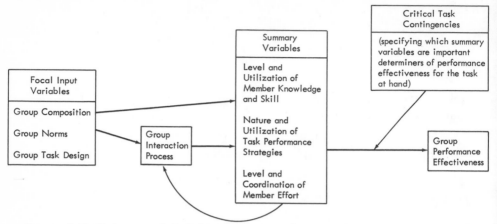

Source: J. R. Hackman, and C. G. Morris, *Group Tasks, Group Interaction Process, and Group Performance Effectiveness: A Review and Proposed Integration* (New Haven, Conn.: Yale University, Technical Report no. 7, August 1974).

tance, feedback, and a chance for individual input.[45] Finally, member knowledge and skill can be changed through selection, training, and ongoing team building interventions.

In summary, groups in organizations provide both positive and negative outcomes. They may be inefficient information generators and various elements of individual initiative or responsibility may suffer. On the other hand, they are often part of the "participation" process and because of our technologies people frequently must interact in groups in order to successfully understand and deal with broad problems. The question is not groups versus no groups but rather a set of questions related to when groups are most effective and how they can be more effective. The implication is that social scientists must begin to handle this complex situation with more complex theories. Studies should be conducted to examine the relative contribution of these variables to outputs. Hopefully the new computer facilities and statistical techniques that can handle highly complex information will facilitate the development of this research.

---

[45] J. R. Hackman, and G. R. Oldham, *Motivation through the Design of Work: Test of a Theory* (New Haven, Conn.: Yale University, Technical Report no. 6, 1974).

But a second implication is applicable for those in organizations. These results show that organizations must first decide upon their goals before introducing various programs or selection procedures designed to increase effectiveness. Attraction and influence can be legitimate goals but they should not be equated with productivity. Competition may hurt you rather than help you. Selecting an exceptionally bright manager (differing greatly from subordinates) may do the same. In sum, there are no simple formulas for assuring high morale and productivity.

part *III*

Organizational Processes

I n the last two parts we discussed the structure of the complex organization and organization behavior. We described various subsystems and some of the factors that affect their performance. This part investigates how certain *strategic processes* contribute to the effectiveness of organizational systems.

It is important to understand the nature of process. In systems theory process contains three elements: activity, change, and function. Activity means courses of action which are normally influenced by human behavior in organization. Given the variety of possible human responses to such organizational activities it is vital to understand, and where possible shape, the nature of these responses. Such activities, aimed at realizing existent or changing organizational components in order to achieve organizational objectives, are greatly dependent on the attitudes and behavior of those who define them and carry them out. Systems are *managed* so that activities are directed toward rational purposes. However, management takes place within the framework of functions, consequently each process has functional subsets which are, in a sense, *specialized* activities. Figure III–1 summarizes the activities, change, and function components of the seven processes we discuss in this part.

Most agree that within human systems people engage in processes such as communication, decision making, and balance. These activities go on in all organizations. They are, indeed, the dynamics that underlie the internal life of an organization, the vital *linking* functions.

189

FIGURE III–1
The Components of Organizational Processes

Process	Activity	Change	Function
Communication	Exchange of meaning among decision centers with feedback.	To alter or influence behavior of the decision centers.	Emotive, motivation, information, control.
Decision making	Quest for alternative courses of action.	To reduce uncertainty.	Search, alternative formation, probability weighing, implementing strategy, evaluating outcomes.
Balance	Maintenance of organizational stability.	To resolve conflict.	Control.
Role and status	Social interaction of divergent centers of authority, power, and specialization.	To modify role expectations; to increase role effectiveness; to reduce role conflict.	Clarification of rights, duties, and obligations; to regularize behavior.
Influence	Social transactions to induce others to do something they would not ordinarily do.	To achieve compliance.	Authority, power, and exchange.
Leadership	Directing, planning, rewarding, punishing.	To affect attitudes and behavior of subordinates.	Authority, feedback, and control.
Technology	Selection of rational means to accomplish ends most efficiently.	To achieve rational goal adjustment in sociotechnical systems.	Scientific method and verification.

In addition to these three linking processes are four other processes we discuss in this part. They are status and role, influence, leadership, and technological processes. While these processes may not occupy quite as prominent a role in organizational life as do the linking processes, they are indispensable forms of human activity because they order relationships among people and organizational functions.

There are many sides to a process. Decision making is a good example. It can be analyzed as choosing among alternatives—the so-called rational choice criteria procedure—or we can focus on individual decisions to participate in and produce for an organization, or we can discuss organizational decisions in terms of routine and innovative classes of activity. Beyond decision making are six other processes that we treat in this part of the book. A full analysis of just one process would require a complete volume.

We have tried in our analysis of processes to present for each a range of concepts that give a fair statement of the nature of the process and its relation to complex organizations and individual behavior. This approach has some deficiencies that should be pointed out. First, we try to avoid giving just one theory about a process. In discussing each process, we review a variety of research and theory pertaining to it. This material is the result of a number of scholars working in an area. Because of an absence of integrated theory in the behavioral sciences, much of the data and the models of behavior may seem conflicting. But this is an accurate reflection of the "state of the art," demonstrating the lack of consensus about the nature and relative importance of the processes' role in complex organizations and individual behavior. Second, each process chapter is a bit like an independent essay on the subject. This again is indicative of the development of the field of organization theory. There is hardly an integrated theory of human systems that forces on us a logical method for arranging this part other than to treat the linking processes first. However, after all of this is said, the topics treated here constitute the crucial internal and interactional activities in organizational life.

chapter 9

Communication Processes

Communication is *the* critical process in organizing because it is the primary medium of human interaction. Communication links individuals, groups, machines, tasks, authority levels, and functional specializations. To effect these linkages requires the exchange of meaning with feedback of understanding between or among decision centers for the purpose of coordination.[1]

Formal communication, written or oral, is goal directed in organizations. Its chief mission is to secure rational management objectives. Thus, the communication process is dynamic, because as objectives change, the content of communication must also *change* in order to alter or to reenforce the actions of various segments of the organization. In the language of the systems model, communication is a linking process that joins various parts and subsystems into a unified, goal-oriented, purposeful activity of organization. It is a managerial tool that has to be used in certain ways depending on the sort of outcomes desired, and like any tool its design and use must be considered carefully. In this respect communication is often programmed according to *functions* performed, which in management are usually classified into four main categories: emotive, motivation, information, control.

COMMUNICATION FUNCTIONS

Page for page, at least as much has been written about communication in management as any other subject in the field of organization theory

---

[1] Lyman W. Porter, Edward E. Lawler III, and J. Richard Hackman, *Behavior in Organizations* (New York: McGraw-Hill Book Company, 1975), p. 95.

and behavior. So it is impossible to deal with this subject in a single chapter. However, its organizationally important dimensions can be described, and they correspond to the functions of communication. Figure 9–1 offers a useful way of conceptualizing the key aspects of this function.

FIGURE 9–1
Functions of Organizational Communication Process

Function	Orientation	Objectives Sought	Theoretical and Research Focus
1. Emotive	Feeling	Increasing *acceptance* of organizational tasks.	Personal and interpersonal satisfaction; resolution of tension; definition of role; expression of attitudes.
2. Motivation.	Influence	Seeking commitment to organization objectives.	Power, authority, compliance; behavioral modification; reenforcement and expectancy theories.
3. Information	Technological	Providing data necessary to rational decisions.	Decision making; assessment of data; organizational intelligence.
4. Control	Structure	Clarifying duties, authority, accountability.	Organizational design and redesign.

Communication functions are not independent of each other. For example, the influence orientation of the motivation function is obviously connected to structure and control. People in authority can extract compliance from those under them by exercising the power inherent in their positions. In another example, the technological data supplied by the information function is often colored by the attitudes and feelings of the people transmitting it. Many instances such as these can be cited. The point is that communication functions are related in organizational systems.

Because communication touches so many facets of organizational life, it is more appropriate to treat some of the theories and research findings pertaining to them in other chapters in this book. Aspects of the emotive and motivation functions are discussed in Chapters 6, 8, 12, and 13 on motivation, group dynamics, status and role, and influence, respectively. This chapter concentrates on the information and control functions of communication. However, for the sake of comprehensiveness a description of each function is given.

Emotive

Intimately involved in organizational communication processes are human senders and receivers of information. The activities in which they engage are fundamental material out of which communication networks are constructed. It is certain, therefore, that some of the communication in organization has little to do with the rational aims of management. Rather, it is concerned with human feeling and emotion.

Nevertheless, communication, whether formal or informal, rational or emotional, is deeply rooted in psychological foundations. People have an inherent need to communicate. Some have explained that this need is based in the ambiguity of human relationships,[2] and that the motivation to communicate arises from the desire for greater clarity, such as illustrated in Figure 9–2.

FIGURE 9–2
Restructuring an Ambiguous Communication Setting

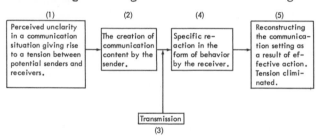

The psychological dynamics at work include a perception of ambiguity between communicating parties that creates a "state of tension or dissonance." This in turn stimulates a specific act or transmission of information in order to resolve the tension. Organizational communication is aimed at clarifying ambiguous situations; such frequently is the purpose of management's communication programs for employees. At one level, these programs are necessary for adequate job performance, because they should provide information to resolve tensions caused by ambiguity in job responsibilities. At another level tension may come from a person's need to know the reason for the job, and its role in the larger organization. The emotive function of communication programs is directed at this level as well.

Apart from these aspects of job and organizational communication,

---

[2] Franklin Fearing, "Toward a Psychological Theory of Human Communication," *Journal of Personality*, 22 (1953–54), 73–76.

people also need to communicate with each other in the organizational setting, but not necessarily about organizational matters. Informal channels of communication exist, often called the grapevine, which carry all sorts of information reflecting feelings, attitudes, and sentiments. The grapevine is discussed exhaustively in much of the human relations literature.[3]

Motivation

Another important function of communication is to influence others to take action in a social setting. The motivation function cannot, therefore, be considered detached from the social network in which it occurs. The relationship between a sender and a receiver is not a simple one in human situations. What the sender transmits is conditioned by what he or she thinks or hopes the receiver will accept. So, in order to move another to action, the sender has to modify constantly the content and the tone of the "message" according to the reactions to them fed back by the receiver.

Frequently, the "sender-receiver" model is expressed in terms of interpersonal, one-to-one relationships. While this model is important in influence theory, it is just one segment of the network in which the motivation function exists organizationally. The study of group dynamics reveals other communication situations. There are group-individual communication and group-to-group communication. Organizationally group-individual communication has two forms—one-to-many which is typical in superior-subordinate relationships, and many-to-one which is found in committee advisory activities. The group-to-group pattern often involves interaction between specialized project teams coordinating their activities, or between groups bargaining over conflicting interests such as those found in labor-management relations.

The research and theory of the behavioral sciences has concentrated on the emotive and motivation functions of communication. By and large this aspect of communication deals with the human actors in organizational settings as we emphasize in other chapters. It involves very close relationships on the microlevel of interpersonal behavior. The next two functions of communication are less personal, and they also tend to be broader in scope, dealing with larger problems of organizational design.

---

[3] Keith Davis, "Management Communication and the Grapevine," *Harvard Business Review*, September–October 1953, 43–49.

Information

The information function of communication provides technical data for rational decision making. Le Breton calls this function administrative intelligence, because it provides the required data necessary for policy formulation.[4]

There are many sources of management information. Very early in the development of organization theory, it was realized that the staff organization existed mainly to advise management through the generation of information in areas of particular organizational importance. Financial information is supreme in this respect and accounting and financial management emerged accordingly. They were followed closely in business organizations with specialized staff groups dealing with production capacity, product output, quality, and design. Marketing staffs came along with sales forecasts and analyses of distribution channels. Without these basic information sources in large organizations rational management policies would be impossible in fundamental areas such as finance, production, and distribution.

As a general rule, the more complex an organization becomes, the more management has to depend upon specialized staff *and* information technology for decision-making data. This dependency raises two very important organization issues. The first issue is organization design for achieving optimum communication effectiveness. The second issue, related to the first, is the use of communication technology.

Changing communication technology has had considerable impact on organizational design and vice versa.[5] Before managements' information needs were accelerated by the size, complexity, and technological sophistication of modern organizations, their information requirements were largely satisfied by organization staff groups generating data with rather primitive techniques. But now management has to consider alternative organization designs to enhance communication effectiveness.

One such alternative is *decentralization*. It amounts to this: If the organization grows so large and so complex that its management cannot centrally control all the information necessary for decisions, then the obvious solution is to break down the organization into semiautonomous

---

[4] Preston P. Le Breton, *Administrative Intelligence—Information Systems* (Boston: Houghton Mifflin Company, 1963).

[5] William G. Scott, "Communication and Centralization of Organization," *Journal of Communication*, March 1963, pp. 3–11.

decision-making units. Thus relevant decision-making information is readily accessible, and it comes in smaller, more easily digestible, packages.

However, the decentralized design is seldom fully implemented. More usually certain categories of decisions are delegated to decentralized units, such as those concerning production control, product quality, maintenance, personnel, and some aspects of marketing. But decisions over major capital expenditures and the evaluation of key management personnel are usually retained by central authorities in the organization. Thus top management has been forced to be selective about the kinds of information it chooses to receive and to act upon out of the total amount of information available in the system. The information that ultimately is reserved for top level centralized decision purposes *is that which gives management the greatest control leverage over the total organization.* Financial and executive performance data are examples of extraordinarily powerful kinds of information for control purposes.

The matrix organization, which is a variation of decentralized design, also has some important communication implications. As we observed in Chapter 3, the matrix organization is a system of relationships that joins specialized "programs" with "functional" departments. The chief reason for this design is better coordination in the allocation of resources among departments and programs in an organization. The matrix design eases the exchange of information at the levels where important activity decisions are made. Consequently much of the communication that goes on in a matrix structure is horizontal among functions of roughly equal authority. However, all matrix structures are in a larger hierarchy, and a position of command authority exists over these structures. This position by its nature is a focal point of communication. It has access to information not available immediately to lower functions in the matrix, but more importantly it can use this information to influence the nature of the decisions made by managers within the matrix.

It is difficult to discuss organizational communication designs without considering information technology at the same time. Scientific developments in electronics have enormously advanced the human capacity to communicate. Without these achievements, which have expanded the ability to generate, transmit, assimilate, store, and retrieve information, the wonders of our technological age would be unknown. With respect to this, we are accustomed to consider the computer as the main electronic marvel. While the computer is in fact the heart of advanced information technology, it is surrounded by larger management information systems that include programming, information distribution methods, simulation techniques, decision models, and so on.

As information demands expand in organizations, the chief problem management faces is to weigh the comparable advantages and disadvantages of expanding its communication technology to satisfy information needs. A commonsense rule is that management should spend no more to obtain information than such information is worth. In other words, investment in information technology must always be subejct to economic justification. While it is possible to work out an elaborate analysis of the economics of information acquisition, it is not necessary to do so here.[6] All we need to note is the obvious—management has in many organizations elected to install progressively more advanced information systems. The organizational effects of such systems are important to stress.

Computer-oriented management information technology biases the organization toward greater centralization,[7] just as technology in general has contributed significantly to the centralization tendencies in society as a whole.[8] However, the patterns of centralization in organization resulting from information technology are not as clear cut as might be supposed. The extreme vision of the centralized, computerized organization is one where all control is vested in a few top managers supported by an elite group of loyal technicians feeding them data. While it makes good science fiction reading, such a condition is unusual. More likely, there are situations of partial decentralization where semiautonomous decision units are retained, but where the scope of authority within these units is reduced. For example, the steady erosion of departmental authority in universities is in part attributable to the expansion of information technology by the central administration of universities. Direct access to information sources is an incalculable advantage when it comes to exercising executive power and influence.

Implicit in our discussion of the information function so far is that one measure of effectiveness is defined by matching information quantity with decision needs. This is partially true, but it obviously does not reduce the need for considering the qualitative character of information as the key variable. Obviously all information is not equal, and more

---

[6] See Herbert A. Simon, "Theories of Decision Making in Economics and Behavioral Science," *American Economic Review*, June 1959, pp. 269–70.

[7] Harold J. Leavitt and Thomas L. Whisler, "Management in the 1980's," *Harvard Business Review*, November–December 1958, pp. 41–48.

[8] Henry S. Kariel, *The Decline of American Pluralism* (Stanford, Calif.: Stanford University Press, 1961).

does not necessarily mean better. The garbage-in-garbage-out phenomenon is frequently mentioned in reference to the computer.

Often it is difficult for management to discriminate in any precise way about the quality of information it acquires for decision purposes. There seems to be an indirect relationship between the ability to assess the quality and the level of the organization at which decisions are made. The higher one rises in the organization, the harder it is to determine the relative merits of data.[9] So executives must rely on experience, judgment, intuition, and knowledge. This is a result of the nature of the data used. Information that is necessary for many top level decisions is likely to be unquantifiable and therefore unsusceptible to computer manipulation. Hence, the quality of the decisions made organizationally depends upon the quality of the executive decision makers, although it must be acknowledged that information technology has extended their range considerably.

Control

The premise that organization design is related to information technology was established in the previous section. The logical extension of this premise is that the communication function is an integral part of the control process of management. Control is exercised by management organizationally in many ways through attitudes, motivation, interpersonal influence, and so on. *Structure,* which we consider in this section, is another dimension of controlling.

Organizational structure can be visualized as a *formalization of communication networks.* The objective of formalization is control over organization activities by making the patterns of information flow uniform and predictable. Various models of communication describe the concepts underlying the control function of communication.

One author says ". . . a model is . . . a structure of symbols and operating rules which is supposed to match a set of relevant points in an existing structure or process."[10] There are three irreducible elements in all communication systems:

1. Sources for generating information and receivers for assimilating it.
2. Vehicles for conveying information—symbols.
3. Channels for distributing information.

---

[9] For interesting examples, see Le Breton, *Administrative Intelligence,* pp. 5–8.
[10] Karl W. Deutsch, "On Communication Models in the Social Sciences," *Public Opinion Quarterly,* 16 (1952), 357.

Using March and Simon's approach the control function of communication applies to all organizationally routinized activities.[11] This includes: the initiation and establishment of activities and the day-to-day coordination of operations; the provision of information for the development of policy strategy; the use of communication to evoke action from various parts of the system; and the provision of feedback on the results of activities.[12] These activities center on the generation, implementation, motivation, and control of organizational programs. Since they are at the heart of organizational life, it is clear that structure must be devoted to their regularization. Such structures are frequently referred to as communication systems.

The simplest way to visualize an organizational communication system is the circuit illustrated in Figure 9–3. The model shows that for commu-

FIGURE 9–3
The Communication Circuit

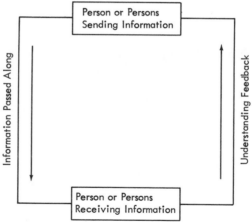

nication to exist both a sender and a receiver are necessary. Additionally, communication in this model relies on a *closed* circuit, requiring both the elements of downward passage of information and understanding feedback to be present. As a first approximation, this model represents

---

[11] James G. March and Herbert A. Simon, *Organizations* (New York: John Wiley & Sons, Inc., 1958), p. 161. March and Simon refer to these as "programmed" activities to distinguish them from all other kinds of informal "nonprogrammed" communications.

[12] March and Simon also include a category of "nonprogrammed" communication activities that contains all individual "listening and talking" in organizations not associated with jobs.

the basic ingredients necessary for effective communication. It should be added that the model is indeed a first approximation.

The circuit model is quadratic, symmetrical, and continuous. It is quadratic in that four elements are basic to it; it is symmetrical because information emitted by the sender (ideally) is balanced by understanding evidence by the receiver; and it is continuous because it portrays communication as an undisrupted interchange between the sender and receiver.

Newman advances the idea that "although communication is . . . a circular process, circular should not be construed as continuous. . . . There need not be an unbroken, continuous relation among the sender, the signal, and the receiver . . . communication may be said to exist wherever there is a relationship effected between any two of the three factors involved, even though the third may be in abeyance."[13] Figure 9–4 explains Newman's point.

FIGURE 9–4
A Dyadic Communication Model

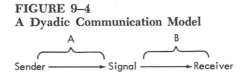

Brackets A and B identify communication dyads. These dyads may eventually link up to form a completed communication circuit. But their linking may be neither direct nor continuous.[14] Instead the two dyads may join at different times and for different reasons in the organization.

The dyadic aspects of communication do not fundamentally change the circuit model. They modify it to accord more with the realities of communication in complex organizations. Certainly not all organizational communication is the personal, direct, and circular interchange which the simple circuit model implies. Management communication is frequently impersonal and is disconnected both in space and time from intended receivers. It is important to appreciate how the communication process operates in the continuous, circular, face-to-face relationship. But it is equally essential to know the circumstances under which dyads link up to form systems in more complex communication networks.

---

[13] John B. Newman, "Communication: A Dyadic Postulation," *Journal of Communication,* June 1959, p. 53.

[14] While the circuit model uses four elements, two of these elements—information and understanding feedback—are carried by the vehicle of a signal to link the sender to the receiver. So, in principle, the same elements exist both in Newman's model and the circuit model.

The subject of communication networks raises the topic of structure and focuses on communication as a linking process—for as Rothstein says, "Organization presupposes the existence of parts, which, considered in their totality, constitute organization. The parts must interact. Were there no communication between them, there would be no organization for we should merely have a collection of individual elements isolated from each other."[15] Similarly, Dorsey points out that administration can be viewed as a configuration of communication patterns relating individuals and groups.[16]

A network is best visualized as a system of decision centers interconnected by communication channels.[17] A network always has feedback features; that is, *control* of the system is accomplished by retroactive mechanisms. Feedback, through a communication network, allows for self-regulation of the system. By sampling the output, the system regulates the input in such a way as to maintain stability in the face of change. Feedback is a basic property of *cybernetic* systems. And the human organization is an example of one of the most complex of all such systems.

Now, the circular model incorporates all the features of a network. In reality this model *is* a highly simplified network because it contains decision centers, information, and a feedback property. However, the network model is far more complex, containing numerous intermeshed loops which do not necessarily behave in a continuous, direct pattern. They act more as dyads than simple circuits. *Further, because of its complexity the network possesses greater capabilities for variety. It is able to assimilate a wider range of inputs, to operate on these inputs in diverse ways, and to produce a larger number of ouputs.*

The network exists to accomplish *goals* set by decision makers. Movement toward these objectives implies the need for control information relative to the progress of the system in achieving its objectives. *Control functions operate through the feedback of information from strategic points of performance to the decision centers.* Therefore, a network is the nervous system of an organization which, in turn, is an elaborate cybernetic mechanism. Cybernetics is not the exclusive property of

---

[15] Jerome Rothstein, *Communication, Organization and Science* (Indian Hills, Colo.: Falcon's Wing Press, 1958), p. 34.

[16] John T. Dorsey, "A Communication Model for Administration," *Administrative Science Quarterly*, December 1957, p. 310.

[17] For an illustration, see Donald F. Schwartz, "A Communication Network in a Formal Organization," in Keith Davis, ed., *Organization Behavior* (New York: McGraw-Hill Book Company, 1974), p. 327.

engineers; rather, cybernetics is concerned with all kinds of control, and all sorts of systems.

Control via the feedback mechanism is the distinguishing feature of a true communication network. Decision centers utilize information feedback to appraise the results of the organization's performance and to make any adjustments to ensure the accomplishment of the purposes of the organization. Additionally, feedback is important for maintaining coordination among the parts of the system.

The communication networks in many modern organizations are complex. Contributing to this complexity are a number of factors, including: organization size, the relationships that exist among functions, advanced developments in technology associated both with organizational processes and products; and the "knowledge-level" of people who work in organizations. These conditions require increased information inputs into communication networks. Obviously, the demand for information to support "space-age" organizations and technology could not possibly be satisfied without change in communication technology itself and this has been discussed in the last section.

In summary, the communication concepts basic to the design of organization structure for the control function are: *regularized channels of communication flow* that increase the degree of predictability of system behavior, *programmed patterns of information* that pertain to specific activities in order to differentiate administrative functions such as planning or motivating, and *feedback of results* for the appraisal and adjustment of programs. These concepts in the final analysis exist for the primary purpose of managerial coordination.

The simplest organization chart is essentially a diagram of a communication model based upon command and functional relationships. However, we have learned that organizational affairs are much more complicated, and therefore networks of communication systems that crosscut lines of authority and functional responsibility have been described. Whatever emerges in formal communication patterns must, however, meet the test of effectiveness; that is, how well does the pattern work.

COMMUNICATION EFFECTIVENESS

There are two things management needs to know about the performance of communication networks. It should know about the speed and accuracy with which a network gets organizational objectives accomplished. It should also know how much satisfaction the participants in the communication process derive from it. In other words, assessment of communication effectiveness must take into consideration how well the process fulfills *both* personal and organizational goals. Obviously these two goal sets are compatible in some situations and incompatible in others. Consequently, the appraisal of communication effectiveness is a contingency problem that requires setting goal priorities for differing situations.

One problem that has been discussed for years in the research literature is the linkage pattern of communication networks.[18] There are three basic types of patterns: the serial, the radial, and the circular, as illustrated in Figure 9–5.

FIGURE 9–5
Network Linkage Patterns

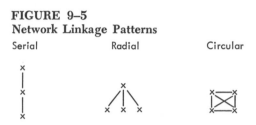

Many combinations of these patterns can be made, but the point is that the fewer the links in a network, the more efficient the communication system is from the standpoint of accomplishing organization goals. However, the minimization of the number of links tends to reduce the degree of satisfaction people find in the communication process. This is because a reduction of links centralizes communication which in turn increases the degree of authoritarianism. The aforementioned research on this subject, which we also discussed in Chapter 8, indicates that the circular pattern contributes more to human satisfaction because it encourages participation. Clearly, the linkage pattern in networks requires tradeoffs; the kind of balancing act management performs depends upon the nature of the environment in which communication occurs.

Another contingency example pertains to the effectiveness of channel selection for sending and receiving messages. What is better—written communication, oral communication, or some combination of the two? Level[19] concludes that for situations he examined the combination of

[18] Robert Dubin, "Stability in Human Organizations," in Mason Haire, ed., *Modern Organization Theory* (New York: John Wiley & Sons, Inc., 1959), pp. 218–32, and Harold J. Leavitt, "Some Effects of Certain Communication Patterns on Group Performance," *The Journal of Abnormal and Social Psychology*, 66 (1951), 38–50.

[19] Dale A. Level, Jr., "Communication Effectives: Method and Situation," *The Journal of Business Communication*, Fall 1972, pp. 19–25.

written and oral communication is most effective for settling work problem disputes, reprimanding for work deficiencies, sending information
requiring immediate action (although oral communication alone ran
a close second), communicating major policy changes, and so on. Actually, oral or written communication by themselves was most effective
in just a limited number of circumstances. As Melcher and Beller observe:

> Administrative effectiveness probably is critically affected by how quickly
> a manager familiarizes himself with the orientation of his superiors, sub-
> ordinates, and members in other departments, the extent to which he
> integrates himself into the social system, and his awareness of the func-
> tional aspects of the alternative channels. He is then in a position to
> use the channels and media that would best fit the nature of the
> communication.[20]

Thus for many management communication decisions, the contingency notion is valid in the sense that the choice of alternative media,
depends on the situation. However, there are, in fact, some communication problems that pervade all organizations. Management control, as
Vardaman and Halterman point out, depends on its ability to cope with
these problems through methods of organization analysis and design.[21]

Distortion Problems

Distortion is largely a semantic problem that can reduce organizational effectiveness. The amount of distortion contained in communication is a function of three variables—the relative efficiency of language,
the type of language employed, and the degree of incongruency in the
frames of reference of the sender and receiver.

Distortion occurs because of the inadequacy of language to carry
precisely the ideas of the sender, and because of the inadequacy of
the sender to frame his ideas in correct language. Not much can be
done to improve the efficiency of language commonly used in ordinary
written or oral communication. However, the human use of language
can be improved although the basic structure of language itself is not
susceptible to rapid change.

Messages sent up and down in an organization have to be *translated*
to suit the levels at which they are received. Top policy makers tend
"to speak a different language" than those on levels below them. But

---

[20] Arlyn J. Melcher and Ronald Beller, "Toward a Theory of Communication:
Consideration in Channel Selection," *Academy of Management Journal*, March 1967,
p. 52.

[21] George T. Vardaman and Carroll C. Halterman, *Managerial Control through
Communication* (New York: John Wiley & Sons, Inc., 1968).

general policies have to be implemented down the line, so a translation process occurs in order to relay policies from top to bottom.

Something is usually lost in the translation. The very nature of language does not allow precise translation of ideas from one level to the next. This inability to bridge organizational levels by precise translations cannot be entirely overcome. However, the distortion resulting from the inefficiency of language can be minimized. One way is to get a feedback from receivers to check whether they have truly understood the content of a message. Redundancy is another technique the sender can use to reduce the distortion in message content.[22]

Distortion also occurs because of differing frames of reference. People in various organizational functions perceive problems differently. Sales people tend to view business problems from the marketing standpoint, the plant manager from the manufacturing standpoint, and so on.

Apart from the differences in jargon of various specialists there also is a difference in the "thinking apparatus" of one organizational group compared with another. The confusion which results from the clash of different frames of reference is apparent in the day-to-day communication of the line with the staff.[23] The staff has been trained to think in terms of the logic of its speciality. For example, establishing or adjusting job standards is a matter of logical procedure. The staff experts want to set, by scientific measurement, fair standards on the job. It is, however, not their responsibility to sell the standards to the workers; this is the supervisor's job. So the supervisor and staff experts may often clash on standards. Both try to communicate their feelings to the other. Neither succeeds, because they are talking on two different planes—two different frames of reference. The staff expert speaks the logical language of work measurement; the supervisor uses the emotive language of operative supervision.

Analogous to the communication barriers erected by differences in technical frames are the social barriers which result in distortion up and down the chain of command. Social barriers arise from *social distance*. For these reasons, the superior does not think the same as the subordinate. The boss has a different frame of reference than the workers. One research study shows that between the boss and subordinate most communication breakdowns occur because:

---

[22] See Harold Guetzkow, "Communication in Organizations," in James G. March, ed., *Handbook of Organizations* (Chicago: Rand McNally & Company, 1965), pp. 558–59.

[23] For an example, see Melville Dalton, "Managing the Managers," *Human Organization*, 3 (1956), 4–10.

1. The two do not rank job responsibilities similarly in order of importance.
2. There is little agreement on relative priorities of job requirements.
3. There is little agreement on future changes in the job content of subordinates. Subordinates see fewer possibilities for change than the boss.
4. There is a great lack of agreement on obstacles and problems the subordinate faces. The boss seldom knows the problems which are of the most concern to the subordinate.[24]

In any event, social distinctions created by authority levels in the organization separate communication groups. This forces each group, and the individuals in it, to adopt a particular frame of reference in forming and interpreting communication. Obviously, the greater the similarity of frames of reference the less likely will be distortion stemming from social distance.

For the reasons just mentioned, distortion is found to move in all directions, organizationally. Filtering, because of its peculiar nature, is more apt to appear in the upward flow of communication.

Filtering Problems

Filtering is the conscious manipulation of "facts" to color events in a way favorable to the sender.[25] It often occurs in upward communication, because this direction of flow carries managerial *control* information. Management evaluates performance as a result of what it hears via the upward channel. The motivation, then, to misrepresent the true situation is strong. Also filtering may happen in lateral and diagonal communication, when individuals in negotiating their transactions with others may present their terms in the light of the "best facts and data" possible to support their position.

The organizational effectiveness problems posed by filtering and distorting information have caused certain large organizations to establish special "audit groups" to improve the quality of information transmitted in the system.

---

[24] Norman R. F. Maier, "Breakdowns in Boss-Subordinate Communication," *Communication in Organization: Some New Research Findings* (Ann Arbor, Mich.: Foundation for Research on Human Behavior, 1959), p. 22.

[25] Charles A. O'Reilly III and Karlene H. Roberts, "Information Filtration in Organizations," *Organizational Behavior and Human Performance*, April 1974, pp. 253–65.

Organizational Audit Groups.[26]   These control groups are allowed to bypass the chain of command and go directly to various points of performance to gather data on operations and relay it to evaluative functions on higher command levels, as shown in Figure 9–6. Even

FIGURE 9–6
Audit Staff Relationships

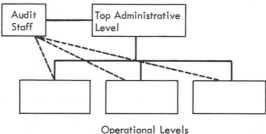

Operational Levels

though these groups are called "audit staffs" they are concerned with more than pure accounting. They gather whatever control information thought to be important by top management. These staff groups may be either established on a permanent or on an ad hoc basis.

Audit staffs provide "instant" and presumably unbiased information on a relatively narrow, often highly technical, range of activities at lower organizational echelons. They are also a positive control factor which helps ensure compliance with organizational regulations. These groups typically are independent of the chain of command, in the sense that they are responsible only to the highest organization authorities.

The channel of upward communication which the audit staff opens is calculated to reduce the tendency and the effects of filtering. In summary, we have observed that this problem becomes particularly acute when (1) the distance between top and lower echelons of the organization widens, (2) the organization grows in size and complexity, (3) the operations of the organization disperse geographically.

However, as a formal organizational device overcomes problems of communication, it also produces dysfunctional consequences of its own. We cannot ignore the fact that the audit staff can be, and in some cases is, a tension-inducing activity. Its extraordinary powers of investigation may create uneasiness among those who are on the receiving end of the audit.

---

[26] For a comprehensive treatment of this activity, see Leonard R. Sayles, *Managerial Behavior* (New York: McGraw-Hill Book Company, 1964), pp. 93–103.

Communication Overload Problems

It is common in complex, bureaucratic organizations that managers are literally buried in communication. Communication at times becomes so heavy that they are saturated. They cannot absorb or adequately respond to all the messages impinging on them. This problem brings up the *principle of sufficiency*.

Sufficiency pertains to the regulation of communication to ensure an effective flow of information to executives. Communication thus should be regulated in terms of both quality and quantity. Sufficiency is implemented by what Dubin calls the "monitoring effect."[27] The monitoring unit acts as a valve which both clears information in order of priority and condenses all messages so that only the relevant information is channeled to executives up the line. In a sense, middle management is a monitor of information between the point of operation and top management.

The principle of sufficiency is supported by the management "exception principle" applied to the field of communication. The exception principle states that only significant deviations from standards, procedures, and policies should be brought to the attention of the superior. Put another way, subsidiary units or subordinate individuals should handle all matters coming in the scope of their jurisdiction. Thus, the superior should be communicated with only on matters of exception and not of standard practice. This principle is implicit in bureaucratic-type organizations. However, in other types of organization structures, like the matrix organization, the principle may not apply because these organizations require free-flowing communication on all manner of subjects. They tend not to isolate "superiors" from "subordinates" by limiting communication to significant departures from standard procedures.

Many other conditions limit communication effectiveness, such as poor timing in the release of information, and short-circuiting the flow of information in communication channels by-passing necessary receivers. The disruption of communication by whatever cause reduces the capacity of management to achieve the goals of the organization. Consequently there is little wonder that so much management attention is given to the communication process. It is the primary instrument for regulating the emotional, motivational, information, and structural components of complex organizations. Those who control the communication process control the organization.

---

[27] Dubin, "Stability in Human Organizations," pp. 247–48.

chapter 10

Decision Processes

Decision making is one of the principal processes engaged in by individuals, groups, and organizations. In Chapters 6 and 8 on motivation and group dynamics, respectively, we discussed certain decision activities as they pertain to some aspects of individual and group behavior. Our intention in this chapter is to treat the decision process as it is related to organizations and as it relates to the individual's decision to function in organizations. Clearly, the material we deal with here is closely connected with the processes we cover in Chapters 13 and 14 on influence and leadership. However, the decision process is sufficiently independent as a body of data and theory to warrant separate treatment.

The structure of this chapter is straightfoward. In it we consider basic decision concepts, individual decision making as it relates the person to organizations, and organizational decision programs. The emphasis of the chapter is on the behavioral dynamics of decision theory. We do not deal with the more technical models in the decision-making field.[1]

INTRODUCTORY CONCEPTS

Regardless of the level of decision making, the process involves certain common ingredients.[2] They are (1) a search process to discover goals;

---

[1] See Donald W. Taylor, "Decision Making and Problem Solving," in James G. March, ed., *Handbook of Organizations* (Chicago: Rand McNally & Company, 1965), pp. 48–86.

[2] See, for example, Stephen H. Archer, "The Structure of Management Decision Theory," *Academy of Management Journal*, December 1964, pp. 269–73, and Theo Haimann and William G. Scott, *Management in the Modern Organization* (Boston, Mass.: Houghton Mifflin Company, 1970), chapter 4.

(2) the formulation of objectives after search; (3) the selection of alternatives (strategies) to accomplish objectives; (4) the evaluation of
outcomes.

The Search Process

In the search process, an individual or organization undertakes to
find a new goal or goals because of dissatisfaction with outcomes within
an existing goal structure. The present payoff structure growing out
of the present set of goals is, in other words, less than an individual's
(or organization's) level of aspiration. March's and Simon's model of
adaptive behavior is useful to demonstrate the role of search in the
decision process.

The search process is evoked by a low level of satisfaction as Figure
10–1 shows. The lower the level of satisfaction the more intensive is

FIGURE 10–1

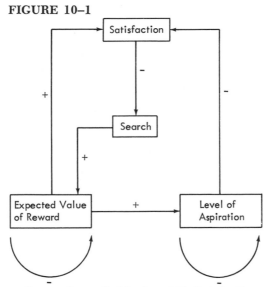

Source: James G. March and Herbert A. Simon,
Organizations (New York: John Wiley & Sons, Inc.,
1958), p. 49. Used with permission.

the search for new goals. The degree of satisfaction depends on the
outcomes (expected value of reward) as well as the level of aspiration.
Satisfaction is achieved when payoffs correspond to the level of aspiration. However, since favorable experience with outcomes from goals

often raises the level of aspiration, a new discrepancy might again appear between rewards and aspiration level setting the search process in motion again.

Formulation of Objectives

Objectives, whether personal or organizational, are values which are desired by the decision maker. Usually, it is useful as a first approximation to view the decision maker as attempting to maximize or minimize values such as profits, losses, costs, salary, rate of advancement, or output. This approach, based largely on traditional economic theory of rationality, has been criticized. Simon, for instance, introduces the concept of "satisficing" which he offers as a substitute for the maximization concept. He observes:

> Psychological studies of the formation and change of aspiration levels support propositions of the following kinds: (*a*) when performance falls short of the level of aspiration, search behavior . . . is induced; (*b*) at the same time, the level of aspiration begins to adjust itself downward until goals reach levels that are practically attainable; (*c*) if the two mechanisms just listed operate too slowly to adapt aspiration to performance, emotional behavior . . . will replace rational adaptive behavior.[3]

We can conceive of goals, out of this framework as "states of tension" providing the motivation of behavior.[4] There is little in psychological theory to suggest that outcomes have to be maximized in order to reduce or even eliminate the intensity of the drive. Indeed the theory of aspiration indicates adaptive flexibility whereby goals may be raised, lowered, or changed in the light of experience.[5]

The theory of value maximization proposes an objective predictive model of behavior within a very narrow framework of adaptive modes. Most of the constraints of this model result from the rigid assumption regarding the relationships among economic variables. Satisficing, ac-

---

[3] Herbert A. Simon, "Theories of Decision Making in Economics and Behavioral Science," *The American Economic Review*, June 1959, p. 263.

[4] See William J. Gore, *Administrative Decision-Making* (New York: John Wiley & Sons, Inc., 1964), pp. 38–41.

[5] The adaptation of organizational goals in the face of changing environment is developed by James K. Dent, "Organizational Correlates of the Goals of Business Management," *Personnel Psychology*, Autumn 1959, pp. 365–94. For a more recent study, see George W. England, "Organizational Goals and Expected Behavior of American Managers," *Academy of Management Journal*, June 1967, pp. 107–17.

cording to Simon, allows a richer model of adaptation which is closer to a more natural (realistic) explanation of decision behavior. For example, simply recognizing the lack of information necessary for rational decisions makes satisficing a more acceptable explanatory device.

Strategies

Once a goal, or hierarchy of goals has been established, the decision maker has partially established a repertory of alternatives for achieving his or her aims. For any given alternative, and there may be an infinite range of possibilities, is associated a decision system composed of an outcome, a probability, and a value. With four alternatives, for example, there is:

$$
\begin{array}{cccc}
A_1 & O_1 & P_1 & V_1 \\
A_2 & O_2 & P_2 & V_2 \\
A_3 & O_3 & P_3 & V_3 \\
A_4 & O_4 & P_4 & V_4
\end{array}
$$

In each case a payoff (outcome) is computed, a probability of payoff occurring arrived at, and the subjective value of the strategy decided.

As an illustration let us suppose that X is bitten by a dog and must make a decision to have rabies shots or not. The shots, as X knows, are painful, inconvenient, expensive, and even dangerous because of the remote chance that death might occur from them. The experience of having shots cast against the possibility of dying from rabies represent extremes on X's value scale.

Given these alternatives, X must have *information* on probabilities and outcomes in order to decide. Assume that a dog is caught that X is fairly sure, but not positive, is the culprit. The presence of doubt about the dog is crucial. If there is certainty in this respect, and the dog is in custody, then the observation period will definitely establish the health of the animal. Based upon what we take as objective probability data, here is X's decision tree.[6]

X, if optimistic, will not undergo shots because the ultimate outcome, the probability of death, is remote in either situation of right or wrong

---

[6] Although these figures are purely imaginary, let us suppose that they represent reliable public health data on rabies for the region in which the incident occurred. The probability information on the right-wrong dog is based on a dog census for the area. We assume that X identified the breed, thus limiting the field of candidates considerably.

FIGURE 10–2
Mr. X's Decision Tree

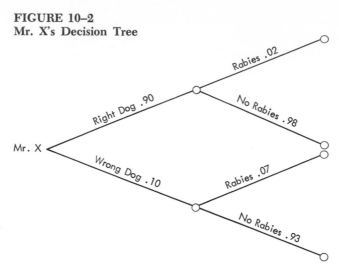

dog. X reasons that in nine chances out of ten the dog is the correct one, and since the dog under observation is a neighborhood pet the probability of it being rabid is very low. And even in the unlikely event the dog that actually did the biting got away the chance that it is rabid is still quite low based on experience factors in the area. Thus according to X's value system incurring the small risk of rabies is more desirable than pain associated with the shots. Thus he chooses the no-shot alternative.

Instead of X, let us assume that Y is in the identical situation, bitten one-half hour later by the same dog. But Y is a pessimist. While the same probability information is available, in Y's eyes a chance of one in ten error about the dog and the higher risk of rabies among strays leads Y, according to her value scale to take shots and endure the pain to secure positive protection. Several important concepts are derived from this simple example.

Risk. The nature of risk is such that the probability of an event occurring or not occurring can be assigned. Both X and Y, we assume, are confronted by the same objective probability data. But X thinks that since the chance of rabies is trifling he avoids the shots. Y perceives the same probability but she still does not want to run even this small chance and so she acts accordingly. This differential behavior does not stem from the probability data per se. Rather, it is a function of the value systems of X and Y, respectively.

This case is analogous to another which has to do with the probability of being killed in an air crash on a commercial carrier. The objective probability data, which has been computed and available to all, is very much against such a calamity happening. Yet there are people who refuse to fly for the very reason that they fear a crash. They choose other modes of transportation, such as driving, even though the danger of accident with injury or death is higher.

Some might argue that optimism or pessimism is reflected in probability data itself. That is, an optimistic person would say, "I think it is a 90 percent chance we got the right dog, *in the absence of any concrete probability data to the contrary.*" Whereas the pessimistic person would be more doubtful feeling the chances were only 50–50. Now while the resulting decisions of X and Y likely will be identical to those postulated in the face of objective data, the line of reasoning is quite different. Under the conditions which we have just stated, X and Y are mixing value data and probability data. This is wholly erroneous in risk analysis, but is quite appropriate in the discussion of uncertainty.

Uncertainty. The nature of uncertainty is such that it is not possible to assign a probability to the occurrence of an event. This is because of either lack of information about the event, or the nonrepeatable character of the event, or both. Archer sums it up this way:

> Uncertainty in decision theory describes all shades of knowledge of the probability distribution of the states of nature ranging from near accurate estimates based upon objective experience to an extreme case in which no knowledge exists. It is this type of model which most frequently applies to management decision. Uncertainty varies from the extreme of no information up to but excluding the condition of risk in which the probability of the states of nature is known. Short of risk conditions, exists uncertainty.[7]

Selection of strategies under uncertainty conditions requires the application of judgment, opinion, belief, subjective estimates of the situation, plus whatever objective data is available. The estimates of probability and payoff (P and O) become hopelessly dependent upon the values of the decision maker. The concept of "subjective probability" is introduced into uncertainty situations as a shorthand notation that a strategy has been selected using decision criteria which are not entirely rational. Hence, subjective probabilities regarding strategies may vary among decision makers confronting the same situation. In short, under risk we can separate O and P from V. We cannot do this under uncertainty.

---

[7] Archer, "Structure of Management Decision Theory," p. 276.

Uncertainty ranges between total ignorance at one end of an extreme to certainty at the other. We dispel uncertainty with information.

Information. There is an inverse relationship between information and uncertainty. Information structures a previously unstructured situation. Information, although imperfectly measured and qualitatively defined in an administrative setting, structures an uncertain environment for the decision maker. It permits him to make better decisions, assuming that effectiveness criteria are measured by the relationship between payoffs and goals. Therefore the decision maker wishes to reduce uncertainty or, if possible, to convert it to a state of either certainty or risk. That this is accomplished through the medium of information is highlighted in Figure 10–3. This figure requires several observations:

FIGURE 10–3
Information and Uncertainty Reduction

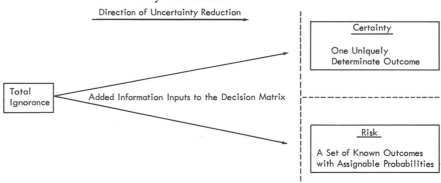

1. The nature of "added information inputs" is data concerning outcomes and probabilities of given strategies. Suppose that decision makers begin acquiring information at the point of "total ignorance" or at some other point to the right of it. They may be unsure at this time whether added information will lead them to the risk state, the certainty state, or for that matter, leave them at some advanced condition within the uncertainty state.

2. Of course it is clear, or should be, that decision makers may never "cross the dotted line" to either certainty or risk states regardless of how much information they acquire. More information may improve decisions within the uncertainty state. Beyond this the decision makers may never learn what the nature of a particular decision is. But they

may avoid the error of using risk assumptions for a decision which more correctly lies in uncertainty.

3. The amount of information the decision makers actually acquire depends on some marginal (or satisficing) calculus, in which they com-- pare information cost to the value of uncertainty reduction. Naturally, we must think incrementally in terms of so many units of information for so many units of uncertainty reduction. It is unlikely that we can go from say total ignorance to some arbitrarily desirable point of uncer- tainty in a single leap.

We discussed the incremental acquisition of information at length in the latter part of Chapter 9 "Communication Processes," so there is no need to deal with it here. But we should note that the *need* for information may be as much *psychological*, in view of the qualitative character of most administrative decisions, as it is technical in some quantitative sense. This then would suggest that the need for information is *satisficed* at points other than where "the cost of information equals the value of uncertainty reduction." The literature leads us to believe that these points are somewhere before the point of maximization.[8]

JUDGMENT

When we are forced to place some sort of rank order or evaluation on priorities, problems, or alternative choices, this process is frequently described as judgment. For example, a university graduate admissions employee has to make evaluative judgments about a whole set of candi- dates before he or she decides on who will be accepted or rejected. Typically, these judgments reflect some combination of separate bits of information into an overall evaluation. Students have Graduate Record Examination (GRE) scores, a college Grade Point Average (GPA), and letters of recommendation, all of which enter into the evaluation. Some universities have a formula which has been validated over the years which provides some standard weighting procedure (called a policy) for these data. For example, GRE may be twice as important as GPA which in turn is twice as important as letters of recommendation. The appropriate weights can be applied and a judgment produced. All students are then ranked on this score and the cut-off point/or acceptance determined.

In some situations, however, no standard formula exists. How do physicians combine all their data for a diagnosis? How do stockbrokers

---

[8] Simon, "Theories of Decision Making," p. 271.

combine information about a company in order to produce an overall evaluation? Well, as it turns out, people have their own subjective formulas which can be made explicit through repeated observations of the judgment task. For example, if stockbrokers are presented with information about different companies and make evaluations of the companies one can mathematically determine how much weight different bits of data are being given.

This information is helpful in many ways. It frequently surprises the individual to see what one is actually doing and often prompts change. It also makes the policy explicit and open to question. Finally, we often find that people think they are using far more information than they actually are. Most evaluations can be predicted from a relatively small number of dimensions.[9]

The Evaluation of Outcomes

The final element of the decision process, after the search has been made, goals set, and strategies determined, is the evaluation of outcomes. This process has been variously called the measurement of effectiveness or the rationality criteria. One of the problems with which we are confronted is that there is apparently no rationality criteria apart from decision rules.

Since there are many families of decision rules (or decision frameworks) there are also many criteria for effectiveness, which do not necessarily carry over from one set of rules to the next. If we accept this position, then one way to measure rationality is to compare the outcomes of decisions to the goals of the decision maker. This yardstick of rationality is based on the *consequences* of decisions. Thus, if the set of rules is "good," that is, if it produces outcomes which meet the objectives of the decision maker, then rationality is established by definition. This is what Bross calls the *pragmatic principle*.[10]

Note that this principle subjects neither the decision process nor the goals of the decision maker to rational scrutiny. It does not insist that a set of decision rules have internal consistency or that goals conform with some "objective" standard of behavior. The presuppositions of conventional logic and conventional culture are *not* standards of rationality so far as the pragmatic principle is concerned.

The pragmatic principle is deceptively simple, since it does away

---

[9] R. J. Ebert, and T. R. Mitchell, *Organizatioal Decision Processes: Concepts and Analysis* (New York: Crane, Russak and Co., 1975).

[10] Irwin D. J. Bross, *Design for Decision* (New York: The Macmillan Company, 1953), pp. 29–32.

with difficult problems by abolishing absolute standards. Goals become merely datum of rationality measurement, not themselves subject to rationality analysis.[11] So we must say that *given these goals,* such and such is a rational strategy to produce the sought for outcomes. If it does not work out so well, then there is a more *rational strategy.* But how about a more rational goal? Since goals are relative, how can one talk about one goal being more rational than another? The pragmatic principle is oriented in spirit toward conservatism. It is more compatible with what is, than with what ought to be.

An excellent example of a model using these concepts has been provided by Vesper and Sayeki.[12] They present a model designed to help the policy maker be consistent in choosing the best of many possible combinations of actions to implement policies related to objectives, which in turn provide the appropriate relative emphasis for the overall goal of the company.

If we conceive of the overall goal as the first level, objectives as the second level, policy areas as the third level, and action alternatives as the fourth level, we can use an hierarchical analysis to understand the interrelationships of the variables at different levels. If importance weights are measured at each level for each element and also an estimate of the relationship between any two elements, one can generate overall estimates of the effectiveness of a specific action. For example, the "goodness" of a new plant being built (action) is jointly dependent upon how well it fits into the policy of the production department (policy areas), how likely these policies are to increase short- and long-term sales (objectives), how likely sales increases are to please the stockholders (overall goal) and how important all of these elements are. One can then compare that action with some alternative and make a choice which should be most likely to satisfy the overall goal of the company.

With these basic concepts behind us, we turn next to the subject of individual decision.

INDIVIDUAL DECISIONS

With emphasis we say that the material covered in this section represents just a humble fraction of available information on individual deci-

---

[11] Rationality analysis can point to the desirability of certain goals over other goals. But again the concept of desirability introduces value systems and so this does not really help much except in scientific fields, and a few administrative situations where the decision field is ethically neutral.

[12] K. H. Vesper, and Y. Sayeki, "A Quantitative Approach for Policy Analysis," *California Management Review,* vol. 15, no. 3 (Spring 1973).

sion processes. Such information ranges in scope from computer simulation experiments in decision analysis, through neurophysiology and biochemistry, to work in psychology. Our concern here is with certain classes of decisions which underlie an individual's choice to (1) participate in an organization and (2) produce for an organization.[13]

Decisions to Participate

An individual undertakes an inducement-contribution calculation when making an organizational participation decision. If she has arrayed before her the alternatives to join or not to join an organization, or several organizations, she weighs what she *perceives* to be:

1. The reward structure of the organization, that is, all the inducements (I), economic, psychological, and social, present and future, against
2. The expectations of the organization which constitute the role structure or the contributions (C) she must make present and future.

Considering for now simply the initial decision to join or not to join an organization, we can say:

(1) $C > I \rightarrow$ the individual will not participate and will continue a search for *alternatives*.
(2) $C = I \rightarrow$ the individual is neutral to alternatives and will continue acquiring *information* on which to base a decision.
(3) $C < I \rightarrow$ the individual will participate in the organization which produces this perception.

Within the dynamics of the organization the individual may change her initial evaluation. If she finds, after experience, that contributions exceed inducements she will resume her search for alternatives and eventually change organizational affiliation. Satisfaction is closely connected to the inducement-contribution relationship. Factors which the individual perceives as lessening the satisfaction she derives from a particular organization will cause her to become mobile. If we are talking about an employment situation, then the ease of movement among organizations is affected by a number of variables, including economic conditions, and the age, sex, and training of the person.

So, the predictions we can make on the basis of $C > I$ and $C < I$ are fairly clear regardless of whether we are considering a person's

---

[13] For this section we rely heavily on James G. March and Herbert A. Simon, *Organizations* (New York: John Wiley & Sons, Inc., 1958), chapters 3 and 4.

initial decision to participate or a decision to remain in an organization as a participant. When we look at the $C = I$ relationship, some interesting problems are posed. For instance, can we expect that an initial $C < I$ perception may change to a $C = I$ perception? If so, what can we say about behavior under these circumstances?

The answer to the first question is, of course! Many after a time are confronted in job situations with the perception that their contributions are about balanced by the inducements offered. Such being the case, what are the consequences? One possibility is that a search for new alternatives either in or out of the organization may be motivated. Another possibility is that the individual may accept the situation at face value, do enough to retain organizational membership, and channel remaining energies elsewhere.

Burns conducted a study of the behavior of executives who experienced a termination of their career progress below the level of their expectations. At times, people will take refuge in a clique, where with the reinforcement of others in similar circumstances, an effective retreat from occupational status is accomplished. Speaking of such an executive clique Burns says, "their clique had a specifically protective reassurance purpose . . . [the executive] . . . furnishes himself and others with assurances that he in fact succeeded but the system was rigged against him, or that failure is not final but an episode in progress towards success, or that the status is one that he has not really claimed, or one in which it would be vulgar to succeed. . . ."[14]

Burns shows in his study how the clique acts as a countersystem to moderate the impact of failure. But more importantly the devaluation of their role in the executive's eyes does not mean they are paralyzed in its performance. The carryover of years of routine in addition to accumulated responsibilities of home and family are sufficient to motivate them to continuing satisfactory performance. They have important stakes in their positions which they are not likely to sacrifice just because their present $C = I$ perceptions do not accord favorably with the optimistic $C < I$ perceptions they had when they first joined the organization.

Thus, while a person's role perception changes, aspirational levels also change often enough to bring about the equivalence between contributions and inducements. As Burns's analysis nicely points out such a change will not necessarily motivate an individual to change formal

---

[14] Tom Burns, "The Reference of Conduct in Small Groups: Cliques and Cabals in Occupational Milieux," *Human Relations*, November 1955, pp. 472 and 474.

organizational connections. Rather efforts which might have been directed toward occupational success may be diverted to interests outside the occupation, including the maintenance of satisfaction producing informal work associations.

There is still another dimension to the inducement-contribution analysis with respect to the individual's acceptance of and compliance with legitimate authority. We may postulate that a person more likely than not will accept the legitimacy of the authority of a superior in a formal organizational setting if the person also sees the participation producing greater rewards than contributions. The reverse holds true as well. The kind of leadership provided has much to do with satisfactions derived.

But we may ask how an individual is apt to respond to authority if he perceives his contributions equaling inducements. Following Barnard's conceptual scheme, he suggests that an individual is confronted by three possibilities when evaluating the orders of a superior.[15] There are those orders which are clearly unacceptable, those on the neutral line of acceptability: i.e., barely acceptable or unacceptable, and those clearly acceptable. Obviously the degree of acceptability or unacceptability of orders depends upon the individual's perception of the legitimacy of the superior person's authority. A high degree of positive compliance is likely to be forthcoming in response to orders from an individual enjoying considerable legitimacy in his position.

Now according to Barnard, the last group of orders, those which are clearly acceptable, lies within the *zone of indifference*. He says that:

> The zone of indifference will be wider or narrower depending upon the degree to which the inducements exceed the burdens and sacrifices which determine the individual's adhesion to the organization. It follows that the range of orders that will be accepted will be very limited among those who are barely induced to contribute to the system.[16]

Barnard's use of the term zone of indifference is unfortunate. It suggests a neutrality or passiveness toward authority and the orders stemming from it. However, this is far from Barnard's intended meaning. To him clearly acceptable orders receive positive compliance because they, ". . . lie within the range that in a general way was anticipated [by the individual] at time of undertaking the connection with the organization."[17]

---

[15] Chester I. Barnard, *Functions of the Executive* (Cambridge, Mass.: Harvard University Press, 1938), pp. 168–69.

[16] Ibid., p. 169.

[17] Ibid., p. 169.

Based on this line of analysis, we diagram in Figure 10–4 the relations which exist among the contribution-inducement variables and the authority compliance variables. Figure 10–4(a) shows authority is not perceived

FIGURE 10–4
The Zone of Indifference and Decision Variables

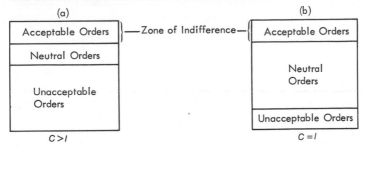

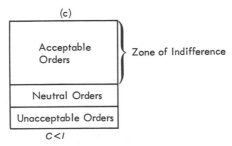

as legitimate and the individual probably will leave the organization as soon as an opportunity appears. Figure 10–4(c) depicts a wide range for the zone of indifference indicating acceptance of authority plus willing compliance to it. The neutral range in Figure 10–4(b) indicates that under circumstances where $C = I$ compliance to orders is secured less because of acceptance of legitimate authority and more as the result of the *power* exercised by persons vested with organizational position.

Decisions to Produce

"Motivation to produce is a function of the character of the evoked set of alternatives . . . the perceived consequences of evoked alternatives . . . , and the individual goals . . . in terms of which alternatives are evaluated."[18]

---

[18] March and Simon, *Organizations*, p. 53.

The evoked set of alternatives means that each individual has frames of reference founded on his or her personality structure. Stimuli impinge upon the individual, evoking certain reactions. The reactions to production motivations depend on the "set" of psychologically based alternatives called forth by a stimulus.

Along with these alternatives are the systems of expectations and values interpreted by March and Simon as the perceived consequences of alternatives which might be selected by the individual as a course of action. Not every alternative will be weighted similarly by the individual. Some alternatives may appear more acceptable than others because of an individual's preconceptions. These preconceptions have strategic importance. Human behavior can be influenced (manipulated!) by changing an individual's value system.

Finally, decisions to produce are partially a function of individual goals. An individual enters an organization with objectives in ordered arrangement. But these objectives are not immutable. Individuals can be, and are more frequently than not, influenced by the groups, formal and informal, with which they come in contact. The influence process conducted by the group is, of course, a method by which it preserves its integrity.

This section treated decisions as internal variables oriented around the individual but affected by ambient conditions of the organizational environment. Looked at this way decisions which an individual makes can be influenced by administrators through modifying organizational structure and climate. The decision process is an independent variable upon which the survival of the organization is based. From this point of view the organization is thought of as having inherent to its structure the ability to maximize survival needs through its decision processes.

GROUP DECISIONS

Many decisions are made jointly in organizations. We are all familiar with committees, conferences, and consultation strategies as devices for sharing information and reaching a consensus. To understand these processes we must not only include individual decision making (IDM) strategies but also how the group interaction impacts on decisions.

We have already pointed out a number of ways in which groups are different from individuals. There tends to be a greater number of resources, people contribute unequally, the processes of conformity and interpersonal attraction may change the interaction, and groups may make more risky decisions. However, some similarities do exist between individual and group decision processes. In most cases, groups proceed through the same phases of generation, evaluation, and choice of alternative resolutions for a decision issue. Thus, while the way in which the decision is made is far more complex with group involvement, the underlying process is similar.

An initial question is simply why should we want group decision making (GDM) and what is involved in using such a strategy. Most organizations utilize GDM because information sources are widely distributed. In order to generate and evaluate feasible alternatives many resources must be tapped. Because of the technical nature of many important decisions, people with different perspectives and expertise are often needed.

A second reason for GDM is the political process in organizations. Since most organizations function as systems with interdependent parts, a decision in one department or area may impact on the policies or routine of another organizational unit. A "democratic" decision process frequently permits everyone to share their perspective of the situation.

Finally, the use of GDM allows a number of group dynamics variables to operate. People become more involved and committed to decisions to which they have contributed. They gain insight into co-workers' views on issues and are more likely to reach a consensus on important goals.

Optimal Group Conditions

A number of qualifying statements are in order. Group decision making occurs in differing degrees and amounts. In some instances the group may participate in only one or two of the decision phases, or a group may contribute in all phases but on a limited basis. Also, different types of people, tasks, and organizational environments facilitate or hinder the GDM process.

In looking at individual characteristics, leadership style plays an important role in determining the amount of shared decision making. Heller and Yukl, for example, describe three such styles: delegative, consultative and joint decision making.[19] Some leaders have stronger needs for independence, or needs for power and influence.[20] Thus, from a leader's

---

[19] F. A. Heller, and G. Yukl, "Participation, Managerial Decision Making, and Situational Variables," *Organizational Behavior and Human Performance*, 4 (1969), 227–41.

[20] V. H. Vroom, *Some Personality Determinants of the Effects of Participation* (Englewood Cliffs, N.J.: Prentice-Hall, Inc., 1960).

point of view the decision to share power and engage in group problem solving is partially dependent upon personal needs. Other researchers have also pointed out that in some cases, urban, blue-collar workers are alienated from middle-class norms and reject participation as a decision strategy. Some people do not want the responsibility.

The decision task also influences the utilization and effectiveness of GDM. Deutsch investigated contrient and promotively interdependent groups.[21] In the former case, one reaches a goal only if other members fail to reach theirs while in the promotively interdependent situations everyone could obtain their goal. Information sharing, satisfaction, and GDM were all more likely in the promotive case. Wood has found similar results for tasks that differed in the amount of attitude and goal similarity of the group participants.[22] GDM was much more likely to occur when people shared similar goals.

Broad organizational parameters have an impact on the tendency to use GDM. In settings where the system is highly interdependent we would expect greater group activity.[23] The managerial philosophy is also important. McGregor, for example, has argued that a Theory Y managerial style is much more likely to lead to GDM.[24] On the other hand, Leavitt has shown how organizational size and complexity places limits on how much and how often GDM can be used.[25]

Practical considerations play a major role as well. If the expertise of one person is too much greater than the rest of the group, GDM may serve to widen the gap between the leader and the followers. Also, time pressure, urgency, and subordinate expertise are related to the feasibility of decision sharing.[26] In summary, the actual use and effectiveness of GDM is dependent on numerous factors, including the types of people, tasks, and organizational settings in which people are placed.

[21] M. Deutsch, "A Theory of Cooperation and Competition," *Human Relations,* 2 (1949), 129–52.

[22] M. T. Wood, "Participation, Influence, and Satisfaction in Group Decision Making," *Journal of Vocational Behavior,* 2 (1972).

[23] J. Marschak, "Efficient and Viable Organizational Forms," in M. Haire, ed., *Modern Organization Theory* (New York: John Wiley & Sons, Inc., 1959), pp. 307–320.

[24] D. M. McGregor, *The Human Side of Enterprise* (New York: McGraw-Hill Book Company, 1960).

[25] H. J. Leavitt, "Applied Organizational Change in Industry: Structural, Technological, and Humanistic Approaches," in J. G. March, ed., *Handbook of Organizations* (Chicago: Rand McNally and Co., 1965), pp. 1144–70.

[26] A. Lowin, "Participative Decision Making: A Model, Literature Critique, and Prescriptions for Research," *Organizational Behavior and Human Performance,* 3 (1968), 68–106.

Vroom's and Yetton's Decision Theory

To date, only one theory has attempted to integrate the various conditions which prompts GDM or IDM. Vroom and Yetton attempted to specify those parameters which influence a manager's decision about whether to include or exclude others in the decision process. They sug-

FIGURE 10–5
Decision Methods for Group and Individual Problems

Group Problems

A1. You solve the problem or make the decision yourself, using information available to you at the time.

A11. You obtain the necessary information from your subordinates, then decide the solution to the problem yourself. You may or may not tell your subordinates what the problem is in getting the information from them. The role played by your subordinates in making the decision is clearly one of providing the necessary information to you, rather than generating or evaluating alternative solutions.

C1. You share the problem with the relevant subordinates individually, getting their ideas and suggestions without bringing them together as a group. Then *you* make the decision, which may or may not reflect your subordinates' influence.

C11. You share the problem with your subordinates as a group, obtaining their collective ideas and suggestions. Then you make the decision, which may or may not reflect your subordinates' influence.

G11. You share the problem with your subordinates as a group. Together you generate and evaluate alternatives and attempt to reach agreement (consensus) on a solution. Your role is much like that of chairman. You do not try to influence the group to adopt "your" solution, and you are willing to accept and implement any solution which has the support of the entire group.

Individual Problems

A1. You solve the problem or make the decision by yourself, using information available to you at the time.

A11. You obtain the necessary information from your subordinate, then decide on the solution to the problem yourself. You may or may not tell the subordinate what the problem is in getting the information from him. His role in making the decision is clearly one of providing the necessary information to you, rather than generating or evaluating alternative solutions.

C1. You share the problem with your subordinate, getting his ideas and suggestions. Then you make a decision, which may or may not reflect his influence.

G1. You share the problem with your subordinate, and together you analyze the problem and arrive at a mutually agreeable solution.

D1. You delegate the problem to your subordinate, providing him with any relevant information that you possess, but giving him responsibility for solving the problem by himself. You may or may not request him to tell you what solution he has reached.

Source: V. H. Vroom and P. W. Yetton, *Leadership and Decision Making* (Pittsburgh: University of Pittsburgh Press, 1973), p. 13.

gest that a manager is faced with the five alternatives[27] in Figure 10–5.

Based on research into the decision process, these authors attempt to identify the properties of the decision itself which would help a manager to select one of the five approaches. These properties and the diagnostic question are provided below.

Thus, a leader must have some idea about what information is needed, how it will effect subordinates, and the degree to which any decision process will affect decision acceptance.

In an attempt to combine the diagnostic questions with the five possible decision strategies, the authors had to order the importance of the questions and then examine the consequences of yes or no answers to each question. Figure 10–6 presents a decision model which Vroom and

FIGURE 10–6
Decision Model

Is there a quality requirement such that one solution is likely to be more rational than another?	Do I have sufficient information to make a high-quality decision?	Is the problem structured?	Is acceptance of decision by subordinates critical to effective implementation?	Do subordinates share the organizational goals to be obtained in solving this problem?	Is conflict among subordinates likely in preferred solutions?
A	B	C	D	E	F

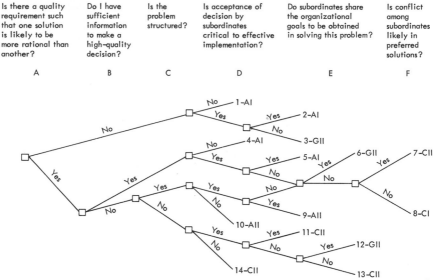

Source: V. H. Vroom and P. W. Yetton, *Leadership and Decision Making* (Pittsburgh: University of Pittsburgh Press, 1973), p. 188.

Yetton suggest will help a manager to choose that decision process which will involve minimum hours of labor with maximum effectiveness.

Combining these answers in the above manner generates 14 different types of decision problems. Case studies of actual decision problems

---

[27] V. H. Vroom, and P. W. Yetton, *Leadership and Decision Making* (Pittsburgh: University of Pittsburgh Press, 1973), p. 13.

were then generated to represent each type of problem and these sce-
narios were presented to many different samples of managers. The task
of the manager was simply to choose a decision strategy to solve the
problem.

Vroom and Yetton report a number of interesting findings from their
research. First, managers tended to use a more appropriate decision
strategy (according to the model) after they had been trained about
the principles of the decision model than managers who failed to receive
such training. Thus, the model should be helpful in increasing the effectiveness of managerial decision making. Second, most managers said
they would use different decision strategies depending upon the situation. That is, managers were not *either* participative or autocratic: They
were both depending upon the decision problem. Variability in decision
strategy was more dependent upon environmental aspects of the decision
itself than personality differences.

In closing, we should note one further point. We have been mainly
concerned with an understanding of the group decision *process*. Whether
participation is effective, the ways in which it has been introduced,
and the overall question of "democratization" as a change strategy will
be discussed later.

ORGANIZATIONAL DECISIONS

Organizational decisions may be considered as the ways by which
organizations adapt to change. March and Simon view such adaptation
decisions as either routine or innovative.[28] The question is, under what
circumstances will an organizational adjustment to change be quasi-automatic or routine, and under what circumstances will the adjustment
be innovative? The answer lies in two interrelated considerations: the
nature of the change itself, and the range of programs available to
the organization for adjusting to changes. (A "program" means an established plan of action.)

The first circumstance deals with the routine adjustment to change.
As shown in Figure 10–7 a change impinges on an organization. It perceives the change and identifies its nature. In this case, the change
is identified as one which can be handled by using a program—program
2—in the organization's repertory of programs, 1, 2, 3, and 4. Thus,
the system's adjustment to change becomes a routine, or quasi-automatic,
matter of selecting one out of an established range of programs to cope

---

[28] March and Simon, *Organizations*, chapters 6 and 7.

FIGURE 10–7

Routine Adjustment of an Organization to Change

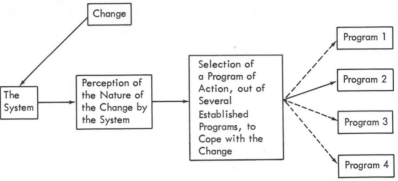

with change. To summarize, if the change is perceived by the system as coming within the purview of established programs of action the adaptation made by the system to the change generally will be routine, or quasi-automatic.[29]

The second circumstance involves innovative or creative adaptation efforts. The need for innovation arises when adaptation to a change is outside the scope of the existing programs that keep the system in balance. The organization has to evolve new programs in order to maintain its internal harmony.

New programs are created by trial-and-error search for feasible alternatives of action to cope with a given change. But innovation is subject to two limitations, at least. First, the organization cannot simultaneously adapt all aspects of its structure to change. That is, certain aspects of an organization's structure have to be held stable, while other, more critically affected areas of the system are adjusted. As March and Simon state, ". . . in order for an organization to behave adaptively, it needs some stable regulations and procedures that it can employ for carrying out its adaptive practices."[30] Therefore, the process of innovation presupposes stability in certain segments of the system. By its very nature innovation cannot immediately extend to the total organization.

Second, innovation is limited by the quantity and variety of information present in a system at a particular time. For innovative purposes, new combinations of alternatives depend on four factors. The first of these is the possible range of output of the system, or the capacity of the system to supply information. Obviously, decision makers are

---

[29] Ibid., pp. 139–40.

[30] Ibid., p. 170.

limited in innovative activity by the capacity of the system to supply data. Alternatives, from which new programs of action are created, arise from the information available in the system. As this information is limited so also are the possibilities for finding appropriate action alternatives.

The second factor limiting innovation is the range of information available in the system's memory. Most human organizations have facilities for storing information, usually in the form of performance records, accounting data, historical information on competition, and the like. Also included in the memory of the system are past solutions to problems of change which appear to be similar but are not identical to the problem at hand. The capacity of the storage centers is not unlimited; therefore, the ability of the system to call on its memory of suitable action alternatives is restricted.

The third factor deals with the operating rules (programs) governing the analysis and flow of information within the system. This limitation on the use of information is similar to the first mentioned above. The use to which information is put for innovative purposes is regulated by the policies of the system. Some action alternatives may be distinct possibilities for change adjustment, but if they fall outside the policies of the firm they will be discarded as unusable.

The fourth factor is the system's ability to "forget" previously learned solutions to problems of change. This interesting limitation means that a system with too good a memory might narrow its behavioral choices to such an extent that innovation is stifled. Previously learned, old programs might be brought into play for an adjustment to change when newly innovated programs are necessary. Often this is what is meant when an organization is termed "inflexible"—it is incapable of learning for purposes of long-range adjustments.[31]

DECISION AIDS

Today's manager is faced with highly complex decision problems. Projections of future needs and demands must be made. Accurate esti-

---

[31] For further discussion, see Mervyn L. Cadwallader, "The Cybernetic Analysis of Change in Complex Social Organizations," *The American Journal of Sociology*, September 1959, p. 156. An interesting example of an organization's inability to forget a previously learned strategy is discussed by Robert E. Kuenne, *The Attack Submarine* (New Haven, Conn.: Yale University Press, 1965). Kuenne reviews the use of the submarine by the Japanese navy during World War II. It was employed as a fleet support (defensive) weapons system, as opposed to an offensive system directed against shipping. As a consequence, Kuenne claims that the Japanese submarine forces were the most underutilized military resource of either side during World War II.

mate of previous activities must be available and all of this must be combined to make decisions about events which are only partially under the control of the individual or the group.

Two major developments in the last 20 years have increased dramatically our ability to deal with such complex problems. First, electronic data processing (EDP) has enabled the decision maker to record, store, manipulate, and call forth vast amounts of information. Twenty years ago the psychological and technical effort expended would have been prohibitive for many commonplace analyses done today. Second, we have developed a number of models or decision aids which help us to deal with this information in a rational manner.

The use of models takes many forms. In some cases, techniques have been developed for making optimum decisions. Given certain data for various alternatives some models predict which alternative would be best. Other models can be used for data organization. How information should best be sequenced, revised, or combined can be described. Finally, models can be used to actually simulate the decision process. In this way, the decision maker may become better aware of how decisions are actually made and ways in which the process can be changed if so desired.

Examples of Models

Two of the more popular models used for planning projects are the program evaluation and review technique (PERT) and the critical path method (CPM). These techniques were developed for management planning decisions and they both attempt to describe the critical units that make up task accomplishments, their proper sequencing, and expected completion times. An example is presented in Figure 10–8 below. Each node at the end of arrow depicts the beginning and end of an activity. Activities further along are dependent upon successful completion of preceding activities. By diagramming such activities the manager learns how activities are sequenced, interdependent, and some idea of the time frame in which completion can be accomplished.

More simplified techniques might be represented by break-even analysis or queuing theory. In the former analysis there is a formula to determine the number of units of a product which must be sold at a specific price in order that the company will incur neither financial gain nor loss. Queuing theory attempts to compute the cost of people waiting for services of some sort compared to the cost of providing additional

FIGURE 10–8
An Example of a Path Analysis

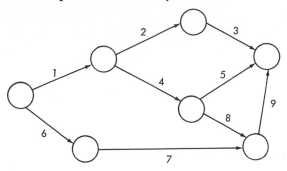

services. An example might be at a service station where the owner must decide whether to add a new gasoline pump. Both of these techniques are helpful for important and reoccurring problems.

A final example of a model used to help in making optimal decisions is labeled goal programming. In this case, goals and their importance, likelihood of attainment, and interrelationships are considered for different decision alternatives. Taking into consideration multiple criteria and organizational constraints, an optimal strategy can be selected.[32] However, the problem occurs in attempting to ascertain reliably the inputs for such a model and much work remains to be done in the area of research.

In summary, we have a fairly good idea of how decisions are made by individuals and groups. That is, we have an accurate description of the decision process. However, the particular inputs to the process such as the reliability of people and information is far from concise or consistent. Hopefully, our better understanding of the process and the use of technical aids will increase decision effectiveness in the future.

---

[32] S. M. Lee, "Decision Analysis through Goal Programming," *Decision Sciences,* 2 (1971), 172–80.

chapter 11

Balance and Conflict Processes

Achieving "balance" is a difficult process in organizing. On one level of abstraction, balance may be treated as a management activity that deals with the techniques necessary to achieve organizational stability and coordination. But on a higher level of abstraction, balance takes on the status of a managerial ideology. It represents an "ideal" state of affairs in that organizational tensions are suppressed and organizational harmony and integration are encouraged. In this respect, balance is the polar opposite of conflict.

Balance is a *desideratum*, ideologically, that has to be constantly sought by managers. They must be alert to the erosive affects of conflict upon the organizational imperative of coordination. In this light, conflict clearly represents—to numerous influential theorists[1]—a condition of deviancy and pathology which must be "managed" and controlled in organizations.

We discuss first the concept of balance largely as it has emerged as an organizational process; then, in the latter part of this chapter, we will treat conflict as an alternative process.

BALANCE

The basic premise upon which the balance process rests is normative. In the eyes of most management practitioners and most organization

[1] For a representative, but not exhaustive example, see Peter F. Drucker, *The New Society: The Anatomy of the Industrial Order* (New York: Harper & Bros., 1950), and Elton Mayo, *The Human Problems of an Industrial Civilization* (Boston, Mass.: Division of Research, Harvard Business School, 1933).

theorists, *order* is the "normal" state of the world, and hence of the organizations which compose it. Thus, balance represents the process by which order is achieved and maintained in systems. The concept of the "black box" is a convenient place to begin to understand the notion of balance.

The Black Box

The *black box* is an interesting idea found in the literature of physics and, more recently, in cybernetics.[2] It is particularly relevant to the analysis of complex organizatons. The black box is a device for converting inputs into outputs. But the operations it employs to transform inputs are quite obscure. Indeed, the black box is never fully knowable! Its inscrutable nature is produced by two important properties:

1.   The internal structure of the black box is highly complex. Elementary cause-effect relationships are impossible to find. The mind simply cannot comprehend the multitude of interconnections and interdependencies which exist among its parts through its linkage system.

2.   The black box defies investigation of its "innards" because if it is tampered with it will change its internal properties. The significance of this statement should not be underestimated. It implies that experimentation with the black box could be futile, since the experimenter is not entirely certain the results are pertinent to the subject of the experiment.

Thus, about all that can be known about the way the box functions is to observe what is put in and see how it comes out. From the changes occurring in the input, inferences can be drawn about the processes within the box which actually wrought the changes. As a consequence, incomplete knowledge of the box is obtained indirectly.

In spite of all this, the black box is not as stubborn as it seems. The black box is a system. And all systems have structures which lend them a certain degree of predictability. Therefore, the black box is not capricious in its behavior. It can be ascertained that in response to certain inputs the black box will produce specified outputs. How this is accomplished is not completely describable; in fact, for practical pur-

---

[2] For an excellent discussion of the black-box concept, see W. Ross Ashby, "General System Theory as a New Discipline," in William E. Schlender, William G. Scott, and Alan C. Filly, ed., *Management in Perspective* (Boston, Houghton Mifflin, 1965), pp. 396–400; see also Stafford Beer, *Cybernetics and Management* (New York: John Wiley & Sons, Inc., 1959), especially chapter 6.

poses it is not really necessary to know much about the internal operations of the box. Desired outputs can be had by modifying *strategic* inputs.

Human organizations are similar to the black box because: (1) they convert inputs of productive factors into outputs of goods and services; (2) they are often highly complex; and (3) they tend to rearrange their structure as a response to the introduction of foreign influences.

To elaborate point three: Assume that an organization is being observed by a detached, objective viewer who is making inferences about its operations. Now, suppose that an experiment is undertaken to check the accuracy and validity of the conclusions arrived at through the observations. No matter how careful the experimenters are they inject a new element into the organization by their presence. In so doing, they rearrange the interactional patterns in such a way that they cannot be positive they are experimenting with the "same" organization previously observed.[3]

Thinking in terms of the subject of this chapter, imagine that a change occurs in an organization. The change is arbitrarily called an input, although some may prefer the word "stimulus." The organization reacts, and an adjustment to the change follows. The adjustment is the output. Figure 11–1 shows that the outside observer can make some deductions regarding the balancing process by knowing the nature of the change

FIGURE 11–1
The Balancing Process as It Appears to the Outside Observer

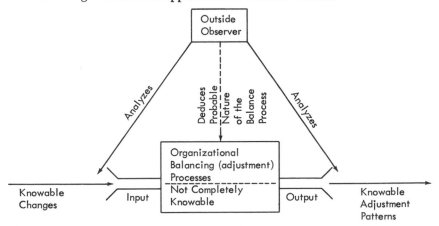

---

[3] This phenomenon is sometimes called the "Hawthorne effect" after the famous Hawthorne studies when the researchers unwittingly changed the experimental conditions by introducing uncontrolled variables into the research setting.

(input) and by dissecting the adjustment (output). Complete understanding of the process, however, is hidden from the observer.

Next the observer decides to include himself as part of the organization to test the validity of his deductions by experiment and to gain a greater insight into the process of balance itself. He cannot, however, be assured that the adjustment process is the same after he has joined the organization. The best which can be said is that if the inputs and outputs are the same under both the conditions of observation and those of experiment, the investigator may be fairly confident that his presence has not affected the balancing process. He feels he has the right to say he understands it. The investigator's confidence is reinforced because his experiments support his observed deductions, *and* he has, in fact, been observing and experimenting with identical situations.[4]

What does all this mean for managers? Is it true that their efforts to facilitate adjustment to change are futile, because organizational reactions to change are complex and unknowable? The answer to this question is no. Desired reactions to change (output) are obtained by controlling the changes (inputs) themselves. Management regulates the nature of changes so that the adjustments accord with the objectives of the organization and satisfy the needs of the people in it.

From an analytical standpoint, balance is an elusive concept. But as a result of observation, deduction, experimentation, intuition, and analogy some things can be said about the black box process of balance. Generally, balance is considered as a process which reconciles and maintains structural interrelationships among the many forces and elements that make up the organization. Balance is a condition where there is accord among the objectives of individuals, the informal organization, jobs, and the formal organization. *It is a process which acts to ensure system stability in face of changing conditions which are either internal or external to the organization.* The first definition treats balance in

---

[4] The problem of observer interference in experimental situations is discussed later in this book. But it should be noted for emphasis that it is an issue not likely to be resolved in the behavioral sciences. The phenomenon of interference, in the form of experimental bias, has been explored in an imaginative study by Robert Rosenthal et al. It was demonstrated in these studies that biases in research results, based upon certain preconceptions of those who formulated an experiment would still appear even though the formal work with subjects was three times removed from the originators of the study. See Robert Rosenthal, Gordon W. Persinger, Linda Vikan Kline, and Ray C. Mulry, "The Role of the Research Assistant in the Mediation of Experimental Bias," *Journal of Personality*, 31 (1963), 313–35; and Robert Rosenthal, "On the Social Psychology of the Psychological Experiment: The Experimenter's Hypothesis as an Unintended Determinant of Experimental Results," *American Scientist*, 51 (1963), 268–83.

a management context specifically. The second definition has greater generality and is found frequently in the literature of the behavioral sciences. In essence the two definitions refer to the same process.

Concepts Related to Balance

Equilibrium and homeostasis are terms often encountered in the behavioral sciences. They pertain to concepts which are similar to balance. Balance, equilibrium, and homeostasis have some important differences. A little closer attention to the latter two ideas casts some light on balance and its administrative applications.

Equilibrium. Equilibrium refers to a state of adjustment between opposing forces. It also describes a tendency of a system to move toward a condition where the forces or influences in it are resolved. Two kinds of equilibrium are applied to social phenomena—static and dynamic.[5]

Static or stationary equilibrium is a situation where the environment of the system is held constant over a period of time. Dynamic equilibrium implies change and the ability of the system to preserve its internal structure of relationships despite a changing environment. Neither of these two forms of equilibrium imply that activities internal to the organization cease.

The equilibrium concept was borrowed from physics and has had a long tradition of application to economics. Somewhat more recently equilibrium has been used to describe processes in psychological and sociological research and theory. Pareto noted the usefulness of the idea in application to social systems, observing that systems have the tendency to return to a state of equilibrium if their original adjustment is disturbed.

Homeostasis. This word is derived from the Greek and means "steady state." It has been borrowed from biology and refers to a process by which a system regulates itself around a stable state. But as Penrose observes, "Strictly speaking, the basic principle [self-regulation] is not a biological one at all in spite of the name given it. It is a general principle of organization, examples of which may be found in biology, in mechanics and in social organization. . . ."[6]

---

[5] For a discussion of various types of equilibrium, see David Easton, "Limits of the Equilibrium Model in Social Research," *Profits and Problems of Homeostatic Models in the Behavioral Sciences* (Chicago: Behavioral Sciences Publications No. 1, 1953), pp. 26–40.

[6] Edith Tilton Penrose, "Biological Analogies in the Theory of the Firm," *American Economic Review,* December 1952, pp. 804–19.

Self-regulation requires feedback and control, both operating in such a way as to minimize the adverse effects of change on a system. On the surface, it appears that equilibrium and homeostasis are quite similar. However, all equilibrium states do not involve homeostasis. *Constancy does not imply feedback.* Davis[7] cites an example of a system moving through several states as follows: 10, 9, 8, 7, 6, 5, 4, 3, 2, 1 . . . . . ! If these states are not dependent on each other, and are equally probable, it is predictable that the next state is 0. The stability or equilibrium of this system is not dependent on a feedback mechanism.

Following Davis, homeostasis has feedback as its basic feature. Some energy must be taken from a latter part of the system and introduced in an earlier part so as to oppose the change produced there by the original input. In human systems information is analogous to energy and is a major part of feedback. Data pertaining to the status of a given result in terms of objective accomplishment are fed back so that modification of action can be made if necessary.

Thus, feedback is a process of retroaction whereby activities are modified in terms of what has been accomplished and what still needs to be done in order to reach a goal. Figure 11–2 illustrates the general principle of feedback.

FIGURE 11–2
The General Principle of Feedback

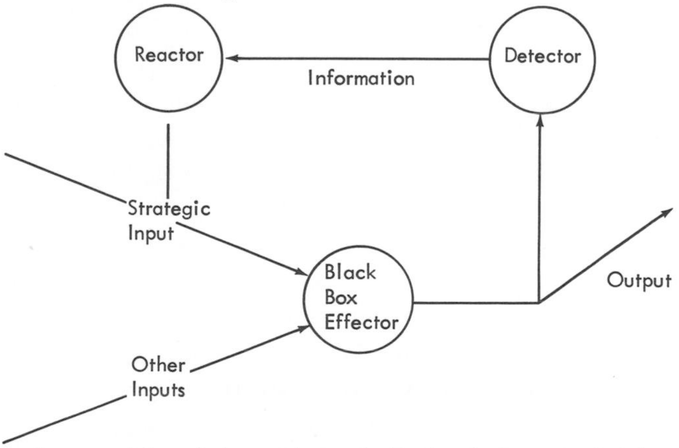

Source: Adapted from Pierre de Latil, *Thinking by Machine* (Boston: Houghton Mifflin Co., 1957), p. 50.

---

[7] R. C. Davis, "The Domain of Homeostasis," *Psychological Review*, 65 (1958), 10.

The operational sequence of a feedback system is as follows:

1. The *detector* is sensitive to variations in the output produced by the black box (the effector); if variations exceed tolerance limits programmed during the planning function, information is sent by the detector to the reactor.

2. The *reactor* is sensitive to the reception of this information and is capable of adjusting the strategic input. It is important to note that in order to achieve outputs which conform to standards it is usually not necessary to change *all* the inputs. There may be one input, or input mix, which, if altered will result in a change to an acceptable output condition.

To summarize what has been said so far, equilibrium has inherent to it the notion of the resolution of opposing forces. Homeostasis also incorporates this idea, but adds to it the matter of self-regulation. Both these concepts offer a useful way of viewing the interdependency of parts of a system. They are, however, not complete in themselves. They describe ends—constancy or stability under changing conditions. They do not specify means whereby these ends are achieved.

Stability in the Simple System

Mills discusses the adjustment process of an uncomplicated system as a first approximation in explaining the means used by organization to preserve stability. He points out that at least three conditions are necessary for stability.[8]

First, all strategic behavioral alternatives, which may emerge in reaction to change, fall within the spectrum of the established control machinery. Control can assume numerous forms, including formal regulation through policies, standards, and rules. The informal organization exercises control over behavior by the group through norms, values, and sanctions of conduct.

Second, the system is able to allow for constructive change even though such a change may deviate from established norms. A discriminating ability between constructive and destructive changes is necessary because stability in a system does not imply stagnation. Indeed, stability may be dependent in some cases on the facility with which an organization is able to adapt to change. Adaptation requires the modification of organizational relationships.

---

[8] Adapted from Theodore M. Mills, "Equilibrium and the Processes of Deviance and Control," *American Sociological Review*, October 1959, pp. 673–74.

Third, the system has a feedback mechanism. Once a change from standards is sensed evaluation action is initiated, and if necessary offsetting strategies are introduced.

Under these circumstances, the simple system would operate something like this:

$$A \qquad\qquad\qquad\qquad B$$

$$1 \quad 2 \quad 1 \quad 2 \quad 1 \quad 2-\text{change}-\text{control}-1 \quad 2 \quad 1 \quad 2 \quad 1 \quad 2$$

Starting with the pattern *A* a change is introduced. The control system is activated offsetting the change and preserving the structure of the system as indicated by pattern *B*.

Obviously, this is an oversimplification. But the example does at least point up some essential features of the stability process. All organizations have internal controls designed to maintain a harmonious relationship among the parts. Any change or deviant form of behavior will be interpreted in terms of the threat it poses to the stability and continuity of the system. If a change is a menace to organizitional integrity, actions will be set in motion to counterbalance the change.

The performance of the simple system is limited by at least four conditions.[9]

First, the effectiveness of the stability process is restricted by lack of information regarding the change. Because of this limitation, change-combating strategies may be totally ineffective for the preservation of stability.

Second, each system, like a formal administrative organization, is composed of subsystems which may be pressed into an unwanted readjustment because of the power exerted by one subsystem relative to the other. For example, a small group could be forced into a realignment of its values, status positions, and standards of conduct because technological change is forced on it by the formal organization. The group may resist and strive to maintain its established structure. But the power exerted by the formal organization is too strong to withstand.

Third, the individual seeking personal ends can undermine stability. Individual goals are not necessarily integrated with organizational goals. The amount and the way in which personal objectives deviate from those of the system determine the extent to which stability is reduced.

Fourth, the system buys stability at a price. Feedback and control cost, if not in dollars, then in some other value. The value of stability

---

[9] Ibid., p. 677.

is weighed against the cost of control. If the cost is too high for the value derived, then some stability is sacrificed.

Some theorists suggest that we look at the human organization as a cybernetic system.[10] Such a point of view is useful particularly in the context of the subjects being considered here and in the previous chapters on decision making and communication.

Cybernetics raises several questions regarding the system.

a. How are decision centers connected, and how are they maintained? Corollary to this question: What is the structure of the feedback system; that is, how is control information transmitted from the point of performance to the decision centers?

b. What information is stored in the system and at what points? Corollary: How accessible is this information to the decision-making centers?

c. How conscious is the organization of the operation of its own parts? To what extent do the policy centers receive control information with sufficient frequency and relevancy to create a real awareness of the operation of the segments of the system?

d. What are the learning (innovating) capabilities of the system?[11]

Answers to the questions posed by cybernetics are crucial to understanding the decision, balancing, and communication processes in systems. Although cybernetics has been applied largely to technical-engineering problems of automation, the model of feedback, control, and regulation in all systems has a good deal of generality.

Balance: A Management Concept

Unlike equilibrium and homeostasis, that are largely automatic mechanical, electrical, or biological processes, balance pertains to the cognitive and administrative properties of open systems such as the human organization.[12] Nevertheless, as we have pointed out, balance theory does rely upon such formulations as feedback, cybernetics, self-regulation, and equalization of opposing forces.

However, balance theory departs from its related concepts in one important way—the goal of organizational harmony is acquired by con-

---

[10] Richard F. Ericson, "Visions of Cybernetic Organizations," *Academy of Management Journal, December* 1972, pp. 427–46.

[11] These questions are adapted from Karl W. Deutsch, "On Communication Models in the Social Sciences," *Public Opinion Quarterly,* 16 (1952), 368–70.

[12] Balance is also an important component of the psychological analysis of tension reduction in individuals.

scious managerial effort. It is not the product of mindless forces. There-fore, balance is uniquely a management phenomenon, sought by managers as a desirable organizational condition. It is achieved by the application of a variety of techniques, many of which are derived from the behav-ioral sciences.

Long before organization theory emerged as a legitimate area of study, scholars were concerned with the problem of balance. The con-cepts related to consensus which we discussed at length in Chapter 1, are concerned with the resolution of organizational forces—i.e., the achievement of balance. The devotion with which the scholars in the human relations movement sought organizational integration is addi-tional evidence of the historical concern of administrative theorists for balance. The purpose of mentioning these historical checkpoints again is simply to stress the traditional bias of administrative theory toward balance and harmony in organizations. This bias still persists.

With the growing complexity of organizations, management's desire for balance has become more difficult to realize. Nevertheless, the terri-tory in which the manager tries to achieve balance, or to "normalize" relationships, may be fairly easily described. There are four distinct components.

1. The *individuals* in organizations as independent "open systems" in themselves.

2. Organizational *tasks* which include jobs, functional processes, and even the physical equipment necessary to do the jobs.

3. *Small groups,* or the informal organizations which supply need satisfactions to their members apart form formal job requirements. These organizations have status and role systems often independent of formal status differentiations.

4. The *formal* organization which is the overall authority hierarchy plus policy-making, and coordination activities.

These elements are interdependent and can be viewed by managers from a number of frames of reference: they can think of these factors in terms of their interaction in the organization as a whole, in a divi-sion, or within their own department. A convenient way of looking at balance is through the patterns-of-balance diagram, Figure 11–3.

As the diagram indicates, there are 12 areas of balance among the major components of the organization. The aim of managers is to har-monize, or to integrate, by their behavioral and technical skills the various goals and objectives of these subsystems. This is to say that the organizational tensions which could arise from divergent goals of

FIGURE 11–3
Patterns of Balance

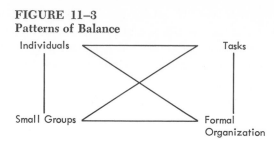

the parts of the system should be eliminated or redirected by enlightened managerial practice.

Further, tensions may also arise among individuals, or between groups, or even between tasks that may be redundant or have overlapping jurisdictions. Such "intracomponent" tensions are not revealed by the diagram, but they are nevertheless sources of disharmony, and consequently need "normalization" through the application of managerial balancing skills.

Balance: A Summary Statement

The balance concept is not an automatic, problem-solving device. It is a way of demonstrating the interdependencies which managers face in complex organizations. Achieving and maintaining balance among organizational components, is, of course, a responsibility of management. The primary obligation rests with those who have supervisory responsibility.

Management is the human instrumentality which consciously acts to produce balanced organizational relationships. While equilibrium and homeostasis are useful for conceptual purposes, they are impersonal. The processes which maintain body temperature at a fairly constant level are homeostatic. But the functioning of sweat glands is hardly similar to the administration of an organization.

An open system like an organization either changes or it fails to survive. The only way to exist in a changing environment is for the organization itself to change. Balance pertains to management's ability to modify formal systems and the operational climate of the organization in face of shifting technological, economic, and social conditions, but at the same time preserve the internal harmony of the system.

Obviously, the caliber of management is a key variable associated with adjustment to change. But even the best management is limited to the extent it can accomplish such adjustment. Limitations are inherent in the system itself. These limitations are very similar to those noted in this chapter with respect to simple systems. Additionally, it can be said that the rate management is able to adjust to change depends on the way in which the organization has designed its method of solving problems. Ideally, the structure should be such that it encompasses the widest range of possible changes which might arise. However, something less than the optimum must be accepted because of limitations on organization resources and human ability to foresee the future.

In addition to all this, balance is a time-oriented concept. A balanced organization is one which:

1. Exhibits continuity with the past. The past contributes to stability by giving the organization an identity.
2. Affords management control over the present direction and amount of change in policy, structure, personnel, and physical facilities.
3. Offers a workable degree of predictability for the future. As we have said before, organizational change is predicated on stability of some parts while undergoing modification of other parts. Predictability of certain balanced relationships is essential to planned change.

Our discussion of balance processes could easily end here, without introducing the disconcerting notion of conflict. However, this subject must be opened somewhere in this volume, and the logical place to do so is in this chapter, because the management of conflict is mostly what balance theory is all about.

CONFLICT

In his book, *Class and Class Conflict in Industrial Society*,[13] Dahrendorf discusses some "recent theories" of class conflict. Most of the scholars he reviews analyze conflict within the range of accepted understanding of the term—that is, conflict is a win-lose struggle between groups or classes with differing interests. This struggle òccurs with varying degrees of intensity according to the means employed. The most intense form of conflict is warfare using the ultimate weapons of violence available to society given the technological state of the art. But conflict may not necessarily be so extreme in that such techniques as strikes, collective bargaining, and even interpersonal trading and exchange can

---

[13] Ralf Dahrendorf, *Class and Class Conflict in Industrial Society* (Stanford, Calif.: Stanford University Press, 1959), Chapter 3.

be considered as more moderate manifestations of conflict relationships. Broadly interpreted conflict presupposes clashes of values and interests between groups or individuals.

While there is a diversity of opinion about the origins, functions, and resolution of conflict among behavioral scientists, there is the generally accepted notion that conflict is an integral component of social relationships. Hence, conflict is a normal aspect of social intercourse, and the problems that it poses are analyzed accordingly from this premise.

However, this premise is typically not the one accepted in management theory. As we have said several times in this chapter, the theoretical bias is in the direction of organizational harmony; i.e., balance. Therefore conditions, such as interest group clashes that cause disharmony and tend to unbalance the organization, are considered pathological. Thus, conflict has tended to be viewed by management theory as an organizational abnormality undermining consensus, rather than as a natural process in social relations.

Dahrendorf notes this facet of management theory in his discussion of Mayo and Drucker. He says, ". . . the central thesis which overshadows all other considerations for Mayo, but is little less important for Drucker, can be summarized in the statement that conflict and tensions such as those which class analysis is supposed to explain constitute but a 'deviation' from a normal state of human attitudes and actions, and can and must therefore be eliminated by 'education.' "[14] Certainly Mayo and Drucker alone are not an adequate sample of administrative theorist opinion, in spite of their considerable stature in the field. Nevertheless, at least insofar as their views on conflict are concerned, they have captured an important theme of consensus.

Indeed, in his book, *The Age of Discontinuity*, Drucker reemphasizes the case he made in earlier works for organizational integration. For example, he observes that the common problem of all organizations, regardless of differences in objectives, is that they share the imperative of ". . . balancing the objectives of the institution against the needs and desires of the individual."[15] In Drucker's mind the fundamental tension between organization and individual still exists, and it is still the major goal of managers to eliminate it or reduce it. But before this truly grand

---

[14] Ibid., p. 111. The works of Mayo and Drucker cited by Dahrendorf are Elton Mayo, *The Social Problems of an Industrial Civilization* (Boston: Harvard University, 1945), and Peter F. Drucker, *The New Society: The Anatomy of the Industrial Order* (New York: Harper and Brothers, 1949).

[15] Peter F. Drucker, *The Age of Discontinuity* (New York: Harper & Row, 1968), p. 195.

achievement of organizational design comes to pass, management still has to deal with the more specific problems of integrating, ". . . men of different knowledge and skills, each making a specific contribution, into one joint venture for common results."[16] Thus Drucker is a contemprorary representative of what is in fact a persistent *continuity* in management theory—the utility of and functionality of *consensus,* and the disutility and dysfunctionality of *conflict* in organizations.

We must quickly emphasize that management theory does not ignore conflict as a process in organizations; since theorists and practitioners alike are constantly questing means for harmonizing and integrating organizations; i.e., reducing conflict. However, if one approaches conflict as an inherent structural element in all social relations, management strategy is likely to be much different than if conflict is viewed as a abnormal departure from a harmonious "state of nature."

A Taxonomy of Conflict Relationships

Even though historically management theory has viewed conflict as deviancy, modern organization theorists appear to be breaking with this tradition. Two major causes are largely responsible for this transition. The first cause is that behavioral science research shows that conflict has differential effects on organizations; that is, given the situation, conflict may have functional, rather than dysfunctional organizational outcomes. Second, the chief dynamic underlying *change* has caused some theorists to gravitate to the Marxian notion of the inevitability of conflict arising from the inequitable and dislocating forces of structure.

Turning our attention first to the differential outcomes of conflict we note that Lewis A. Coser is one of the main architects responsible for building a "positive theory" of conflict. He says: "Conflict may serve to remove dissociating elements in a relationship and to re-establish unity. Insofar as conflict is the resolution of tension between antagonists it has stabilizing functions and becomes an integrating component of the relationship. However, not all conflicts are positively functional for the relationship. . . ."[17]

While Coser may overemphasize the utility of conflict in organizations, he, in effect, suggests that the functionality of conflict can be interpreted situationally. Figure 11–4 offers some alternative outcomes of conflict as they are derived from research in conflict settings.

---

[16] Ibid., p. 198.

[17] Lewis A. Coser, *The Functions of Social Conflict* (Glencoe, Ill.: The Free Press, 1956), p. 80.

FIGURE 11–4
Conflict: Types and Effects

Internal

Type	Effect
1. Conflict among individuals in a group centering on subordinate or minor goals, but not questioning the basic values of the organization.	Serves a positively useful function of reevaluating established norms of behavior and facilitating movement of individuals in the status system of the organization.
2. Conflict where parties no longer endorse basic values of the organization.	Tends to destroy the fabric of the organization.
3. Conflict in a closely knit organization.	Generates greater intensity, thus tending to be destructive.
4. Conflict in a relatively loosely established organization.	Tends not to be destructive since it is not as intense as the previous situation, because people are less personally committed to the organization.
5. Conflict in flexible organizations.	Tends to have relatively minor localized conflicts, obviating rifts which may split the organization into antagonistic camps.

External

Type	Effect
1. Groups continually in conflict with outside organizations.	Demands greater conformity of members—tends to reduce internal conflict so as to focus all organizational energy on the antagonist.
2. Organization not involved in continual external struggles.	Makes fewer demands on members.
3. Conflict of a rigid organization with outside organizations.	Tends to suppress internal adaptation to the conflict, refuses to change to cope more adequately with a dynamic environment.
4. Conflict of the flexible, more loosely structured organization with outside organizations.	Modifies its internal relationships to meet the exigencies of external conflict.
5. External conflict in general.	Tends to vitalize organizational values and makes members of the organization interested in the activities of the opponent.

While by no means inclusive, the types of conflicts and their consequences shown in Figure 11–4 do point up some patterns. First, internal
conflict is beneficial to the extent that it promotes:

a. The circulation of leadership: The advancement of new, vital
leaders who are better equipped to reflect the values of the organization
and to serve its purposes.

b. The modification of old goals: The modification of previously
held values to facilitate organizational adjustment in the face of change.[18]

c. The institutionalization of conflict: The establishment of outlets
so that people can "blow off steam" without damaging the structure
of the organization.

Second, the benefits of internal conflict accrue more to the loosely
structured rather than the rigid organization. Rigid organizations demand greater personal involvement of the individuals in them. By so
doing, conflicts, even minor conflicts, become more intense and increase
the likelihood of dangerous factional splits. Further, rigid organizations
tend to suppress instead of institutionalizing conflict. Smothering conflict
can be costly, and as tension builds even the most elaborate method
of control may not be able to contain expression of pent-up feelings.

Third, conflict with outside organizations serves four purposes by:

a. Promoting closer bonds of unity among individuals within the
organization.

b. Building new life into organizational objectives and values.

c. Making organizational members aware of the strategy and tactics of
the antagonist.

d. Acting as an agency of social control. Conflict in this case results in
a countervailing power relationship in which organizations will tend
not to transcend limits of propriety because if they do they will be
set back by another equally powerful organization.

Fourth, the effect of external conflict on internal organizational structure is not clear-cut. External conflict builds *esprit de corps,* but continual conflict requires the organization to make greater conformity
demands on members, reducing internal conflict. This reaction may or
may not result in rigidity in the structure. Military organizations are

---

[18] Torrance notes that task-oriented disagreements serve beneficial purposes by
increasing the range of judgments, by reducing chances for misunderstanding because
each person's position is expressed, and by increasing willingness to take calculated
risks because each person knows where others stand on issues. See E. Paul Torrance,
"Group Decision-Making and Disagreement," *Social Forces,* vol. 35 (1957), pp.
314–18.

extremely rigid relative to advertising agencies. But both organizations are geared to a continual conflict type of situation. In general, internally rigid organizations seem less able to adapt to a changing conflict environment while flexible organizations can more readily make adjustments. Thus, conflict serves the flexible, loosely structured organization better than a rigid one.

The second current line of analysis relates conflict to change. However, there seems to be little agreement on whether conflict is the cause or the consequence of change. Coser believes that conflict prevents social calcification and is, therefore, a cause.

> Conflict within and between groups in a society can prevent accommodations and habitual relations from progressively impoverishing creativity. The clash of values and interests, the tension between what is and what some groups feel ought to be, the conflict between vested interests and new strata and groups demanding their share of power, wealth and status, have been productive of vitality.[19]

Other writers, notably Toffler,[20] think that change results in conflict by accentuating disparties in interests and values—for instance, between young and old, men and women, blacks and whites—to say nothing of conflicts between line and staff, managers and technicians, and workers and supervisors in organizations.

Regardless of the interpretation of the cause or effect state of conflict contemporary management theorists generally agree that it is a major element in the process of organizational adaptation. We will return to the question of change and adaptation. In the next chapter, we discuss role processes that are related to balance through E. Wight Bakke's notion of organizational fusion.

---

[19] Lewis A. Coser, "Social Conflict and Social Change," *The British Journal of Sociology*, September 1957, p. 197.

[20] Alvin Toffler, *Future Shock* (New York: Random House, Inc., 1970).

chapter 12

Role and Status Development Processes

Role and status are processes of social interaction in organizational systems. Role definition primarily involves the relationship between organizational rights, duties, and obligations with the perceptions and expectations of individuals within systems. The study of status development and/or mobility is mainly devoted to the institutionalization of roles in organization structure and with the regularization of behavior with respect to these roles. While role and status are intimately linked to each other, it is useful to discuss them separately in order to highlight their importance as organization processes.

ROLE

Role definition is a collection of activities peculiar to a position or function in society at large, a community, an organization, or a social club. Thus an individual occupies many roles as a citizen, parent, student, manager, and group leader. Each of these roles, and all the others that an individual plays, has a counterpart status. Each role as it is socially defined carries rights, duties, and obligations which create the costs and the benefits of social participation.

Dimensions of the Concept of Role

Role has three dimensions.[1] The one stressed depends often on the behavioral science persuasion of the people discussing the subject. If

---

[1] The three "usages" of role are adapted from Daniel J. Levinson, "Role, Personality, and Social Structure in the Organizational Setting," *Journal of Abnormal and Social Psychology*, March 1959, p. 172.

they are sociologists, or perhaps anthropologists, they will approach role as something outside the individual. Role would be considered as a set of social pressures which direct and support an individual in the action he takes in an organization. Coutu defines role in this sense. Role is a ". . . socially prescribed way of behaving in particular situations for any person occupying a given social position or status."[2]

Behavioral scientists who have a psychological orientation probably will look upon role as an individual's conception of the part he or she plays in an organization. Using this point of view in an experimental situation, Gerard observes that in any social situation an individual will tend to evaluate the degree to which behavior has fulfilled the expectations of the role played.[3]

The third view of role, which is popular currently, is that of social psychologists. The ". . . concept of role concerns the thoughts and actions of individuals, and, at the same time, it points up the influence upon the individual of socially patterned demands and standardizing forces."[4]

The reciprocal and normative nature of role is stressed in the social psychologist's point of view.[5] For example, a small work group has expectations of the type of behavior it anticipates from members of the group. These expectations are values or norms commonly held by members of the group.[6]

An individual who seeks association with a group must sense what its values are and modify behavior accordingly. But, as Bakke observes, the individual is also capable of modifying the expectations of the group.[7] What results is a "fusion process" which changes both the group and the individual so that their separate values may be reconciled.

From these definitional dimensions, we can develop a topology for role concepts as shown in Figure 12–1. We assume that each dimension defines role similarly, but the effect of role on the individual is inter-

---

[2] Walter Coutu, "Role-Playing versus Role-Taking: An Appeal for Clarification," *American Sociological Review*, April 1951, p. 180.

[3] Harold B. Gerard, "Some Effects of Status, Role Clarity, and Group Goal Clarity upon the Individual's Relations of Group Process," *Journal of Personality*, 25 (1956–1957), 475.

[4] Levinson, "Role, Personality, and Social Structure," p. 170.

[5] See Aidan Southall, "An Operational Theory of Role," *Human Relations*, 12 (1959), 17–34.

[6] Frederick L. Bates, "Position, Role, and Status: A Reformulation of Concepts," *Social Forces*, vol. 34 (1955–56), p. 319.

[7] E. Wight Bakke, "Concept of the Social Organization," in Mason Haire, ed., *Modern Organization Theory* (New York: John Wiley & Sons, Inc., 1959), pp. 60–61.

FIGURE 12–1
Dimensions of the Role Concept

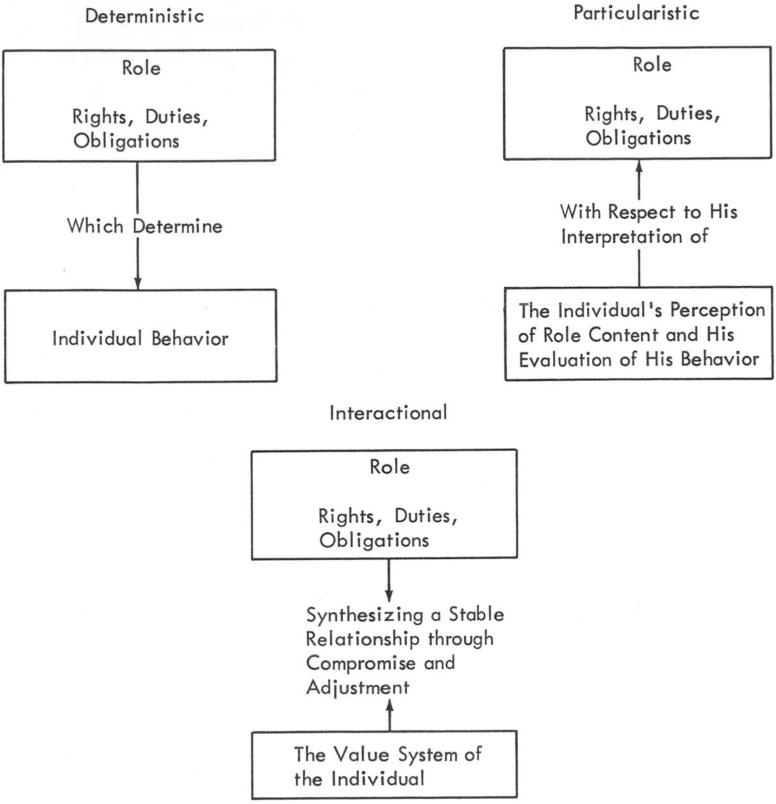

Deterministic   Particularistic

Role
Rights, Duties, Obligations

Which Determine

Individual Behavior

Role
Rights, Duties, Obligations

With Respect to His Interpretation of

The Individual's Perception of Role Content and His Evaluation of His Behavior

Interactional

Role
Rights, Duties, Obligations

Synthesizing a Stable Relationship through Compromise and Adjustment

The Value System of the Individual

preted differently, from deterministic, particularistic, and interactional points of view.

Deterministic. Role is seen here as a dominant influence on behavior. The assumption is that if the content of the role is known, the behavior of individuals playing the role is predictable. *Behavior is role determined.* Thus, if we know the role content of, let us say, "father" in a primitive society, then we would be able to predict the behavior of all fathers playing this role in that society. Similarly the content of jobs which is highly specified in modern organizations permits us to predict what any individual performing these jobs will be doing when occupied with the formal aspects of the functions.

Particularistic. This view of role focuses not so much on the formal content of the role as specified culturally and organizationally, but upon how the individual *perceives* the role or roles played and how the individual *evaluates* performance in light of this perception.

Interactional. This approach concerns outcomes resulting from the merger of individual-group behavior. The *mutual modification* individual and group behavior is the chief matter of attention. Bakke's concept of the fusion process nicely summarizes this interpretation of role.

This topology is an oversimplification. The three role dimensions as presented tend to admit only a one-sided interpretation of the behavioral consequences of the relationships depicted. For example, a "stable relationship" is not always the outcome of the interactional dimension. Compromise and adjustment may never occur in some individual-group transactions. Conflict could be the behavioral product of this case. Or, role may be ambiguous. It may present an individual with contradictory obligations. Hence, behavior cannot be predicted in the sense implied in our initial discussion. Rather, anxiety, or in extreme cases, action paralysis may occur in the individual.

Some Organizational Implications of Role Processes

For management purposes human behavior cannot be approached only with the view that an individual's actions are determined by social pressures. The psychological approach of individual perception of expectations is not a complete explanation of role behavior either. Probably the most satisfactory point of view is the one offered by the social psychologists, which stresses the reciprocal relationship that exists between the individual and the role expectations.

Following this approach, the individual is influenced in actions by two major sources of role expectations—the formal demands made by the organization, and the informal ones made by the groups contacted by the individual in the work situation. Thus both formal and informal expectation forces make behavioral demands on the individual.

As a result of these demands, individuals attempt to structure the social situation and to define their place in it. This process is called *role definition*. Role definition, as Levinson notes, is an aspect of personality and is expressed in terms of basic values, opinion of one's self, objectives in life, and attachment to an occupation.[8] The purpose of role definition is to guide individuals in the pursuit of goals and to help obtain work satisfaction.

This approach, however, is somewhat oversimplified. For as Sarbin

---

[8] Levinson, "Role, Personality, and Social Structure," p. 178.

observes, "role expectations are bidimensional. . . ." For every expectation a formal or informal group might have a reciprocal expectation or demand is made by the individual on these groups.[9] Additionally, as could be anticipated, the groups themselves can be expected to interact, each affecting the other's expectations. Figure 12–2 shows the interacting of relationships these preliminary remarks suggest.

FIGURE 12–2
Role Expectations and Their Interactions

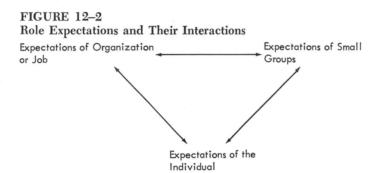

The outcome of the pattern is the fusion process, which, in turn, is a fragment of Bakke's total theory of social organization. He says that the reconciliation of expectancies brought by the fusion process acts ". . . to maintain the integrity of the organization in the face of divergent interests of individuals, groups, other organizations, and the organization itself. . . ."[10]

The necessity for balance in organizations requires that management consciously modify and regulate role behavior. This means that management has to intervene in the fusion process in order to define rationally a role and to influence the way an employee perceives a role. Successful interventions are designed strategies that management uses to increase communication acceptance, build empathy, resolve role conflict, and improve role effectiveness.[11]

Communication Acceptance. Receipt of information does not guarantee acceptance. Acceptance is a psychological phenomenon based on, among other things, the needs, motives, experience, and education of

---

[9] Theodore R. Sarbin, "Role Theory," in Gardner Lindzey, ed., *Handbook of Social Psychology* (Cambridge, Mass: Addison-Wesley Publishing Co., 1954), vol. I, p. 255.

[10] Bakke, "Concept of the Social Organization," p. 60.

[11] For a discussion of organization development-type interventions, see Wendell L. French and Cecil H. Bell, Jr., *Organization Development* (Englewood Cliffs, N.J.: Prentice-Hall Inc., 1973), chapter 9.

the receivers, plus the environment in which they find themselves. Escher comments that, "Since unconscious selection [of information] is closely allied to our psychological needs and desires, it may be said quite aptly that we hear what we want to hear and reject what we don't want to hear."[12]

Assuming that the content of a message is understood, acceptance of the message's statement is a desirable—but not a necessary—prerequisite of effective action. From the standpoint of "democratic leadership," acceptance carries the force of a value; that is, people will be happier doing things they accept. Nonacceptance, however, does not preclude effective action. People do many things quite efficiently even though they neither agree nor accept the rightness of their act. Managers may not "accept" a sales policy, but they operate under it because of loyalty, or fear of the loss of their jobs, or the transient nature of the undesirable policy.

Several factors condition human acceptance of communication.[13] They are:

1. Reality. This very important factor refers to peoples' appraisal of their situation. Reality is a person's definition of this environment. Reality for one may not be reality for another. But the relevant reality in this case is the one which the *receiver* defines for purposes of acceptance or nonacceptance of the contents of a message.

2. Ambiguity. All communication is susceptible to varying interpretations. The receiver may not have a clear idea of "reality," or the content of the communication may be unclear in itself. In any event, lack of clarity results in ambiguity. And the more ambiguous a communication situation the less likely the receiver will be to accept a message.

3. Credibility. A good deal of communication is accepted as a "matter of faith" in the sender. The trustworthiness of the source of information is an important variable promoting or hindering acceptance.

4. Congruency. The congruency factor applies to the relevancy of the communication to the needs, motives, and values of the receivers. Acceptance in this case depends on whether the information in a message conflicts with or reinforces the receivers' values and their social, psycho-

---

[12] Albert J. Escher, "But I Thought . . . ," *Supervision,* July 1959, p. 24.

[13] These factors are adapted from Franklin Fearing, "Toward a Psychological Theory of Human Communication," *Journal of Personality,* 22 (1953–1954), 81–84; and Robert Zajone, "Distortion at the Receiving End." *Communication in Organizations: Some New Research Findings* (Ann Arbor, Mich.: Foundation for Research on Human Behavior, 1959), p. 6.

logical, and economic needs. Obviously, conflict between the contents of the message and the receivers' value-need system lowers the probability of acceptance. These factors are clearly interrelated. A person's view of reality defines what information is ambiguous, who is credible, and what communication is congruent with his or her needs and values.

The legitimacy of management in any organization is measured by the acceptance of their communication.[14] Interventions into role processes are aimed at increasing communication acceptance by subordinates through modifying their perceptions of management leadership and through altering their expectations of the official functions performed in the organization. However, such changes are not achieved merely by command or by overt manipulation. Empathy has an important part to play in the role process.

The Significance of Empathy.   Empathy refers to role-taking ability whereby individuals are able to "put themselves in others' shoes." Role-taking persons allow the attitudes of others to become their own, consciously adjusting their behavior as they see others reacting to it. This is a reflexive or an adaptive action in which one's behavior is modified in response to the counteractions of others.[15]

Empathy is an interpersonal and an interactional skill, that is essential to effective interventions into role processes. It is difficult to modify role perceptions of others, if one does not have a "feel" for how roles are being perceived by people in the organization. A considerable amount of training in management, as we discuss later, is aimed at improving this skill.

Role Effectiveness and the Reduction of Role Conflict.   Role conflict results when an individual is faced with two roles which are incompatible.[16] The person cannot meet the expectations of these roles simultaneously, and thus a conflict ensues between them. The seriousness of the conflict depends on two factors:

1.   The nature of the situation, including the degree to which the roles are incompatible, and the rigidity with which the expectations are enforced.

2.   The personality of the individual, including adjustment to the

[14] Chester I. Barnard, *The Functions of the Executive* (Cambridge, Mass.: Harvard University Press, 1938), pp. 165–68.

[15] Ralph H. Turner, "Role-Taking, Role Standpoint, and Reference Group Behavior," *American Journal of Sociology*, January 1956, pp. 318–21, 326.

[16] See John T. Gullahorn, "Measuring Role Conflict," *American Journal of Sociology*, January 1956, pp. 299–303.

situation and the ability to ignore some of the demands of one role or the other.[17]

An individual in an organization is required to play a number of roles. Managers try to ensure that role conflict does not occur, because of the resulting inefficiencies and dissatisfactions. However, modern organizations are so complex that it is practically impossible to eliminate all sources of role conflict. One example is the production supervisor who is faced with certain productivity demands by the immediate line superior. At the same time, a staff organization—quality control, for instance—is making demands on the supervisor in terms of quality expectations. Frequently these two demands are inconsistent and the supervisor is faced with a quality-or-quantity dilemma. Whichever route the supervisor chooses is likely to result in an accusation of incompetency.

In addition to role conflict between functions, there is also the problem of role conflict between the expectations of the organization versus the expectations of the group. Output restriction is a convenient example of this situation. Output restriction is a deliberate effort, informally enforced by the group, either to produce below standards or not to produce as much as possible under the standard for fear it may be unfavorably revised.

An individual coming into such a situation is faced with two sets of demands. Management wants as much output as possible. The group pressures the individual to restrict output to some limit that they, not management, consider appropriate. Hence role conflict results!

What does the individual do? On the one hand he or she may go to either extreme: join forces with the output restricters, or become a rate-buster. On the other hand, the individual may vacillate or try to find a niche somewhere between these two extremes. In speaking of restricters and rate-busters Whyte notes that by far the majority of employees in a particular situation studied by him were "men in the middle." They were pulled in one direction by the goal of higher productivity and in the other by the goal of the restricting work group.[18]

Management's responsibilities for organizational balance falls within the effectiveness aspect of role theory. Role effectiveness and conflict reduction require organizational consensus building. This crosscuts many management activities ranging from heightening the levels of interper-

---

[17] J. W. Getzels and E. G. Guba, "Role, Role Conflict, and Effectiveness: An Empirical Study," *American Sociological Review*, April 1954, pp. 164–66.

[18] William F. Whyte, *Money and Motivation* (New York: Harper & Bros., 1955), pp. 46–9.

sonal competency within organizations to designing rational relationships among organizational functions.

Role effectiveness is the counterpart of role conflict. Management's organizational intervention strategies are supposed to increase role effectiveness by anticipating and modifying the perception of roles held by employees. Through organizational design management attempts to reduce conflict by clarifying role content. The expectation is that improved role effectiveness raises the level of organizational rationality, because if roles are clarified, people's ability to perceive them accurately and to play them better is improved. Ever since the invention of organization, status systems were an important part of design.

STATUS

Acquiring status is one of the foremost objectives of human behavior. People devote countless hours and considerable energy trying to achieve it. But status while *sought* by individuals, ultimately cannot be created by individuals; it is something like honor, which is disposed by others. Status is socially defined and granted and therefore its development must be viewed as a dynamic process.

Status has two connotations. First, it may be thought of as a ranking of positions, or a relative ordering of rights and duties, like those found in the formal structure of an organization. This view of status is objective. Second, status has a private, subjective connotation. One can judge another in one's own mind. This personal status judgement is not necessarily related to the formal status position that the person being judged holds in the organization.

Thus status may apply to a position in a social structure distinct from the individual who occupies it; or it may apply to a private evaluation of one individual by another. These judgments are not unrelated, of course, because these private evaluations may very well affect careers in the formal organization.

The Objective Connotation of Status

In the objective sense, status is considered as a position involving rights and duties arranged in a structure of human interrelationships. A particular status is something apart from the individual who occupies it.[19]

---

[19] Linton points out that role is the dynamic counterpart of a status position. An individual is given a status through a social process; but when he begins to discharge

Status systems refer to the total structure of an organization, including a hierarchial pattern of rights and duties. The rights and duties, and their relative position in status hierarchies, are determined by the value systems of institutions.[20] An organization has various positions carrying rewards, authorities, and obligations. These positions are ordered in relation to each other according to the importance assigned to them by management.

Thus, a president and vice president in a business organization have specific functions to perform, but the value placed on the president's job is greater than that given the vice president's position. The point to keep in mind is that both the *specific* obligations and rewards for status positions, as well as the relative values assigned to them, are determined by management. *Management imposes the formal status hierarchy.*

The Subjective Connotation of Status

The subjective aspect of status concerns how people make status judgments of others. People constantly evaluate those with whom they come in contact. This is a process of making *status judgments*. From these private judgments an individual receives a status in a hospital, office, or student group.[21]

People base their judgments of others on "status measuring criteria," of which Parsons has identified five standards: parentage, personal qualities, achievements, possessions, and authority.[22] People will not weigh these standards the same. This accounts for the fact that an individual can have a "high" status in one situation and a "low" status in another situation. Thus granting status is rather arbitrary. People do not apply status-measuring criteria uniformly in ordinary circumstances where interpersonal relations are often informal and casual. But the organizational need for order, requires that formal status systems are imposed

---

the obligations of this position he is said to be playing a role. Status and role, thus, are inseparable. Ralph Linton, *The Study of Man* (New York: D. Appleton-Century Co., 1936), pp. 113–14.

[20] The hierarchial aspect of status is discussed at length by Emile Benoit-Smullyan, "Status, Status Types, and Status Interrelations," *American Sociological Review*, April 1944, pp. 151–61.

[21] The status one receives may be translated into a position in the formal organization, or a position in an informal organization, or it may simply remain one person's opinion of another.

[22] Talcott Parsons, *Essays in Sociological Theory Pure and Applied* (Glencoe, Ill.: The Free Press, 1949), pp. 171–72.

so that people "know where they stand" relative to others in terms of authority and responsibility.

Status Systems

Every formal organization is a composite of two status systems: the functional and the scalar. Barnard observed that each status position is actually a point on an organizational matrix relative vertically and horizontally to other status points on the same matrix.[23]

Functional status positions correspond to specializations in the organization, and lie on a horizontal plane. These positions derive their status from the *level and type of expertise* required by the organization of those who perform them. Functional status does not include command authority. The essential feature of scalar status is that it carries the right to command. Scalar status bestows command authority on those occupying positions in the vertical plane of organizational relationships. It is obvious that scalar and functional status systems are the counterparts of the scalar and functional processes that we discussed earlier in our treatment of classical organization theory in Chapter 2.

The purpose of status systems, which when combined often result in the traditional organization pyramid, is to institutionalize two important organizational roles: the role of coordination and the role of specialization. Specialized roles differentiate the organization into segments of expertise, that then have to be coordinated by roles performing integration functions. The classical structure of organization is a clear example to the interaction of these two roles, although there are alternative structural designs for achieving the same objective—a rational combination of integration and differentiation activities.[24]

Status Symbols

People are status conscious, although it is probably more accurate to say that people are conscious of the status symbols they possess or lack. Status symbols are externalizations of the basic social processes of ranking regardless of whether the processes are subjective, objective, or a combination of the two.

Once a status position is acquired, "badges of office" are granted.

---

[23] Barnard, *The Functions of the Executive*, pp. 207–44.

[24] Paul R. Lawrence and Jay W. Lorsch, *Organization and Environment* (Homewood, Ill.: Richard D. Irwin, Inc., 1969).

These badges are status symbols and act as tangible evidence of the rank and function of people in an organization.

The symbols of formal organizations are easiest to describe. In business, titles serve as status indicators. The title "vice president of sales" has a twofold message. First, "vice president" says the individual occupies a high rank in the *chain of command.* Second, "sales" tells interested parties the function or job the individual performs in the company.

But titles relate only part of the story of an individual's status. At best they are rough indicators, particularly when the middle management "jungle" is viewed. Here other symbols tend to become more important. External trappings of office such as the size of the desk, name in the company telephone directory, a secretary, the floor on which the office is located, gold, silver, or brass spitoons—all are evidence of a rank in the formal structure. While subtle, these symbols are quite tangible. They show the shading of status gradients in an organization.

A description of status symbols in a bank is given by John P. Marquand in his novel *Point of No Return.*

> Though you seldom talked of salaries at Stuyvesant, your social status was obvious from the *position* of your desk. Charles occupied one of the *two flat mahogany desks* that stood in a sort of *no man's land* between the *roll-top desks* of the officers and the *smaller flat-tops* of lesser executives and secretaries crowding the floor of the bank *outside* the cages. A *green rug* extended from the officers' desks, *forming a neat and restricted zone* that *just included* Charles's desk. . . .[25]

Without knowing any more about Charles and the Stuyvesant bank than this passage reveals, it is still easy to pinpoint his position in the status structure of the company. Even the old-fashioned roll-top desks used by the bank officers indicated a reverse snob appeal.

Although fun can be made of the elaborate forms and rituals connected with the use of status symbols, their importance as a social phenomenon must not be disregarded.[26] Status symbols, as the concrete product of judgmental and ranking processes, have real significance for organizational participants. Rewards are often made in other than money terms. People weigh external evidence of success heavily. Accomplishments do not taste so sweet unless others know about them. Status

---

[25] John P. Marquand, *Point of No Return* (Boston: Little, Brown & Co., 1949), p. 29. Reprinted with permission. Italics are ours; they indicate the symbols mentioned in this short paragraph.

[26] For a further discussion of status symbols, see Erving Goffman, "Symbols of Class Status," *British Journal of Sociology,* December 1951, pp. 294–304.

symbols represent achievement; if symbols are not awarded, many would suffer from severe cases of "status anxiety."

In summary, the importance of status symbols may be expressed as the organizational purposes which they serve.

1. Motivation. Status symbols act as honors or rewards for achievements. As such, they provide incentives to motivate people toward greater accomplishments.

2. Identification. Status symbols make it easier to determine who holds authority and performs differentiated functions. The greater the degree to which specialization of functions is carried the more important status symbols become in order to identify who does what in an organization.

3. Dignification. Status symbols add dignity to a position and support authority in it.

4. Stabilization. Status symbols solidify rank, authority, and areas of functional specialization, and this facilitates regularization of work patterns.

While this discussion implies formal organizations, it should not be inferred that status symbols are their exclusive property. Indeed, status symbols are used by small groups in less obvious ways. But they are present nonetheless and perform the same four functions just mentioned.

Status Passage

Status passage is a basic social process by which the change of status of an individual is regularized.[27] The route of status change for a child who matures from schoolchild, to college student, to a career in business, to marriage, to parenthood, and eventually to death is lined with cultural road marks showing the way to travel to ease the passage as status transitions are made. Now, of course, not all pitfalls are clearly indicated. Some may be obscure. Others may not exist at all. Often, to help with these rough segments, the older person who has traveled the route comes to the aid of the younger. It is common in many walks of life for the young person to have a patron, a high-status friend, act as a coach as his or her career evolves.

Because there are specified functions to be performed in organizations and because the people who are presently filling these functions will change, most organizations institutionalize the process of status mobility.

---

[27] This discussion is drawn from Anselm L. Strauss, "Transformations of Identity," in Warren G. Bennis, Kenneth D. Benne, and Robert Chin, eds., *The Planning of Change* (New York: Holt, Rinehart and Winston, Inc., 1961), pp. 548–58.

This means that organization design prepares the way for individuals who must undergo status changes. The person's passage is made easier by indicators showing where an individual is going and where he or she should be at certain points of time. Now the route of status passage is not necessarily the same as the hierarchy of status positions shown on the organizational chart. The literature on career progress makes this clear.

Martin and Strauss present a study of status passage patterns in business organizations.[28] In their view, as an organization matures it evolves career lines which are open to individuals seeking advancement. They describe these lines as branches on a tree, with some terminating at lower management levels, fewer moving through middle management, and still fewer going all the way to top management.

The status passage of an individual in an organization requires a series of vertical and horizontal steps. Horizontal movement from one function to another is designed to give a broader background in the organization. Vertical mobility, of course, constitutes the payoff by status changes to positions of greater authority and responsibility. But each move is, in a sense, ritualized since it is considered a training and testing point. If individuals perform well they are in line for another move. If they do not live up to expectations, their mobility probably is terminated.

The interesting feature of established career progressions is the timetable by which individuals can gauge their progress. Martin and Strauss observe, "Acceptable age ranges are identifiable for the various strata. . . . A person who does not progress in accordance with these age timetables may know . . . that his potential for higher levels of management has been judged unfavorably."[29]

Even within this model of a structured career system the individual retains some discretion and control. In any organization a person has available a number of alternative channels or career lines from which to select. It is largely up to the individual to appraise these alternatives and select the channel which will be the most beneficial. In the stable organization, however, *persons select from established career lines; they do not make their own.*

---

[28] Norman H. Martin and Anselm L. Strauss, "Patterns of Mobility within Industrial Organizations," *Journal of Business,* April 1956, pp. 101–10. A study of mobility patterns which stresses the element of independence from ritualistic passage routes is by William R. Dill, Thomas L. Hilton, and Walter R. Reitman, *The New Manager* (Englewood Cliffs, N.J.: Prentice-Hall, Inc., 1962).

[29] Ibid., p. 109.

Thus far, individual progress is based on technical competence, favorable judgment of others, and appropriate selection of a career alternative. Another factor emphasized by Martin and Strauss is the role of sponsorship. Sponsorship is the support lent by one person to another in order to facilitate a career. The sponsor pulls protégés up the ladder.

Here again, the judgement of the protégé enters into the promotional pattern. A career often is greatly enhanced by the happy wedding of a protégé and a powerful sponsor. But there are also dangers in these arrangements. A sponsor may lose ground in organizational transitions and power shifts, in which case the protégé is placed in an extremely tenuous position. It is not only high-level persons who are affected by organizational personnel changes; also affected are constellations of people, high and low, who have formed alliances.

One consequence of organizational reshuffling is, of course, being fired. However, an individual who at one time appeared to be a "hot prospect" in the organization is perceived as less desirable. Instead of being fired, failure to perform up to expectation or loss of power might result in a person being "cooled out." "Cooling out" is a face-saving device by which an individual is "kicked upstairs" or "banished" to an innocuous position. The cooling-out process may be only temporary, or it may represent a terminal point in a career.

Status Congruency and Perceived Status Differentials

The reader should not leave the last section with the idea that status passage somehow *effortlessly* allows an individual to make positional changes in a social matrix. Anyone who has experienced life realizes this is not true. Change, even under the most desirable circumstances, causes social and psychological dislocations that must be restored in new status positions.

As one changes status, one often changes reference groups. This is routine in organizations. The extent to which one making passage into a new group perceives the status of the group as compatible, and the group concurs in this perception, we have status congruency. The individual has a high degree of social certitude because the position is unambiguous in terms of the subjective status judgment of associates. This condition is important in formal organizations. As Homans says, "Congruence facilitates social ease in the interaction among men, and so when they are working together as a team, a congruent relationship between them, by removing one possible source of friction, should encourage their joint efficiency. Up at least to middle levels of congruence . . ."[30]

While group dynamics is treated at length in Chapter 8, we must not pass the opportunity to note the function played by status congruency in formation of these groups. People tend naturally to group where they perceive status congruency. The basis of the perception may be occupational—secretaries will associate with secretaries, not with file clerks. Or it could be 101 other socially differentiating factors which condition choice of affiliation in small groups such as age, sex, race affluence, and education.

Strategies designed to rationally shape role and status definitions are crucial to management's desire for organizational balance in the form of consensus and integration. Related as well to the need for balance are various influence processes, which we treat as authority and power in the next chapter.

---

[30] George C. Homans, *Social Behavior: Its Elementary Forms* (New York: Harcourt, Brace & World, Inc., 1961), p. 264. Beyond the middle point of congruency task performance will fall off, see Stuart Adams, "Status Congruency as a Variable in Small Group Performance," *Social Forces*, vol. 32 (1953), pp. 16–22.

chapter 13

Influence Processes: Authority and Power

Influence involves a series of social transactions by which a person or group is induced by another person or group to act in conformance to the influencing agents' expectations to do something other than what would be done ordinarily. In this chapter we treat influence mainly as a matter of power and authority that is exercised in the context of formal organizations. However, this process is not so limited, as we will show.

Sources of influence for persons or groups in organizations are found in positional status, control, or reward and punishment systems, financial (budgetary) control, possession of information, and access to communication channels. Influence is also obtained from the functional expertise and the personal magnetism of the influencing agent. In brief, the question—"How and why are people induced to perform certain actions and to strive for certain goals?"—has been for years the center of attention of many behavioral scientists and management theorists.

As a theoretical background we will return to our earlier description of motivational behavior. We believe that an individual chooses to respond to an influence attempt because he feels that it will maximize the positive consequences (or minimize the negative ones). These consequences may be internal (e.g., feelings of legitimacy), controlled by one's supervisor (e.g., monetary rewards or punishment), or related to co-workers or the environment (e.g., liking from peers). In the following review of the literature, we will attempt to use this conceptualization to organize the diverse material presented in the area.

ELEMENTS OF THE INFLUENCE PROCESS

Cartwright, in his comprehensive summary of influence research and theory, presents a useful outline of the subject.[1] The influence process includes three elements: (1) the agent (O) exerting influence; (2) the method ($\rightarrow$) of influence; (3) the agent (P) subjected to influence. The shorthand describing the influence process is $O \rightarrow P$. Following the conventional terminology, if O is able to get P to behave in certain ways, or to adopt certain attitudes and opinions, it is said that O has influenced P; or variously, O has power over P; or O controls P.

Methods of Influence

Based upon his analysis of the literature, Cartwright concludes that O has essentially four means available to influence P.[2] Taking the form of power, they are physical, positive or negative sanctions, expertise, and charisma.

Physical power as a means of coercion is probably the crudest form of influence. It involves the *threat* or the actual *use* of force to influence action and to obtain compliance. Extracting a wallet at gunpoint is one example; executing a political opponent is another example. Such extreme measures are not ordinarily employed by the typical administrative system. The exercise of power through the control of sanctions is a more common, and subtler, method.

Positive and negative sanctions are simply the means to reward or punish. Thus, O is able to influence P by withholding, withdrawing, or distributing the resources at O's command. This capability implies that O occupies a strategic organizational position and has legitimacy as well. The matters of positional power and legitimacy are discussed later in this chapter.

O may also be able to influence P by applying his expertise as an "authority" in an area of knowledge. Hence, if O is an expert in Asiatic affairs and P is ignorant in this area, O by virtue of his learning may be able to impress P sufficiently to mold his opinions. However, the process of opinion change need not always be a function of expert knowledge. Authorities recognize that opinion change through the use of prop-

---

[1] Dorwin Cartwright, "Influence, Leadership, Control," in James G. March, ed., *Handbook of Organizations* (Chicago: Rand McNally & Co., 1965), pp. 1–14.

[2] Ibid., pp. 11–22.

aganda and manipulation of information are distinct possibilities which fall within the scope of this aspect of influence.[3]

Finally, influence may be accomplished by personal magnetism. *O* can influence *P* charismatically. Cartwright also acknowledges that within this category it is appropriate to include the influence that can be achieved by position or rank in an organization. Such a position may carry with it awesome qualities (as viewed by those of lesser rank) quite apart from the personality of the individual occupying the position. The presidency of the United States is just such a position.

The Territory of Influence

The above methods of influence are- exercised in many situations. This is evident especially if we reflect on the fact that *O* and *P* can be construed as *groups* as well as individuals. Therefore, the territory of influence includes the following relationships:

1. One on one (discussed here and in Chapter 9, "Communication Processes").
2. Group on one (discussed mainly in Chapter 8, "Group Dynamics," and Chapter 9).
3. Group on group (referenced in Chapters 8 and 9, discussed in Chapter 12, "Role and Status Development Processes," and Chapter 20, "Organizational Governance").
4. One on group (discussed mainly in this chapter).

The above classification of influence into the various chapters in the book is by no means mutually exclusive. It is merely a way of bringing into focus a very complex subject. So while our interest here is most often with a more traditional view of organizational power and authority, which directs us to a "one on group" relationship, we cannot ignore the fact that the "one on one" relationship is very much a part of the authority and power concepts conventionally held by management. Further, "the group on group" relationship, while basically political in nature, often arises out of structural causes. With all this said, our main concern nevertheless is with items 1 and 4 above.

---

[3] G. Gilman, "An Inquiry into the Nature and Use of Authority," in M. Haire, ed., *Organization Theory in Industrial Practice* (New York: John Wiley & Sons, Inc., 1962).

POWER AND INFLUENCE

The purpose of this section is to discuss certain contemporary interpretations of power and influence relationships, particularly as they appear organizationally. The French-Raven approach is probably best known as representing the social-psychology stream of analysis. We discuss their analysis, and then proceed to the work of Etzioni and Nisbet as reflecting the sociological approach.

French-Raven Analysis of Power and Influence

French and Raven define power in terms of influence, and influence in terms of psychological change. Influence is the *control* which a social agent exercises on others.[4] They say that the strength of power a person possesses in a given system is the maximum *potential* ability to control. Obviously it is a matter of discretion how much of this potential a social agent chooses to exercise. An important concept is based on this idea. *Power is latent influence; while influence is power in action.*

The basis upon which power rests is a crucial part of the French-Raven analysis. They see power stemming from five sources.

1. Reward Power. Reward power is the number of positive incentives which the social agent is able to offer others. Reward power depends not only on some absolute quantity (of money, for instance) but also on the *perception* by those influenced of the number of positive rewards they think a potential social agent can muster. Thus, a manager may have a certain amount of absolute power to offer salary incentives within the established range on a given job. But this person may or may not be perceived as possessing the ability within the organization to get the ranges changed or to have a positive influence in advancing the careers of subordinates.

2. Coercive Power. The analysis of coercive power is similar to reward power, only it is the opposite side of the coin. It stems from both the absolute and perceived expectations that punishment will follow if one does not comply with the aims of the power agent.

Reward and coercive power have positive and negative outcomes. But it is difficult to predict them. Often management strategy requires

---

[4] Much of the following material is based on John R. P. French and Bertram Raven, "The Bases of Social Power," in Dorwin Cartwright and A. F. Zander, eds., *Group Dynamics*, 2d ed. (Evanston, Ill.: Row, Peterson and Company, 1960), pp. 607–23.

the use of both to secure compliance. Depending on the situation, too much coercion may cause those subject to power to leave the social agent's field of influence entirely.

3. *Legitimate Power.* Legitimate power stems from "internalized values . . . which dictate that [a social agent] has a legitimate right to influence . . . and that [one] has an obligation to accept this influence."[5] This kind of power rests upon cultural values, acceptance of a social structure, and the delegation of power by one possessing it to another to act as his or her agent.

4. *Referent Power.* Referent power is based on the identification of those influenced with one who is influencing. This feeling of value oneness may be, but is not necessarily, reciprocated.

5. *Expert Power.* Possession of functional expertise is the foundation of this form of power. The strength of power in this instance is a function of an individual's perception that the influencer possesses superior knowledge in a given area, and will therefore act in ways suggested by the influencing agent.

These "sources" can be construed as means for achieving compliance to authority in organizations. Thus, O can obtain P's compliance if P feels that this behavior is likely to lead to rewards or because P feels O has the expertise or the legitimacy to make demands. What is omitted, however, is an analysis of "other possible consequences." More specifically, whether P obeys O is not only a function of the outcomes provided by P but also by other environmental demands. French and Raven have omitted these sources of influence.

The Etzioni Analysis of Power and Influence

While French and Raven treat power and influence as latent and active elements of the same process, Etzioni finds it useful to separate these concepts.[6] He points out that the use of power by O may change P's behavior, but it may not change P's *preferences*. "Resistance," he says, "is overcome not because the actor subjected to the use of power changes his 'will' but because resistance has been made more expensive, prohibitive, or impossible."[7] Conversely, successful influence results in

---

[5] Ibid., p. 616.

[6] Amitai Etzioni, *The Active Society* (New York: The Free Press, 1968), pp. 359–60.

[7] Ibid.

a change in *P*'s preference system, such that *P* "wills" a change in his behavior, opinions, and attitudes in order that they conform to his newly arranged preference priorities.

The distinction here seems to be dependent upon the consequence of compliance. In some cases, *P* will obey *O* to avoid negative consequences. However, *P* will continue to find the activity distasteful. On the other hand, if obeying *O* results in positive consequences, then *P* may change his attitude about the behavior in question. A thorough analysis of just how much pressure *O* should exert in order to increase the chances of creating a positive attitude change in *P* was discussed previously in relation to attitude change.

Etzioni, then, is more concerned about whether *P* likes what he is doing for *O* rather than if *P* complies or does not comply. The notion of *P*'s "willful" acceptance of behavioral change leads us directly to the concept of authority which we introduce by discussing Nisbet's analysis.

The Nisbet Analysis of Power and Influence

Robert Nisbet has an interesting approach to the subject of power. He sees it as the antithesis of authority. The latter concept, authority, is treated by Nisbet as one of the "unit-ideas" of sociology.[8] Unlike social psychologists, Nisbet observes that in the "sociological tradition" there has been a standing distinction between authority and power. The concept of authority parallels in a rough way the social-psychological notion of influence. That is, authority has been viewed as the "willful" acceptance by people of behavioral modifications induced by their leaders.

Power, on the other hand, typically has been treated as domination or coercion, by which people are forced to behave in certain ways without any real or lasting effect on their preference systems. A further distinction frequently made by sociologists is that authority is tied to the rewards inherent in the position occupied by *O*. These rewards could be the coercive, reward, and legitimacy sources discussed by French and Raven. Power, on the other hand, is seen as the rewards that might be available to the individual *O* such as expertise, charm, or charisma. This distinction leads us to a more thorough review of the concept of authority.

---

[8] Robert A. Nisbet, *The Sociological Tradition* (New York: Basic Books, Inc., Publishers, 1966), pp. 107–73.

AUTHORITY AND THE NATURE OF THE OBEDIENCE RELATIONSHIP

Many attempts have been made to explain the nature of authority in organizations. One of the most important statements on this subject was presented recently by Stanley Milgram. His analysis of behavior under authority grew out of his experiments with people in stress situations. In these experiments, the subjects were led to believe that they were administering painful, even dangerous, electrical shocks to a "reluctant victim."[9]

One of the observations Milgram made was that ordinary people will continue to give shocks, at increasing voltages, even though the "victim" is screaming in protest. Milgram thinks that part of the reason for this behavior can be explained by authority; that is, subjects acting under what is perceived as legitimate authority will tend to shock the "victim" on orders, even when such orders run counter to their (the subjects') espoused moral beliefs.

This critical findings raises a question that is basic in organization theory: What causes people to comply with authority in hierarchial systems? The answer, or at least part of the answer, is found in the nature of hierarchy and in the nature of obedience. Both hierarchy and obedience are closely related.

According to Milgram, hierarchy, and therefore, hierarchial authority has its origin in evolution. Apparently, the human propensity to form hierarchial authority relationships is a genetic trait, selected out by the evolutionary process because it has survival value for the species. But this is not the whole story. Pointing to human psychological development, Milgram observes that individual self-control is also important to survival. Thus, the emergence of conscience to regulate destructive impulses is another aspect of the evolutionary phenomenon. However, conscience is a highly individualized thing which tends to inhibit to varying degrees, one person from doing harm to another. As society becomes more complex, and as organizations emerge, people become

---

[9] A complete description of the experiments are found in Stanley Milgram, *Obedience to Authority* (New York: Harper & Row, Publishers, 1974). For the sake of clarity, "the victim" was an actor who pretended to be shocked, the "subjects" were people chosen from all walks of life who administered the shocks to the "victim" although there were no electrical discharges whatsoever, and the "experimenter" acted as the authority figure. Thus, the "experimenter" and the "victim" know that the "experimental" situation into which the "subject" was introduced was a hoax. The behavior studied was of the person who manipulated the machine that was supposed to shock the "victim."

willing to submerge the dictates of their individual consciences to the "larger conscience" of the authority structure of the organization for the sake of coordination. Consequently authority originates in hierarchy, and it, in turn, provides the *controls* that are necessary for human survival in society.[10]

Obedience to authority follows as part of the socialization process of individuals. Society places high priorities on the development of compliant behavior. Children are expected to be obedient, and they are rewarded or punished depending on how they act toward authority figures. Throughout life obedience is reenforced positively, whereas deviency is punished.

However, extracting obedience is not so simple a matter that it can be converted to reenforcement schedules. The individual is often confronted with the need to decide who must be obeyed, in what kinds of situations, and when. In other words, one has to know what is the *legitimate* authority pertinent to the situation. Organization theory has given a great deal of attention to the matter of perception of legitimacy.

Origins of Organizational Authority

Hierarchial authority in organizations makes sanctions available to individuals occupying them which permit managers to extract compliance from subordinates. Organization theory has two major explanations of how such positions of authority in hierarchy come into existence: They either originate at the top of the organization and are delegated downward, or they emerge from the bottom of the organization as a result of the consent of those managed.

The Top-down Theory. Where does manager X in some executive function of an organization get authority? The answer most likely would be "from the superior next in line in the chain of command." If we trace the roots of delegated authority they lead us to the chief executive. Assuming a business organization, we can push beyond the executive hierarchy to the board of directors, from there to the stockholders, and if we persist we find the ultimate legitimacy for authority in the laws of the land supporting the rights of private property.

This theory of authority is closely allied with the concept of traditional legitimacy. Every organization which has a formally structured system of authority rests upon tradition to some extent. This is so regardless of whether one traces authority to private property or to God, as in the case of the divine right of kings.

---
[10] Ibid., chapter 10.

Society recognizes the ultimate source of authority as legitimate and accepts the outcomes of the distribution of this authority throughout social institutions. So as people at one time widely accepted and complied with the "ruling and teaching" powers of the church exercised through the stewardship of the clergy, now they comply with the formal prescriptions of professional managers who are agents of the owners of property.

The Consent Theory of Authority.   Authority is proposed in this theory as coming from those led rather than from the delegation process in hierarchical systems. This theory, as the name indicates, is based upon the acceptance by followers of the authority exercised by those in superordinate positions. The idea essentially is that authority is meaningless unless consent is secured from subordinates. Action is impossible without the willing cooperation of those who are led to act.

In the strict sense, the only possible origin for authority is the consent of those who follow. Bottom-up as it were! But Milgram's warning should be heeded, that authority once granted is very difficult to retrieve by those governed. Consent is institutionalized in bureaucratic authority structures which are resistant to constituent demands for change. For example, at one major university, control was increasingly centralized "by consent" in its administration. A movement to change the terms of this consent was started by the faculty. Basically, procedures were sought by which the consent of the faculty to administrative authority would be periodically reaffirmed by votes of confidence in the administration. This effort to achieve change was suppressed by the administration, and the faculty saw fit not to pursue the issue. Thus, while authority may originate by consent of subordinates in organizations, ". . . its withdrawal does not proceed automatically or without great cost."[11]

In spite of managerial failings in some institutions, it is clear that in organizations the willing compliance of subordinates with authority is desirable and rational. The purpose of authority is to summon obedience efficiently; and this can be accomplished only when authority is perceived to be legitimate.

Authority and Legitimacy

Max Weber made the classic study of authority. He saw it as the willing, unconditioned compliance of people resting upon their belief that it is legitimate for the superior to impose his will on them, and it is illegitimate for them to refuse obedience.

---

[11] Ibid., p. 143.

The key word in this statement is legitimate. The extent to which people *believe* in the legitimacy of authority determines the amount of positive incentives or coercive measures a superior must employ to secure compliance to his aims. Blau points out that the very use of incentives or sanctions is evidence that authority is not accepted either altogether or in part.[12] The question is what conditions are necessary to produce the perception of legitimate authority? According to Weber there are three grounds for legitimating authority: tradition, charisma, and legal (or rational).

Tradition

Traditional authority rests in the perception that a certain person, class, or caste is destined to rule by some preordained right. This perception may be found in the acceptance of a political system or it may be based on religious belief. Regardless, those who are in the ruling position obtain compliance by virtue of the fact that those who follow subscribe to the cultural values which support the ruling structure.

Charisma

Charisma is tied in with the notion of change usually brought about by an individual who has the personal ability to enlist the support of followers who believe in the goals prescribed. Change may be directed against the established traditional system of authority. Charismatic authority is legitimate in the sense that the followers make it so. The property of charisma is thought to be a configuration of personality traits which enables a person to obtain compliance of followers because they believe that the goals sought by the leader ought be the goals they should strive for as well. Charisma is grounded in the personal magnetism of the leader.

Legal (Rational)

Rational authority also involves change. But the change evoked by this process is not in response to a particular person. Rather it is change based on the emerging needs of an organization. People possessing rational legitimate authority secure compliance to their goals because they are technically (functionally) equipped to spell out what sort of ends

---

[12] Peter M. Blau, "Critical Remarks on Weber's Theory of Authority," *The American Political Science Review,* June 1963, p. 312. See also Robert Presthus, *The Organizational Society* (New York: Vantage Books, 1962), pp. 141–42.

are necessary to be pursued for the good of the system. Followers accept these prescriptions because of the acknowledged expertise of the decision maker who is technically qualified to perform those functions required to further the rational progress of the organization.

These concepts of legitimate authority stand in juxtaposition. On the one hand is tradition, which is static, preserving the established order. On the other hand are charisma and rational authority dedicated to change. In a concrete organizational setting all three types of authority are present.

The Use of Organizational Authority

The reader may have observed that we changed the rules of the semantic game with respect to our treatment of power. Our discussion in the initial pages of this chapter dealt with power as an influence phenomenon. It carried no value connotations as being good or bad, organizationally effective or ineffective.

However, we shifted ground later by noting that the predominant opinion in administrative theory stresses the utility of authority as a means of influencing and de-emphasizes power as such a means. The reason for this shift is based simply on the fact that power has implied to management theorists a form of domination and coercion. Whereas authority is interpreted by them to imply democracy and willing compliance. Power has assumed a negative connotation, and authority has taken on a positive connotation. Out of this has grown an enormous body of research and literature which has "demonstrated" the values of democratic leadership and noncoercive motivational techniques.

However, more is involved here than semantic mixups. The application of authority includes a considerable range of tangible organizational design alternatives and leadership styles of behavior. A case in point is the confusion between authority and authoritarianism. Authoritarianism is a leadership style, a personal way of implementing power, which has acquired a negative connotation largely because it is thought less able to achieve organizational goals and to produce human satisfaction than other leadership forms. In our analysis authoritarianism is more closely associated with power than with authority.

We must remember that power is connected with such practices as the use of incentives or coercion to secure action toward goals. The more superior is required to use incentives or coercion the less subordinates have accepted the legitimacy of his or her authority. Naturally, the most efficient and economical way of gaining compliance is by voluntary, willing submission to authority. Coercion and incentive programs are always more costly than if people are spontaneously motivated to achieve goals which they perceive as created by legitimate authority.

Chester I. Barnard was one of the first in management circles to give a systematic statement of the consent theory of authority.[13] However, it is not entirely clear whether his position was a reaction to the dysfunctional consequences of *authoritarianism* or a reaffirmation of Weber's concept of bureaucratic rationality. There are elements of both in his analysis. But there is strong evidence indicating his preference for a democratic explanation of the authority phenomenon. His argument runs that since all formal organizations are founded on the consent of those governed the managers of these organizations should act with maximum regard to the inputs from their constituencies. In other words, managers would be better able to achieve goals of the cooperative system if they tapped the democratic roots of authority in the decision process rather than unilaterally imposing their will on the people subordinated to them. Based upon a democratic assumption about the origins of authority, Barnard prescribes the kind of management style required, which of course includes a greater degree of decentralization and participation designs than allowed by autocratic practices.

Beyond this Barnard caught the effectiveness-efficiency implications of legitimate authority versus the use of power to motivate subordinates. He believed the main vehicle for legitimating authority in organizations is communication. If people think that messages they receive are legitimate, they will accept the source which issues them as a legitimate authority and act accordingly to pursue goals which will satisfy their needs and the organizational needs. This holds whether the authority is rational, traditional, or charismatic.

But Barnard, like other writers during his period, had a strong bias toward a concept of legitimate authority rooted in rationality. This is because in many instances their personal experience was tied to large bureaucratic systems which relied heavily on functional expertise. Mary Parker Follett, as another example, was also inclined toward the rational view of authority as the basis of legitimacy.[14] She stressed that

---

[13] Chester I. Barnard, *The Functions of the Executive* (Cambridge, Mass.: Harvard University Press, 1939), chapter 12. But for an earlier work, see Mary P. Follett, *The New State* (London: Longmans, Green and Co., 1920).

[14] Mary P. Follett, "The Illusion of Final Authority," *Bulletin of the Taylor Society*, December 1926, p. 244.

the expertise required in a function stays with it regardless of personnel changes. The rational demands of the formal organization are not based upon the particular abilities of individuals available at any one time, but upon the activities themselves which persist over time, and which may even transcend the traditional command hierarchy of authority. This point is developed by Feld in a research study dealing with information and authority in military organizations. The access to intelligence and operational data by functional staff specialists at times endows these people with the authority to command, if not officially at least instrumentally, because their superior information often "takes precedence over formal rank as a determinant of organization status."[15]

Charismatic authority presents a somewhat different problem is application. Steming from the character of the individual, it is a personal thing. However, Shills makes an important point noting that people will often attribute the property of charisma to a person in a position of vast authority such as president, pope, dictator, or king.[16] This may happen even though the individual does not in fact have the magnetism which Weber implied as necessary in the charismatic personality. Thus, the source of charisma is in some instances the impersonal authority possessed by a few individuals in political and economic life. But in most other circumstances the personal interpretation of charisma is likely to be the correct one.

ORGANIZATIONAL EFFECTIVENESS AND CONTROL

Whether an individual or a group complies with a superior's wishes depends upon the consequences of this compliance as compared to the consequences for noncompliance. Different approaches to the study of power have emphasized the content of these consequences. The social psychological analysis of power has typically emphasized those consequences that P feels are controlled by O. The sociological approach has placed more emphasis on the organizational or situational factors involved as well as on the attitude P has about his compliance. This latter point has emphasized the willingness of P to do what O asks of him.

The discussion of authority centered more on the institutionalized rewards available to P independent of personal characteristics. Since these

---

[15] M. D. Feld, "Information and Authority: The Structure of Military Organization," *American Sociological Review*, 24 (1959), 20.

[16] Edward Shills, "Charisma, Order, and Status," *American Sociological Review*, April 1965, 199–213.

are in some sense allocated to positions, the distribution of these rewards in an organizational hierarchy has also been an important topic. What is needed now is an integration of these various facets of the relationship between O and P in a more comprehensive theory.[17]

Price[18] sets forth an inventory of propositions, illuminated by empirical research, discussing the relationship between organization effectiveness and control systems. Organizational effectiveness in this context is taken in the sense of Barnard[19] who defines it as the dispatch with which an organization achieves its goals. Note that the concept of effectiveness does not specifically include the individual's satisfaction derived from organizational participation, although such satisfactions are not excluded specifically from the concept either. It is just that if organizational control systems happen to produce high levels of participant satisfaction, this is a happy but not an inevitable consequence of their existence and implementation.

Integral with control systems are, of course, the means or techniques by which an organization exercises influence over participant behavior. Price discusses several such techniques.

1. The availability of *sanctions* to reward or punish employees is the first obvious system of control. Naturally, such means may be positive or negative, i.e., promotion versus firing. The point is that the use of positive rewards and the availability of a wide range of differing kinds of positive rewards for a manager to chose from seem to contribute substantially to organizational effectiveness.

2. Organizational effectiveness also is served better if the sanction system is *graded*. This means simply that rewards (or punishments) ought to be scaled according to the scale of contributions (or disservices) rendered by the employee.

3. Sanction systems which reward or punish on the basis of *group* performance, as opposed to individual performance, seem to result in the greatest organizational effectiveness.

4. Organizations which are designed so that their norms, policies, and standards are enforced *uniformly and impersonally* appear to have greater effectiveness.

5. Organizations which have intense communication aimed at the

---

[17] See William Pollard and Terence R. Mitchell, "A Decision Theory Analysis of Social Power," *Technical Report #71–15* (Seattle, Wash.: Organizational Research Group, University of Washington).

[18] James L. Price, *Organizational Effectiveness* (Homewood, Ill.: Irwin-Dorsey Press, 1968), chapters 5 and 6.

[19] Barnard, *Functions of the Executive,* pp. 19–20.

acculturation and socialization of employees seem to have higher degrees of effectiveness.

6. High levels of *vertical and horizontal communication* in the structure contributes more to organizational effectiveness than low degrees of such communication.

7. Organizational effectiveness is achieved better if communication flowing through its vertical and horizontal channels is *formal, contains information about job content and problems, and is transmitted face-to-face* between people who are directly concerned with task accomplishment.

The research upon which these propositions are based appears to support the more-or-less traditional techniques for organizational integration, given effectiveness as the primary goal. It is important to keep in mind that these control techniques are also means of influence. Thus, the refinement of the sanction systems and the function of communication appear to be critical to organization effectiveness.

This reinforcement of the usefulness of traditional organizational influence techniques is valuable in the light of current fashion in management theory that tends to downplay them. Nevertheless, we must be aware of the modes of organizational influence on situational contingencies. We dwell more on this point in the next chapter dealing with leadership.

chapter 14

Leadership Processes

The traditional view of leadership holds that the success or failure of a group is largely determined by the effectiveness of its leader. When a business or a military campaign is successful, it is the top manager or general who often receives the credit. When baseball or football teams have a losing season, the manager or coach is the first to go. Most organizations recognize the importance of leadership and have, therefore, devoted a great deal of time and energy to the task of identifying and developing good leaders.

Because of this practical interest and the concurrent financial commitment the research in the area of leadership is voluminous. There is plenty of evidence that when supervisors or managers are changed group morale and productivity also fluctuate.[1] The critical questions of how and in what directions these outputs will fluctuate however, have as yet been only crudely determined. We will review the approaches that have been utilized to study these questions with special emphasis on the implications of the research findings for the attainment of leadership effectiveness.

DEFINITIONAL PROBLEMS

Just what is meant by "leadership" is hard to say. Suppose that you were asked to go into an organization and select their leaders for some

---

[1] For a review of this literature, see V. Vroom, *Work and Motivation* (New York: John Wiley & Sons, Inc., 1964), chapters 3 and 4.

sort of study. Listed below are pertinent criteria which you might use:

1. Employees could be asked to point out their leader. Most people could do this without reference to any other information.
2. You could obtain the organization chart and select individuals who fill certain positions that have formal authority or power over a large set of employees.
3. Observers could view the groups on the job and select individuals based upon their fulfillment of certain functions. For example the individual who makes procedural decisions is frequently thought of as the leader.
4. Some people have suggested that the leader of the group would be the individual who has the greatest influence on the group's productivity. One could obtain this information through records, ratings, or observations.
5. You might ask employees whom they like by means of questionnaires and select the individuals that were most frequently mentioned.
6. Observations or questionnaires could determine who influences whom within the group. Leaders are often described as having power and influence over their subordinates.
7. Finally, you might inquire about the "charisma" of the various individuals; that is, who is respected and with whom do the employees identify?

All of these suggestions have been used in empirical investigations to define who is a leader. In attempting to organize these definitions it becomes apparent that they differ on three or four important dimensions. First, some of the definitions might produce more than one leader in a group. There might be two individuals who are equally liked or equally productive, for example. To have multiple leaders causes difficulties conceptually and methodologically. A second distinction can be made according to who makes the selection. In some cases the choice is based upon employee information; in other cases it can be done by observers. The question here is whether leadership must be tied to the feelings of subordinates—i.e., does he or she have to be perceived as the leader by the rest of the group? A third difference is that some definitions emphasize the personal characteristics of the individual (e.g., likable, charismatic) while others stress behavior (e.g., influential; makes decisions). Is leadership tied to personality traits or to observable behaviors? Finally, there seem to be some definitions that emphasize the willingness of the employees to be led (e.g., likability) versus the use of some other criterion (e.g., productivity).[2]

The point of this exercise was simply to show that investigators do not agree on what is meant by the term leadership. However, certain research approaches described above have been tested and found inadequate for a variety of reasons which we will discuss in our review of leadership theory and research. It will be suggested at this point that the best way to study leadership is to select those individuals who hold a specific position within the organization (this could be front-line supervisors or vice presidents) and then compare those who are high performers with low performers in terms of their traits or behaviors. Leadership then becomes the characteristics or behavioral skills of individuals in a relatively specific job and a specific setting. We will attempt to show the usefulness of this approach.

THEORY AND RESEARCH

The two main questions that intrigue most leadership researchers are the identification of who will become a leader and the ability to select those leaders that will be most effective. We will deal with both of these issues.

Leadership Emergence

Most observations of newly formed groups confirm the fact that groups exhibit certain systematic phases of development.[3] One of the early phases of development suggests that group members feel tense and competitive until the status structure and leadership pattern emerges and that groups that fail to generate such patterns frequently are unable to engage in effective task performance.[4] Thus, the emergence of a leader is central to group functioning.

Recent reviews by Hollander and Stogdill[5] discuss the general charac-

---

[2] Many of these ideas were formed through personal communication with Ivan Steiner.

[3] R. F. Bales, *Interaction Process Analysis* (Reading, Mass.: Addison-Wesley Publishing Co., Inc., 1950).

[4] B. W. Tuckman, "Developmental Sequence in Small Groups," *Psychological Bulletin*, 63 (1965), 384–99.

[5] E. P. Hollander, "Processes of Leadership Emergence," *Journal of Contemporary Business*, 3 (1974), 19–34, and R. M. Stogdill, *Handbook of Leadership* (New York: The Free Press, 1974).

teristics that are likely to distinguish leaders from followers. A number of interpersonal variables are important. First, those individuals who talk more both in terms of quantity and quality are likely to become leaders. Also, the degree to which group members are similar and compatible tends to facilitate the emergence process and the stabilization of the group structure. In general, those individuals that seem confident, speak up, and have a past history of successful influence are more likely to become leaders.

A number of group characteristics also are important. We find, for example, that as the group size increases the number of acceptable leaders *decreases*. Apparently, the larger the group the greater the demand for greater skill and competence in the leadership position. This makes sense when you consider the fact that as a group grows larger the impact of any one follower is proportionally less. Probably as one feels that their own impact decreases it becomes more important that the leader is effective.

There are also a number of studies which suggest that one's physical location in the group is important. The more central the individual is in terms of access to people and information the more likely he is to emerge as the leader. Also, individuals who take leadership positions (e.g., the chair at the head of the table) in group discussions are also likely to be chosen as leader. Thus, a number of personal interpersonal, and situation characteristics all influence who will become a leader.

Leader Effectiveness

But given that a group has a leader, how can we tell which leaders will be most effective? This is our second question and a number of major approaches have been suggested through the years.

The Trait Approach

The early research in the area of leadership contained an underlying bias that the individual was the origin of his actions.[6] Effective leadership was a function of the personal qualities of the individual, not of the situation, the technology, or the supporting cast.

Research attempting to discover the traits that are possessed by great leaders can be traced back to historians of ancient Greece or Rome

---

[6] Dorwin Cartwright and Alvin Zandar, *Group Dynamics* (New York: Harper & Row, Publishers 1968), pp. 301–18.

such as Herodotus or Tacitus. The belief is that people make the times and great successes can be attributed to the personal characteristics of the one in charge. The research that has utilized this approach has investigated two major questions: What distinguishes leaders from followers and what makes certain leaders better than others?

Hundreds of studies have been conducted on the topic with very little agreement or support for specific characteristics being generated. Reviews by Stogdill in 1948, Gibb in 1954, and Mann in 1959 with their critical evaluation of the findings effectively discouraged this approach.[7] Their findings are similar for both questions mentioned above and have been reviewed by Stogdill in his recent *Handbook of Leadership*.[8] They can be summarized as follows:

Physical Characteristics. Historical traditions would lead one to believe that effective leaders would be tall, strong, physically dominating types of individuals and the reviews by Stogdill and Mann generally support this notion but with severe qualifications. They report that a majority of the studies analyzing these variables did find leaders to be slightly heavier, taller and neater in appearance. However, the differences that are reported are very small and were not consistent over different situations. The findings for physique and health were even more confusing. In general, it appears that physical characteristics will be helpful only when they are demanded by the job. Therefore the usefulness of these characteristics as methods for differentiating leadership skills is limited.

Intellectual Factors. These factors are perhaps the most well documented as contributing to leadership status and effectiveness. Reviews of the research show that intelligence is positively correlated with these characteristics and that the relationship is fairly consistent. However, it is also not very strong. The average correlation across studies is in the low 20s. One possible interpretation of these results is that leaders are usually somewhat, but not too much, brighter than other group members.

Personality Traits. The list of personality measures that have been related to leadership effectiveness and status is very long and for the

---

[7] See R. Stogdill, "Personal Factors Associated with Leadership: A Survey of the Literature," *Journal of Psychology,* 25 (1948), 35–71. Also R. D. Mann, "A Review of the Relationships between Personality and Performance in Small Groups," *Psychological Bulletin,* 56 (1959), 241–70. Finally, see C. A. Gibb, "Leadership," in G. Lindzey, ed., *Handbook of Social Psychology,* vol. 2 (Cambridge, Mass.: Addison-Wesley Publishing Co., Inc., 1954).

[8] R. M. Stogdill, *Handbook of Leadership* (New York: The Free Press, 1974).

sake of brevity will be broken down into three categories: responsibility, sociability, and dominance. The research has generally supported the idea that leaders should be responsible, sociable, and somewhat dominant. Again, however, the findings across settings are inconsistent and those results that are reported are generally weak.

Criticisms of the Trait Approach. Clearly, the above results leave a lot to be desired. The trait approach has been highly criticized for the following reasons:

1. The trait approach dominated leadership studies prior to World War II and paralleled to some extent the methodology of the instinct theories which dominated sociology and psychology at the turn of the century. Whenever distinctive behaviors occurred that were not explained by existing traits, a new trait was posited, until it became apparent that that which included everything discriminated nothing. Traits became mere tautologies due to the fact that no independent measures of the traits were available. The strategy then turned to developing measures of these traits or personality characteristics, but this also presented problems.

2. There are a number of methodological problems with the measures which were developed to assess leadership traits. The reliability and validity coefficients of most personality tests are uniformly low (.25 — .50). Also, the concepts which are supposedly being measured are often poorly conceptualized and therefore mean different things to different people. As our knowledge about the nature of personality improves and as our techniques of measurement become more dependable, it is possible that traits will be specified which regularly distinguish leaders from followers or good leaders from poor ones. However, any empirical results supporting this approach will always be limited by the final criticism which discusses situational demands.

3. It has become apparent that the variance in performance due to leadership traits is only a very small percentage of the total variance. Many other factors such as technological equipment and facilities, along with member characteristics and situational demands are important. These variables are often situationally determined and different in different situations. It would also seem logical that different traits are more effective in different situations than are other traits.

A related fact is that the attainment of leadership status is often a function of sociological, political, or economic factors such as age, financial status, social class, or chance circumstances. More specifically, it appears that the attainment of a leadership position is influenced by personality variables to a small degree and probably much less than is believed by most laymen.[9]

In summary, then, the trait approach was confronted with many theoretical, methodological, and practical problems. And in general, across a number of situations, traits do not consistently distinguish the leaders from the followers or the good leaders from the poor ones.

The Behavior Approach

Dissatisfaction with the trait approach to leadership led to a new tactic which focused on leadership behavior. The methodological and theoretical emphasis was on reliable observations rather than internal states or traits. Leadership was viewed as the performance of those acts which helped the group achieve its preferred outcomes (e.g., improving the quality of interaction, building cohesiveness, making resources available to the group, or increasing effectiveness).

Three main schools of research have been identified with the above theoretical orientation. They will be discussed briefly, and the major methodological and substantive problems will also be reviewed.

Bales's research at Harvard has emphasized that leadership behavior may be performed by any group member; yet early in the life of a group, certain persons engage in such behavior to a greater degree than others.[10] By means of a detailed observation system, Bales observed the behavior of newly formed laboratory groups and discovered what he felt were three distinct facets of leadership behavior: activity, taskability, and likeability. In a number of studies, Bales had indicated that the individual who is both the best idea person and the best liked member is the *best* leader (i.e., has better performance).

A distinctly different approach was directed by Shartle and his co-workers at Ohio State University.[11] Their source of data on leader behavior comes from the Leader Behavior Description Questionnaire (LBDQ), a questionnaire which is distributed to group *members* and

---

[9] W. L. Warner and J. C. Abegglen, *Big Business Leaders in America* (New York: Harper & Row, Publishers, 1955).

[10] R. Bales and P. Slater, "Role Differentiation in Small Decision-Making Groups," in T. Parsons, *et al.*, eds., *Family Socialization and Interaction Process* (Glencoe, Ill.: The Free Press, 1955).

[11] C. L. Shartle, *Executive Performance and Leadership* (Columbus: Ohio State University Research Foundation, 1952). Also R. M. Stogdill and A. E. Coons, "Leader Behavior: Its Description and Measurement," *Research Monograph No. 88* (Columbus: Ohio State University, 1957).

on which the members rate how often their leader uses particular behaviors. The two main facets of leadership behavior are labeled *consideration and initiation of structure* and account for about 80 percent of the common factor variance. The work has generally been done in organizational settings and the leader who is high on both factors is generally seen as more effective than those seen as deficient in one or both of these behavior factors.

The third group includes the work of Likert and his colleagues at Michigan and is similar to that of the Ohio State group.[12] However, the information about behavior is frequently gathered from a questionnaire distributed to group *leaders*. The two main categories of leader behaviors are called *job centered* and *employee centered,* and in general the employee-centered supervisors and managers tend to have higher productivity.

Evaluation of the Behavior Approach. The finding which seems to be most agreed upon is that there are two styles of leadership: task orientation and interpersonal orientation. Although the three groups of researchers might have minor disagreements about specific behaviors, they would probably concur on the conceptual similarities of the styles. Further research by these groups has attempted to specify more clearly the styles which appear to mix the two extremes (i.e., pure task orientation versus pure interpersonal orientation) and some research has discussed ways in which these styles could be broken into more differentiated groupings for a more refined analysis.[13] The research emphasis, however, still centers on these two main styles.

There are two major problems with the behavior approach. First, the different schools of thought have used different sources to assess the leader's behavior: leaders, members, and observers. Some investigators have found that there is little agreement among different raters of an individual's behavior. Therefore, it becomes difficult to assess what the leader is actually doing. More specifically, it is hard to tell whether it is more important to know what the leader thinks he or she is doing,

---

[12] R. Likert, "An Emerging Theory of Organization, Leadership and Management," in L. Petrullo and B. Bass, eds., *Leadership and Interpersonal Behavior* (New York: Holt, Rinehart and Winston, Inc., 1961), pp. 290–309. Also R. L. Kahn and D. Katz, "Leadership Practices in Relation to Productivity and Morale," in D. Cartwright and A. Zander, eds., *Group Dynamics: Research and Theory* (New York: Harper & Row, Publishers, 1953), pp. 612–28.

[13] See R. M. Stogdill, *Manual for the Leader Behavior Description Questionnaire—Form XII.* (Columbus, Ohio: Ohio State University, Bureau of Business Research, 1963), and G. A. Yukl, "Toward a Behavior Theory of Leadership," *Organizational Behavior and Human Performance,* 6 (1971), 414–40.

how the members perceive his behavior or how nonparticipating observers categorize his acts.[14]

A second shortcoming is the lack of agreement about what sort of style is most effective. Reviews of the empirical findings show that in some cases being interpersonally oriented is related to effectiveness while others support a task-oriented style and some find that the leader who

FIGURE 14–1
Summary of Leadership Style Relationships with Satisfaction and Performance Criteria

		Considerate Style	Structuring Style
	Positive	48	14
Satisfaction	Zero	9	8
	Negative	7	11
	Positive	47	47
Productivity	Zero	32	26
	Negative	14	7

is high on both dimensions is best.[15] Figure 14–1 presents a tabulation of the research relating leadership style to performance and satisfaction.[16] The leader behaviors are divided into the person-oriented and work-oriented behaviors and perhaps the most convincing finding is that person-oriented behavior is positively related to follower satisfaction.

The relationships with productivity suggest that it is perhaps better in general to be high on one of these dimensions than to be low on them but it is not convincing as to which style is best and when it is most effective. None of the approaches takes into account the fact that varying situations require different behavior from the leader in order for him to be effective.

In summary, then, it appears that the behavior approach pointed out some important aspects of leadership. A combination of the behavior

[14] T. R. Mitchell, "The Construct Validity of Three Dimensions of Leadership Research," *Journal of Social Psychology*, 80 (1970), 89–94.

[15] A. K. Korman, "Consideration, Initiating Structure and Organizational Criteria: A Review," *Personnel Psychology*, 19 (1966), 349–63.

[16] Stogdill, *Handbook of Leadership*.

or trait approaches in conjunction with an emphasis on task and situational demands was tried next.

The Situational Approach

There are three major theories of leadership which try to combine information about the leader and the situation in which he or she finds himself. Two of these theories, Fiedler's contingency model and the path-goal theory will be discussed in more detail shortly. The other theory is known as the "open-systems" approach.

This latter theory begins by identifying and mapping the repeated cycles of input, transformation, output, and renewed input which compose the organizational pattern. Organizations are seen as being greatly entwined with the environment, and as constantly being able to change through feedback and other mechanisms.[17]

Leadership is defined as any act of influence on a matter of organizational relevance which goes beyond routine and utilized bases of power which are decreed. These acts are seen as different for different organizational levels and situations and each requires for successful use a different cognitive style, different kinds of knowledge, and different characteristics.

The theory, then, is rather broad and to date very little empirical evidence has been presented either for or against its position. The evidence that does exist seems to suggest that skills in the interpersonal area are more important at higher levels of management while a more task-oriented approach may be more applicable at lower levels. A somewhat different approach was taken by Fiedler.

THE CONTINGENCY MODEL

An extensive research program by Fiedler since 1951 resulted in the development of "The Contingency Model of Leadership Effectiveness." This model suggests that an effective leader must match his "style" with the demands of the situation. To provide support for this model it was necessary to define effectiveness, leadership style, and the situational demands. We will describe the model, the data on which it was based, validation evidence, and the implications of using such a model.[18]

---

[17] D. Katz and R. L. Kahn, *The Social Psychology of Organizations* (New York: John Wiley & Sons, Inc., 1966).

[18] Fred E. Fiedler, *A Theory of Leadership Effectiveness* (New York: McGraw-Hill Book Co., 1967).

Effectiveness. By *effective* leadership, it is meant that the leader's group has performed well, or that it has succeeded in comparison with other groups. In other words leadership effectiveness, as the term is defined here, is measured on the basis of group performance.

Leadership Style. Relationship-oriented versus task-oriented leadership styles are measured by means of the Least Preferred Co-worker Scores (LPC). The individual is asked to think of all the people with whom he or she has ever worked and then describe the Least Preferred Co-worker (or LPC) on 17 bipolar scales in the form of Osgood's Semantic Differential.[19] A favorable description of the least preferred co-worker indicates a relationship-oriented style: an unfavorable description indicates a task-oriented style of leadership.

This leadership style measure, or variants of it, has been used in a wide variety of interacting groups, ranging from high school basketball teams and surveying parties to military combat crews, research and management teams, and boards of directors. The results, however, failed to indicate that one type of leader was consistently better than another. To interpret the results it was necessary to have some sort of assessment of the situation.

Factors Determining Situational Favorableness. Fiedler has argued that the basic component of leadership is influence. That is, leadership is defined as a relationship in which one person tries to influence others in the performance of a common task. Therefore, his situational assessment consists of one underlying dimension: the degree to which the leader can influence members.

Fiedler argues that this dimension is composed of three major factors. The first and most important variable which contributes to the leader's influence is defined as the leader-member relations. In situations where these relationships are positive the leader is believed to have greater influence than where he is disliked. The second factor is the leader's formal power. The more positive and negative actions that he can use, the more influence he will have. The final factor is defined by the degree to which the task is structured or unstructured. The greater the structure, the easier it is for the leader to tell his subordinates what to do. Dichotomizing these three dimensions leads to the classification of group situations shown in Figure 14–2.

Note that this says nothing about how intrinsically difficult the task itself may be. A structured task, say building an electronic computer,

---

[19] C. E. Osgood, G. J. Suci, and P. H. Tannenbaum, *The Measurement of Meaning* (Urbana, Ill.: The University of Illinois Press, 1957).

FIGURE 14–2
A Model for the Classification of Group-Task Situations

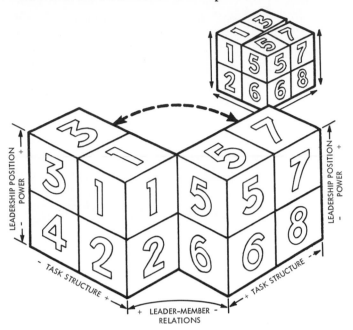

Source: *Harvard Business Review,* September–October 1965, p. 117.

may be much more difficult than an unstructured job of preparing an entertainment program. But the leader's problem of influencing the group will be greater in the volunteer committee than in the task of building a computer. It will obviously be easier to lead if you are the liked and trusted sergeant of a rifle squad (cell 1) than if you are the informal leader of a recreational basketball team (cell 2), and it will be very difficult indeed to be the disliked and distrusted leader of a volunteer group which is asked to plan the program of an annual meeting (cell 8). In other words, the cells can be ordered on the basis of how favorable or unfavorable the situation will be for the leader.

Empirical Results. Fiedler then asked what kind of leadership styles various situations required. To answer this question, the leadership style score was correlated with the performance of the leader's group in a variety of situations for which there were data (Figure 14–3).

The correlation between the leadership-style score and group performance is shown on the vertical axis of this graph. The difficulty of the situation is shown on the horizontal axis. There are over 500 different groups represented on this plot.

FIGURE 14–3

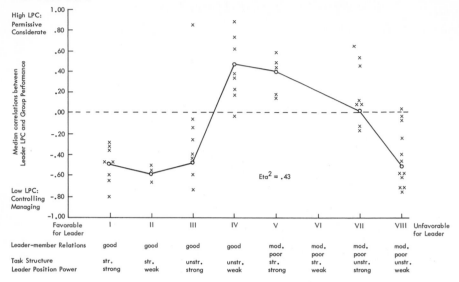

Source: *Harvard Business Review,* September–October 1965, p. 117.

What does this figure show? Positive correlations; that is, points falling above the midline of the graph, indicate that the relationship-oriented leaders performed better than did task-oriented leaders. Negative correlations, represented by points falling below the midline of the graph, indicate that the task-oriented leaders performed better than did the relationship-oriented leaders.

Taken as a whole, the plot shows that the task-oriented leaders are more effective in situations in which the leader has very little or very much influence. The relationship-oriented person is most effective in situations which are only moderately favorable for the leader. Fiedler argues that in the very easy or difficult situations, strong task-oriented leadership is needed to be effective. In situations of moderate difficulty, the leader who spends time being concerned about the interpersonal relationships in the group will be most effective.

Criticisms of the model have also appeared.[20] These critiques have

---

[20] See Terence R. Mitchell, Anthony Biglan, Gerald R. Oncken, and Fred E. Fiedler, "The Contingency Model: Criticisms and Suggestions," *Journal of the Academy of Management,* September 1970, pp. 253–67. Also Fred E. Fiedler, "Validation and Extension of the Contingency Model of Leadership Effectiveness: A Review of Empirical Findings," *Psychological Bulletin,* 76 (1971), 128–48. Also see G. Graen, D. A. Alvares, J. Orris, and J. Martella, "The Contingency Model of Leadership Effectiveness," "Antecedent and Evidential Results," *Psychological Bulletin,* 74 (1970) 285–96.

suggested the use of other personality characteristics[21] or cognitive variables[22] and proposed various ways to match these characteristics with the situation.[23] Other problems have dealt with methodological concerns[24] and alternative interpretations of the favorability dimension.[25] Clearly more research is needed but as a first step the model has been a valuable contribution to our understanding of leadership.

One recent attempt to extend the finding of the contingency model has dealt with organizational processes designed to train or rotate leaders to improve their performance.[26] The contingency model would predict that any general training or rotation experience that was similar for all the trainees would increase the effectiveness of some leaders and decrease the effectiveness of others. For example, if all the upper level managers of an organization gain interpersonal skills through sensitivity training this will in some cases make a better match between leaders and their situation and produce an equally poor match for other leaders. Stogdill's review in fact suggests that no studies have shown strong support for systematic changes in behavior and increases in performance.

The crucial point, Fiedler argues, is that the contingency model can help to predict what type of training will be most effective for different types of people in different situations. For example, a task-oriented leader in a situation of moderate favorability (where an interpersonal style is required) might profit from human relations training. If the same person was in a highly favorable situation however this type of training might decrease effectiveness. Fiedler has recently presented data from a number of studies which successfully make such differential predictions. Potentially, the theory may be very useful in dealing with some areas of leadership which have been confusing to date.

[21] A. R. Bass, F. E. Fiedler and S. Krueger. "Personality Correlates of Assumed Similarity (ASO) and Related Scores" (Urbana, Ill.: University of Illinois, Group Effectiveness Research Laboratory, 1964). Also, see M. Fishbein, Eva Landy, and Grace Hatch. "Some Determinants of an Individual's Esteem for His Least Preferred Co-Worker: An Attitudinal Analysis" (Urbana, Ill.: University of Illinois, Group Effectiveness Research Laboratory, 1965).

[22] Terence R. Mitchell, "Cognitive Complexity and Leadership Style," *Journal of Personality and Social Psychology,* 16 (1970), 166–74.

[23] U. G. Foa, T. R. Mitchell, and F. E. Fiedler, "Differentiation Matching," *Behavior Science,* 16 (1971), 130–42.

[24] Alan Posthuma, "Normative Data on the Least Preferred Co-Worker and Group Atmosphere Questionnaires," *Technical Report No. 70-8* (Seattle, Wash.: Organizational Research, 1970).

[25] G. E. O'Brien, "Group Structure and the Measurement of Potential Leader Influence," *Australian Journal of Psychology,* 21 (1969), 277–89.

[26] F. E. Fiedler, and M. M. Chemers, *Leadership and Effective Management* (Glenview, Ill.: Scott, Foresman & Company, 1974).

THE PATH-GOAL APPROACH

Another major theoretical orientation that attempts to match the leader's style with certain interpersonal and situational variables is called the path-Goal approach.[27] The major concern of the theory is how the leader's behavior is motivating or satisfying because of its impact on a subordinate's perception of his or her work and personal goals and the paths to goal attainment.

The approach has its roots in expectancy theory which was discussed earlier. An individual is supposedly motivated to work hard if (1) he believes that working hard will lead to various outcomes and (2) he highly values the outcomes. Thus a leader can influence both the type of outcomes experienced by the subordinates as well as clarify the behavior-outcome relationship.

House and Mitchell advanced a fairly complex statement of the theory and a diagram of the main relationships are presented in Figure 14–4.

FIGURE 14–4
Summary of Path-Goal Relationships

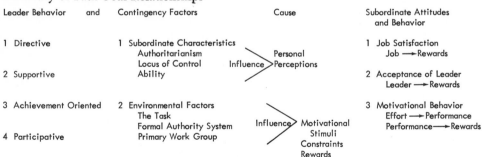

Four types of leadership styles are analyzed along with contingency factors relating to environmental factors and subordinate personality profiles. These three main factors cause various perceptions and determine the setting which eventually leads to the motivation and satisfaction of subordinates. Reviews of the empirical results to date have provided a number of interesting generalizations. For example, directive types of behavior tend to clarify path-goal relationships and lead to greater satisfaction and performance when subordinates are more authoritarian

[27] R. J. House, and T. R. Mitchell, "Path Goal Theory of Leadership," *Journal of Contemporary Business*, 3 (1974), 81–98. Also, see R. J. House, "A Path Goal Theory of Leadership Effectiveness," *Administrative Science Quarterly*, 16 (1971), 21–38.

(i.e., they like directions) and the task is fairly unstructured. However, the same style is ineffective when the task is already fairly structured or when the subordinates prefer more freedom of action. A supportive, interpersonal style appears to be most effective when the task already is fairly structured. Most subordinates are satisfied with this style in structural situations, regardless of their individual personalities. This is especially true when work conditions are stressful or frustrating. Thus the interpersonal style provides supplementary rewards while a structuring directive one clarifies paths to goals. The overall theory helps us to predict when and under what conditions different styles will be most effective.

IMPLICATIONS FOR IMPROVING LEADERSHIP PERFORMANCE

The major thrust of what has been said is not new. People differ widely in the characteristics, skills, and attitudes they bring to a job. It is also true that the kinds of jobs that exist are numerous. With such variability in people and work settings some sort of matching procedure is necessary. Clearly the optimum strategy would be to place people in positions that would maximize their potential and society's needs. Attempts to implement these ideas have major implications for the areas of personnel selection and training.

Selection

Traditionally, psychologists have used a rather simple model of selection. Dunnette points out that "this model has sought to link *predictors* (that is, various measures of individual differences) directly with so-called *criteria* (that is, various measures of organizational consequences or job "success") through a simple index or relationship, the correlation coefficient. This traditional validation model directed that persons on any given job be divided on some global measure (such as sales volume, overall rating of "success," or potential for promotion) into successes and failures and that they be compared on test scores, biographical information, or any other personal measurements available."[28] Such an approach overlooks at least two major considerations. First, numerous behavioral styles might be used to acquire success, some of which would

---

[28] Marvin D. Dunnette, *Personnel Selection and Placement* (Belmont, Calif.: Wadsworth Publishing Co., 1966), p. 104.

be more in line with the position of company policy. That is, two sales representatives might have equally good sales records but one might be diligent, courteous, and highly motivated while the other might practice various forms of deception. A second problem is that certain characteristics might be helpful in most situations but not in all. There are data, for example, which show that hiring bright people for certain kinds of routine jobs leads to a high level of turnover. Yet, it would be hard to convince an employer to hire the applicant who is not as bright as another, equally qualified candidate.[29] The result of this process is that most selection devices correlate with performance at best in the 20s and low 30s.

What is needed is a thorough analysis of the jobs and the behaviors required to be successful on that job. Various selection techniques can be used to determine what types of people are most likely to display these behaviors. Such a model has been suggested by Dunnette and is presented in Figure 14–5. Some recent research using this approach

FIGURE 14–5
A Model for Test Validation and Selection Research

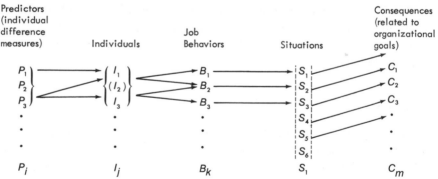

Source: Marvin D. Dunnette, *Personnel Selection and Placement* (Belmont, Calif.: Wadsworth Publishing Co., 1966), p. 105.

has been completed. Dunnette discusses research with managers at Standard Oil, with a small electrical goods company, with district marketing managers and with Farmer Mutual Reinsurance Company.[30] All of these studies showed support for the model. However, it is also true that

---

[29] Marian Bills, "Relation of Mental Alertness Test Scores to Positions and Permancy in Company," *Journal of Applied Psychology*, 7 (1923), 154–56.

[30] Dunnette, *Personnel Selection.*

people and jobs change over time and people frequently change positions. To match people with positions when both might change has implications for training.

Organizational Training

Our review of the training literature is presented in Chapter 17 so we will not discuss this topic in detail. The findings suggest, however, that very few training programs have been shown to change systematically the behavior or increase the effectiveness of managers. It should be made clear that this summary statement is only applicable to those programs aiming at attitudinal and interpersonal changes.

After our review of the leadership literature the reasons for this lack of positive findings should be more clear. Some styles are good in some situations and not in others. Assuming that changes can be made through training, then making everyone more interpersonally oriented simply makes some people more effective and some people less effective depending upon the situation. To train people without knowledge of what they are being trained for is probably unwise.

The above assumption that major changes in interpersonal styles can be induced through training is tenuous and therefore leads us to a second possible solution. Rather than changing people to fit the situation, why not train people to change the situation? More specifically, if a manager is task oriented, it might be easier to train him to make the situation fit his style rather than the reverse.

Through selection devices groups can be made more or less harmonious. A manager can be given more or less power and he or she probably can determine to some extent the environment wherein he might be able to avoid a mismatch between personal style and work setting.

One clear implication is that we must gain more knowledge about the effects of structural change on attitudes and behavior. Lawrence and Lorsch's data as well as their treatment of a "Contingency Theory of Organization" reviews the research in this area.[31] Most of this research, however, covers very broad structural topics and little insight is provided as to how individual leaders could manipulate their specific environment in optimal ways.

In summary, the empirical findings on the area of leadership suggest that styles of personal characteristics must be matched to the situation.

---

[31] Paul R. Lawrence and Jay W. Lorsch, *Organization and Environment* (Homewood, Ill.: Richard D. Irwin, Inc., 1969), pp. 187–203.

Three ways to attain this match are through (1) selection techniques tied to the job requirements, (2) training managers to change their leadership styles, and (3) training managers to change the situation to match their style. Based upon past results it is suggested that the first and third strategies may hold more promise than the second alternative which is based on more traditionally held ideas of training philosophy.

chapter 15

Technological Processes

W e began our discussion of organization theory by labeling rationality as *the* pivotal concept. We do not intend to reopen this subject here, other than to say that rationality has grown to mean, in both elementary and advanced discourse in organization theory, *productive efficiency*. Technical rationality is a form of practical reason in management. *Its chief characteristic is the selection of means to accomplish ends most efficiently by the method of scientific verification.* Hence, technical rationality is almost exclusively devoted to the discovery of means, or to the elaboration of techniques; *it is not particularly applicable to the discovery or elaboration of ends.* Thus:

> Organizations that achieve their ends efficiently are functionally rational; decisions leading to efficient goal achievement are substantially rational. A technically rational organization is one in which each expenditure of energy or other material makes a maximum contribution to a productive sequence, culminating in a given goal. A technically rational decision is one in which each step of a productive sequence is chosen because it is the best fitted to move the sequence along to a given goal.[1]

Since the Industrial Revolution, the main, if not the exclusive, concern of administrative organizations has been with production or output of material goods and services. Thus organization theory and research in organizations have taken the technical rationality of these systems as

[1] Paul Diesing, *Reason in Society* (Urbana: University of Illinois Press, 1962), pp. 9–10.

a given, either explicitly or implicitly. More generally, technological progress—the discovery of improved means for increasing productivity—is a powerful social value in industrially advanced nations. The economic systems of these nations are geared to reward those organizations, and their managers for successful quests of technical rationality.

The reason why organization theory is intimately involved with technological processes is evident. The organization structure is one means for advancing productive efficiency. A functionally rational organization promotes technical rationality; it does not impede it. While this observation is a truism, its implications for organization theory and research have not been clearly perceived by scholars until fairly recently. The proposition that technological change precedes structural change—or alternatively, that technology is an independent variable and structure is a dependent variable—has received its just prominence only within the last 14 years. It is appropriate to investigate some of the leading models used by scholars in their analysis of technology.

TECHNOLOGICAL TYPOLOGIES

One cannot help but be struck by the fact that many scholars whose work has been done in the area of technology and organization have their "feet mostly in a manufacturing reality." In other words the kinds of organizations studied with greatest frequency were manufacturing firms. This is a limitation to the usefulness of theoretical models. For example we cannot say whether or not Woodward's classification of technology into unit, batch, and process systems is applicable also to nonmanufacturing organization such as hospitals, libraries, banks insurance companies, or government agencies.

In spite of these difficulties, it is fruitful to review the various descriptions of technological systems for two reasons: (1) manufacturing is still the focal activity of industrial nations, and (2) research in their technological processes may provide valuable conceptual clues for the analysis of the technologies of nonmanufacturing organizations.

The Thompson Model[2]

We begin with Thompson's model because his classification of technical systems is not bound exclusively to a manufacturing setting. He

---

[2] See James D. Thompson, *Organizations in Action* (New York: McGraw-Hill Book Company, 1967), chapter 2.

suggests three types of technology: long-linked, mediating, and intensive.

·Long-Linked. Long-linked technology is the kind found most often in mass-production, fabricating industries, such as the automobile industry or the appliance industry. As Thompson observes, this system of technology is based upon the "serial interdependence" of tasks necessary to the completion of a product. For example, a steering wheel can only be put on a car after the steering column is in place. More generally, the performance of task D depends upon task C being completed first, and it upon B, and so on. Thus, long-linked technology requires the sequential performance of a large number of interrelated tasks. Such a system is illustrated in Figure 15–1.

FIGURE 15–1
Long-Linked Technology

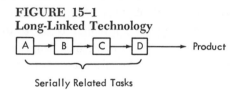

Serially Related Tasks

Mediating Technology. Mediating technologies are found in organizations that provide a linking service between customers or clients. Freight companies are good examples of such organizations since they offer the link of transportation between a shipper and a receiver of merchandise. Banks and savings and loan associations tie depositors and borrowers together. Insurance companies offer a service link for pooling risks of underwriters. Advertising agencies sell time or space, bringing advertising clients together with media owners or management.

There are multitudes of organizations offering a mediating technology to clients. Their general form is shown in Figure 15–2. With growth

FIGURE 15–2
Mediating
Technology

of service organizations such as these, the practice of mediating technology is increasing rapidly. One consequence has been the explosion of paper work, causing many service-type organizations to introduce new information processing technologies.

These technologies have had differing impacts upon structure. In some instances, however, organizations that are nominally mediating such as gigantic insurance companies or credit companies, have become analogous in the way they handle their paper work to the way manufacturing firms mass-produce products. Thus, such organizations may depart in a technological sense only superficially from their manufacturing counterparts.

Intensive Technology. The focusing of a wide variety of skills and specializations upon a single client is the characteristic of an organization using an intensive technology. The hospital is an example of this sort of an organization. The general contracting firm in the construction industry is another such example. Figure 15–3 illustrates intensive technology.

FIGURE 15–3
Intensive Technology

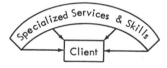

Intensive technology seems particularly conducive to a project design organization, in the sense that for a "case" or a building the appropriate skills needed can be identified and mustered at the strategic time.

The Galbraith Model[3]

Unlike Thompson's, Galbraith's view of technology is drawn almost exclusively from the manufacturing side of the large corporation. Galbraith describes the following imperatives of this type of an organization.

1. Long time span between the start and completion of a task.
2. Large investment commitment to capital equipment and plant.
3. Corresponding inflexibility of the organization in relation to its investment in fixed resources.

[3] See John Kenneth Galbraith, *The New Industrial State* (Boston: Houghton Mifflin Company, 1967), chapter 2.

4. Specialization of the work force.
5. Bureaucratization.
6. Long-range planning.

Galbraith's opinion is that technology has placed the above imperatives on corporations. These imperatives are such that large manufacturing organizations are required to do intensive long-range planning. Because of the vast economic and political power of the gigantic corporation, these plans have the force of self-fulfilling prophecies. Thus, a corporate commitment to a particular strategy, policy, or product means that it will be carried through to the public without its expression of acceptance or rejection in the marketplace or halls of government.

The Woodward Model[4]

Joan Woodward is largely responsible for the regeneration of interest in technology as a vital element in organization theory. We will have more to say about her work in the next section. For now we will just describe her model of technology. Woodward, like Galbraith, draws exclusively upon the manufacturing environment for the classification of technology. She identifies three types of manufacturing, each with its own technological system.

1. Process Production System. Organizations falling in this category are in what is commonly called continuous manufacturing industries. Included are petroleum refineries and producers of chemicals. The makers of highly standardized goods such as tennis balls, flashlight batteries, and some electronic components frequently are also part of this overall category.

Typical of process manufacturers is production in anticipation of demand, rather than in direct response to customer order. Paralleling anticipatory production is making goods to inventory so that production can be maintained at a fairly constant level over a substantial period of time. The product itself is made uniformly to a standard. The length of the production run is relatively long and the lot sizes manufactured are relatively large.

Process technology lends itself to mechanization or automation. Consequently, there is a high degree of capital-labor substitution in these industries, whereby labor costs represent a relatively small proportion of the total cost of the product manufactured.

---

[4] See Joan Woodward, *Industrial Organization: Theory and Practice* (London: Oxford University Press, 1965), chapter 3.

2. Unit and Small-Batch Production System. This category is often called job-order manufacturing. In the broadest sense, this production system allows a manufacturing organization to customize a product for the buyer. The characteristics of job-order manufacturing are almost exactly the opposite of process manufacturing. The products are heterogeneous, varying according to different customer specifications. Production is undertaken only as a result of demand—specifically, the receipt of an order. Products are not manufactured to inventory. Production runs are relatively short, and the lot sizes are small. The nature of the technology is largely nonrepetitive. And labor cost represents a fairly high proportion of total costs for a product.

Some examples of firms in job-order manufacturing may be found in the machine-tool industry, the construction industry, and in the electronics industry where an organization might be making exotic components for a missile guidance system.

3. Large-Batch Production System. This type of manufacturing is a hybrid of job order and continuous. Sometimes called intermittent manufacturing, it is the commonest in American industry since its technology embraces nearly all mass-production assembly firms. The most refined examples of this technology are found in the automotive industry.

In large-batch production systems the manufacturing of the components of a particular product are made for inventory, although the final product can be assembled to reflect different component combinations specified by the customer. For example, an automobile dealer can request the color, body style, and equipment he needs to fill the order of a customer. Each dealer order accompanies the car through the assembly process. Thus, the car is "made to order" by putting together a certain combination of components selected from a wide variety of standardized options.

Therefore, in large-batch manufacturing parts are usually produced on a continuous, repetitive basis for inventory. The finished product, however, is not produced to inventory. Typically batch production is in part in response to customer demand and in part in anticipation of demand. The finished product is heterogeneous, but it is heterogeneous within a range of standardized options established by the manufacturer.

All in all, the large-batch manufacturer has a number of complex technological problems to solve, including scheduling, forecasting demands, coordination of production activities, and balancing inventories.

Within the large-batch category fall most of the durable consumer goods manufacturers in American industry.

The Technological Process

In its rudimentary form the technological process is nothing more than the methods used to obtain a result.[5] As we have suggested above, the methods used by organizations will differ depending upon the nature of the industry in which a manufacturing firm is doing business. The technological processes for firms in large-batch production are substantially different from firms in job-order manufacturing. Likewise, the technologies used by nonmanufacturing organizations in mediating service industries or intensive health and welfare undertakings will also be variegated. Thus, on the level of *technical operations* the range of technical practices in organizations is so broad that it is nearly impossible to come to know them all.

However, this kind of knowledge is not particularly important for our purposes. Fortunately we are able to observe certain generalizable aspects of the technological process that have strong normative, theoretical, and organizational implications.

First, technical rationality has become practically synonymous with efficiency. Thus, organizations, although they are nonmanufacturing, or nonprofit for that matter, frequently use efficiency counters to keep score in the game of organizational effectiveness. So pervasive is efficiency that it supplies the *normative criteria* by which managers of organizations are measured. Such is the case, even though they do not run conventional business firms to which these standards traditionally have applied.

Second, technological processes in the name of progress create incentives for managers of all kinds of organizations to quest better and better means for improving the effectiveness of their undertakings, but always within the boundaries of the normative criteria of productive efficiency. To suggest to many university administrators, for example, that the interests of learning might be advanced further with less emphasis on the efficiency of their organizations is to voice virtual heresy in their estimation.

The endless search for improved means to achieve instrumental

---

[5] Jacques Ellul, *The Technological Society* (New York: Alfred A. Knopf, Inc., 1965), p. 19.

ends—building cars, getting educated, curing the sick, prosecuting wars, burying the dead—have tended to blind managers and theorists to crucial philosophical problems of humans and society. While we grant Diesing's point, that technical rationality is the exercise of practical reason, we believe that more is needed now from practitioners and theoreticians than simply the perfection of means to create more goods and better services. Pressing upon us with urgency are theoretical issues concerning the nature of humans in organizations, the appropriate character of social goals, and the relationship between people and their environment. These are not subjects peculiarly susceptible to examination by practical reason alone. More is said about this in the last section of this chapter.

Third, technological processes have the property of determining the nature of organizational structure and organizational behavior. While our understanding of the influence of technology on structure and behavior is rudimentary at present, some attempts to illuminate these matters have been made. The relationship between structure and technology is in some respects a question in theory. But in a larger part, it is an empirical question, that must be approached through research. In the next section we discuss several selected studies pertaining to this aspect of technological processes.

SOCIOTECHNICAL SYSTEMS

The expansion of research literature concerning interrelations among technology, structure, and behavior is impressive.[6] Since the early 1960s it has been popular to label this type of inquiry as research in sociotechnical systems. A sociotechnical system is one in which the rational impersonal processes of technology interact with human factors such as (1) work behavior and attitudes, (2) small-group organization, and (3) formal organization structure.

Given such a broad definition it is evident that the great proportion of research in the behavioral sciences could be slotted into one or more of these three categories. Certainly the research associated with the human relations movement seems to fit the requisites for study of sociotechnical systems. However, a large proportion of human relations and behavioral science research lacks a focus on work and the technology surrounding work. Guest points out:

---

[6] For an excellent review article summarizing the research literature, see Raymond G. Hunt, "Technology and Organization," *Academy of Management Journal*, September 1970, pp. 235–52.

> . . . the social scientist often makes the error of concentrating on human motivation and group behavior without fully accounting for the technical environment which circumscribes, even determines, the roles which the actors play. Motivation, group structure, interaction process, authority—none of these abstractions of behavior takes place in a technological vacuum.[7]

Further, as both Hunt and Guest emphasize, research in sociotechnical systems has at its nucleus a concern with the practical problems of organization design. This action orientation is stressed by Guest in the introduction to his book when he says, "This is a study of a patient who was acutely ill and who became extremely healthy. The 'patient' was not a Man but a Management, the management of a large, complex industrial organization."[8]

Thus, research in sociotechnical systems has three qualities that distinguish it from other kinds of behavioral studies: (1) the reinstatement of technological, as well as behavioral and structural variables in the study of organizations, (2) the use of research and consultancy methods to design the human and technological relationships in organizations, and (3) a commitment to action by consultants and management with the objective of redesigning organizations to cope with change.

A great deal of this type of research has been concentrated in three groups. While by no means inclusive of all the studies that have been done, the Yale Technology Project, the Tavistock Studies, and the work of Joan Woodward and her followers, represent a fair sampling of the research on sociotechnical systems.

The Yale Technology Project

It is fair to say that the Yale Technology Project had as its main concern the welfare of the individual worker in confrontation with the leviathan of mass-production technology. The studies that grew out of this project covered a period from approximately 1950 to 1960. These are among the earliest of the kind of research investigating relationships among men, machines, and technological processes. The Yale Project, conducted under the leadership of Charles R. Walker was almost anthropological in research design. The researchers studied mainly the

---

[7] Robert H. Guest, *Organizational Change: The Effect of Successful Leadership* (Homewood, Ill.: Irwin-Dorsey Press, 1962), p. 4.

[8] Ibid., p. 1.

attitudes and feelings of factory workers toward their jobs and the organizational technology in which they labored.[9]

The delineation of the technological environment was rather crude in these studies. The environment often selected for research had a mass-production, assembly-line technology. In Thompson's classification, it was a long-line technology, or in Woodward's a batch technology. In any event, the workers studied generally had low skills, did relatively simple repetitive jobs, and were paced in their work by machines or conveyor systems.

Frequently, the researchers used the interview method to gather data on workers' sentiments toward jobs, their chances for promotion, or the desirability of leaving their present job and moving to another company. They used the same techniques to get information about various kinds of interactional behaviors as who talks to whom, who initiates job action, feelings toward the union and union leadership, feelings toward management, and so on. Sometimes the interview data were paired with statistical data, such as absenteeism and job turnover rates.

While such research does not lend itself to forming generalizable propositions, especially since this work has not been widely replicated, it does have the quality of giving a "feeling" for the situation of people engaged in a dehumanized technological process such as that found in a mass-production industry. Words stemming from the interviews of workers such as "lonely, scared, cog in a wheel, being trapped, pressure for output, dead-end job, exhaustion, tension" express the alienation and hopelessness surrounding work in a mass-production technology.

Further Walker and Guest found that by scaling the degrees of: (1) repetitiveness of work, (2) mechanical pacing of work, (3) the skill required to do the work, (4) the frequency of breaks in job routine, (5) the frequency of social interaction, and (6) the size of the interacting group they could establish a index of mass-production technology. They discovered that the higher the index, or the more intensive the application of mass-production principles, the higher also were the rates of job turnover and absenteeism. In other words, turnover and absenteeism were behaviors directly related to the degree of mass-production technology present in a job.[10]

---

[9] Extracts of these studies may be found in Charles R. Walker, *Modern Technology and Civilization* (New York: McGraw-Hill Book Company, 1962), pp. 96–134. The research methods used in these studies is reminiscent of some of Whyte's work; see, for example, William F. Whyte, *Men at Work* (Homewood, Ill.: Irwin-Dorsey Press, 1961). A recent example of this approach is Studs Turkel, *Working* (New York: Pantheon Books, 1974).

[10] This study is extracted in Walker, *Modern Technology*, pp. 104–9.

Out of the Yale Studies came action recommendations that are familiar in present management literature and practice. One such recommendation—job enlargement—is discussed later in this book. These recommendations, that also include worker control over job pacing, variation in job assignments, and participation in job decisions, required not so much total organizational modification, as they involved redesign of the job itself.

The purposes of job change were to increase worker discretion, reduce monotony and repetitiveness, increase worker control over the immediate job environment, and increase interaction with other workers in order to reduce feelings of loneliness and anonymity. Part of the motivation behind making these job changes was to increase worker productivity and reduce labor cost. However, this was not the entire rationale, since many humanist researchers at this time believed that factory work was demeaning. While vestiges of this attitude still prevail among modern behavioral scientists and action-oriented change agents,[11] the plight of the factory worker is less a *cause célèbre* than it was 15 or more years ago. Because of this decline in fashionableness and because of the advent of more advanced behavioral research techniques, the Technology Project has fallen into obscurity. Nevertheless it must be recognized as a landmark of research into sociotechnical systems.

The Tavistock Institute of Human Relations

Around the same period as the Yale Technology Project was active in the United States, the Tavistock Institute in Great Britain was sponsoring a number of studies of the social consequences of technological change. While the Yale Project was primarily focused on the effect of technology on the individual worker, the Tavistock studies were oriented toward the impact of technology on social organization, both on the small-group level and the larger formal organizational level. We discuss in this section two early Tavistock studies which have become "classics" of their type of research.

Technological Change in Coal Mining.[12] The coal mining industry in England underwent massive technological change following World

---

[11] For example, consider the Argyris-Simon Discussion, Chris Argyris, "Some Limits of Rational Man in Organization Theory," *Public Administration Review*, May/June 1973. Herbert Simon, "Organization Man: Rational or Self-Actualizing," *Public Administration Review*, July/August 1973, and Argyris' "Reply" in the same issue.

[12] The full account of this study including all the technical information may be found in E. L. Trist and K. W. Bamforth, "Some Social and Psychological Consequences of the Longwall Method of Coal-Getting," *Human Relations*, vol. 4, No. 1 (1951), pp. 3–38.

War II. These changes were not without their social influences as Trist and Bamforth reported.

Before the introduction of the longwall, mass-production techniques of coal getting, the mining technology was largely a handicraft undertaking. Typically, two miners worked the coal face as a team, supported by one or two other people who moved the coal from where it was taken to a spot in the mine shaft from where it would be hoisted to the surface. These groups tended to become highly cohesive autonomous teams. The handicraft mining technology required great individual skill, resourcefulness, and independence. At the same time, the team provided a good many social satisfactions to its members. Thus the social and task structure, that had evolved in mining for many years prior to mechanization, created as Trist and Bamforth put it, "a dynamically interrelated system that permitted enduring social balance."[13]

The introduction of mass-production technology changed all this. Whereas the two-man team worked on what was called a short-face segment of the mine, the new production techniques allowed longwall methods to be applied. That is, machinery was developed that would gouge out vast lengths of a coal seam, and then automatically convey the coal to a central location in the mine where it could be moved to the top. Right at the start this change in technique destroyed the old patterns of social relationships. Further, it reduced the level of skill required, eliminated the entrepreneurial character of the mining operation at the coal face, and finally ruptured the social balance that had been functioning for centuries in the mining industry and the mining communities.

New jobs associated with the new technology emerged, necessitating the evolution of new sets of task and human interdependencies in the mining process. The overall technological activity was far more complex than the old. But new forms of social organization to replace those that had been disrupted or destroyed did not come immediately with the new technology.

Consequently a period of adjustment followed wherein the miners exhibited behavior associated with workers in typical mass-production technology. Without the support of their traditional work groups, and without the confidence of their old skills, the workers began to behave dysfunctionally. Informal organizations appeared, but they did not completely satisfy the absence of the old two-man team. In fact some of these groups acted antisocially with respect to other groups and indi-

---

[13] Ibid., p. 8.

viduals who were isolated from group membership. Also "reactive individualism" appeared to replace the old entrepreneurship of the miners. Such practices involved "deception and intrigue" which pitted one miner against another or the development of practices by miners to "beat the system." Additionally, abdication of work responsibility and absenteeism appeared as miners reacted against the new technology.

In their report Trist and Bamforth observe that in some experimental situations during the transition period these dysfunctional results of technological change were offset by innovations in organizational design. These innovations were aimed at integrating workers and roles that had been highly differentiated by the new mining technology. In cases where experimentation with social planning for integration occurred greater social cohesion resulted along with reduction of absenteeism and destructive competitiveness.

The Ahmedabad Experiments in the Textile Industry.[14] Rice, in his book, discusses his work with an Indian textile firm in the mid-1950s. Part of his assignment was the reorganization of the looming processes, which like the coal mining processes, had been handicraft. With the introduction of automatic equipment, the traditional patterns of social organization underwent enormous change. The task was to build new forms of association to replace those that had been disrupted by technology.

However, Rice's report goes far beyond the redesign of the social climate on the manufacturing floor. It discusses the renovation of the entire organization from top management down. Rice's work was among the first examples of organizational development, and it grew out of recognition of the fact that technological change is not a localized phenomenon. Successful adaptation to change has to involve the entire organization. Management needs to be educated to new patterns of organizational design and leadership behavior. The organization itself has to be restructured in ways to permit flexibility.

From Rice's research and experience in the sociotechnical systems of the textile firm came the first statement of organizations as open systems—a statement based on empirically gathered evidence. This concept has become a leading idea in organization theory, an idea which we examine in work of Burns and Stalker.[15]

---

[14] See A. K. Rice, *The Enterprise and Its Environment* (London: Tavistock Publications, 1963).

[15] See Tom Burns and G. M. Stalker, *The Management of Innovation* (London: Tavistock Publications, 1961).

Innovation and Change in Sociotechnical Systems. With a background of research and consulting experience with the Scottish and British electronics industry, Burns and Stalker announced an approach to the analysis of organizations that became a lasting construct in organization theory. The electronics industry underwent dramatic changes in the years following World War II. These changes were the result of a technological explosion in the electronics field. For a firm in this industry, adaptation to change meant the difference between success or failure. Partly success of a firm dependent upon scientific and engineering innovation; and while these innovations were mandatory, a management climate and an organizational system designed to foster innovation was also essential. The vitality of a firm depended as much on social and administrative innovation as it did upon technical discovery.

The problem, on the behavioral side, is one of determining those management and organizational characteristics that facilitate adaptation. In responding to this problem, Burns and Stalker, stated their well-known classification of managerial style—the mechanistic and organic systems.

The mechanistic organization, which seems suitable for stable environmental conditions, parallels the formal bureaucratic model of organization. The organic organization, which is similar to Rice's open system, seems the better equipped to adapt to a turbulent environment.

Because of its flexibility and its lack of dependence upon a rigid hierarchy, the organic organization is able to make exchanges with its environment more effectively than the mechanistic system. Environmental exchange is the essence of adaptability for living systems, as it is for organic organizations.

Thus, the task of social consultant is to recommend to management of organizations in turbulent settings new types of organizational strategies that will make their organizations more flexible. A few of the many recommendations suggested by Burns and Stalker include:

1. Emphasis on functional expertise.
2. De-emphasis of hierarchy.
3. Encouragement of lateral organizational communication.
4. Discouragement of vertical communication.
5. Communication content should stress information and advice.
6. Communication content should de-emphasize instructions and decision.

7. The ad hoc centers of authority should be around technical expertise rather than around nominal positions of authority in hierarchy.[16]

These, and other recommendations made by Burns and Stalker, have been largely accepted by action-oriented behavioral scientists and incorporated into their programs for organizational change.

In summary the amount of influence Tavistock has had on organization theory is considerable. Its work on sociotechnical systems, and the strategies of social consultancy is pioneering. Joan Woodward's research is also of this nature.

THE HUMAN RELATIONS RESEARCH UNIT

The original studies which culminated in the book, *Industrial Organization: Theory and Practice*[17] were conducted by Joan Woodward and her colleagues at the Human Relations Research Unit of the South East Essex College of Technology in England. These studies, begun around 1954, were specifically related to the effect of technology upon organization structure, differing from the Yale and Tavistock studies that largely were concerned with the impact of technology on the individual and the small group.

We have described Woodward's unit, batch, and process classes of technology. These were the classificatory basis for her comparative analysis of structural differences among manufacturing firms. Assuming that these technologies represent an ascending scale of complexity, Woodward found direct connections between them and certain structural variables along the following dimensions.

1. Firms in process industries tended to use top policy committees for decision making more frequently than firms in unit or batch industries. Thus in a process technology, the chief executive acted as a committee chairman rather than as a unilateral decision maker.

2. A linear relationship was found between the complexity of the technology and the number of levels of management in an organization. In direct production activities, unit manufacturers had fewer levels in the management hierarchy. Process manufacturers had the most levels, with batch firms in between.

3. The span of control tended to be wider for unit producers and narrower for process producers. This causes a tall pyramidal shape for

---

[16] Ibid., pp. 121–22.

[17] Woodward, *Industrial Organization*.

process organizational structure and a flat shape for unit organizations. While the number of workers controlled in batch industries was large, this did not necessarily result in a wide span of control producing greater freedom for workers. Actually the *effective* span of control in batch industries is quite narrow, since the supervisor is supported by automatic control systems built into the production process and by a large number of staff support groups that exercise control authority of line-production workers.

4. Not surprisingly, labor costs as a percentage of total costs was smaller in process technologies as compared to batch and unit systems. The relationship was on the order of 12.5 percent of total cost for process technologies compared to 26 percent for batch and unit.

5. The ratio between management and nonmanagement personnel is interesting. In process production firms the ratio was 1:8; while in batch production it was 1:16, and in unit, 1:23.

6. Also as the complexity of technology rises, the ratio of indirect to direct workers increases. The "burden" of administrative and clerical workers grows in relation to production workers, Woodward found, as one moves from unit to process technolgy.

Probably one of the most intriguing findings reported by Woodward is what she calls, "similarity at the extremes." On the one hand, along several important organizational parameters—numbers of employees controlled by first-line supervisors, skill levels of workers and management, and the use of organic management systems—unit and process firms seemed to have similar structural characteristics. On the other hand, batch manufacturers—typical of mass-production technology—appeared to have many of the features of mechanistic systems, such as elaborate production control techniques, separation of structure into line and staff functions, low skill of production workers, the use of many specialists in a variety of control activities, and a proliferation of written orders, rules, and memoranda.

Woodward's findings are strongly suggestive of the fact that the nature of structure and the style of management depend upon the technological character of the industry in which a firm is engaged. This generalization is challenged by Hickson, et al. whose research indicates that size of the organization may be a more important determinant of technological effect on structure than Woodward's studies show.[18] The

---

[18] See David J. Hickson, D. S. Pugh, and Diana C. Pheysey, "Operations Technology and Organization Structure: An Empirical Reappraisal," *Administrative Science Quarterly,* September 1969, pp. 378–97.

structural impact of technology is likely to be more dramatic on smaller organizations. Larger organizations seem to be better able to absorb technological change without significant structural modifications.

With their sights on technology, action research, and change, the people associated with the study of sociotechnical systems have made an enormous contribution to organization theory. Modern societies are desperately trying to solve problems of human dislocation spawned by technological change. Technological problems have been fostered by organizations. That their solutions will be a product of organizational effort is an inevitable conclusion. All this makes the juncture between organization theory and technology that much more important. We consider next some of the wider implications of the technological process.

TECHNOLOGICAL ASSESSMENT

Sterling M. McMurrin pointed out that two kinds of people live in a technological society—the technophiles and the technophobes.[19] The technophiles admire technology for its wonders, because it, and virtually it alone, has made possible the material advantages enjoyed by a very large proportion of the earth's population, while most of those who do not have technological advantages measure their deprivation in terms of it. The technophobes fear technology, believing it to lodge the ultimate danger to mankind. Its products of war, and its drain on the world's resources and environment threaten to destroy humans at the very moment they luxuriate in the material pleasures of their technological surroundings.

The technophiles and the technophobes both have impressive cases to offer. The former think that the solution to humanity's problems—famine, disease, overpopulation, indeed even nuclear warfare—is continuous expansion of technology. The latter find hope only in the reversal of technological development, in the gearing down of the technological machine and the returning to a simpler life of material asceticism. Neither case, in the extreme, is particularly realistic nor desirable. Callahan argues that the likelihood of our becoming less a technological society is remote, while, at the same time, there has to be upper limits beyond which technological development should not be pushed.[20]

---

[19] Sterling M. McMurrin, "The Quality of Life in a Quantitative Society," *Conference Board Record*, January 1968, pp. 2–4.

[20] Daniel Callahan, *The Tyranny of Survival* (New York: The Macmillan Company, 1973).

The difficulty lies in establishing limits, because our understanding of the impact of technology on society is meager. It has been just within recent years that some attempts have been made to sketch the outlines of the problem through technological assessment. While they are by no means exhaustive, three levels of technological assessment are emerging—the first pertains to technology and rational management decision making, the second involves technology and public policy, and the third includes the vague, but crucial, considerations of technology and social values.

Technology and Rational Management Decision Making

This level of technological assessment is an extension of the rationality paradigm into the domain of technological forecasting. Its objective is to assess the effect of technological change upon managerial strategy, with the ultimate purpose of providing guidelines for better utilization of technology. Roman observes that, "The real innovation [in technological assessment] is in the decision process on how technological development might best be exploited."[21] In order to conduct such a rational assessment of technology, Roman proposes a model showing a multitude of factors influencing the management decision process. The model, illustrated in Figure 15–4, indicates the contingency factors that have to be weighed in the appraisal of technology.

Essentially the process of technological assessment at the management decision level is the rational calculation of the impact of technological change, and the accounting for the primary, secondary, and tertiary effects of such change on the organization and also on its external environment. In some respects, there is really nothing new in the form of assessment. Management has always been interested in the subjects of technological feasibility, efficiency, and profitability. However, what is new in this approach is the concern for the wider social, economic, and environmental effects of technological development. Evidence of this interest is reflected in various aspects of public policy as a result of heightened citizen awareness of technological change.

Technology and Public Policy

We are familiar with agencies such as the EPA which attempts to control the extent of damage that the use of technology does to the

---

[21] Daniel D. Roman, "Technology Assessment: Perspective from the Managerial Position," *Public Administration Review*, September/October 1973, p. 394.

FIGURE 15–4
Technology Assessment Model

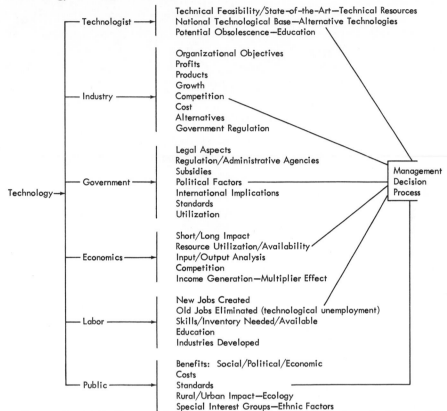

Source: Daniel D. Roman, "Technology Assessment: Perspective from the Managerial Position," *Public Administration Review,* September/October 1973, p. 397. Used with permission.

environment. Standards regulating the emission of pollutants from automobiles is a case in point; the imposition of building codes for the Alaska pipeline on federal land is another example. Lesser known, at the federal level, is the Office of Technology Assessment (OTA) which was established in 1972, with the responsibility for researching technology related problems. One objective of the Technology Assessment Act is to provide Congress with information about developments in the physical, biological, behavioral, and social sciences so that informed legislation could be offered for the regulation, support, and management of scientific innovations.

While the mandate of the OTA is far from clear, and while its field of responsibility is not well defined, the probability is high that it will operate from a model of decision making closely approximating the rational model described previously. The OTA will be subject to the same kinds of pressures for technical rationality as are imposed upon other types of managerial systems.

One possible exception raised by Kloman is that a practical format of citizen participation can be introduced into the workings of this agency.[22] The prospects for this happening are not bright. The politicization of the OTA, indeed, could force it to take other than technically rational paths of assessment; but at the same time, participation could reduce the agency's effectiveness in the accomplishment of its mission as a congressional information resource. In other words, congressmen might end up reading the minutes of a debating society, rather than reading the appraisal of an innovation by scientists best qualified to make technical judgments.

Technology and Social Values

Thoughtful scholars, such as Jacques Ellul, have written extensively about the value crisis created by technology. For Ellul, the *least* of the dangers that people face from technology is an assault upon their person or the destruction of their physical environment. Rather the real menace of technology is its potential to destroy the human spirit.

Ellul argues that *la technique* engenders values of its own.[23] Ellul distinguishes between technology and *la technique*. The concern of technology is with means required to solve practical worldly problems. We have been so successful in our application of technology, that we have elevated our devotion to means to the level of an ethic. This ethic has an implicit premise that good means (processes) automatically will produce good results. Thus, Ellul believes that the quest for better and better means for advancing material progress is leading humans to be dominated by process—the process of *la technique*. So pervasive and unyielding is this process that it excludes the possibility of deviancy from its core value of rationality.

Put another way, technique and the managers that serve it must be able to engineer human behavior so that it expedites the progression

---

[22] Erasmus H. Kloman, "Public Participation in Technology Assessment," *Public Administration Review*, January/February 1974, pp. 52–61.

[23] Jacques Ellul, *The Technological Society* (New York: Alfred A. Knopf, Inc., 1965).

of rationality. Thus the values that *la technique* unfolds are those values that people *must* hold, and will be induced to hold, in order to guarantee that the rational imperative is expressed at every level of human existence. Ellul is emphatic about this. He reasons that people have led themselves to believe that the method and the values of science should be applied to all phases of life, because its models of rationality have succeeded so well in bending nature to human will. Hence, little promises to be untouched by the rational processes of *la technique*. It applies to all aspects of human existence: the social, the cultural, the education, the recreational, the economic, and the organizational. But the greatest danger is the application of *la technique* to political problems, because the result will be the conversion of politics to administration. In other words political problems will be transformed by *la technique* into technical problems susceptible to managerial puzzle solving. This is the surest route to totalitarian goverance which we discuss in the last chapter.

Ellul foresees that science and technology in the service of *la technique* may be able to eradicate those things that have been historically characterized as human. Before the onslaught of technique, "human" history stands to be replaced by "technical" history, in which case humanity loses its distinctiveness and nobility. People, like machines, will become an accessory to the process of *la technique*.

It is difficult to understand from the reading Ellul's *The Technological Society* alone, what exactly are the human values he believes are jeopardized by *la technique*. However, a review of his many works suggests that it is in fact the value system of Western society commonly grounded in Christianity. Regardless of whether or not Ellul is correct in this interpretation, it is obvious that we are experiencing an extension of technical rationality that began with the Age of Enlightenment. Traditional institutions, such as the family, church, and education, are failing as the paradigm of technical rationality expands into the qualitative and normative aspects of contemporary life.

Standing athwart these changes are the managers of the organizations that deliver to people the goods and services which result from the application of science, engineering, and technology. Managers are the human intermediaries between social values and the technological apparatus who: (1) facilitate the rational expression of technological within organizations, (2) provide a bridge between such abstractions as rationality, technology, and organization and the mass of humanity, (3) marshal and control the vast amount of technical expertise and other resources necessary to advance the material progress of society, and (4) possess among themselves a peculiar expertise that is quite apart from the more conventional forms of scientific and engineering skill. Therefore, to expect managers to assume a moral posture, apart from rationality, in their direction of the course of technology is not to demand something unreasonable; but for them to actually do so might be impossible.

part *IV*

Organization Change

W arren G. Bennis is fond of pointing out that in the social sciences there are theories of change, but not theories of changing.[1] This was, probably, an accurate appraisal of the state of affairs in the social sciences up to the end of the last decade. However there are reasons to believe that the situation is different now. Theories, or more accurately techniques, of *changing* organizations are beginning to appear because the management of complex organizations requires reliable methods for the control of human behavior. In order to appreciate what is behind this development, it is necessary to understand the reason why Bennis makes a distinction between theories of change and theories of changing.

Theories of change, and there are many of them, have one thing in common. They hold that change arises from the very nature of physical, biological, and social existence. As the sociologist Pitrim Sorokin put it, to be is to change. In other words, change is *immanent* to existence. Those who take this view are among the most honored scientists and philosophers in history. They include Darwin, Spencer, Chardin, Hegel, and Marx. With a few exceptions, immanent change theorists believed that the processes of change worked to better the system in which they operated. Thus, evolution and the dialectic, both of which are examples of immanent change theories, brought about improvement. They are teleological in that change is end-directed. As the change

---

[1] Warren G. Bennis, *Changing Organizations* (New York: McGraw-Hill Book Company, 1966), p. 99.

323

processes worked their way toward ends, the condition of humanity, or whatever else, improved.

While immanent theories of change generally were optimistic ("Everyday in every way we are getting better and better"), the concept of immanence attributes hidden, unknowable forces to change; that is, the phenomenon of change is almost mystical, its conditions are virtually unknowable, and our power to explain it and to control it is limited.

Immanence is, consequently, opposed to science and the spirit of logical positivism. The heart of scientific explanation lies in its abilty to ascribe causality, and thereby predict and control events. So the question is how do we cope with a concept like immanence that has so many irreconcilable differences with science? The best approach is to ignore philosophical problems, and hope they go away. This is in fact what has happened with the theories of change. The old ideas of immanence have yielded to new explanations of change that we can group under the label *externalism.*

Externalistic theories offer hypotheses about the causes of specific changes, but they make no statements about the principle of change itself. Change arises from forces, causes, factors, and contingencies that lie as variables outside the system. This explanation of change has become so important that it represents the basis for theories of *changing.*

The triumph of externalism in organization theory is the result of four exceedingly important conditions of modern life.

1. The acceleration of the pace of events and the consequent compression of decision makers' time horizons.
2. The growing complexity of technological and human systems.
3. The increasing power of technology to regulate specific, input variables that are responsible for system outputs.
4. The abandonment of values that gave high priority to immanent forces as being causal to change.

The enormous complexity that we perceive in the physical, biological, human, and organizational events surrounding us has seemingly placed understanding of the essential character of change outside the range of human comprehension. Complex things such as the brain, the organization, genetic structure, and even the atom are consigned to the status of the "black box"—essentially unknowable, *but not necessarily uncontrollable.* As we discussed previously, many complex phenomenon can be regulated by manipulating their contingencies.

Black-box thinking, which is intimately a part of the triumph of externalism, has downgraded philosophy that seeks the essence of things and has exalted technology which requires the manipulation of things. This is nowhere more obvious than in the behavioral sciences that pertain to management. They are applied technologies devoted to planning, designing, redesigning, and changing organizations, and, of course, the behavior in them. Thus, externalism of the sort that we are discussing forces an engineering perspective on management scientists, theorists, and practitioners. Dealing as they do with *external causation* absolutely requires a *contingency approach*. The two terms mean the same thing, and we have expanded on this point in previous chapters.

Thus, management theories of changing rely upon external concepts of behavioral causation. However, there is at present little that we can point to as a coherent theoretical system of knowledge called "changing theory." The best management has now is the contingency approach which is a heuristic of muddling through with technological assistance. Nevertheless the evolutionary direction in the management of changing organizations is fairly clear. The imperative of rationality requires that management has access to techniques of preemptive behavioral control, so that the human response to changed environmental contingencies can be anticipated and regulated. Little else is more important to the management of complex organizations than to be reasonably certain that the people in the system will behave reliably.

The following chapters treat organizational and individual change techniques. Chapter 16 reviews behavioral technologies in the areas of organization development, job design and redesign, job enlargement and enrichment, participation, and management by objectives. Chapter 17 is concerned with training. Again, the lack of an overarching framework for these "theories of changing" indicates that management has just begun its quest for effective means of preemptive control.

chapter 16
Organizational Change Techniques

The press, other media and social science literature is filled with stories about alienation, the "blue-collar blues," white-collar crime, sabotage at work, and other examples of malaise in the workplace. The explanations for these problems are equally numerous. People are different today: They want different things. Organizations are too big; they're less human. Society is changing too rapidly; we can't adjust.

There is some truth in most of these explanations. People are different. Education levels have risen along with corresponding expectations and abilities. People are generally more affluent and have greater security in this country. The role of the church and the family has decreased and there is some evidence that obedience to authority has declined as well. Society has begun to emphasize cooperation and self-actualization over competition and hard work directed to organizational goals. All these changes suggest that people come into the work setting with different values and expectations than in the past.

But what do they face at work? Walton has suggested the following discrepancies between worker expectations and organizational realities.

1. Employees want challenge and personal growth, but work tends to be simplified and specialties tend to be used repeatedly in work assignments. This pattern exploits the narrow skills of a worker, while limiting his or her opportunities to broaden or develop.
2. Employees want to be included in patterns of mutual influence; they want egalitarian treatment. But organizations are characterized by tall hierarchies, status differentials, and chains of command.

3. Employee commitment to an organization is increasingly influenced by the intrinsic interest of the work itself, the human dignity afforded by management, and social responsibility reflected in the organization's products. Yet organization practices still emphasize material rewards and employment security and neglect other employee concerns.

4. What employees want from careers, they are apt to want *right now*. But when organizations design job hierarchies and career paths, they continue to assume that today's workers are as willing to postpone gratifications as were yesterday's workers.

5. Employees want more attention to the emotional aspects of organization life, such as individual self-esteem, openness between people, and expressions of warmth. Yet organizations emphasize rationality and seldom legitimize the emotional part of the organizational experience.

6. Employees are becoming less driven by competitive urges, less likely to identify competition as the American way. Nevertheless, managers continue to plan career patterns, organize work, and design reward systems as if employees valued competition as highly as they used to.[1]

Finally, the world around us is changing at an increasing speed. Toffler's *Future Shock* discussed this phenomena in detail and its resultant impact on the individual's ability to cope and adjust to new environments.[2] We are highly interdependent on other cultures, economies, regional groups, and small segments of the work force. A strike in one occupation (e.g., garbage collectors, police officers, truck drivers) can seriously alter our lives as can the whim of a Middle East political leader. Communication media brings us instant reporting with films transmitted by satellite. Our changes and everyone elses changes are exposed immediately. And through communication individual differences in life-styles, norms and habits are more apparent and acceptable. One consequence is that organizations are finding it more difficult to reconcile individual or group differences through a powerful "efficiency imperative." What's good for General Motors is not necessarily good for the country.

Somehow organizations have to adapt to these different environments and to the different types of demands made by their participants. Over the last 20 years, numerous change strategies have evolved, been tested,

---

[1] R. E. Walton, "How to Counter Alienation in the Plant," *Harvard Business Review*, November–December 1972, p. 72.

[2] A. Toffler, *Future Shock* (New York: Random House, Inc., 1970).

implemented, and evaluated. The rest of this chapter will deal with these strategies and the current "state of the art."

PERSPECTIVES ON CHANGE

The demand for a better working life has resulted in a proliferation of change technologies. These technologies are designed to make people more satisfied and productive in the work setting. Some of them deal with issues of job status, job content, relationships with peers and supervisors, reward systems, working conditions, and numerous other aspects of one's job.

In order to discuss these strategies systematically we have imposed a crude system of categorization. In general we see two major aims of the change process: (1) restructure or redesign the job; and (2) modify the communication and interpersonal relationships. On the one hand, we have attempts to make jobs more meaningful through enlargement, rotation, increased responsibility or autonomy. On the other, we have strategies designed to make relationships more honest and open, with free exchange of feedback and ideas.

There are also two schools of thought that have developed these techniques: (1) scientific management; and (2) industrial humanism. The former is based more on the principle of rationality while the latter is a more clinical, value-oriented approach. Combining the background and strategies generates the picture illustrated in Figure 16–1.

FIGURE 16–1
Historical Referents of Current Change Strategies

	Change the Structure	Change the Process
Scientific Management	Job Design	Management by Objectives
Industrial Humanism	Job Enrichment	Organizational Development

Before describing and evaluating these technologies in detail we should first provide a summary perspective. While hundreds of research and case studies have been conducted dealing with organizational change, few good pieces of research exist. Most of the studies involve self-report measures and correlational statistics both of which seriously weaken our ability to make inferences about the effects of a given change attempt.

However, a recent report by Cummings and Salipante does provide a good review of the more technically adequate research.[3] They found in their review of the literature 57 studies which had at least passable research designs. They divided the .studies into four different types: autonomous work groups; job restructuring; participative management; and organizational change. They also categorized the kinds of changes introduced into nine independent variables and looked at the impact on five criteria or dependent variables. Figure 16–2 presents a summary of the findings of these studies.

One must be struck by the overwhelming degree of favorable findings. No matter what was changed or introduced, the chances were invariably better than .50 that there would be some positive impact on performance (costs, productivity, quality) or satisfaction (withdrawal, attitudes). At first blush, these data are very impressive. However, the results must be scrutinized from two perspectives. First, a more detailed analysis will help to discover which sorts of interventions were most successful and on what criteria. Second, a thorough review of the methodologies employed may lessen our confidence in the overall impact of these figures. We will return to these topics throughout the chapter.

THE DATA GATHERING PROCESS

The mutual phases of any organizational change effort typically include some sort of diagnostic measurement procedures. These data are used to highlight those areas that are in need of change or where change will be most effective. The early research tended to be rather unsystematic in this regard: a few interviews, some subjective impressions or some discussion groups. However, in the last five years a number of more thorough strategies have emerged. The results that are generated frequently point out both what is wrong and suggest ways that the problems can be corrected.

1. Survey Feedback

Many of the practitioners involved in organizational change utilize an action research—survey feedback technique. In general, a question-

---

[3] T. G. Cummings, and P. Salipante, Jr., "The Development of Research-Based Strategies for Improving the Quality of Work Life" (Paper delivered at the NATO Conference on Personal Goals and Work Design in York, England, August 1974).

FIGURE 16-2

A. Independent Variables

A summary of the percentage of field experimental studies that manipulated a particular variable.

	Pay/Reward Systems	Autonomy/Discretion	Support	Training	Organization Structure	Technical/Physical	Task Variety	Information/Feedback	Interpersonal/Group Process
Sociotechnical/Autonomous Groups (n = 16)	56% (16)*	88% (16)	31% (16)	44% (16)	19% (16)	63% (16)	63% (16)	63% (16)	75% (16)
Job Restructuring (n = 27)	14% (27)	92% (27)	22% (27)	33% (27)	14% (27)	22% (27)	79% (27)	45% (27)	4% (27)
Participative Management (n = 7)		100% (7)		14% (7)	14% (7)				
Organization Change (n = 7)	29% (7)	43% (7)	43% (7)	43% (7)	100% (7)	29% (7)	14% (7)	71% (7)	43% (7)

* Numbers in parentheses indicate the base number of studies on which the percentage is based—i.e., the denominator.

B. Dependent Variables

A summary of the percentage of field experimental studies that produced totally positive results.†

	Costs	Productivity	Quality	Withdrawal	Attitudes
Sociotechnical/Autonomous Groups (n = 16)	88% (8)	93% (15)	86% (7)	73% (7)	70% (10)
Job Restructuring (n = 27)	90% (10)	75% (20)	100% (17)	86% (7)	76% (21)
Participative Management (n = 7)	100% (1)	57% (7)	100% (1)	80% (5)	80% (5)
Organization Change (n = 7)	50% (2)	100% (4)	100% (2)	67% (3)	50% (6)

† The percentages represent those studies which reported no negative, mixed, or zero-change findings for the dependent variable in that column.

naire or group discussion is used to generate data to explore, clarify, and identify problem areas. These sessions actively involve the client systems in the data generation process. The next step is to actively engage the client in the problem-solving process. This is done through a survey feedback technique. The data that has been collected is tabulated and organized by the consultant but not interpreted or evaluated. Instead, these data are fed back to the client groups for the purpose of problem solving.

The client is actively involved in the whole process. He or she helps to generate, interpret, and act on the data. In the long run, it is hoped that this process will be maintained after the initial effort and the consultant is gone.[4]

The actual choice of measuring devices is variable. Different types of instruments are used by different people and not every "change agent" engages in all the steps of the action research survey feedback process. Three fairly important measurement tools are discussed below.

2. Leadership Pattern Systems

One set of measurement tools have been developed by Rensis Likert to assess the type of leadership pattern typically being employed by management. Managers are asked to describe the highest and lowest producing departments about which they have had some knowledge. Likert finds that these descriptions generally fit into four distinct patterns (presented in Figure 16–3).[5] From reading the descriptions of the styles it is clear that system 4 is loaded with positive words and system 1 with negative ones. Likert and his colleagues, while recognizing that system 4 leadership may not be the most efficient in all situations, believe this style is way ahead of whatever is in second place. Based upon the data generated, a consultant can recognize areas where the leadership pattern may be inadequate and suggest possible remedies.

3. Organizational Climate

A somewhat broader concept revolves around the climate of the organization. Hellriegel and Slocum define climate as "a set of attributes which can be perceived about a particular organization and/or its subsys-

---

[4] Wendell L. French, and C. A. Bell, Jr., *Organization Development* (Englewood Cliffs, N.J.: Prentice-Hall, Inc., 1973).

[5] R. Likert, *The Human Organization* (New York: McGraw-Hill Book Company, 1967).

FIGURE 16–3
Likert's Systems of Management Leadership

Leadership Variable	System 1 (Exploitive Autocratic)	System 2 (Benevolent Autocratic)	System 3 (Participative)	System 4 (Democratic)
Confidence and trust in subordinates	Has no confidence and trust in subordinates.	Has condescending confidence and trust, such as master has to servant.	Substantial but not complete confidence and trust; still wishes to keep control of decisions.	Complete confidence and trust in all matters.
Subordinates' feeling of freedom	Subordinates do not feel at all free to discuss things about the job with their superior.	Subordinates do not feel very free to discuss things about the job with their superior.	Subordinates feel rather free to discuss things about the job with their superior.	Subordinates feel completely free to discuss things about the job with their superior.
Superiors seeking involvement with subordinates	Seldom gets ideas and opinions of subordinates in solving job problems.	Sometimes gets ideas and opinions of subordinates in solving job problems.	Usually gets ideas and opinions and usually tries to make constructive use of them.	Always asks subordinates for ideas and opinions and always tries to make constructive use of them.

Source: Adapted from Rensis Likert, *The Human Organization* (New York: McGraw-Hill Book Company, 1967), p. 4. Used by permission.

tems, and that may be induced from the way that organization and/or its subsystems deal with their members and environment."[6] The underlying assumption is that some consistent organizational style exists and that people agree about what it is. While some researchers have questioned these assumptions, measures of climate have proliferated and are being employed in a substantial number of organizations.

A recent article by Lawler, Hall, and Oldham suggests that the climate is a joint function of the organizational structure and organizational processes.[7] Climate, in turn, is related to organizational performance and job satisfaction. Thus, climate is seen as a moderator between these sets of variables (see Figure 16–4).

FIGURE 16–4
The Proposed Model for Organizational Climate

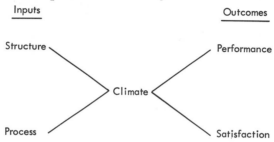

Their data generated from about 300 scientists in 21 large research and development laboratories seem to confirm their supposition. Both structural and process variables impacted on climate although the process variables had a somewhat greater impact. Climate seemed to have a greater effect on job satisfaction than on performance. It appears as if climate measures are more related to the interpersonal and affective aspects of the job than the more structural, efficiency oriented aspects.

4. Job Diagnostic Survey

Recently, a questionnaire labeled the Job Diagnostic Survey has been developed by Hackman and Oldham.[8] The instrument assesses five

[6] D. Hellriegel, and J. W. Slocum, Jr., "Organizational Climate: Measures, Research and Contingencies," *Academy of Management Journal*, 17 (1974), 256.

[7] E. E. Lawler III, D. T. Hall, and G. R. Oldham, "Organization Climate: Relationship to Organizational Structure, Process and Performance," *Organizational Behavior and Human Performance*, 11 (1974), 139–55.

[8] J. R. Hackman and G. R. Oldham, "The Job Diagnostic Survey: An Instrument for the Diagnosis of Jobs and the Evaluation of Job Redesign Projects," *Journal of Applied Psychology*, 60 (1975), 159–70.

key job dimensions: skill variety; task identity; task significance; autonomy; and feedback. Also assessed are a number of psychological states having to do with the meaningfulness of the job and one's responsibilities along with some assessment of the affective reactions to the job overall and its subparts.

The authors argue that the questionnaire can be used first as a diagnostic device and then as an instrument for evaluation. In the latter case one can monitor the impact of various changes that have been implemented. Since a well-developed theory of job enrichment underlies the construction of the instrument, we will discuss the Hackman and Oldham research more fully in the next section.

CHANGING THE JOB

Given that problems exist in an organizational setting, there are a number of alternative remedies. One set of strategies revolve around changing the job while the other focuses on the interpersonal relations and group processes. We will deal with the job changes first.

Job Design: Scientific Management

Two somewhat different schools of thought have contributed to the emphasis on job design: scientific management and industrial humanism. The first systematic attempt to discover the principles of matching the individual to the job in some optimal fashion was carried out by Frederick W. Taylor. His "scientific management" approach suggested that through scientific methods we could design jobs and train people to attain maximum output. While Taylor's ideas included a rather broad ideal of management and workers involved in a cooperative effort to increase productivity, his followers were more restrictive in their approach. They concentrated on two main aspects of Taylor's ideas: determining the one best way to do a job and the use of incentive pay to ensure compliance with the prescribed work methods.

This emphasis on the one "best way" led to what is referred to as time and motion studies. This research was designed to do the following:

1. Find the best way for people to move, stand, and generally physically deal with a task.
2. Break jobs down into easily repeatable, learnable tasks.
3. Arrange tools and equipment in a manner that minimizes effort and lost time.

4. Construct the plant environment in such a way that noise, ventilation, and other support facilities do not reduce effectiveness.
5. Design special tools for specific jobs such as conveyors, clients, and other machines to reduce unnecessary actions.
6. Eliminate all activities that are fatigue producing, which are unrelated to the task at hand.

The underlying idea is clear: The worker and his job are to be treated as machines. The time and motion studies markedly increased our knowledge about how people fit with machines. Certain aspects of an individual's physical endowment were emphasized such as the amount of work space that was easily accessible, the fact that symmetrical movements were easiest to carry out, and that a sequence or rhythm to physical movements is best. Circular movements were found to be easier than back and forth movements; picking things up is harder than moving them.

All of this activity had a number of profound implications. Jobs were timed and there was a "best way." Jobs became simpler and more repetitive. But probably most important was the fact that many of the benefits originally hoped for went unrealized. Scanlon provides an excellent listing of the unanticipated consequences of early approaches to job design. (See Figure 16–5.)

People disliked the work; they had greater education and higher expectations. They spent a large part of their lives working at dull repetitive tasks. Technology had been used in a rather limited fashion with a narrow perspective and more and more people began to realize that there was a new and more important function for technology. "Everyone accepts the obvious notion that new technology can and must eliminate dumb-dumb jobs."[9] The question was "how?"

Job Enlargement and Enrichment

In the late 1950s and 1960s, there was a change in the emphasis of job design. Louis Davis stated quite early that "the assembly line has designed out of the job virtually everything that might be of personal value or meaning to the workers."[10] There was an increased interest in the human problems associated with work. It was at this point that

[9] R. N. Ford, "Job Enrichment Lesson from AT&T," *Harvard Business Review,* January–February 1973, pp. 96–106.

[10] L. E. Davis, "Job Design and Productivity: A New Approach," *Personnel,* 33 (1957), 418–13.

FIGURE 16–5
Anticipated Advantages and Actual Results of the Historical Approach to Job Design

Anticipated Advantages	Actual Results
1. Jobs can be learned quickly, thus little training is required.	1. Savings in training cost fail to materialize because of excessively high turnover.
2. Jobs can be filled with unskilled people— presumably an inexpensive, readily available commodity.	2. High rates of absenteeism require that extra workers must be available on a standby basis. This increases labor costs.
3. Because of low skill required and ease of training, workers are interchangeable.	3. Because assembly line work is so dissatisfying in nature, a high wage must be paid just to get people to accept jobs on the line.
4. Because of mechanization, workers do not become physically tired.	4. Substantial quality problems occur because of a lack of commitment on the part of workers.
5. Standardization permits ease of quality control. Also, the chance of mistakes is minimized.	5. Because of turnover, costs of recruiting and selection of workers are also increased.
6. Mechanization makes production predictable.	6. Problems of supervision develop as the gap between labor and management broadens.
7. Management has control over workers and to a degree can supervise by observation.	

Source: B. K. Scanlon, *Principles of Management and Organizational Behavior* (New York: John Wiley & Sons, Inc., 1973), p. 326.

the theorists from the second "school" joined in. Industrial humanists and those people who participated in the human relations movement brought their knowledge to bear on the job design problem. The approaches fall into two main categories: Job enlargement and job enrichment. Lawler describes the former as first-aid approaches to redesigning jobs and the latter as major surgery.[11] Under the heading of job enlargement we usually include those changes designed at horizontal job enlargement (widening the scope of the job) and some other job features such as the hours of work.

The name most readily paired with the job enlargement and later enrichment ideas is Frederick Herzberg.[12] While there is some disagreement in academic circles about the validity of a number of aspects of his theory (described as arguments "akin to medieval church dis-

---

[11] E. E. Lawler, III, "Motivation and the Design of Jobs," *ASTME Vectors*, 1968, pp. 14–25.

[12] F. Herzberg, *Work and the Nature of Man* (Cleveland, Ohio: World Publishing Company, 1966).

putes" by Sirota[13]), there is little doubt about his impact on the general idea of job enlargement. Four major ways to enlarge jobs have generally been discussed:

1. Challenging the employee. The emphasis is on asking employees to work up to their potential. Obviously, this will work only if other aspects of the job are changed as well.
2. Replacing difficult, repetitive, and boring tasks by machines where possible. This would leave the employee the more interesting aspects of the job.
3. Assigning more tasks or more operations to the job. There is less monotony and more variety.
4. Using job rotation to allow the employee to learn new skills and to engage in a variety of tasks.

Frequently combined with these ideas is the relatively recent flexibility in work hours. The modifications of the workweek may take the form of four-day weeks or more flexible hours over a five-day week. This latter approach usually allows the employee some discretion in choosing his work hours as long as a specified minimum is attained.

The research results for many of these enlargement strategies are generally supportive.[14] In most cases, there is a more recognizable impact on satisfaction than on productivity. While increased satisfaction should reduce turnover and absenteeism many people felt that more inclusive changes were needed.

Job enrichment was the response. The concept of enrichment entails both horizontal and vertical restructuring of jobs in an effort to increase the meaningfulness and satisfaction of work. It is more than just an expanded job, it is a new job. New skills and abilities can be used and the job is upgraded. Figure 16–6 lists the principles of vertical job loading.

Job enrichment is more comprehensive than job enlargement. The employee has more responsibility and discretion. There is feedback about performance, communication is two-way, and there is some attempt at having an individual do a whole job. That is, there is an attempt at closure. Through these practices, motivation, performance, and satisfaction are hoped to increase.

---

[13] D. Sirota, "Job Enrichment—Is It for Real?" *Advanced Management Journal,* April 1973.

[14] See B. E. Sandler, "Eclecticism at Work; Approaches to Job Design," *American Psychologist,* 29 (1974), 767–73.

FIGURE 16–6
Principles of Vertical Job Loading

Principle	Motivators Involved
1. Removing some controls while retaining accountability.	1. Responsibility and personal achievement.
2. Increasing the accountability of individuals for own work.	2. Responsibility and recognition.
3. Giving a person a complete natural unit of work (module, division, area, and so on).	3. Responsibility, achievement, and recognition.
4. Granting additional authority to an employee in his activity; job freedom.	4. Responsibility, achievement, and recognition.
5. Making periodic reports directly available to the worker himself rather than to the supervisor.	5. Internal recognition.
6. Introducing new and more difficult tasks not previously handled.	6. Growth and learning.
7. Assigning individuals specific or specialized tasks, enabling them to become experts.	7. Responsibility, growth, and advancement.

Source: B. K. Scanlon, *Principles of Management and Organizational Behavior* (New York: John Wiley & Sons, Inc., 1973), p. 330.

A fairly specific theory of job enrichment has recently been developed by Hackman and Oldham. They suggest that certain core job dimensions have an impact on a number of psychological states which in turn relate to attitudes and behavior on the job. Figure 16–7 presents their theory.

There are some important implications of this theory. First, changing only one job dimension may have only a minor impact on eventual behavior. Second, changing the job will change behavior only by changing the critical psychological states. Third, the theory will vary in effectiveness depending upon individual needs. It would be expected to work better for people who highly value autonomy, growth, and responsibility. There is currently an increasing amount of data being presented on job enrichment projects. Robert Ford has published the results of enrichment projects conducted at AT&T; Herzberg has introduced enrichment at a number of large corporations; and Lawler has done similar work in a variety of settings.[15] The summary of data presented at the beginning of this chapter was also generally supportive of these attempts to redesign jobs. It is not surprising therefore that many theorists and

---

[15] Ford, "Job Enrichment Lesson"; Herzberg, *Work and the Nature of Man;* and Lawler, "Motivation and the Design of Jobs."

FIGURE 16–7
The Relationships among the Core Job Dimensions, the Critical Psychological States, and On-the-Job Outcomes

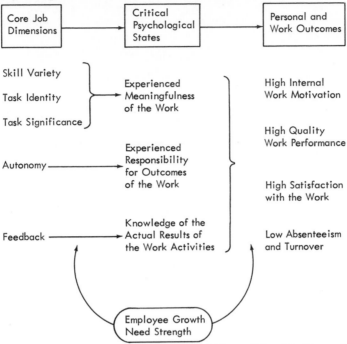

Source: J. R. Hackman and G. R. Oldham, "The Job Diagnostic Survey: An Instrument for the Diagnosis of Jobs and the Evaluation of Job Redesign Projects," *Journal of Applied Psychology*, 60 (1975), 160.

practitioners are enthusiastic about the possibilities of job enrichment. There are some reservations, however, and we will deal with them at the end of the chapter.

CHANGING INTERPERSONAL PROCESSES

There is another whole set of change technologies which have a somewhat different thrust. The emphasis is on the interpersonal communications and relationships. How open and honest is the communication? What are the secret agendas? Who has really got the clout and why? What is the group process all about?

With an increased realization of the fact that human needs, desires, fears, and hopes were operating in the workplace came attempts to understand their impact on organizational life. Bennis has pointed out that we are also faced by turbulent, uncertain, and dynamic environ-ments[16] and we must learn to cope with them. Complicated people are working in complicated environments; and constant adjustments by both are demanded frequently if the meshing of organizational goals and human needs is to be sought as a means of increasing efficiency.

The response has been a set of change strategies designed to improve the group process and the interpersonal organizational climate. Some attempts focus on rather specific communication processes such as par-ticipation in decision making or management by objectives (MBO). Other approaches are broader in nature such as organizational develop-ment (OD). Similar to the theorists who were interested in changing the job, there seem to be two general "schools" of thought. Those who emphasize the goal setting, MBO-type approaches seem to place a greater emphasis on rational, empirical, more scientific management-type approaches. The people interested in OD seem to be more explicit about the value orientation of their industrial humanism background. Even though their implementation strategies may overlap, the underlying theory may be very different. We will point out these differences where it is important.

Organizational Development

A variety of definitions of OD exist. We have chosen the one by French and Bell because of its inclusiveness. They see OD as "a long-range effort to improve an organization's problem-solving and renewal processes, particularly through a more effective and collaborative man-agement of organization culture—with special emphasis on the culture of formal work teams—with the assistance of a change agent or catalyst and the use of the theory and technology of applied behavioral science, including action research."[17]

Notice the key parts of this definition. There is an emphasis on the "long-range" effort. OD is more than a one-shot intervention. The main targets of the effort are group interaction processes, not structures, rules, or regulations. And the way to change these processes is through the work team climate. Finally, note that the use of a change agent and

---

[16] W. G. Bennis, *Organizational Development: Its Nature, Origins, and Prospects* (Reading, Mass.: Addison–Wesley Publishing Co., Inc., 1969), p. 77.

[17] W. L. French and C. H. Bell, "A Definition and History of Organization Devel-opment: Some Comments," Proceedings of the Thirty-First Annual Meeting, Academy of Management, Boston, 1972, p. 146.

of the action research data gathering strategy are formally built into the definition. Thus, both the content and the process of intervening are important for determining what constitutes an OD effort.

Two main historical trends contributed to the development of OD: laboratory training and action research. Laboratory training focuses on the interpersonal relationships that exist in the small work group. Through group interaction participants learn about how they are perceived by others as well as the impact they have on their peers. The action research contribution is a data gathering process which we discussed earlier. There is a preliminary diagnosis, some data gathered, some feedback and discussion, some action plans and implemented change. These two technologies were joined to form the broader organizational development strategy.

The general characteristics of the OD approach have been specified by Eddy.

1. Focus on the total system of interdependent sub-organizational groupings (work units, teams, management levels) rather than upon individual employees as the object of training. Team development is frequently a major component of the change process.

2. The approach to change is "organic." It seeks to establish a climate in which growth, development and renewal are brought about as a natural part of the organization's daily operation, rather than superimposed unilaterally.

3. Experimental learning techniques (role-playing, problem-solving exercises, T-groups) in addition to traditional lecture methods are utilized. Subject matter includes real problems and events that exist in the organization and often in the training groups, as well as hypothetical cases or examples. Often there is gathering and analysis of organization data—either formally or informally.

4. Emphasis is placed upon competence in interpersonal relationships rather than upon task skills. Much of the content and method is based on the behavioral sciences rather than upon management theory, operations research, or personnel techniques—although these may be included as part of the program.

5. Goals frequently have to do with developing behavioral competence in areas such as communication, decision-making, and problem-solving, in addition to understanding and retention of principles and theories. The trainer often sees himself more as a consultant or change agent than expert-teacher.

6. The value system is humanistic. It is committed to integrating individual needs and management goals, maximizing opportunity for

human growth and development, and encouraging more open, authentic human relationships.

7. There is less intention to refute the traditional structural-functional conception of the organization than to augment this conception with newer data and help remedy some of its major dysfunctions.[18]

Again, one can see the emphasis on long-term changes in the interpersonal climate as the summary goal. However, to add some more specifics to this discussion, we will briefly describe some of the interventions used by OD consultants.

Figure 16–8 presents a typology of OD interventions as compiled by French and Bell.[19]

Some of the techniques are designed to improve individual effectiveness while others emphasize dyadic, group, intergroup, or total organization relationships. For example, the life and career-planning activities ask the individual to indicate what he or she would like to be doing at different points in their career. One's goals, successes and failures are explored in an attempt to help the individual accurately evaluate his strengths, weaknesses, and potential. T-groups or sensitivity training also focus on the individual and will be discussed in detail in Chapter 17 on training.

Some of the group activities include approaches such as team building or the role analysis technique. In team building data is generated from the group about various types of interpersonal or communication problems. These data are openly discussed and action plans formulated. The role analysis technique requires the group to pick a role (say, the role of group leader or supervisor) and analyze how that role should be carried out in the most efficient manner. The person who actually fills that role may or may not be present depending upon the group relations. However, the role occupant can use the data to analyze those areas which need the most improvement.

An intervention for intergroup relations is called organizational mirroring. This technique requires that each group indicate how they view their own behavior, the behavior of the other groups involved *and* how they think the other groups view them. These data are then exchanged and a given group can see two main discrepancies: The difference between how they see other groups and how those other groups see themselves, and the difference between how they see themselves and how

---

[18] W. B. Eddy, "From Training to Organization Change," *Personnel Administration*, January–February 1971, pp. 37–43.

[19] French and Bell, "Definition and History of Organization Development."

FIGURE 16–8
Typology of OD Interventions Based on Target Groups

Target Group	Types of Interventions
Interventions designed to improve the effectiveness of INDIVIDUALS	Life and career-planning activities.
	Role analysis technique.
	Coaching and counseling.
	T-group (sensitivity training).
	Education and training to increase skills, knowledge in the areas of technical task needs, relationship skills, process skills, decision-making, problem-solving, planning, goal-setting skills.
	Grid OD phase 1.
Interventions designed to improve the effectiveness of DYADS/TRIADS	Process consultation.
	Third-party peacemaking.
	Grid OD phases 1, 2.
Interventions designed to improve the effectiveness of TEAMS and GROUPS	Team-building:
	Task-directed.
	Process-directed.
	Family T-group.
	Survey feedback.
	Process consultation.
	Role analysis technique.
	"Start-up" team-building activities.
	Education in decision making, problem solving, planning, goal-setting in group settings.
Interventions designed to improve the effectiveness of INTERGROUP RELATIONS	Intergroup activities:
	Process-directed.
	Task-directed.
	Organizational mirroring (3 or more groups).
	Technostructural interventions.
	Process consultation.
	Third-party peacemaking at group level.
	Grid OD phase 3.
	Survey feedback.
Interventions designed to improve the effectiveness of the TOTAL ORGANIZATION	Technostructural activities.
	Confrontation meetings.
	Strategic planning activities.
	Grid OD phases 4, 5, 6.
	Survey feedback.

Source: W. L. French and C. H. Bell, "A Definition and History of Organization Development: Some Comments," *Proceedings of the Thirty-First Annual Meeting,* Academy of Management, Atlanta, Georgia, 1971, pp. 146–152.

the other groups see them. Again, action plans can be designed to remedy the problems that emerge.

Finally, some techniques are designed to deal with total organizational problems. For example, strategic planning and survey feedback involve getting together the different segments of an organization and making explicit the various needs, demands, and resources required for effective functioning. In summary, the OD interventions are highly heterogenous in nature. There are different kinds of remedies for different types of problems. In this sense, it is somewhat of a clinical approach in that data gathering, diagnosis, feedback, interventions, and follow-up are designed around a specific problem or set of problems.

Because of this eclectic emphasis very little systematic research has been conducted on OD intervention activities. Research per se is not part of the process and there are many practitioners who feel that evaluative research would spoil the OD process. However, what data does exist is not very supportive. Porter, Lawler, and Hackman summarize these results by stating that "the number of well-documented instances in which an organization has been substantially 'turned around' by interventions which have relied solely [or primarily] on direct intervention into interpersonal processes and social attitudes is relatively small."[20]

Participation in Decision Making

A change strategy with a somewhat more narrow focus is to have employees participate more in the process of decision making. It has been pointed out in many places that organizations would perform more effectively if higher groups left to lower groups within the same system decision powers and functions which they could handle best. Not only would organizations work better achieving their goals, but the dignity and freedom of people in these organizations would rise to higher levels, and human satisfaction concomitantly would advance. This is the *principle of subsidiarity* and it is identical in spirit to the philosophy of participative management and decentralization. It promotes, as Golembiewski keenly observes, "a sense of partnership in and responsibility for" the affairs of the organization.[21] In short, it allows self-determination instead of lockstep conformity to the whims of a central authority. Thus the prinicple of subsidiarity must be a pivotal doctrine of industrial humanism and the cornerstone of the modified organization. It is the road to democracy in administration. Its chief form of expression in the literature is as participation and decentralization.

Cost, product line, market area, and communication are technicoeconomic determinants which underlie decisions to disperse production facilities, distribution activities, and administrative centers in order to

---

[20] L. W. Porter, E. E. Lawler, III, and J. R. Hackman, *Behavior in Organizations,* (New York: McGraw-Hill Book Company, 1975), p. 471.

[21] See Robert T. Golembiewski, *Men, Management, and Morality* (New York: McGraw-Hill Book Company, 1965), chapters 7 and 8.

achieve efficiencies in the performance of an organization. Now, of course, *true* decentralization requires more than merely spreading out the operations of an organization. However, there is some confusion in the literature, as well as in public relations press releases, about what happens in the decentralization process.

An organization with geographically or functionally distinct divisions may still be centralized. *The responsibility for the judgmental aspects of work is retained by central authorities.* The result is a tall organization, close supervision (imposed either by immediate superiors in the chain of command or elaborate staff control groups responsible to higher central authorities), and narrow spans of control.

The only valid estimate of decentralization is the degree to which *decision making* is delegated to subordinate command units, and, in turn, to individuals in these units. The qualitative results of decentralization are flatter organizations, more general supervision, and wider spans of control.

The *process* by which decentralization is achieved is unequivocal. It is accomplished by the *delegation of authority.* Delegation, which is the dynamic behind the scalar process, is the method by which the authority of subordinate command units (and managers) is conferred and defined. Now the degree of decentralization is a function of the amount of authority delegated. In Golembiewski's words:

> How much authority is conferred and what conditions hedge that grant: these determine the degree of "centralization-decentralization." When much is conferred and the grant is not restricted by detailed controls, then the delegation is decentralized. While delegation cannot be avoided, the specific pattern of delegation can run the full spectrum from rigid centralization to extreme decentralization.[22]

In its broadest sense participation implements the aims of democratic administration by enhancing the degree of self-determination had by people in organizations. It is a reaction to repressive autocratic leadership. This reaction is expressed in all kinds of organizations regardless of whether their purposes are educational, religious, governmental, or economic. What exactly happens in this participative process? Well, we would anticipate at least two major benefits.

> 1. Participation can increase the amount and the accuracy of information workers have about work practices and the environmental contingencies associated with them. In one study . . . , for example, some

---

[22] Ibid, p. 256.

groups themselves designed new reward systems keyed on coming to work regularly (a task clearly affected by employee effort—i.e., trying to get to work every day). These groups responded both more quickly and more positively to the new pay plans than did groups which had technically identical plans imposed upon them by company management. One reason suggested by the authors to account for this finding was that the participative groups simply may have understood their plans better and had fewer uncertainties and worries about what the rewards were (and were not) for coming to work regularly.

2. Participation can increase the degree to which group members feel they "own" their work practices—and therefore the likelihood that the group will develop a norm of support for those practices. In the participative groups, . . . , for example, the nature of the work-related communication among members changed from initial "shared warnings" about management and "things management proposes" to helping members (especially new members) come to understand and believe in "our plan." In other words, as group members come to experience the work or work practices *as under their own control or ownership*, it becomes more likely that informal group norms supportive of effective behavior vis-à-vis those practices will develop. Such norms provide a striking contrast to the "group protective" norms which often emerge when control is perceived to be exclusively and unilaterally under management control.[23]

The research evidence seems to support these suggests. Vroom's review of experiments on participation indicate that both job satisfaction and productivity are effected positively.[24] And Mitchell has shown how this technique can be directly tied into expectancy theories of motivation.[25] Both theoretical and empirical support is available.

However, some limiting conditions have been discovered which impact on the implementation of such approaches. First, the topic of participation should be related to something about which employees are generally interested. To ask for participation on irrelevant topics may lead to hostility and rejection of the program. Second, the topic should be concerned with an area in which the employees have some expertise. Their participation will only be truly useful in those areas where they can best contribute. Finally, the participation should have some impact. Employees should be able to see the impact of their participation in

---

[23] Ibid, p. 419–20.

[24] V. Vroom, *Work and Motivation* (New York: John Wiley & Sons, Inc., 1964).

[25] T. R. Mitchell, "Motivation and Participation: An Integration," *Academy of Management Journal,* December 1973, pp. 670–79.

the form of modified policies and work norms. To introduce the program without actually utilizing the ideas generated will eventually lead to rejection.

Over the last few years, the participative approach has become formalized in many countries in the form of workers councils, or joint committees of employees and management. Western European countries such as Germany and Sweden as well as Eastern European countries such as Yugoslavia and Russia have utilized these ideas with positive results. So, these participative approaches may have some validity for both American and non-American cultures.

Management by Objectives (MBO)

In Chapter 6 on "Motivation," we discussed goal setting as a major example of theory and practice. The process of setting goals is frequently included as an integral part of an overall change technology called management by objectives. MBO is both a general philosophy of management and a fairly well-defined process. It is a philosophy which is highly rational in nature and suggests a proactive rather than a reactive management climate. Overall goals for the organization and its interrelated parts are jointly developed and specified at different organization levels. There is an emphasis on the observable and quantifiable, and also on improvement, on doing better. It encourages participation and tries to anticipate change. It is an overall philosophy designed to deal with current organizational problems.

As a process, MBO is broader in scope than goal setting. It requires not only the setting of clear, concise objectives, but also the development of realistic action plans and the systematic measurement of performance and achievement. Finally, there are built-in corrective measures to deal with problems of goal changes or inattainability.

Historically, Peter Drucker is generally cited as the first person to clearly describe the MBO process.[26] Management's job is to provide goals, jointly set and monitored, in order to increase both motivation and effectiveness. As an overall system, MBO includes three major phases: Performance appraisal; planning and control; and integrative management systems. Figure 16–9 provides an overview of the MBO process.[27]

---

[26] P. F. Drucker, *The Practice of Management* (New York: Harper & Row, Publishers, 1954).

[27] A. P. Raia, *Managing by Objectives* (Glenview, Ill.: Scott, Foresman & Co., 1974), p. 20.

FIGURE 16–9
MBO as a System

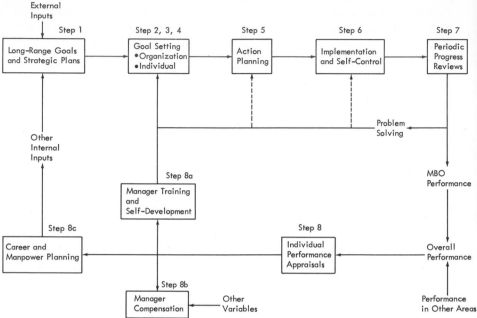

Source: A. P. Raia, *Managing by Objectives* (Glenview, Ill.: Scott, Foresman & Co., 1974), p. 20.

The actual setting of objectives and goal-setting process can occur at all levels. Top management should specify the overall mission and central purpose of the organization as well as some more short-run performance objectives for the organization as a whole. These objectives should include some statement of resource and time commitments. These broad objectives can then be translated into more specific objectives at the department level and further on down the hierarchy. Obviously, at this top levels, there must be explicit statements about what resources can be committed, what are the priorities for the objectives, and what are the tradeoffs for these decisions.

Specific job objectives are of a more individualistic nature. Behaviors that are important must be specified and deadlines made clear. However, throughout the process there must an element of flexibility and negotiation. Interruptions occur and unforeseen events may disturb the timetable. Goals and objectives are flexible targets, not written in stone. They can and should be changed when the situation requires it.

Another integral part of the MBO process is the need for performance appraisal. In order to set goals, monitor them, and evaluate goal attainment, we must know what sorts of behaviors are important for good performance. The MBO system requires a fairly rigorous procedure for evaluation. Goals are written down, recorded, clearly specified, and they have time constraints. Thus, the performance appraisal system can be built upon a well-established, goal-setting program.

Finally, reward systems must be designed around the performance appraisal process. People who reach attainable goals should be recognized and rewarded for goal attainment. Bonus plans or other reward strategies can be tied to the MBO philosophy.

There are some problems with MBO which should be raised. All too frequently, goals are set which are not specific such as "improving customer service." These types of goals lead to frustration on the part of the employee. They are too subjective. It also frequently occurs that goals are unilaterally rather than jointly sent. This tactic may lead to resentment or rejection of the goals. The crucial factor seems to be that MBO usually does well in a climate which is generally supportive and trusting; that is, an environment that is fairly well off to begin with.[28]

PROBLEMS IN CHANGING ORGANIZATIONS

Social scientists have obviously been hard at work attempting to develop technologies to remedy the problems of worker alienation and dissatisfaction. The attempts include a two-pronged attack on both the design of jobs and the interpersonal environment. And some reviews of the research literature such as the one by Cummings and Salipante cited at the beginning of this chapter, are obviously favorable.

But there are many researchers who advocate caution. They feel that there are reasons to doubt the validity of the empirical studies and that many problems in implementing change programs have not been thoroughly discussed. Sirota states that "job enrichment today is being sold as a panacea for just about every business ill. This is dangerous nonsense."[29] Hackman has said that "What we have seen out there in the 'organizational heartland' is not very encouraging' and that "job enrichment is failing at least as often as it is succeeding."[30] Porter

---

[28] Porter, Lawler, and Hackman, *Behavior in Organizations.*

[29] Sirota, "Job Enrichment," p. 279.

[30] J. R. Hackman, "On the Coming Demise of Job Enrichment," *Technical Report No. 9* (Department of Administrative Sciences, Yale University), p. 2.

et al. also suggested that there is little support for long-term process changes attributed to OD.[31]

What is the problem? Why do these differences of opinion exist. As a concluding section, we would like to catalogue some of the problems that recur in changing organization and perhaps suggest some remedies.

Characteristics of the Setting

Two main problems concern the types of people involved in the change process. First, as has been clearly pointed out by Reif and Luthans, there is frequently some resistance to change.[32] In some cases, employees are anxious or afraid that they will not be able to master the new skills required of an enlarged or changed job. Related to this fear is a fear of failure on the job. Finally, some employees are simply against changing the system. They prefer familiar habits to unfamiliar ones. A second set of individual variables refer to the types of people involved in the changes process. As Hulin and Blood pointed out many workers may simply reject the value premise on which these change technologies are built.[33] More specifically, for some employees, job content may be unrelated to job satisfaction. They may feel that social interaction is the primary source of job satisfaction and have no desire for more autonomy, responsibility, or enrichment.

Characteristics of the Change Process

We have described changes for both the job and the interpersonal relations and the problems which occur in both areas with regard to the implementation process. Hackman has listed a number of things that may go wrong in redesigning jobs.[34] First, in some cases, the work itself does not actually change. There is a lot of motion but very little substance. Another issue is that job design requires attention to the whole system of interrelated units. Whenever a change occurs in one area we should expect change in related areas as well. Also, in many

---

[31] Porter, Lawler, and Hackman, *Behavior in Organizations.*

[32] W. E. Reif, and F. Luthans, "Does Job Enrichment Really Pay Off?" *California Management Review,* 15 (1972), 30–37.

[33] C. L. Hulin, and M. R. Blood, "Job Enlargement, Individual Differences and Worker Responses," *Psychological Bulletin,* 69 (1968), 41–55.

[34] Hackman, "Coming Demise of Job Enrichment."

cases, a systematic job diagnosis is rarely undertaken before the changes are implemented. Finally, in many situations, the line and staff people who are introducing change are poorly informed about how it should be conducted or evaluated. The feedback may be biased and unsystematic and the management of the change may regress to more traditional bureaucratic practices.

The OD process also has problems.[35] In many cases, too much emphasis is placed on individual problems in the "informal" organization. The total organization and its formal structure may be de-emphasized, yet both should probably change together. On occasion certain steps in the OD process are omitted or underrepresented. For example, in many cases too little time is spent on diagnosis and task analysis with an overemphasis on change interventions. Finally, OD practitioners sometimes assume that they know more about the organization's problems than the organization's participants.

The implications of these criticisms are rather explicit. To do a good job changing tasks or interpersonal processes takes a lot of time, effort, and commitment. It requires continual planning and evaluation. And most of all, it requires a slow, step-by-step feedback procedure. The consultant must really know the organization and be intimately involved with the planned change in order to assure effectiveness.

Criticisms about the Evidence

The Cummings and Salipante study seemed to indicate that most research studies were highly supportive of planned change strategies. However, their analysis of the research designs employed to generate these data was fairly discouraging. They evaluated each study in terms of the possible confounding interpretations of the data. The designs were generally poor, the conclusions generally unwarranted and they summarized by saying:

> In summarizing about internal validity, we must conclude that the hypotheses reviewed in the report have not been very thoroughly probed. The multivariate nature of the experiments and the looseness of the designs make it impossible to present any conclusive results. The overall trend is positive, but far more rigorous research is necessary before we can have confidence in the validity of the results.[36]

---

[35] L. E. Greiner, "Red Flags in Organization Development," *Business Horizons,* June 1972, pp. 17–24.

[36] Cummings and Salipante, "Development of Research-Based Strategies."

Future directions are unclear. In general, there seems to be more correspondence between the more rational "scientific management" people and the clinically oriented "industrial humanists." Attempts at job enrichment and organizational development are more frequently including interventions from both schools of thought. However, we are still basically ignorant about what works, when it works, and why it works. We suspect that just as in other areas, there will develop a contingency approach to organizational change which will specify what kinds of interventions are best with what sorts of people dealing with certain types of problems.[37] However, this goal will be realized only through more systematic evaluation of the implementation process and of the goals actually achieved.

---

[37] See Victor H. Vroom and Philip W. Yetton, *Leadership and Decision Making* (Pittsburgh: University of Pittsburgh Press, 1974), for a current example of such an approach.

chapter 17

Organizational Training

The word "training" has many meanings. To some writers in the field of personnel management training means developing work force for particular jobs.[1] Other writers interpret it more broadly, including training for adequate job performance *and* extending an employee's intellectual range through general education.[2] Still other writers speak of an overall area called development, which they divide into education and training. Training in this instance means fitting the person to the job, whereas the purpose of education fits the person to the environment off and on the job.[3]

Searching management literature for an operative definition of management training in the behavioral sciences is quite futile. By their nature, such programs crosscut the definitions of training and education given above. In one sense, an understanding of the behavioral sciences at the skill level and at the level of concept fulfills the requirement of the training definition because the presumption is that knowledge and ability in this area will help a manager do a better job. In another sense, a knowledge of the behavioral sciences is essential for the executive from the standpoint that organization theory, and the theory of

---

[1] Dale Yoder, *Personnel Management and Industrial Relations*, 4th ed. (Englewood Cliffs, N.J.: Prentice-Hall, Inc., 1956), chapter 9.

[2] William W. Waite, *Personnel Administration* (New York: The Ronald Press Co., 1952), pp. 219–40.

[3] Arthur M. Whitehill, Jr., *Personnel Relations* (New York: McGraw-Hill Book Company, 1955), pp. 121–51.

personality is essential for executives who are moving in complex social and business environments.

These remarks provide a background for a definition of training programs oriented toward the behavioral sciences. Training in the behavioral sciences is an activity which has as its goal individual achievement of greater job effectiveness, improved interpersonal relationships in the organization, and better adjustment of an executive to the total environment.

Thus, the immediate goals of training aim at improving individual job effectiveness and the climate of interpersonal relations. The purpose of training in the behavioral sciences is to equip executives with the knowledge and attitude toward human behavior that will improve their ability to run their own command unit and relate it successfully to others in the organization. In short, training seeks a change in the behavior of the trainee.

UNDERSTANDING TRAINING NEEDS

To produce the desired changes one must be familiar with the needs of the organization, the kinds of changes possible, and the ways in which one brings about these changes. These preliminary topics will be discussed before turning to a description and evaluation of various programs.[4]

Discovering Training Needs

Before an organization chooses a training program for any of its employees there are some preliminary questions which should be asked. A thorough analysis of the organization, the jobs involved, and the employees affected should be conducted in order to discover what is needed in the way of training.

Organizational Goals. A general consideration of both the long- and short-term goals of the organization is important for developing a broad perspective of one's training philosophy. How does the organization feel it will grow? How will both the social and physical environment be related to this growth? In general, what sort of "climate" and "image" is being sought?

---

[4] See Herbert J. Chruden and Arthur W. Sherman, Jr., *Personnel Management* (Cincinnati, Ohio: South-Western Publishing Co., 1959), pp. 153–54.

If the organization wishes to hire minority group members living in the neighborhood this may affect the selection of a training program. Or perhaps management wants to emphasize the relationship between the organization and the physical environment. What sorts of waste products are there? How does the firm handle these issues? Since organizations are constantly being forced to plan their production or services years in advance the same emphasis should be placed on their goals and training philosophy. Otherwise, they will fail to correspond to one another and the training will be of limited value.

Job Analysis. In the consideration of training procedures management must also keep in mind the jobs for which people are being trained. An analysis of these jobs requires knowledge of the kinds of skills, attitudes, behaviors, and personality characteristics that are most effective for those positions. These data would spell out rather clearly the tasks that constitute the job.

It should be pointed out that in some cases this may be a very difficult task because of the flexible nature of some managerial positions. But it is just this difficulty that makes it crucial. We know that different kinds of situations require different types of people with different attitudes, behaviors, and skills. There are three possible consequences of training: greater effectiveness, no change, and less effectiveness. Since two of these are costly, it pays for the organization to know what is needed.

Work Force Analysis. The final assessment of the functioning of the organization involves the employees currently filling the positions of interest. Some attempt should be made to find out if performance is substandard to begin with. Second, it may be true that the problems with performance are due to nontrainable factors. More specifically, technological or mechanical changes may be needed—not changes in the employees. It would also be important to determine if the employees currently in the positions are capable of improvement through training or whether new personnel is needed. In short, a thorough look at the goals, jobs, and job occupants is needed before one decides what and how to train.

Kinds of Changes Induced by Training

Like most forms of training, programs in the behavioral sciences aim to transmit information, develop attitudes, and improve skills.[5] Another

---

[5] Ibid., pp. 153–54.

facet of training, representing a fairly recent shift in emphasis, is the marked interest in the development of managerial conceptual abilities in the behavioral sciences. Each of these training facets is discussed separately, but it should be recognized that there is a considerable amount of overlap among them.

Transmitting Information. The essential element in most training programs is content. The purpose of training is to impart to the trainees information drawn from a body of knowledge. Training in the behavioral sciences, therefore, transmits to participants information about human personality and motivation, the process of communication, organization theory including small group processes, leadership, and so on. Fields such as sociology, psychology, social-psychology, and anthropology are relied upon by the program developers and conference leaders to supply the material.

Development of Attitudes. Closely linked to the imparting of knowledge is the development of attitudes. Actually, it is more accurate to say *changing* the attitudes of participants. People go into training programs with certain preconceived ideas about leadership, the grapevine, the function of status, and the informal organization. The attitudes management trainees have regarding these factors and others in the organization environment determine executive effectiveness of a leader.

Experts in behavioral science training feel it is not sufficient just to impart knowledge in these fields. It is also necessary to work on changing the participants' attitudes on human behavior. Thus, the training aspect of attitude development is an important part of programs. It is, however, one of the most difficult to execute effectively.

Development of Skills. Assume that in a given training program a considerable amount of information has been transmitted to participants, and that in the progress of training their attitudes have been changed. In other words, the first two aspects of training were accomplished well. Is the program then a success? The answer probably is "no," because the trainees have not yet had an opportunity to develop "human skills" in the application of the material imparted to them. Consequently, the next logical phase of training is skill development.

Some argue that the development of skills in the use of human tools derived from training must come from on-the-job experience. Classroom simulation of human problems through case studies and role playing, it is claimed, is inadequate even when conducted under the supervision of a training expert. Nevertheless, those in the training field are constantly working on new devices and techniques which endeavor to fill the need for realistic forms of classroom experiences where skills can be developed.

Conceptual Level. The notion that training or education in the application of the behavioral sciences to management practice should be conducted on a higher level of abstraction is a fairly recent development. The objective is to move training a step or two beyond direct application to a level of greater generalization. The idea is to develop managers who can *think* in behavioral science terms.

Although not specifically mentioned, it can be seen that different aspects of training are emphasized at different organizational levels. Managerial development may concentrate on changing some attitudes, concepts, and interpersonal skills, whereas the training of front-line supervisors might emphasize the transmission of knowledge and the development of certain motor skills. The important point is that the trainees change their behavior in some way.

Principles of Learning

We have already defined training in terms of changes in behavior, and we have mentioned some kinds of changes that might take place. The changes are facilitated through the process of learning which Bass and Vaughn define as "a relatively permanent change in behavior that occurs as a result of practice or experience."[6] This is a broad definition which would include learning to walk, driving a car, painting, or doing addition. It would also include changes in interpersonal behavior, attitudes or one's conceptual framework. To bring about these changes one must understand some of the basic principles of how behavior is modified.

Motivation. Perhaps the best starting point is to state that the trainee should want to learn. This is not to say that participation in a training program without motivation would result in no learning. However up to a certain point, wanting and trying to learn (paying attention, and so on), will increase the amount learned. Certain types of programs may be interesting and motivating by themselves or external rewards can be provided. One principle used to make training intrinsically interesting is to assure the active participation of the trainee. Rather than read a case study, a trainer could have the trainees play the roles of the characters mentioned in the case. Some authors even suggest that

[6] Bernard M. Bass and James A. Vaughn, *Training in Industry: The Management of Learning* (Belmont, Calif.: Wadsworth Publishing Co., 1966), p. 8.

the trainee participate in the planning and formulation of the training program itself.[7]

For external motivation, a variety of financial or social rewards could be used. Ingenohl, for example, argues that the competitive nature of training will serve as a good motivator for managers.[8] In any case, the desire to do well is an important determinant of how much one receives out of a training program.

Reinforcement and Feedback. One of the most powerful principles of learning says that when one receives positive rewards, information, or feelings for doing something that it becomes more likely that he or she will do the same thing in the same or similar situations. On the other side is the fact that punishment for a particular response will decrease the probability of its occurrence in similar settings. The trainer should thus be able to increase the frequency of desirable behavior through the correct use of various rewards (praise, money, status, and so on). The major problem, however, is to determine what will serve as reinforcers. Different people want different things and the use of rewards which an individual does not desire will not affect learning in the manner anticipated.

Coupled with the idea of reinforcement is the very similar idea of giving individuals feedback or knowledge of when they are correct or incorrect. Providing this information in an explicit manner lets the trainees correct their mistakes and often makes the task more rewarding or stimulating. Vroom reviews a number of studies where individuals show greater performance on a variety of tasks when they have feedback than when it is absent.[9] Ayers reports a study on a management training course where those receiving feedback showed greater changes in their behavior than those without this information.[10] The two principles together suggest that trainers should tell trainees when they are doing poorly or well, why that is the case, and provide attractive or unattractive consequences as a result of the trainees' behavior.

Practice and Repetition. The greater the opportunity to repeat or practice something we learn the better it is learned. With practice indi-

---

[7] See C. Argyris, "Puzzle and Perplexity in Executive Development," *Personnel Journal,* 39 (1961), 463–65. Also E. H. Schein, "Forces Which Undermine Management Development," *California Management Review,* 5 (1963), 23–34.

[8] I. Ingenohl, "Blueprints for a Successful Management Development Policy," *Personnel,* 41 (1962), 491–94.

[9] Victor Vroom, *Work and Motivation* (New York: John Wiley & Sons, Inc., 1964), pp. 242–43.

[10] A. W. Ayers, "Effects of Knowledge of Results on Supervisors' Post-Training Test Scores," *Personnel Psychology,* 32 (1955), 152–55.

viduals may become more familiar and at ease with what they are supposed to do. Also by the judicious use of various ways to teach similar things the trainer may illustrate the generality of the information to be learned. For certain managerial training courses there could be multiple chances to play roles or practice behavioral skills. For other types of supervisory training involving motor skills the trainee should be allowed to repeat the correct responses over and over. These behaviors are "overlearned to ensure smooth performance and a minimum of forgetting at a later date."[11]

Meaningfulness of Material. There are at least three ways that the organization and presentation of the material is important. First, the material should be meaningful in the sense that it is understandable and interpretable by those participating in the training. There are certain techniques available to trainers and Kolasa mentions a few: "Organizing meaningful units, creating association with familiar terms, and providing a conceptual basis or logical reason for the material are some of the practical possibilities."[12]

A second related topic is the amount of the information presented at one time to the trainee. The question here is whether to split the information into smaller parts or present it as a whole. Surveys of the literature suggest that the trainer should use as large a unit of information as can be handled and meaningfully presented. Too much information or too broad a scope may confuse the trainee. The major problem with this principle involves the determination of the "correct" unit.

Finally, it has been argued that training should space out its learning periods rather than present them all together. When all the information is presented together it seems to couple the problems of not breaking the information down into smaller units and probably presents limitations of practice time. By spacing out the sessions the material is easier to assimilate and practice. One study of managerial training procedures indicated that managers who received their training over a two-week period made fewer mistakes than those who received their training in three successive days.[13]

---

[11] John P. Campbell, Marvin D. Dunnette, Edward E. Lawler, III, and Karl E. Weick, Jr., *Managerial Behavior, Performance, and Effectiveness* (New York: McGraw-Hill Book Company 1970), p. 257.

[12] Blair J. Kolasa, *Introduction to Behavioral Science for Business* (New York: John Wiley & Sons, Inc., 1969), p. 186.

[13] W. R. Mahler, and W. H. Monroe, "How Industry Determines the Need for and Effectiveness of Training," *Personnel Research Section Report*, No. 929, 1952, Department of the Army.

Transfer of Training. Clearly, the purpose of training employees is to prepare them for some position in the organization. One important aspect of any training program, therefore, is the degree to which the material to be learned can be transferred to the job. There are at least two possible strategies for obtaining transferability. The first is to make the training situation similar to the actual job in terms of the physical characteristics of the situation. Training on the job would therefore maximize this similarity. Simulations that attempt to physically represent the situation in which one will work would also display this similarity. However, most management and leadership training takes place off the job and requires a somewhat different approach.

The second strategy is the teaching of *principles* that may be applied on the job. One may learn about the interdependence of organizational parts or the complexity of individual decisions through a series of case studies, role-playing sessions or simulations. It is hoped that the trainee will carry these principles onto the job. However, as we shall see, this hope is often not fulfilled.

TRAINING PROGRAMS

The training and development of employees has been on the increase for a number of years. A study in the 30s reported that only about 3 percent of the companies surveyed had executive training programs.[14] In 1954, Tricket reported a figure of 50 percent and Serbein reported in 1961 that out of 277 firms with 10,000 or more employees, 255 had some type of training program.[15] Campbell, et al. reported a few years ago that the aircraft industry spent about $34 million per year on training. In a recent interview they discovered that that much was now being spent by just one company.[16]

These figures reflect changes for different types of training and are therefore, difficult to compare. More specifically, some studies have looked at all forms of training while others have gathered information only on managerial development. However, there are three broad trends

---

[14] S. Habbe, "College Graduates Assess Their Company Training," *National Industrial Conference Board Studies in Personnel Policy*, No. 188, 1963, cited in D. S. Bridgeman, "Company Management Development Programs," in F. C. Pierson et al., *The Education of American Businessmen* (New York: McGraw-Hill Book Company, 1959), pp. 536–76.

[15] O. N. Serbein, *Educational Activities of Business* (Washington, D.C.: American Council on Education, 1961). Tricket's study is reported in D. S. Bridgeman, "Company Management Development Programs," pp. 536–76.

[16] Campbell et al., *Managerial Behavior*, pp. 40–43.

that seem to be justified. First, training is increasing. Firms are spending more money on developing and maintaining the effectiveness of their employees. Studies by Bailey and by Wickstrom both report that organizations are training employees to improve their performance or prepare them for promotion.[17]

A second trend is that training is now taking place to an increasing extent outside the organization. Many training programs are run by an outside agency or institute that provides the service for a fee. The implications of this trend are that specialists in training now exist and that providing this service has become a big business in itself.

The third point is tied to the first two: training is currently broader in scope than it used to be. Numerous training programs today emphasize the learning of complex emotional and behavioral skills. Sensitivity training is one of these. Other programs emphasize attitudinal and informational issues. Training is no longer used just to teach motor skills to assembly-line employees. There are feasible programs for employees at all levels in the organization.

Because of the multiplicity of programs developed we will only describe some of the more representative types of programs both for on-the-job and off-the-job training. The programs will generally be evaluated in terms of the utilization of learning principles discussed earlier.

On-the-Job Training

One of the most common procedures over the years has been to train a person while on the job. A practical reason for this approach is that the individual is producing while being trained. No special space or equipment need be used. There are, however, some shortcomings associated with these approaches. A competent trainer or coach must be provided from within the organization. If the trainee must work at a reduced pace then certain equipment or facilities may be tied up. The trainee must experience some of the stress and pressure of the job while trying to learn. In short, the use of such training should be carefully evaluated in terms of needs, costs, and effectiveness.

Job Instruction. Most firms have some means of introducing the employee to the work environment. Traditional programs would include a general survey of the firm, personal introductions to the people with

---

[17] J. K. Bailey, "The Goals of Supervisory Training: A Study of Company Programs," *Personnel*, 32 (1955), 311–26. Also, W. S. Wickstrom, "Developing Managerial Competence, Changing Concepts—Emerging Practices," *National Industrial Conference Board Studies in Personnel Policy*, No. 189, 1964.

whom the trainee will work, and some instruction about the job. During World War II, The War Manpower Board formalized some of the procedures involved for introducing the new trainee to a variety of technical jobs. Bass describes these steps as follows:

> After an introductory statement of the purposes of the job, the trainee receives a step-by-step review and demonstration of the job operations. He then tries to perform the operations himself, explaining as he proceeds. The instructor is encouraged to ask the trainee questions during this demonstration and to correct mistakes as they occur. Practice continues until the trainee reaches a satisfactory level of performance; then close supervision is removed. However, the trainer is cautioned to check back later to insure that his performance continues to be satisfactory.[18]

Notice that repetition, feedback, active participation, and easily transferable experiences are built into this type of training. However, no matter how well the materials or job are organized, the skills of the trainer are potential problems. It should also be pointed out that this type of training is suited best for jobs that have fairly specific content. It also requires close supervision, which means that the trainer's time and potential productivity are being used for this task.

Coaching. A less formalized procedure than the one described above is often called coaching. In this type of program, the trainee may have one person who is the tutor or "big brother" in the organization. The coach will attempt to help the trainee by providing feedback, setting goals, and discussing any problems that may occur. Training of this kind may be used for positions at many different levels within the organization.

A study by Goodacre of certain coaching practices used by General Electric indicated that coaches (who had been trained how to coach) increased their ability to set performance standards, provide feedback and assistance for trainees.[19] The major problem with the coaching approach is that it is dependent upon the skills of the coach. The amount and kinds of feedback and reinforcement, as well as the way the material is presented, are possible difficulties. And again, to the degree that the coach spends time coaching he or she is not doing other things.

Job Rotation. When the trainee is required to work in a number of assignments before assuming a permanent position he or she is involved in a job-rotation program. Many law firms and certainly the

---

[18] Bass and Vaughn, *Training in Industry*, p. 89.

[19] Daniel M. Goodacre, "Stimulating Improved Management," *Personnel Psychology*, 16 (1963), 133–43.

medical profession require this sort of training. In large organizations the trainee may become familiar with the existing divisions or departments. The program may provide not only scope but also allow the trainee to work at different levels within the organization. This variety of experience is designed to give the trainee an overall view of the organization and the interrelationships of its parts.

There are a variety of problems with this approach. The supervision or feedback that the trainee receives is often spotty or inconsistent. It is also worth arguing that some of the experiences are nontransferable; that is, not useful for the permanent position. Finally, it is one of the more long-term and expensive procedures for training.

To be effective, a trainee should be able to have a flexible job-rotation program. Different positions in the organization should require different training and the job-rotation program for an individual should reflect these needs. The organization should also provide consistent feedback, reinforcement, and goal-setting procedures through the use of competent managers, coaches, or advisers.

Junior Boards. A shorter and less involved strategy than job rotation is to assign the trainee to a committee or junior board which deals with programs concerning the whole organization. In this way the trainee is able to learn information about the different departments or subunits of the organization and how they operate. In some cases this board may be set up for the explicit purpose of serving as a training device. These assignments are often used as supplements to the programs already described. Their effectiveness depends upon the degree to which the task is related to activities that the trainee will have to perform later and the degree to which he learns the correct information.

Assistantship or Apprenticeship. In these types of programs the trainee is often assigned as an assistant or apprentice to an individual in the organization. In most cases this trainer holds a position similar to the one the trainee hopes to eventually hold. So, for example, a trainee (in graduate school) may be a teaching or research assistant or in occupations such as plumbing or carpentry an individual may serve an apprenticeship before assuming the position.

These programs have some rather distinct features. The trainee is usually assigned to one person and for a given length of time. Before assuming the position there are typically a number of tests or competencies that the trainee must display. It is precisely these features which may weaken this type of training. First, the dependence on one coach or trainer demands that he or she be good in providing feedback and reinforcement. Second, the rigidity of the program often restricts the individual from moving along faster than the program allows. It is just this problem that is being contested by many minority groups. They argue that the apprenticeship programs can be completed sooner than the union may allow. A third and related point is that the competencies or tests may not reflect what the individual needs to know for the position to be assumed. More specifically, the wrong material may be emphasized.

In summary, most on-the-job techniques have the advantages of being similar to what the trainee will actually be doing (transfer of training) and they allow the organization to obtain some benefit from the trainee who is working while being trained. The degree to which the materials are effectively organized, and feedback provided are generally matters which require attention as does the motivation of the trainee. In some cases, organizations have decided that this function is handled more effectively by outside trainers.

Off-the-Job Training: Informational Techniques

In many cases the organization wishes to provide training that would supplement its on-the-job efforts or facilities. In these situations off-the-job techniques are used. The advantages for this approach are numerous. The trainee is not obliged to perform under the stress or anxiety of the actual work setting. Removal from the setting may provide opportunities for the trainee to practice various skills and test acquired knowledge without the possibility of dire consequences.

The organization is, of course, obliged to pay for these services. This cost, however, may be lower in the long run than the cost of using the organizations' existing personnel and perhaps risking major mistakes while on the job. Finally, it is an opportunity for the organization to utilize the skills of specialists in the field of training. More specifically, the organization may not have people with the skills or facilities to conduct the training.

The major problem with most off-the-job training is just that: it is off the job. When the training is not similar to the actual work requirements it becomes questionable as to how much of the training is actually transferable. The trainee may learn a lot but is he learning the right thing?

In recent years there has been an increase in these supplementary programs. Changing needs, widened interests, and technological advances have all influenced this increment. We will break these programs down into two categories; those that deal with the dissemination of information and those that attempt to change behavior. Although this distinction is not applicable for all the programs, it is useful in terms of identifying the major emphasis and actual applications of the training technique.

Lectures. This technique typically involves a trainer reading and organizing some material which is presented orally to a group of trainees. It is probably the most widely used method of training and this is because it is an inexpensive way to distribute information to a large number of people. In fact, in its economy lies its chief positive point.

It has been suggested, however, that lectures became obsolete with the invention of type. It is argued that the trainee could read the material himself. While this may be true it still does not account for the difference in work hours expended when each member of a class reads some information versus one individual reading it and passing along the important information. It is also true that the trainer should have expertise in the area and will therefore be able to organize and synthesize the material in the most meaningful fashion.

Bass and Vaughn present some more important criticisms. They point out that:

> The lecture generally consists of a one-way communication: The instructor presents information to a group of passive listeners. Thus little or no opportunity exists to clarify meanings, to check on whether trainees really understand the lecture material, or to handle the wider diversity of ability, attitude, and interest that may prevail among the trainees. Also, there is little or no opportunity for practice, reinforcement, knowledge of results, or overlearning.[20]

In short, the organization pays heavily for the economy.

Discussion or Conference. This type of training typically involves trainees discussing preselected topics that are related to the work setting. It is very often used to teach principles of communication, problem solving, and decision making and it is perhaps the most frequently used method of training for managers.[21]

The advantages over a lecture are numerous. The trainer may provide feedback and the trainee can be actively involved in the learning process. The communication is two way. Also important is the fact that the trainee may learn from others or his own errors by receiving positive or negative reinforcement that corresponds to the way in which he has behaved. Levine and Butler describe a study where 27 managers were

[20] Bass and Vaughn, *Training in Industry*, p. 94.
[21] D. Yoder, *Personnel Management and Industrial Relations* (Englewood Cliffs, N.J.: Prentice-Hall, Inc., 1962).

placed in 3 groups to deal with a problem that had arisen in the evaluation system for subordinates.[22] Nine people discussed the problem, nine received a lecture, and nine served as a control group. The lecture and control groups showed no change in their rating procedures while the discussion group made significant changes toward reducing the problem.

This technique requires a highly skilled trainer. It is difficult to control a discussion without hindering the desired freedom. The trainer must know what to say to different people and must be ready for unanticipated events. The major problems with this method occur when the trainer is not able to properly carry out the functions. In these situations the discussion may get off the topic or may dwell on one point too long. When the material is poorly organized or poorly covered it reduces the chance of transfer from the session to the work setting.

Films and TV. Both television and films are examples of technological advances that are used in training. The use of a video tape or actual film is skillfully done and has some distinct advantages. First, the tape can be used again. The organization is not dependent upon a given lecturer or dicussion leader. Second, certain scenes or visual effects may be used to maximum advantage. For example, pictures of actual accidents in industry are used in safety films. Third, films often heighten the motivation and interest of the trainee. Fryer and Edgerton report a study comparing the information learned from a film on aerial gunnery to that learned from a manual and from a lecture on the same material.[23] The film was superior to the other two techniques.

The major problem with the material presented in this form is that there is no two-way communication. It is effective in the distribution of information but seldom provides for the active participation of the trainee. Feedback and reinforcement processes are also absent. One way to circumvent some of these problems is to couple discussions with films or lectures or TV presentations and in fact, this is often done.

Special Study. Some training programs consist of a special format of study that the individual pursues off the job. These special study courses may be given by universities under the label of "continuing education" or they may be tailor-made for a given set of managers or executives. Usually, there are specific reading lists and lectures pro-

[22] J. Levine and J. Butler, "Lecture versus Group Decision in Changing Behavior," *Journal of Applied Psychology*, 36 (1952), 29–33.

[23] D. H. Fryer and H. A. Edgerton, "Research Concerning 'Off-the Job Training'," *Personnel Psychology*, 3 (1950), 261–84.

vided as well as discussion groups. The readings and discussions are topic oriented and focus on a wide variety of issues. Viteles reports data on a program run at the University of Pennsylvania for some managers from Bell Telephone.[24] These managers received information on art, history, music, city planning, business history, and other topics. Their attitudes about innovation and change were reported to be much more favorable after the course when compared to a control group that had not received the program. Probably the most important consideration for this type of program is its organization. If it is poorly organized or the material is poorly selected there may be very little transfer of information to the real organizational setting.

Off-the-Job Training: Behavioral Programs

In recent years, a number of new types of training programs have been developed for off-the-job use. Although in certain cases the differences between these methods and some of those already described may be slight, the basic underlying goal of the new programs is to change behavior through active involvement and experiential learning. One of the major problems with the traditional techniques that involved lectures or films was that the communication was one way, the trainee was not involved, and the applicability of the material was not always apparent. The programs that evolved, specifically addressed themselves to the use of one or more of these principles in an atttempt to improve the training.

Case Study-Role Playing. The typical case study used for business purposes is a thorough description of some events that actually occurred in an organization. Cases have been included in training programs because it is believed that leadership effectiveness can be achieved through the study of situations with which managers have been actually confronted.

The application of the technique is flexible with a few basic processes seen as standard procedures. The trainee or trainees read the case and present some alternative solutions or lines of action. These suggestions may then be discussed in a class session where the individual is able to obtain information about how others viewed the case. The trainee is therefore actively involved and is working in a setting which is supposedly similar to a setting he or she might encounter.

---

[24] M. S. Viteles, " 'Human Relations' and the 'Humanities' in the Education of Business Leaders: Evaluation of a Program of Humanistic Studies for Executives,' *Personnel Psychology*, 12 (1959), 1–28.

In discussions of the case method many authors point out that there is no one correct solution to the case.[25] The trainee is encouraged to consider a variety of alternatives and actively encouraged to explore different points of view. He should project himself into the case to some extent by asking "What would I do if I were in this situation?" The emphasis on flexibility however, creates some problems. To the degree that there are no answers, it is difficult to use effective reinforcement techniques and to judge objectively whether the trainee has done a good job. Hopefully, the trainee is learning to come up with both numerous and constructive plans of action.

In an attempt to increase the participation and involvement in case studies, trainees are sometimes asked to play the roles of the case participants. That is, they act out a case as if it were a play. This technique is known as role playing and a comparison between the role-playing and case study techniques is presented in Figure 17–1. As one can

FIGURE 17–1

Case Study	Role Playing
1. Presents a problem for discussion.	Places the problem in a lifelike setting.
2. Derives problems from previous events.	Involves problems with ongoing processes.
3. Typically deals with problems involving others.	Typically deals with problems involving the participants themselves.
4. Deals with emotional and attitudinal aspects in an intellectual frame of reference.	Deals with emotional and attitudinal aspects in an experiential frame of reference.
5. Emphasizes the importance of facts.	Emphasizes the importance of feelings.
6. Typically involves discussion from a psychological position "outside" the problem situation.	Deals with participants who are psychologically "inside" the problem situation.
7. Facilitates intellectual involvement.	Makes for emotional involvement.
8. Furnishes practice in analysis of problems.	Provides practice in interpersonal skills.
9. Provides for development of ideas and hypotheses.	Provides for testing ideas and hypotheses.
10. Trains in the exercise of judgment.	Trains in emotional control.
11. Defines the action or solution.	Provides for execution of the action or solution.
12. Involves action whose consequences are usually undetermined.	Involves continuous feedback.

Source: Bernard M. Bass and James A. Vaughn, *Training in Industry: The Management of Learning* (Belmont, Calif.: Wadsworth Publishing Co., 1966), p. 101.

[25] J. D. Glover and R. M. Hower, *The Administrator: Cases on Human Relations in Business* (Homewood, Ill.: Richard D. Irwin, Inc., 1973).

see the trainee gains both information and experience through this technique. By switching roles one may gain insight into "how the other guy feels." Although the content is not necessarily tied to cases, the emphasis seems to be similar in that both techniques are designed to provide practice in the development of one's interpersonal insights and skills.

There are some shortcomings however with the procedure. The trainer must be careful in the way in which the group plays out their roles. Some individuals may become too involved in the "acting" and lose sight of the purpose of the exercise. The trainer must also be careful that the trainees receive correct feedback and reinforcement: More to the point, he must be sure that trainees are not reinforced for doing the wrong thing. Finally, some sort of supplemental discussion period is probably necessary to discuss the feelings and insights experienced by the trainee.[26] Without this supplement the trainee will not be able to provide necessary information about an individual's reactions during the training.

Simulations.   Simulations attempt not only to involve the individual but also to duplicate the environmental setting in which the trainee will eventually work. A list of the typical features of a simulation is presented in Figure 17–2. A well-developed simulation would, therefore,

FIGURE 17–2

1. The essential characteristics of a real-life organization or activity are abstracted and presented as a case—not to be studied and analyzed as in the usual case method, but to be experienced by the trainee as a realistic, lifelike circumstance.
2. Trainees are asked to assume various roles in the circumstance and to solve the problems facing them. They are asked to be themselves—*not* to act.
3. A simulation often involves a telescoping or compressing of time and events; a single hour may be equated with a month or a quarter of a year in real life, and many events are experienced in a relatively brief period of time.
4. Trainees are required to make decisions that have a real effect in the simulation and about which they receive rapid feedback.
5. The simulation is followed by a critique of what went on during the exercise.

    Source: Bernard M. Bass and James A. Vaughn, *Training in Industry: The Management of Learning* (Belmont, Calif.: Wadsworth Publishing Co., 1966), p. 105.

maximize the use of many of the learning principles which we have described.

Examples of simulations for business fall under two major headings, those that deal with games of some sort and those that attempt to dupli-

---

   [26] C. H. Lawshe, Jr., R. A. Bolda, and R. L. Brune, "Studies in Management Training Evaluations: II. The Effects of Exposures to Role Playing," *Journal of Applied Psychology*, 42 (1958), 396–98.

cate a task setting. In the case of business games an environment is designed to replicate the economic and administrative functioning of an actual organization. This duplication is based on various principles linking inputs with processes and then with eventual outcomes or output which in turn change the inputs. The trainees make decisions (as individuals or in teams) about the market, the budget, personnel policy, or so on, and these decisions modify the situation and more decisions are required. The games are typically conducted over a series of sessions or trials where the trainees are given some information and some general statements about how to use the information (e.g., economic principles, probability estimates). The trainees must then make a variety of decisions, and a given session will end when this is done. The trainer must then figure out the implications of the decisions that were made according to the preestablished relationships underlying the game. He then gives this information back to the trainees and another trial begins. It should be mentioned that the sophistication of these games is highly variable. Some use computers to provide rapid and continuous feedback while some use the discrete steps described above.

There are a few drawbacks associated with these games. Under certain circumstances trainees may discover some gimmick or principle which allows them to win or to perform successfully. This gimmick, however, may not be a good strategy to employ in an actual organizational setting. A similar problem occurs when trainees become so involved in winning the game that they fail to learn the major principles that are being taught. Finally, where the simulation is inaccurate in its representation of the environment the trainee may actually learn the wrong thing.[27]

The type of simulation designed to represent a more specific task setting is best illustrated by the "in-basket" technique.[28] The trainee is presented with a situation where he or she must take over for a manager who is absent. He is provided with an in-basket full of materials with which he must deal. These materials may be phone calls, meetings to set up, complaints to handle, orders to make, and other demands, which supposedly duplicate the tasks he would face if he held such a position. These materials are typically gathered by assessing what a manager of a certain type of firm actually does during a day. The

[27] C. J. Croft, J. Kibbee, and B. Nanus, *Management Games* (New York: Reinhold, 1961).

[28] N. Frederiksen, D. R. Saunders, and B. Ward, "The In-Basket Test," *Psychological Monographs*, 71: 9 (Whole No. 438) (1957).

trainee must go through the material and deal with it as best he can. This may require a list of priorities and in fact, may result in some demands to which he will not attend. After the session is completed the trainer and trainee should meet to discuss and evaluate the trainee's performance. Similar techniques may have people working together as a management group or may supplement the task with films.[29] Again, the same strong and weak points that were applicable for business games are applicable here. The trainer must be sure that the trainee is learning the correct material.

Programmed Instruction. A relatively new approach to training has emphasized a technique known as programmed learning. The characteristics of this type of instruction are:

1. The material to be learned is broken down into small units called "frames" which are presented to the trainee one at a time (in a book or on a screen).
2. The trainee is required to respond to each frame as to a multiple choice question. That is, read the frame and then respond to a question about it.
3. The trainee then receives immediate feedback and reinforcement. If the answer is incorrect the trainee usually must reread the frame and choose again.
4. Material is sequenced according to its complexity with more difficult items dependent upon knowledge acquired in the earlier stages of the program.

These principles emphasize the organization of the material, feedback, reinforcement, and the active participation of the trainee. Modification of the basic format, called linear programming, has allowed the trainee to progress at his or her own speed. That is, if a trainee shows that he knows certain material by his responses on a set of separate frames he may be "branched" to more complex material. The trainee who has trouble may be given an extra set of frames to help him master a given topic.[30]

Although the technique seems to be most applicable for the teaching of factual material there are a number of examples where it has been

[29] C. W. Gibson, "A New Dimension for "In-Basket" Training," *Personnel*, 38 (1961), 76–79.

[30] N. Growder, "Automatic Tutoring by Means of Intrinsic Programming," in E. Galanter, ed., *Automatic Teaching: The State of the Art* (New York: John Wiley & Sons, Inc., 1959).

used for training behavioral skills. One report by Lysaught describes the use of this technique to teach motivational principles to managers and another study used programmed instruction in an attempt to teach certain supervisory skills in the delegation of responsibility, the scheduling and handling of work flow, and the chairing of meetings.[31] Another series of studies has used programmed instruction to teach managers about other cultures in which they are soon to work.[32] This device, called the "culture assimilator" presents frames consisting of intercultural encounters between Americans and the people from the culture of interest. Studies conducted in Greece, Iran, Honduras, and Thailand show that this technique produces better interpersonal relations, adjustment— and in certain cases—productivity than that produced by other training techniques.

There are a number of considerations, however, which limit the use of this type of program. First, it can be very expensive, both to develop and to maintain. If the programs are to be placed on computers and presented on teaching machines (small consoles with a screen and a variety of buttons on which one can respond) the cost may be prohibitive. It is also important to note that the transfer of the training may be questionable. Just because some information is learned does not necessarily mean that one will behave in the fashion desired.

Laboratory Training. In the 1967 edition of this book the chapter on management development had the following introductory sentence: "Management development has two distinct eras: BST (Before Sensitivity Training) and AST (After Sensitivity Training)."[33] It is our opinion that this sentence still reflects rather accurately the importance of this technique and its impact on management training.

Sensitivity or laboratory training is a fairly recent innovation in executive development. It has grown out of the work of applied group dynamics[34] and is often associated with the program of the National Training Laboratory in Group Development.[35] The training approaches developed

---

[31] J. P. Lysaught, *Programmed Learning: Evolving Principles and Industrial Applications* (Ann Arbor, Mich.: Foundation for Research on Human Behavior, 1961).

[32] F. E. Fiedler, T. R. Mitchell, and H. G. Triandis, "The Culture Assimilator: An Approach to Cross-Cultural Training," *Journal of Applied Psychology,* 55 (1971), 95–103.

[33] William G. Scott, *Organization Theory: A Behavioral Analysis for Management* (Homewood, Ill.: Richard D. Irwin, Inc., 1967), p. 323.

[34] See D. Cartwright and A. Zander, eds., *Group Dynamics: Research and Theory* (Evanston, Ill.: Row, Peterson and Co., 1960).

[35] See National Training Laboratory in Group Development, "Explorations in Human Relations Training: An Assessment of Experience, 1947–1953" (Washington, D.C.: National Education Association, 1953).

by researchers in these activities have been applied to industrial pro-grams in a number of forms.[36] The objectives of sensitivity training, however, are basically the same.

It has been repeatedly observed in this chapter that the purpose of training is to change behavior. In the realm of *human* interrelation-ships as in no other sphere of human interest attitudes are fixed and loaded with explosive content. The aim of most human-relations training is to accomplish organizational goals through the efforts of people. It is something of a self-evident truth that executive behavior in human undertakings is a matter of attitudes which are effective or ineffective from the standpoint of motivating people. Therefore, human-relations training attempts to change attitudes so that ultimately behavior itself will change. However, programs in the past enjoyed a rather low level of success in effecting anything like a lasting or even initial change in attitudes.

Sensitivity training attempts to accomplish the end of behavioral change through a philosophy and technique of training which is best described as a concern with the "how" of things—how trainees appraise themselves, how a group behaves, how another would react in a given situation. In short, sensitivity training has as its purpose the development of an executive's *awareness* of himself, of others, of group processes, and of group culture.

The core of a laboratory program is the T-group. From the standpoint of those who design and sponsor the program, the T-group's purpose is to help people: "(1) to explore their values and their impact on others; (2) to determine if they wish to modify the old values and develop new ones; and (3) to develop awareness of how groups can inhibit as well as facilitate human growth and decision making.[37]

To the trainees the T-group, or the small group into which they are put, appears objectiveless and structureless at the start. But as they interact, structure and objectives emerge. In viewing this, the trainees can get an understanding of small group processes and their impact on them. At the same time, through communication and feedback with and from other members of the group, the trainees learns about them-selves as seen through the eyes of others. By being told frankly how

---

[36] For example, see Irving R. Weschler, Marvin A. Klemes, and Clovis Shepard, "A New Focus in Executive Training," *Advanced Management*, May 1955, pp. 19–22; and Michael G. Blanfield and W. F. Robinson, in "Variations in Training Laboratory Design: A Case Study in Sensitivity Training," *Personnel Administration*, March–April 1961, pp. 17–22, 49.

[37] Chris Argyris, *Interpersonal Competence and Organizational Effectiveness*, (Homewood, Ill.: The Dorsey Press, 1962), p. 156. This is a basic reference in labora-tory training.

their behavior and attitudes are "read" they have opened alternatives for change.

From this experience, hopefully an individual will see behavioral shortcomings in himself and others which impair interpersonal relationships. If a person experiences failure in relating with other members of the group, and is told why by the group, he or she then may change his attitudes, and ultimately, his behavior in order to interact more successfully. Obviously these kinds of laboratory experiences can generate a high degree of individual involvement because a person's basic assumptions about his own behavior and the behavior of others is directly challenged.

The end of lab training is to enhance *authenticity* in human relationships. This can only be accomplished in a setting where there is a high degree of individual awareness and acceptance of other people. In Argyris's words, ". . . an individual's growth and learning (on the interpersonal level) is inexorably tied up with his fellow man."[38] Thus authenticity comes from the *relationship* between aware and sensitivie individuals who have reached maturity in interpersonal transactions.

Laboratory programs differ widely in design. They may incorporate varying amounts of lecture, conference, case studies, and role playing. They may vary also in the degree of structuredness. But to repeat, the central feature of these programs is the T-group which exists to accomplish the purposes mentioned above. The trainee is actively involved and receives feedback about his action. However, due to the lack of structure in the situation, the organization of material and its transfer is questionable.

Evaluation of Training Programs

In the beginning of this chapter it was suggested that an organization should make a thorough analysis of its goals, people, and positions *before* choosing a training program. It is equally, and perhaps more, important that the program itself be evaluated both before and after it has been introduced. It is silly to choose a training program when one is not sure of his needs, it is wasteful and sheer folly not to evaluate it. Two useful areas of information would include knowledge of both the use of learning principles and methodology. After a brief discussion of these principles we will present a summary of some of the empirical findings on the effectiveness of management training programs.

---

[38] Ibid., pp. 20–21.

Learning Principles. Given that one's needs are known, the next step would be to evaluate a set of possible training programs. Our review of the use of learning principles is presented in Figure 17–3. Different programs have different strengths and weaknesses and the organization should take this into account in its choice. In general, with on-the-job training, one runs the risk of having poorly organized material and of using a coach who is not properly trained for the administration of the program. The major difficulties with those programs conducted off the job are their expense and the fact that conditions are not optimal for a transfer of the learned material to the work setting.

Methodology. There are two important methodological issues that should be discussed. First, one must choose a measure that reflects the changes desired by the organization. These measures may range from a multiple choice test of information to detailed observations of behavior on the job. Interviews, performance ratings, or attitude questionnaires are frequent choices as well. The use of any technique should depend on what one is trying to do with the training: provide information? change attitudes? teach interpersonal skills? increase effectiveness? Different criteria should be used to assess whether the training has helped the organization in obtaining these goals.

The second important consideration is the experimental design used to evaluate the program. Whenever possible, some sort of control group (employees who do not get the training) should be used so that a comparison can be made between those who receive training and those who do not. It is also desirable to assign employees randomly to these two conditions. The use of these two techniques would produce one of the two designs illustrated below depending upon whether a pretest was used. (O stands for observations, X symbolizes the training program, and R means random assignment.)

Training Group— O X O   X O where X = Training
            R   R
Control Group— O   O   O   O = Performance
                                             Appraisal

In some cases the use of a control group or randomization will not be feasible. In these situations it may still be possible to gain some control through the use of multiple measures or other procedures.[39] The more controls one is able to introduce the more confidence he or she

---

[39] Donald T. Campbell and Julian C. Stanley, *Experimental and Quasi-Experimental Designs for Research* (Chicago: Rand McNally and Co., 1963).

FIGURE 17–3
Extent to Which Training Techniques Utilize Certain Principles of Learning

	Motivation: Active Participation of Learner	Reinforcement: Feedback of Knowledge of Results	Stimulus: Meaningful Organization of Materials	Responses: Practice and Repetition	Stimulus-Response: Conditions Most Favorable for Transfer
On-the-job techniques:					
Job-instruction training	Yes	Sometimes	Yes	Yes	Yes
Apprentice training	Yes	Sometimes	?	Sometimes	Yes
Internships and assistantships	Yes	Sometimes	?	Sometimes	Yes
Job rotation	Yes	No	?	Sometimes	Yes
Junior board	Yes	Sometimes	Sometimes	Sometimes	Yes
Coaching	Yes	Yes	Sometimes	Sometimes	Yes
Off-the-job techniques:					
Vestibule	Yes	Sometimes	Yes	Yes	Sometimes
Lecture	No	No	Yes	No	No
Special study	Yes	No	Yes	?	No
Films	No	No	Yes	No	No
Television	No	No	Yes	No	No
Conference or discussion	Yes	Sometimes	Sometimes	Sometimes	Sometimes
Case study	Yes	Sometimes	Sometimes	Sometimes	Sometimes
Role playing	Yes	Sometimes	No	Sometimes	Sometimes
Simulation	Yes	Sometimes	Sometimes	Sometimes	Sometimes
Programmed instruction	Yes	Yes	Yes	Yes	No
Laboratory training	Yes	Yes	No	Yes	Sometimes
Programmed group exercises	Yes	Yes	Yes	Sometimes	Sometimes

Source: Bernard M. Bass and James A. Vaughn, *Training in Industry: The Management of Learning* (Belmont, Calif.: Wadsworth Publishing Co., 1966), p. 131.

may ascribe to the findings. Since training may easily cost hundreds of thousands of dollars a year it would seem advantageous to provide these controls when it is feasible.

Empirical Findings. In a recent review of all the empirical literature on management training, five headings were used to categorize these programs.[40] (See Figure 17–4.) ·It should be pointed out that these

FIGURE 17–4

		General Management Programs	General Human-Relations Programs	Problem Solving and Decision Making	T-Group and Laboratory Education Programs	Specialty Programs	
External Criteria	Some Controls	2	–	–	6	5	
	Few Controls	1	3	1	3	–	
		3	3		9	5	21
Internal Criteria	Some Controls	8	10	3	8	3	
	Few Controls	5	6	–	9	–	
		13	16	3	17	3	52
		16	19	4	26	6	73

Source: John P. Campbell, Marvin D. Dunnette, Edward E. Lawler III, and Karl E. Weick, Jr., *Managerial Behavior, Performance, and Effectiveness* (New York: McGraw-Hill Book Company, 1970), p. 322.

headings reflect the goals of the programs and not necessarily their content. For example both human relations and T-group training might include conferences or role-playing techniques.

Seventy-three different studies were reviewed according to their goals and two other factors: criterion measures and amount of control. Those studies that provided information about changes in the trainee as a function of the training (learning, attitudes, opinion, and so on), are said to have internal criteria. Those that assess changes in actual job behavior (absences, effectiveness, reported grievances, and so forth), are classified as having external criteria. Those studies defined as having some experimental controls used a control group, while those with only a pretest-posttest comparison (no control group) are classified as having few controls. A breakdown of the 73 studies reviewed is presented in Figure 17–4.

One can see from the figure that a majority of the studies used internal criteria and have some control over the evaluation process. It is also

---

[40] Campbell et al., *Managerial Behavior,* chapter 13.

clear that human-relations and T-group training programs have been evaluated more extensively than the other types of training.

A review of the experimental results prompted the following general statements.[41]

1. Approximately 80 percent of the human-relations and general management programs produced significant changes in the anticipated direction. Most of the studies, however, used internal criteria which focused on attitudinal information and may not have produced actual behavioral changes back on the job.

2. The results for T-group training, although generally supportive, are not as one-sided as those above. Most of the studies that show support are of the internal-criteria, few controls type. The two most well-known and thorough reviews of this literature are also cautious in their overall evaluations of T-groups.[42] Millions of dollars are being spent on this type of training every year and yet the evidence for its effectiveness is minimal. At best one might say with confidence that certain types of T-groups are helpful for certain types of people working in certain types of settings. It behooves us to find out these contingencies.

3. Very few studies have been designed to test problem-solving or specialty programs and in general, the results are inconclusive or not supportive of those that have been done. Either the programs are ineffective or their changes have not been accurately assessed. Both alternatives require further evaluation.

In summarizing the literature, two things should be noted. First, most of the programs evaluated contained combinations of lectures, cases, role playing, conferences, or T-groups. The implications are twofold. Numerous kinds of training techniques discussed earlier, such as business simulations, programmed learning, and on-the-job techniques, have been assessed infrequently. A related implication is that since many programs combine techniques, perhaps we should assess particular *combinations* of training rather than gloss over these combinations by classifying them by their goals. Both the specific techniques and particular combinations may be useful in certain situations.

Finally, as mentioned earlier, most of the studies evaluated the training with either internal criteria or few controls and of the 13 that had

---

[41] Ibid. pp. 321–25.

[42] See R. J. House, "T-Group Education and Leadership Effectiveness: A Review of the Empirical Literature and a Critical Evaluation," *Personnel Psychology*, 20 (1967), 1–32 and J. P. Campbell and M. D. Dunnette, "Effectiveness of T-Group Experiences in Managerial Training and Development," *Psychological Bulletin*, 70 (1968), 73–104.

external criteria and some control, only four are considered by Campbell *et al.,* to have been experimentally sound with broad, general measures. The authors conclude,

> Thus with regard to the bulk of the literature on training effects, it remains to be demonstrated whether the changes in the criteria used to measure training effects have any importance for the organization's goals. It unfortunately follows that the present empirical literature on the relationship of training content to managerial performance tells us very little about what kind of knowledge and skills contribute to managerial effectiveness. In order for this to happen, it must be demonstrated that "what is learned" in a training program contributes to making an individual a better manager.[43]

If social scientists are to avoid being accused of selling "snake oil," they should demand more frequent and better designed assessment of their peddled product.

---

[43] Campbell et al., *Managerial Behavior*, p. 325.

part V

Organizational Research and Methodology

Throughout our analysis we have drawn on the works of numerous authors. Some of these writings were based on personal observations, others provided theoretical insight, and some utilized empirical investigations. Perhaps the most striking commonality was their approach to the acquisition of knowledge; most of these authors were influenced by the social sciences and a rational set of rules for how one comes to "know" something.

In Part V we shall describe both the philosophical and methodological principles on which most of the writings about organization theory and behavior are based. The major purpose of Chapter 18 is to acquaint the reader with some general statements about the philosophy of science and the "scientific method." Two general themes are presented. First, it is important to note that the rational approach to understanding is only one of many possible approaches. A "scientific" analysis, although certainly the most frequently used in the area of organizational behavior, is not the only way to acquire knowledge. We shall, however, attempt to point out both the strong and weak points of using this analysis.

The other theme for Chapter 18 is to present the variety of types of research that are included in the "social sciences," using the "scientific method." Using science is often confused with a particular type of work. The scope, however, of topics, tools, and settings is extremely broad. It is the process that makes the investigation "scientific," not necessarily the content. Finally, a detailed analysis of the research methodology most frequently used for organizational studies is presented. Included are discussions of how research questions are asked, the types of research designs needed to provide answers, the settings in which the research is conducted, and the types of inferences that can be made about the findings.

The purpose of the scientific analysis is to provide: (1) a general agreement about the meaning of our observations in such a way that investigators can communicate with each other and build on the work of others, and (2) to generate statements about phenomena of interest that are generalizable to a variety of settings and people. These objectives are clearly important to those interested in understanding what goes on in organizations.

Chapter 19 discusses a number of research problems related to the conduct of the investigator and the investigation. Experimenter bias and the "Hawthorne effect" are described and remedies suggested. Ethical conduct is examined in terms of who participates in research and what types of studies are justified. In general, there is agreement that investigators must be cautious about how they conduct their research and how research results are used.

chapter 18

Organizational Theory and the Behavioral Sciences: Conceptual Issues

I t is probably true that most people spend at least 50 percent of their lives in organizational settings (work, school, church, and so on). We not only work in or for these organizations, we also belong to them. The relative newness of this phenomena has a number of implications. First, we are just now beginning to see some of the effects of this type of involvement (social, economic, and ecological). Second, we are still in the process of developing scientific procedures to study the behavior of the individuals in these settings.

Attempts to explain the behavior that goes on in organizations requires some knowledge about individuals, groups, and the surrounding environment. Our interest in this book, then, has been with the sciences such as sociology, psychology, and anthropology, which have produced information and generalizations about human behavior in organizations. These fields are called the behavioral sciences. To some extent they are "interdisciplinary." But the point of view taken here is that there is not a *behavioral science approach,* which is defined as a master science combining in a *gestalt* fashion all the subsidiary sciences of human behavior.

So ours is not an interdisciplinary orientation in the sense that there is an integrated science of behavior. We agree with Roethlisberger's statement that ". . . the behavioral sciences are not yet one."[1] This view

---

[1] Fritz J. Roethlisberger, "Contributions of the Behavioral Sciences to a General Theory of Management," in Harold Koontz, ed., *Toward a Unified Theory of Management* (New York: McGraw-Hill Book Company, 1964), p. 41.

is reinforced by a content examination of Berelson's and Steiner's book, *Human Behavior: An Inventory of Scientific Findings.*[2] There is little here to cause one to suppose that the findings presented are interdisciplinary in character. Indeed, the sources chosen by the authors as representative of "hard data" lead one to the conclusion that psychology dominates the other behavioral sciences in the production of valid and reliable scientific findings.[3] Most of the experimental results reported in this book have been therefore from the fields of social, industrial, and organizational psychology.

The behavioral sciences have values for management on at least three levels. First, they formulate abstract concepts and explanations about human behavior in open systems of interdependency. This is the conceptual contribution to management. Second, they provide a way of gathering data and thinking about these relationships. This is the methodological contribution. Third, they contribute to administrative policy decisions with respect to change. This is the action contribution. All three of these levels also have ethical implications both for the people involved in doing the research and those participating in the research. It is the conceptual and methodological issues with which we will concern ourselves in this section.

One of the allures of the behavioral sciences to managers is the word science itself. Science has produced wonderments in our understanding and control of nature. Why not in the sphere of human behavior as well? It is useful to look at certain scientific presuppositions and relate the behavioral sciences to them as far as possible in a short section. We will concern ourselves next with what is science, what it proposes to do, and what sorts of special problems we encounter in the behavioral sciences.

THE SCIENTIFIC APPROACH

Braithwaite says that science seeks to establish ". . . general laws covering the behavior of empirical events or objects with which the science in question is concerned, and thereby enable us to connect together our knowledge of the separately known events, and to make reli-

---

[2] Bernard Berelson and Gary A. Steiner, *Human Behavior: An Inventory of Scientific Findings* (New York: Harcourt, Brace & World, Inc., 1964).

[3] Of the journals cited in their bibliographical index, over 60 percent of the total were psychological.

able predictions of events yet unknown."[4] Science attempts to simplify into general laws the processes which govern the external objects of sense perception. It does this by setting forth a set of general strategies for making inferences about observations. These strategies or characteristics of scientific inquiry reflect a certain spirit as to how we pursue knowledge that is distinct from the "scientific method" which will be discussed later.

First, it is important to point out that when a scientist is doing research he or she is *systematically planning* in an *unbiased* way how a particular question will be answered. Second, he usually gathers some sort of record of his observations. These records are his *data* and although they may be gathered in a variety of ways—questionnaires, observation, interviews, and so on—they emphasize the empirical nature of the process. Third, these data are usually subjected to some sort of *unbiased analysis* which addresses itself to the kinds of inferences that can be made. That is, how much confidence can one have in the results? Fourth, the findings are usually *public* in the sense that they are communicated to others through various media (journals, speeches, and so forth), and can therefore be replicated or extended if necessary. Fifth, because of its systematic and public nature, the knowledge can be *cumulative*. One can build on what others have done.[5]

How does this process differ from common-sense procedures for gaining knowledge? There are a number of important differences worth mentioning. Scientists are more *systematic* and less selective in the ways that they gather information. Hopefully, *both positive and negative support* for one's ideas or theories are recorded. It is also true that scientists often *actively pursue* certain relationships. That is, they actually set up situations to test their ideas. By setting up these situations, they are also *establishing some control* over the setting which is often missing in our everyday experiences. Finally, scientists usually attempt to *rule out metaphysical (not testable) explanations* of observed phenomena. An example of this last point comes from the early work on leadership where observational studies were made of successful leaders or managers. In many cases, the behavior of these individuals was attributed to instincts or inherited characteristics. The list of instincts became so

---

[4] Richard Bevan Braithwaite, *Scientific Explanation* (London: Cambridge University Press, 1953), p. 1.

[5] Blair J. Kolasa, *Introduction to Behavioral Science for Business* (New York: John Wiley & Sons, Inc., 1969).

long that the approach did little to further our understanding or prediction of successful leaders because of the nontestable nature of the explanation.

The scientific process therefore requires a method of inquiry that actively seeks out information, both supportive, and nonsupportive, in a systematic and unbiased manner and reports this information in a way that can be used by others. Before leaving this topic, two further points should be made.

Along with the above way of thinking there are often statements related to the "autonomy of inquiry," which implies that the pursuit of truth through the scientific method is accountable to nothing and to no one not a part of that pursuit itself. In a society where resources are scarce and problems abound, this autonomy is at best questionable.

It should also be mentioned that although the above process of inquiry may indeed lead to great increases in knowledge, it is not the only route to knowledge nor is it always done well. A poorly run experiment contributes very little more to our knowledge than any other person's personal assumptions about behavior. Because it is "scientific" does not necessarily make it good or right.

THE SCIENCE OF BEHAVIOR

The scientific work on human behavior has been carried out in a number of different academic areas which together are known as the behavioral sciences. We will attempt to define this area more clearly, give some historical background, and point out some of the problems that exist in these areas. As mentioned earlier, three disciplines—anthropology, sociology, and psychology—have contributed most to our knowledge of behavior. Each of these disciplines, however, is concerned with both more and less than these behavioral areas of study.[6] Much of the research in psychology concerned with animal behavior or the biological aspects of vision might not be included. Areas of study in anthropology concerned with certain artifacts, per se, or sociological studies of organizational structures without reference to the behavior of individuals within them might be excluded. On the other hand, certain areas of political science, history, and economics might be included. The boundaries are complicated further with the addition of new interdisciplinary areas such as social psychiatry, communication or cybernetics, and psy-

---

[6] Bernard Berelson, ed., *The Behavioral Sciences Today* (New York: Basic Books, Inc., Publishers, 1963), p. 2.

cholinguistics. It is therefore difficult to speak of a behavioral science approach in any meaningful fashion. Psychology has made most of the contributions in the area of organizational behavior and we have drawn heavily on the findings of that discipline. Findings of numerous other disciplines have been described when appropriate.

Historical Perspective

A brief overview of the scientific interest in human behavior should probably start with the Greek philosophers Aristotle and Plato. The latter's *Republic* is one of our earliest speculations on human nature and one of the first attempts to understand the relationship between one's mind and one's body. Aristotle was one of the world's greatest thinkers, with works on logic, biology, physics, psychology, politics, and so on. Both he and Plato emphasized the importance of logic and the belief that one can discover truth by the use of reason.

The Greeks seem to have regarded the human race as an integral part of nature. Through the Middle Ages, however, humans were perceived to have a soul and free will, and attempts to study their behavior were frowned on. During the 17th and 18th centuries, philosophers such as Descartes and La Mettrie presented radical ideas. They saw human beings as machines that moved and behaved in predictable ways. Through the work of a number of Europeans such as Comte, Helmholtz, and Wundt in the 19th century the study of human behavior began to emerge as a more distinctive set of ideas. Psychologists such as Titchener at Cornell and James at Harvard opened laboratories in this country and began experimentation on problems in the area of human behavior.

Research continued through both major world conflicts but it was not until after World War II that the term *behavioral science* was used with any real frequency.[7] Great increases in money made available by private agencies such as the Ford Foundation and by the government stimulated both the education and research output of behavioral scientists. Merton has pointed out that probably 90 percent of all behavioral scientists who have lived are still alive, and that we have "a very new science of a very ancient subject."[8]

---

[7] P. Seen, "What Is Behavioral Science—Notes toward a History," *Journal of the History of the Behavioral Sciences,* 2 (1966), 107–22.

[8] Robert K. Merton, "The Mosaic of the Behavioral Sciences," in Berelson, *The Behavioral Sciences Today,* p. 249.

Special Problems

There are a number of problems faced by behavioral scientists which are not faced by those doing research in the so-called hard sciences to the same degree or in quite the same way. First, they must often attempt to distinguish between the meaning of an act to the actor as well as its meaning as subject matter. Is aggression the intent to hurt someone or the actual pain or harm inflicted? If a supervisor corrects a subordinate's mistake with the intent to be helpful and supportive is it a supportive act if the subordinate does not view it that way? Objects of study in other scientific disciplines do not typically display this characteristic.

All sciences need to be able to have some control over the phenomenon of interest. Behavioral science is different to some degree in its ability to impose these controls and this is true for at least two reasons. The consent and time of subjects must be obtained and, second, there are some ethical considerations about what can be done or asked of those that have agreed to participate.

A third problem has to do with the degree and type of quantification that is possible. Behavioral scientists have relatively weak mathematical tools with which they can work. More specifically, most behavioral measures are rather crude in their scaling techniques. They allow the investigator to talk with confidence about more or less of some characteristic but that is all. This problem is more apparent when you think about other more familiar measurement scales, such as height or weight, which have zero points and precise intervals.

A final problem, which is frequently cited, is that the phenomena studied by behavioral scientists are more complex than those of other disciplines. There are two issues here. First, there is the sheer number of variables that might be influencing behavior: The number is infinite. A second problem is the fact that many of the influences on behavior are lost forever; that is, they occurred in the past. To some extent these problems are ones of degree but the implications are clear—progress is difficult and time consuming.

The Scientific Method

The scientific way of thinking usually proceeds through a regular progression of logical steps. There is some time spent in formulating ideas and stating hypotheses. There is a period during which the actual experiment is carried out and there is some final work which involves the conclusions that can be drawn and their public presentation. We will discuss these steps in more detail with particular reference to issues discussed by philosophers of science.

Generating Ideas

Usually the first step in the process of scientific investigation is simply that there is some question for which the scientist wants an answer (e.g., What makes an organization effective?). To provide possible suggestions may require intuition, reference to some sort of model, or the development of an elaborate theory. To communicate these suggestions requires the clear usage of language.

Terms. The whole problem of definition centers around the meaning which we ascribe to a given term. The words in a theory may refer to observable objects (e.g., number of people in the organization) or unobservable states (such as the level of anxiety of the managers). It is fairly clear what one means by the first variable (i.e., number of people) because people agree on such things as how to count and everyone can observe the objects of study.

The issue is not as clear for the second variable of interest. Different people may not agree on what they mean by anxiety. It is definitely true that we cannot see it. Therefore, the two things that make the first term clear—that it can be seen and that there is agreement on how it should be measured—are not available for the second term. We remedy this problem by developing theories or by the use of models.

Theories. There are numerous definitions of what is meant by theory We shall begin with a rather simple statement presented by Mandler and Kessen and elaborate on its meanings. "Theories are set of statements, understandable to others; which make predictions about empirical events."[9] There are three critical elements of this definition.

First, theories are understandable statements. This means that they are communicable and public. Other people can read one, test it or discard it. The crucial thing is that they can see how and why you did what you did. They may not agree with your theory, but then, the answer to the problem is a matter of empirical support.

Second, theories make predictions. That is, they are to some extent anticipation systems. They may also interpret or unify established laws

[9] George Mandler and William Kessen, *The Language of Psychology* (New York: John Wiley & Sons, Inc., 1959), p. 142.

or enable one to fit unanticipated data into their formulation. Anticipation does not necessarily mean that the theory must be used for future events; simply that it correctly accounts for events that have been, are, or would be unaccountable without the theory.

Finally, theories deal with empirical events. At some point every theory must be tied to events and objects or some sort of observable referent about which people agree. If one has a theory about how a manager's anxiety is related to performance, then at some point he or she must specify what would happen if the relationship existed. For example, he might suggest that a small amount of anxiety increased output, whereas large amounts hindered output. If the measurement of anxiety (some questionnaire, for example) is related to actual productivity measures in the way that the theory predicts, then the manager has increased our confidence in his conceptualization of anxiety and in the theory as a whole.[10]

Models. In conceptualizing an area of interest more clearly, it may be helpful to use a model of some sort. Models are systems which represent an area of interest in terms of the structure but not of the content. Comparing the behavior of a human being with that of a machine is an example mentioned earlier. Supposedly, whenever a relation holds between two elements of one system, a corresponding one holds for elements of the other system.

There are different kinds of models. Some of them might present a physical representation of one's interests. Simulations such as those seen on space flights are good examples. Business games also attempt to simulate the actual setting. One may have symbolic or conceptual analogies such as people as a machine or ideal structures somewhat similar to Weber's early work on organizations. There are also models of and for theories which show how theories should look as a structure of uninterpreted symbols.

Models are therefore guides in the process of formulating and understanding a problem. They may help to organize one's thoughts, show us gaps in our knowledge, or guide us in what and how to look for relationships.

One must be careful, however, of the possible shortcomings of models.[11] Occasionally an overemphasis is put on either the symbols or the form of a model. Because a model is elegant does not mean

---

[10] For a good discussion of theories, see Abraham Kaplan, *The Conduct of Inquiry* (Scranton, Pa.: Chandler Publishing Co., 1964), pp. 294–325.

[11] Ibid., pp. 258–91.

it is correct. Another problem with models is that they may be oversimplified or narrow a person's perspective in ways which cause him to overlook critical issues related to his theory or observations. In general, then, it must be remembered that models are analogies and that analogies are not expected to be completely accurate.

Data Gathering

Suppose that one has developed a theory of organizational effectiveness and wishes to test it. He or she wants some empirical support for the predictions he has made. To obtain the answers he must address himself to two major issues: methodology and practical problems.

Methodology. We have suggested that there are a variety of techniques or steps in scientific inquiry and that these methods or steps include such procedures as theory building, generating hypotheses, designing and running experiments, and providing explanations. These methods are sufficiently general to be common to most scientific inquiry.

The aim of methodology, as Kaplan has said so appropriately, is

> To describe and analyze these methods, throwing light on their limitations and resources, clarifying presuppositions and consequences, relating their potentialities to the twilight zone at the frontiers of knowledge. It is to venture generalizations from the success of particular techniques; to suggest new applications; and to unfold the specific bearings of logical and metaphysical principles on concrete problems, suggesting new formulations. It is to invite speculation from science and particularly from philosophy. In sum, the aim of methodology is to help us to *understand,* in the broadest possible terms, not the product of scientific inquiry but the process itself.[12]

Some of the issues, such as the generation of ideas or the use of models have been discussed already. A discussion of the decisions that must be made about measurement, research settings, and experimental design will be presented in the following sections. The critical point is that methodology involves the whole scientific process and that it should be viewed not as a hurdle or an inhibitor of imaginative ideas, but as a process that facilitates our understanding.

Practical Problems. Hand-in-hand with methodological problems is a set of practical issues that must be resolved. Decisions must be made in terms of how much money can be spent. The elegance of design,

---

[12] Ibid., p. 23.

number of subjects tested, and the type of analyses performed are often determined by the amount of money or time available.

Lastly, the social scientist must be concerned about the ethical implications of the way the reseach is conducted. The use of human or animal subjects requires certain precautions about which social scientists should be aware. We shall discuss these ethical issues at length in Chapter 19.

Explanation

After generating a theory and conducting an experimental test of this theory one must attempt to make some statements about the experiment that will describe what has been found. It has been observed that certain managers are more effective than others and we ask for an *explanation* of that phenomena. Mandler and Kessen have suggested that "we are expressing a demand for the context of general statements into which the phenomenon may be fitted."[13] Hopefully, our theory will present these statements.

The problems, however, are twofold. First, one must ascertain the degree to which his or her observations have indeed been supportive of the theory. This process involves both the ruling out of alternative hypotheses and some indication of the strength of the support provided. The elimination of other interpretations can be partially handled by the way in which the study is designed and this will be discussed later in detail. The strength of the support is typically inferred through the use of statistics. That is, mathematical tools provide us with probabilistic estimates of support. The analyses essentially ask, "How probable is it that we should find this relationship (e.g., that very anxious managers had low productivity) if in reality these two factors are unrelated (anxiety and productivity)?" More specifically, statistics help one to determine the likelihood that information has just been gathered from an unrepresentative group. If this likelihood is small one puts more confidence in the findings, and therefore in his theory. This confidence is always probabilistic, never absolute.[14]

The second problem deals with the generality of the findings. Are the findings just applicable to the kinds of managers with whom the experiment was conducted or are they applicable to all managers? To answer this latter question may require numerous experiments in numer-

---

[13] Mandler and Kessen, *The Language of Psychology*, p. 216.

[14] See the writings of David Hume, "An Inquiry Concerning Human Understanding," in E. A. Burtt, ed., *The English Philosophers from Bacon to Mill* (New York: Modern Library, 1748 [1939]).

ous settings, using various observation techniques. The final acceptance of a theory as an explanation probably stops when our curiosity rests and the new law is in some sense coherent with the rest of the findings on areas relevant to our theory (e.g., leadership, anxiety, and so on).

BEHAVIORAL SCIENCE RESEARCH: DESCRIPTIVE DIMENSIONS

Research in the behavioral sciences today is extremely varied with respect to the scope, methods, techniques, and applications that are used. Numerous classifications could be suggested but a recent conceptualization by Helmstadter seems relatively inclusive and appropriate.

A Research Taxonomy. The purpose of this taxonomy is twofold. It points out rather well the critical dimensions on which research may vary and secondly, provides perspective for those that believe that one type of research is the "only way" or the dominant theme in behavioral science. The three dimensions shown in Figure 18–1 require further explanation.[15]

FIGURE 18–1
A Taxonomy of Research in the Behavioral Sciences

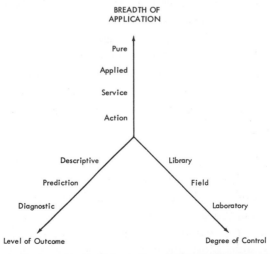

Source: G. C. Helmstadter, *Research Concepts in Human Behavior* (New York: Appleton-Century-Crofts, 1970), p. 28.

---

[15] Many of these ideas were presented by G. C. Helmstadter, *Research Concepts in Human Behavior* (New York: Appleton-Century-Crofts, 1970), pp. 27–38.

Breadth of Application.   This dimension is perhaps the most discussed and in our opinion perhaps the most misunderstood. The motivation for doing pure or *basic* research is essentially one of curiosity. The scientist is interested in understanding some phenomenon without particular reference or thought as to how the findings could or should be used. Hovland, in describing this approach as used by the Bell Telephone System's laboratory at Murray Hill, N.J., said: "Basic research provides a fund of new knowledge to be drawn upon by those interested in its development and application. The responsibility for potential utilization of research does not rest with the researcher. The researcher's responsibility is that of creating new knowledge and conferring with those who see possibilities of its utilization concerning its varied and deep implications."[16]

Research which would be termed *applied* is typically concerned with not only the explanation of observations but the use of these explanations. The popular image of science is that applied sciences use and adapt the abstractions, laws, and generalizations of the pure sciences to solve concrete problems. While this may be true in the case of engineering and physics, and this is not altogether certain, it is not applicable to the behavioral sciences. As Gouldner says, "Any metaphor which conceives of applied social science as the offspring, and of the basic disciplines as parents, is misleading. It obscures the point that the applied sciences often contribute as much to pure science as they receive from it."[17] Indeed, if the applied branches of the behavioral sciences stood in dependent and subsidiary relation to pure science, administration would derive little of value from them. However, because of the strong emphasis on doing functional or usable research (which is part of the Protestant ethic tradition) the applied areas have flourished and will continue to do so.

The two other points on this dimension are even more problem oriented. We typically mean by *service* research that an administrator, government official, or practitioner hires investigators to solve a specific problem. The results of this type of research may be somewhat limited in their scope simply because a specific problem is under investigation.

Another type of research that falls under this classification is called evaluation research. Most government departments have an Office of

---

[16] C. Hovland, "Two New Social Science Research Units in Industrial Settings," *American Psychologist*, 16 (1961), 87–91.

[17] Alvin W. Gouldner, "Explorations in Applied Social Science," *Social Problems*, January 1956, p. 19.

Evaluation which is responsible for assessing the impact of various government programs. For example, the Department of Labor may regularly evaluate the effectiveness of various training programs such as Job Corps or Operation Mainstream (government programs designed to increase the skills and employability of young people and "hard core" unemployed). These efforts usually involve a clear statement of program goals, some agreed-upon sample of the participants and research methodology dictated by both situational demands and scientific principles. This research strategy is becoming increasingly sophisticated and has attracted numerous social scientists as advocates. It is a valuable addition to our understanding of the research process and has added substantially to the effectiveness of policy making.

The term action research as used by Helmstadter seems to imply not only the investigation of a problem but also the introduction of various techniques, changes, or strategies which will promote change and, hopefully, solve the problem. The relevant consideration is to avoid changing things for change's sake.

Before moving to a discussion of the next dimension we believe that it is important to emphasize that none of these orientations are necessarily any better than any other. They may have both favorable and unfavorable consequences. Studies that are more action oriented may be limited in scope, whereas pure or basic research may be broad in scope but lacking in utility. One must judge the products by the goals that were set for the research and the way in which it was done.

Level of Outcome. In a sense the level-of-outcome dimension is related to what goals have been set for the research. If one simply wishes to know what something is like she may call it *descriptive*. For example, a variety of measures have been developed to describe organizational structure in such a way that the measures are useful for any organization.

When one is seeking to anticipate what will happen in the future, given that certain conditions exist, he will be doing research that is *predictive*. For example, the ultimate goal of selection tests is to enable the personnel manager to predict whether a prospective employee will be successful in the company.

Finally, in some situations one is not only concerned with the relationship between two variables (e.g., high anxiety being related to low productivity) but he is also interested in the direction of that relationship. Does high anxiety cause low productivity or is the reverse true? An investigation of this type is frequently called *diagnostic*.

Degree of Control. The topic of research settings in terms of methodological considerations will be discussed in the next chapter. It is useful, however, to point out how these settings vary in the amount of control which can be used by the investigator. Research done in the *library* typically involves the use of data or observations over which the investigator has had no control. In *field* settings control is usually limited to the time and place that the observations are made. *Laboratory* studies, on the other hand, provide control for most of the variables of interest to the extent that the setting in which the experiment is carried out is created by the investigator. There are typically trade-offs for this control, in that scope and potential information are frequently sacrificed. Again, the study must be judged in terms of its purpose.

Use of Behavioral Science in Business

The applications of behavioral science to organizational behavior cover almost the whole range of organizational concerns. The organization is composed of some people, some technology (machines, supplies, etc.), and—to some extent—an output or product of its endeavors.

Research from industrial psychology has been concerned with topics such as selection, management training, job satisfaction and morale, and job performance. Some of the findings from psychology, anthropology, and social psychology have been concerned with the areas of personality, perception, and motivation; the specialized interests of attitude change and persuasion are important for marketing both the organization's image and product.

Other disciplines, such as sociology and anthropology, have looked at organizational structure as it is related to effectiveness. Engineering psychology has produced research on the optimal fit between man and machine.

Problems of bargaining, legislation, budgets, grievances, and leadership are of interest to economists, sociologists, lawyers, and political scientists. Other areas, such as consulting and mental health research, are also applicable. In sum, the interests of behavioral scientists cover rather comprehensively the problems with which managers and organizations are concerned.

THE RESEARCH PROCESS

The extent to which research findings are important to the public is increasing all the time. Advertisements frequently cite their "independent study" in support of their product. Most organizations utilize selection or assessment devices which they believe will increase their efficiency at choosing or evaluating people correctly. The form in which products are marketed is often based upon research. In short, research is being used more and more as an integral part of our every day lives.

Types of Experiments

The research process involves numerous stages of observation, theory building, and empirical verification or testing.[18] In most instances it is these latter types of studies which are most publicized. In these cases the experimenter is usually interested in one of two questions: (1) Is one variable or factor *related* in some way to some other variable or (2) Does one variable *cause* some other variable to assume certain values? For example, one may wish to know if intelligence and income are related for a group of upper level managers. It would not be suggested that intelligence caused one to have a certain income level but simply that they were related. The research strategy for this type of question usually involves the gathering of data, through questionnaires, observations, or other recording techniques relevant to the two or more variables of interest. These types of studies are usually called surveys or field studies in organizational settings.

Investigations that attempt to infer causality usually involve a different strategy. Here, some variable is introduced or changed and the resulting impact on some other variable observed. For example, one might introduce a new training program for upper level managers to see if it could cause an increase in performance. These studies are usually called field experiments of laboratory investigations and they require a thorough understanding of research design to be done effectively.

RESEARCH DESIGN

When a behavioral scientist is reviewing or criticizing a research study there are two basic questions that he or she asks. First, he will examine the study to see if there are alternative suggestions as to why the results turned out the way they did. If there are no equally likely interpretations of the results other than the one reported the study is said to have *internal validity*. The inferences made by the original investigator seem to be warranted for the study in question.[19]

[18] Helmstadter, *Research Concepts.*

[19] Donald T. Campbell and Julian C. Stanley, *Experimental and Quasi-Experimental Designs for Research* (Chicago: Rand McNally & Company, 1963).

But there is a second question. Would the results have been the same if different people had participated? Would another method of observing the behavior in question produced similar findings? More specifically, if the results seem to be generalizable—that is applicable to a wide range of people and situations—then the study or studies are said to have *external validity*. The inferences are not only applicable for the specific study but for a wider range of phenomena.

To assure that a study has both internal and external validity requires that the investigator have some knowledge of research design. Since the applications of the necessary principles are somewhat clearer for experimental settings, our discussion will begin there and then move to the relevant issues for correlational research.

Experimental Design: Internal Validity

Campbell and Stanley state "Internal validity is the basic minimum without which any experiment is uninterpretable: Did in fact, the experimental treatments make a difference in this specific instance?"[20] To understand the answer to this question more fully, we will present the example of a human relations course being presented to a group of first-line supervisors. The objective of the investigator is to assess the degree to which the course influenced the productivity of these supervisors. Certain symbols will be used and their meaning is as follows:

S = Subjects, the people participating in the experiment.
O = Our observation techniques, the measurement device.
X = The experimental treatment, the manipulated variable.
R = The process of randomization.

Three poor designs will be described and their problems pointed out. Three good designs will be presented that remedy these problems. A summary of these designs is presented in Figure 18–2. Finally, some "quasi-experimental" designs will be discussed for situations where the proper controls are not available to the investigator.

Poor Designs. Suppose that our personnel manager gave the human relations training course to *all* of the supervisors. How would he or she evaluate it? The manager could not compare their performance scores to earlier performance scores (before training) nor could they

---
[20] Ibid., p. 5.

FIGURE 18–2
Some Types of Research Designs

Type	*Characteristics*
1. The one-shot design: $X \quad O$	Subject to error due to history, maturation, testing, instrument decay, selection.
2. One-group pretest-posttest design: $O_1 \quad X \quad O_2$	Subject to error due to history, maturation, testing, instrument decay, regression.
3. Static group comparison: $X \quad O_1$ $- \quad - \quad -$ O_2	Subject to error due to selection, regression, mortality
4. Pretest-posttest control group design: $R \begin{cases} O_1 \ X \ O_2 \\ O_3 \quad\ \ O_4 \end{cases}$	Subject to error due to interaction of testing and X.
5. Posttest only control group design: $R \begin{cases} X \ O_1 \\ \quad\ O_2 \end{cases}$	Controls for but does not measure effects of history, maturation.
6. Solomon 4-group design: $R \begin{cases} O_1 \ X \ O_2 \\ O_3 \quad\ \ O_4 \\ \quad\ \ X \ O_5 \\ \quad\quad\ \ O_6 \end{cases}$	Combines features of designs 4 and 5. Controls for and also measures effects of history, maturation, and testing.

be compared against a group that did not receive the training. This is called a *one-shot* design and is diagrammed below.

$$X \qquad O$$

Here, X stands for the treatment, the course, and O for the observation, the performance measure which would probably be presented in the form of an average score. The investigator has no way of knowing whether the performance scores are good or bad and if the training influenced these scores. This type of design is rarely used because of its obvious weaknesses.

Perhaps our manager from personnel was aware of some of these problems and used the following design.

$$O_1 \qquad X \qquad O_2$$

He gathered performance measures on the supervisors, gave them the training course and then remeasured their performance and found $O_2 > O_1$. This design is called a *one-group pretest-posttest* design. A pretest is given, then the treatment, a posttest administered and differences between averages on the pretest and the posttest are attributed to the treatment.

There are numerous problems with this design. What if at the same time that the course was given, completely new machinery was installed in the organization? Would it not be an equally plausible explanation to say that the new machinery caused the changes in performance? This type of alternative hypothesis is called a *history* factor. Definitions of this type of confound along with seven others are presented in Figure 18–3. *Maturation* might also be a confound in that the supervisors are

FIGURE 18–3
A Summary Table Illustrating Some Classes of Factors Which Confound Experimental Results

History:	Events other than the experimental treatment (X) which occurred between premeasurement and postmeasurement.
Maturation:	Changes in the subject population which occur with the passage of time and which are independent of the experimental treatment (X).
Testing:	Changes in subject performance which occur because previous measurement of his performance sensitized him regarding that area.
Instrument decay:	Changes in measures of subject performance that arise because of changes in the measurement instruments or conditions—such as wear of parts for physical instruments; learning, boredom, or fatigue for human observers.
Selection:	If subject assignment to different groups (i.e., experimental and control groups) in the design is on any basis other than random assignment from a common pool, those other bases of selection will represent *systematic* biases making for differences between groups which are unrelated to effects of experimental treatment X—or which may interact with X.
Mortality:	If some subjects who initially start the experiment drop out before its completion, the experimental and control groups may not be comparable at the end even though they were in the beginning.
Interactive effects:	Any of several of the above factors may *interact* with experimental treatment (X) making for confounding effects. For example, pretesting may only sensitize the subject when it is followed by X. Or, the types of subjects who drop out of a study (mortality) may differ for the group receiving X (experimental) and the group not getting X (control).

three months older and more familiar with their surroundings. This familiarity with his people and environment might have produced increased performance regardless of training.

One might also argue that the first performance measure made the supervisors aware of the fact that some type of evaluation of their performance was being made and most of them decided to work extra hard over the next six months in case they were being monitored for one reason or another. This type of confound would be due to *testing*.

Perhaps the first performance observations were recorded in the afternoon when the observers were somewhat tired and the second evaluations were done in the morning when they were more alert. Differences in the two observations due to changes in the measurement device is called *instrument decay*. All four of the possible confounds discussed above would provide alternative explanations to the suggestion that the training course had made the supervisors more effective.

A third design which also has many problems might be set up as follows: The personnel manager announces the possibility of taking the course to the supervisors and lets them sign up for the course. When 50 percent have signed up he or she discontinues registration and begins the course. Three months later the manager compares the ones who took the course against those who did not. This design is called a *static group comparison* and is symbolized as follows:

$$X \qquad O_1$$
$$\overline{} \; \text{--} \; \text{--} \; \overline{}$$
$$O_2$$

The dotted lines mean that the supervisors were not randomly assigned to the two groups and it points out the first major problem with the design: *Selection*. Is it not possible that the people who volunteered were more highly motivated and better supervisors to begin with?

The addition of a comparison group (called a control group) is laudable and it rules out many of the errors discussed in relation to the first two designs. For example, the increments in performance due to new machinery should occur for both groups so differences between O_1 and O_2 could not be attributed to history. However, when individuals are not randomly assigned to the experimental group (the one that receives the treatment) and the control group (the one without the treatment), differences may exist betweeen the two groups other than the treatment.

What if the course is a very difficult one and some of the supervisors who have signed up find it frustrating and quit their job? Not only would you have only highly motivated supervisors but you would also now have only the brightest ones taking the training. When there are systematically different dropout rates for the experimental and control groups, differences between the two groups may be attributable to errors of *mortality*.[21]

---

[21] For a discussion of regression and interactive effects, see Campbell and Stanley, *Experimental and Quasi-Experimental Designs*, pp. 9–12.

Three Good Designs

The first good design simply adds a control group to the one-group pretest-posttest design and randomly assigns individuals to the two group. It is called a *pretest-posttest control group* design.

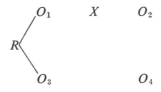

The comparison made is one of change scores. That is, were the changes from O_1 to O_2 greater than the changes from O_3 to O_4? Change scores are used because the investigator can then rule out alternative interpretations due to history, testing, maturation, and so forth. More specifically, anything that happens to the experimenal group should also happen to the control group, so that any difference in the *degree of change* should be attributed to X, the treatment. By randomly assigning people to the two groups, there should be no initial bias as to why an individual ends up in a given group. The only possible error is the interactive one suggestel in Figure 18–2. Perhaps being observed the first time makes everyone work a little harder but the experimental group also works hard at doing well in the training program. The differences in change scores may indeed be due in part to the training course but only when the individuals know that it is partially related to their performance ratings. The people in the experimental group are in some sense more receptive to the training because of the pretest. This is a relatively minor problem and can be corrected with a design called a *posttest only control group* design.

In this design, people are randomly assigned to the two groups, the treatment administered and scores on posttests compared. It remedies the minor problem with the previous design by not administering a pretest. However, this omission also means that the investigator does not have a group which receives a pretest and a posttest without the treatment. This can be a useful group because it provides information on the effects of history, maturation, instrument decay, and so on.

Occasionally, an investigator will combine the last two designs to form a *Solomon 4-group* design.

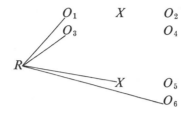

The supervisors would be randomly assigned to four groups, two of which would receive the training course (one with a pretest, one without). This provides the investigator with a lot of information. He can examine history effects (O_3 to O_4) testing effects (O_4 to O_6) the interaction of testing and the treatment (O_2 to O_5), and so on. However, in some cases this type of design requires the use of more personnel, more subjects and therefore, more money. The added information must be weighed against the cost.

In summary, then, the investigator wants to *conduct* a study with a design that will allow him to answer the questions he wishes to ask. By ruling out alternative interpretations of his results he can produce an internally valid study. The two most important components of the good designs discussed are that a comparison group is needed (one that does not get the treatment or receives some other treatment) and the random assignment of subjects to the two groups so that theoretically no initial differences will exist for the two groups. The differences that are found can then be attributed to the manipulated variable—the experimental treatment.

Experimental Design: External Validity

The three components of experimental research consist of the subjects, the treatment, and the observation techniques. When the results of a study are tied to the specific people, treatment or measurement device or situation which produced the results, then the study lacks *external validity*.

Subjects. People come to or serve in experiments for different reasons. Some volunteer, some are paid. College students often are asked to serve as part of an introductory psychology course and much of the research in psychology has consequently been performed on the American college sophomore. It can and has been argued that this is not a representative group.[22] The results generated with the subjects may tell us a lot about college sophomores but very little about other groups. Investigators should use subjects from the larger group of people to whom they wish to generalize their findings. This may require that an experiment be replicated a number of times with different types of people coming for different reasons but it should be done if one is to argue that his findings are general in nature.

Treatments. In certain cases the experimenter makes broader generalizations about his treatment than is justified. For example, certain types of human relations training is probably good for certain types of people but to argue that all "group experiences" are good is not justified based on the results of one experiment. Another example would be helpful. Suppose that some employees on the shop floor of some industrial plant thought that music would be nice to listen to while they work and an industrial psychologist tries out two levels of loudness of the music to see which is most conducive to hard work. He obtains the following results:

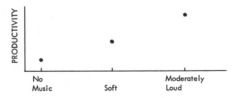

He has randomly assigned employees to the three conditions and he concludes that his results represent the following relationship: Increases in loudness increase productivity.

He, therefore, recommends that the music be played at the loudest possible level, and the employees suffer ear damage as a consequence.

---

[22] Robert Rosenthal, "The Volunteer Subject," *Human Relations,* 1965, 18, 389–408.

The problem arises because the experimenter attempted to generalize his results to loudness levels other than those he had tested. A more logical guess might have produced the following curve:

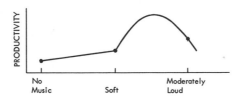

Again, the remedy for generalization is to try out a wider range and different presentations of the manipulated variable. If the results still hold one has more confidence in the generalizability of the findings.

Observations. Occasionally results can be attributed to the specific measurement procedure. For example, subjects respond differently on multiple choice tests where guessing is allowed then when it is penalized. [23] An attempt should be made to try out various procedures such as questionnaires, interviews, and observers, and if the findings are still replicated the results are more externally valid.

Reactive Effects. Particular situational characteristics (specific experimenter, the room in which people worked, the time of day, and so on) that might explain the results are called reactive effects.[24] By conducting the experiment at different times in various places with different experimenters the results again become more generalizable.

Quasi-Experimental Designs

In some settings the investigator is not able to obtain a control group or randomly place the subjects into one condition or another. Although there are a variety of ways one can deal with these problems, only one representative example for each will be presented. Modifications of these examples are available if one wishes to pursue the topic.[25]

Time Series. In the case where a control group is not available the investigator is mostly concerned about changes that occur between a pretest and posttest that might confound the results (history, matura-

---

[23] L. Cronbach, "Response Sets and Test Validity," *Educational and Psychological Measurement,* 6 (1946), 475–94.

[24] Campbell and Stanley, *Experimental and Quasi-Experimental Designs,* pp. 20–21.

[25] Ibid., pp. 34–63.

tion, instrument decay). One possible solution to his problem is to use a time series design where multiple pretests and posttests are used.

$$O_1 \quad O_2 \quad O_3 \quad O_4 \quad O_5 \quad X \quad O_6 \quad O_7 \quad O_8 \quad O_9 \quad O_{10}$$

If there are no differences between O_1 and O_2 or O_2 and O_3 or O_7 and O_8, and so forth, and there is a large difference between O_5 and O_6 the investigator may have some confidence that the treatment made some difference. For example, the manager might monitor performance ratings before and after some training program and then examine the relationship over time. If something like what is plotted below occurred then he might have some support for the use of his program (especially if he is relatively sure that nothing dramatic, like new machinery, occurred at the same time as the training).

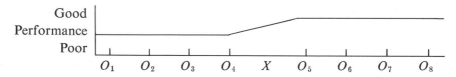

Nonequivalent Control Group. When the investigator cannot randomly assign people to experimental and control groups he can still have some control over selection or mortality errors. The design below calls for extensive pretests which help guard against both of these types of errors.

$$
\begin{array}{ccc}
O_1 & X & O_2 \\
\hline
O_3 & & O_4
\end{array}
$$

Randomization is an attempt to get rid of systematic bias between the experimental and control group. If it cannot be done then having information (pretests) on the variables which would be critical if a difference existed is available. Statistical techniques would allow the proper comparison to be made (adjustments can be made for original differences). Also, if people dropped out of one group or another, similar people could be chosen to be dropped from the other group in order to maintain their comparability. The central point is that pretests give you information about the similarity of the groups *before* the experiment. When they are dissimilar corrections can be made for the original differences. When they become dissimilar (people drop out) adjustments in the other group can again be made. Since one cannot measure everything you are never sure if they are completely comparable but it is better than not having the information (at which point the design would be a static group comparison).

Correlational Design: Internal and External Validity

The other type of research, where we are simply interested in whether variables are related, is called correlational. In correlational studies, the results are in the form of correlation coefficients and the question of internal validity has to do with alternative explanations of the implied inference. If one found a high correlation for students between weight and reading ability, one might suggest that a possible confound—age— was responsible for the relationship. Ruling out the possibility that a correlation between two variables is due to their relationship to a third, however, is by and large an intuitive process rather than a process that can be systematically introduced into the design (except by measuring everything).

Other alternative interpretations can mostly be ruled out by having confidence in one's measures. By making sure that they are both reliable and valid the investigator may be relatively sure that the relationship found did indeed exist for the group that was tested.

The problems of external validity are largely the same as for experimental studies. The investigator must ascertain whether the relationship exists for other groups of people, under other conditions, with the use of alternative observation techniques.

MEASUREMENT AND DESIGN: A COMPARISON

Two basic ideas run through the problems of measurement and research design: reproducibility and generalizability. A reliable measurement device is one that gives us the same score on repeated observations. An internally valid study is one where alternative hypotheses are ruled out. If the experiment were run again the same results should occur. Both the ideas of reliability and internal validity emphasize reproducibility—if one did it again, he would get the same results.

Both measurement validity and external validity of research design emphasize the content or generalizability of the measures or design. Is one measuring what he says he's measuring? Who are the people, places, and observation techniques used in the design? These are questions of content and generalizability. That is, do we get similar findings with different measures or different components of the design?

The reason for their emphasis is that these dimensions underscore two of the important aspects of scientific inquiry. This inquiry should be public, reproducible, understandable in terms of content, and augmentable. Being able to reproduce one's work and understanding its meaning contributes greatly to these goals.

chapter 19

Experimentation: Methodological and Ethical Considerations

The purpose of almost all scientific inquiry in the behavioral sciences involves the observation of human beings. These observations may be unobtrusive measures such as personnel or attendance records or they may be simply observations recorded in the fashion of a diary.[1] More frequently they involve questionnaire interviews or other intrusions into the lives of those people participating and this intrusion raises two major questions.

Do individuals behave differently because they are in an experiment? The Heisenberg principle states that in the process of studying anything we change it. This is certainly the case for behavioral science and only lately have attempts been made to deal adequately with the problem.

Also, what rights does the subject or investigator have in the process of experimentation? What sorts of questions can be asked? Other ethical questions are related to the source and types of financial support and the general professional behavior of the researchers. It is the purpose of this chapter to examine these questions and their implications for research conducted on organizational behavior.

PARTICIPATION IN AN EXPERIMENT

In conducting an experiment there are two aspects of the situation which might produce data that was not representative of how one would

---

[1] E. Webb, D. Campbell, R. Schwartz, and L. Sechrest, *Unobtrusive Measures: Non-Reactive Research in the Social Sciences* (Chicago: Rand McNally & Company, 1966).

behave in "real life." First, there is the situation. That is, the degree to which the experimental *setting* causes the individual to behave differently. These possible confounds are called "demand characteristics."[2]

A second problem is caused by the experimenter. In some cases he may unwittingly convey his expectations about the experiment to the participants. For example, interviewees for jobs often try very hard to say what they think the interviewer wants to hear. These confounds are called "experimenter bias."[3] effects. The effects of both of these errors on organizational research is potentially very great and will be discussed in more detail.

Demand Characteristics

In the early 1920s a group headed by Elton Mayo[4] conducted a series of research projects in the Hawthorne plant of the Western Electric Company. Their original intent was to examine the effects of various physical characteristics of the work environment on the workers' output. In one study, a group of women were selected to work together under various lighting intensities. The investigators soon discovered however, that the output produced by this group was not related to the lighting conditions. The situation has been described as follows, "the girls felt 'it was fun' and, even though the number of observers was greater and their attention higher in the test situation than in the ordinary work environment, the girls felt no sense of anxiety because of tight control."[5] They became highly motivated to work hard, and developed warm relationships with each other and their supervisors. In short, the setting and attention changed their behavior, not the experimental variable of interest (illumination in this case).

Even with this auspicious beginning, social scientists continued to believe that the individual that participated in an experiment was a passive responder. The subject was treated as if he or she were behaving in exactly the same way that he would outside of the experiment. This

[2] Martin T. Orne, "On the Social Psychology of the Psychological Experiment: with Particular Reference to Demand Characteristics and Their Implications," *American Psychologist*, 17 (1962), 776–83.

[3] Robert Rosenthal, *Experimenter Effect in Behavioral Research* (New York: Appleton-Century-Crofts, 1966).

[4] Elton Mayo, *Social Problems of an Industrial Civilization* (Cambridge, Mass.: Harvard University Press, 1945).

[5] Blair J. Kolasa, *Introduction to Behavioral Science for Business* (New York: John Wiley & Sons, Inc., 1969), p. 463.

idea has recently been challenged by Martin Orne who has presented data to support his contentions. Orne cites one experiment (the most tedious and boring task that he could imagine) where participants were asked to do 224 simple additions from each of a large stack of printed papers, record their answers on another sheet and then tear up this answer sheet into 32 pieces. This task was to be repeated for 2,000 sheets: clearly a task that few individuals would ever undertake in a "real life" setting. In one case, Orne reports that a subject continued work for 5½ hours and that the experimenter gave up!

Possible Confounds. The possible "demands" of an experimental setting are numerous. The one aspect they have in common, however, is that the participant behaves differently *because he is in an experiment.*

1. Looking good. An example of this type of problem has already been mentioned: the interviewee. It is clearly important to "look good" to a prospective employer in habits, dress, appearance, and background. How many job applicants say, "Oh yes, I drink a lot on the job and I'll probably be absent once a week"?

2. Helping science. In certain settings the participant may feel that he is furthering the cause of social science and try very hard to do a good job. The Hawthorne studies can be partially viewed in this light. That is, the women knew they were being observed and wished to do well both for themselves (looking good) and for the observers.

3. Problem solving. Many experimental studies of leadership utilize tasks specifically set up for an experiment.[6] Subjects may approach these tasks with a bent at "problem solving" or "gaming" rather than perceiving them as tests of their leadership skills.

4. Unknown effects. Imagine a setting where employees know they are being observed. Then, one day, new guidelines for doing a job are established and more observations take place. Orne states that even the dullest college student is aware that change is expected after a pretest, treatment, posttest sequence. The subject may choose to help or hinder the experimenter or he or she may choose to do something else. The point is that investigators are usually not sure about the motivational incentives under which their subjects are operating.

Possible Solutions. Since the investigator is by definition changing the situation through experimentation, the problem cannot be solved altogether. There are, however, a few strategies which can be suggested:

1. Unobtrusive measures. One possible solution is to make the experi-

---

[6] See Fred E. Fiedler, *A Theory of Leadership Effectiveness* (New York: McGraw-Hill Book Company, 1967).

ment as unnoticeable as possible. Webb suggests the use of records already available, either printed, published, filed, or physical indications of behavior.[7] He cites an example of a situation where an owner of a museum was interested in which displays were viewed the most. Rather than place an observer to watch people as they watched the displays, he measured the wear of the tile in front of the displays. In many cases, some of the data which are needed are on file or can be gathered with a minimum of intrusion.

2. Ask participants. If the investigator must carry out the study with questionnaires, experimental tasks, or other methods of direct contact with subjects, he or she might ask them about their behavior when the experiment is completed. If it turns out that most of the subjects respond by saying that they behaved in a way that was not representative of their everyday actions, then the investigator should question the generality of his findings.

3. Dry-run the experiment. A third strategy is to simulate the experiment with some volunteers. More specifically, the investigator could present a group of individuals with exactly what he is going to do. He would then ask them: "If you were to serve in this experiment, what would you think was going on? How naturally would you behave?" This method has the advantage of giving the investigator information before the study has actually been completed. Again, there is no solution, but there are certainly some ways in which the effects of demand characteristics can be measured or minimized.

Experimenter Bias

Not only is an experimental subject often placed in an unrepresentative setting, he or she may also interact with an investigator that influences his or her behavior. When the subject behaves differently than he ordinarily would because of contact with the experimenter, it is an example of what is termed "experimenter bias." McGuigan points out that "while we have traditionally recognized that the characteristics of an experimenter may indeed influence behavior, it is important to observe that we have not seriously attempted to study him as an independent variable."[8]

---

[7] Webb et al., *Unobstrusive Measures*, chapters 1 and 2.

[8] F. J. McGuigan, "The Experimenter: A Neglected Stimulus Object," *Psychological Bulletin*, 60 (1963), 421.

There are a number of ways that experimenter effects may operate. In studies with only one investigator the experimenter may convey his expectations to the experimental group. That is, he may behave toward one group differently from another and differences between an experimental and control group could be attributed to the interaction with the experimenter and not the variables of interest. In cases of multiple data collectors one investigator may gather data from the experimental group and one from the control group. Once again, the differences between groups may be because of their differential treatment by the investigators. An article by Woods pointed out that almost 45 percent of a large sample of journal articles (722) had two or more authors.[9] Estimates by McGuigan would lead one to believe that almost none of these articles included any information about possible experimenter effects.[10]

Another set of similar problems may be traced to the experimenter making systematic mistakes in favor of his hypothesis. More specifically, in situations which require the judgment of the investigator (observations, interpretations of answer) mistakes may be recorded that favor the support of one's theory. Although in most cases these errors are not done on purpose, it is worth noting that checks for this type of problem are often not reported.

Possible Bias. Numerous studies have been conducted which show the effects of experimenter bias and reviews of this literature are available.[11] Some of the most important variables effecting this bias are listed below:

1. Personality. A variety of personality characteristics of experimenters may influence the behavior of subjects. Research has been reported showing that subjects behave differently for experimenters with different anxiety levels, neuroticism levels, and other personality traits.

2. Person characteristics. Information about the experimenters' religion, sex, or research experience may also produce systematically different data. One survey report indicated that Christian experimenters when interviewing subjects found that 50 percent of the participants believed that Jewish people had too much influence. Jewish interviewers working

---

[9] P. J. Woods, "Some Characteristics of Journals and Authors," *American Psychologist*, 16 (1961), 699–701.

[10] McGuigan, "The Experimenter," p. 428.

[11] See B. L. Kintz, D. J. Delprato, D. R. Mettee, C. E. Persons, and R. H. Shappe, "The Experimenter Effect," *Psychological Bulletin*, 63 (1965), 223–33, or Robert Rosenthal, "Experimenter Outcome, Orientation and the Results of the Psychological Experiment," *Psychological Bulletin*, 51 (1964), 405–12.

with a similar sample reported that only 22 percent of their subjects felt that way.[12]

3. Expectations. Rosenthal has presented a number of striking findings which illuminate the importance of experimenter expectations.[13] He has reported data indicating that teachers' expectations as to the amount of potential held by their students influences the student's actual performance. More specifically, teachers were told that some students would improve markedly while others would not. In reality, the students were randomly placed into these two groups. However, at the end of the year, Rosenthal reports that the students for whom the teachers held high expectations did indeed, show improvement in comparison to the other group.

Experimenters that were told they were dealing with "maze bright" rats recorded significantly better maze performance for these animals than the reports of experimenters dealing with "maze dull" animals. The animals were not different for the two groups and had been randomly assigned to the two conditions.

Clearly, the important question is how these expectations get translated into systematically different treatment for the experimental and control groups, without the investigator's active attempts to do so. Rosenthal suggests a number of possibilities: tone of voice, facial expressions, unintentional verbal reinforcement, misjudgment of responses, and so forth. Although there have been some legitimate criticisms raised about both the generality of his findings and the ways in which certain studies were conducted, it is still true that this type of bias does exist and may influence the empirical results.

Organizational Settings. There are a number of settings in organizational research where these types of bias may be operating:

1. Selection. Both selection interviews and personality tests put the interviewee in a situation where he or she wishes to please a possible employer. Clearly it is to his advantage to not only ascertain what is expected of him but to meet these expectations as well. This is one of the reasons that many of these tests or interviews have very little relationship to how the individual eventually behaves in the organization.

2. Guidance. On a more positive note, some investigators have reported that clinical psychologists or vocational guidance experts find positive expectations to be a powerful determinant of eventual mental

---

[12] H. H. Hyman, W. J. Cobb, J. J. Feldman, C. W. Hart, and C. H. Stember, *Interviewing in Social Research* (Chicago: University of Chicago Press, 1954).

[13] Rosenthal, "Experimenter Outcome," pp. 407–10.

health.[14] However, the opposite would also be true; those expected to fail often do.

3. Experimental research. Campbell and Dunnette report studies of the effects of T-group training where bias may have existed.[15] Some reports of managerial training have the following design: Managers attitudes about a set of issues are assessed as pretest material, the company spends $1,000 to send an employee away for two weeks of training, he returns and is asked "Did it change your attitudes? Did it do you any good?" The expectations of the investigator are rather explicit. The argument as to whether real effects indeed occurred is not at issue here. The problem is that bias was built into the investigation.

4. Survey research. Much of the research on consumer behavior has involved elaborate surveys of public opinion. As pointed out earlier, the experimenter's sex or religion may influence the responses he receives. It has also been found that contingent questions or open-ended questions on surveys increase the likelihood of error. The greater the flexibility allowed in the questions the greater the probability of bias.

Possible Remedies. In experimental settings where there are experimental and control groups there are three major ways to correct for experimenter bias. First, experimenters can be run blind. More specifically, experimenters can be assigned to collect data without knowing to which group the subject belongs. A second, similar strategy is to randomly assign individuals to experimenters so that conditions and experimenters are mixed. Finally, in situations where different experimenters are carefully assigned to different groups, questions may be asked or analyses conducted to see if any bias did indeed occur. Although far from satisfactory, this last alternative should be done whenever multiple investigators are involved.

In interview or survey settings there are also a couple of possible ways to control experimenter bias. One important strategy is to structure interviews or surveys so that relatively few decisions or judgments are left up to the investigator. This procedure minimizes error. A second technique is to interview your interviewers; that is, find out what characteristics might bias a given study (the Christian, Jewish example) and eliminate certain investigators from collecting data in that setting.

---

[14] R. Sanders and S. E. Cleveland, "The Relation between Certain Experimenter Personality Variables and Subject's Rorschach Scores," *Journal of Projective Techniques,* 17 (1953), 34–50.

[15] John P. Campbell and Marvin D. Dunnette, "Effectiveness of T-Group Experiences on Managerial Training and Development," *Psychological Bulletin,* 70 (1968) 73–104.

In summary, both demand characteristics and experimenter bias will always exist. It should be clear, however, that these effects in some cases can be measured or controlled and that these procedures should be used if possible. These precautions will increase our confidence in the investigators' results.

ETHICAL ISSUES IN EXPERIMENTATION

In designing and planning research that involves human subjects, the investigator must be concerned not only with issues pertinent to experimental design, but with questions of ethics. The most important topics for research on organizational behavior are those of deception, testing, financial support, and general professional behavior.

Most professional disciplines, such as psychology, sociology, or anthropology have some sort of professional association which provides ethical standards. The American Psychological Association (APA) has a Committee on Scientific and Professional Ethics and Conduct, for example. This committee hears and investigates complaints, recommends action, and formulates rules or principles of ethics. These principles are distributed to all members of the APA in the form of a "Casebook on Ethical Standards of Psychologists" which provides examples referred to the committee dealing with the various principles and the action recommended. Even with these precautions, errors of judgment occur. We will present some examples and possible remedies.

Deception-Mistreatment of Human Subjects

One of the earliest articles on ethics in human experimentation was written by Vinacke in 1954. In this paper he raised a number of questions about experiments in which "the psychologist conceals the true purpose and conditions of the experiment, or positively misinforms the subjects or exposes them to painful, embarrassing, or worse, experiences, without the subject's knowledge of what is going on."[16] The number of studies in which physical harm is possible for the participant are minimal but the same is not true for the other areas of concern mentioned by Vinacke. A relatively recent article by Seeman points out that samples of articles from the *Journal of Personality* and the *Journal of Abnormal and Social*

---

[16] Edgar Vinacke, "Deceiving Experimental Subjects," *American Psychologist,* 9 (1954), 155.

Psychology showed around 10 percent using deception in 1948 and 30 percent in 1963.[17] Seeman states that: "It seems safe to conclude that to some degree deception has come to be the method of choice in this area of research."[18]

Research on organizational behavior has included studies utilizing false information. Mulder and Stemerding studied the effects of threat on group attraction using independent food merchants in a number of Dutch towns.[19] These merchants were told that there was a high probability that a new supermarket would open in their town and that they might go out of business. Their reactions were studied and they were never informed about the falseness of the information they had received. In another set of studies reported by Berkun, Bialek, Kern, and Yagi, army recruits were told they were aboard a plane that was about to "ditch" or crash-land.[20] Literally, hundreds of studies on attitude change, interpersonal attraction, and conformity use some sort of deception in the introduction of an experimental manipulation.

Implications. Dishonesty in any form of research requires some sort of justification. The implications of not having some justification raise ethical, methodological, and professional problems.[21] Social scientists have no *right* to cause any physical harm to the subject but this has not been as clear with respect to psychological harm. Most investigators who use deception argue that it must be used because it is the only way that they can test their theories. It is hard to imagine doing experimental research on managerial stress or anxiety without creating this discomfort. It is also argued that the possible knowledge to be gained is important in some wider sense (i.e., to society or people). And, it should probably be mentioned, that most investigators provide elaborate debriefing procedures after an experiment. Whether these arguments serve as justification is questionable.

There are also methodological considerations that are important when deception is used. What happens if the subject discovers the use? Should

---

[17] Julius Seeman, "Deception in Psychological Research," *American Psychologist*, 24 (1969), 1025–28.

[18] Ibid., p. 1025.

[19] M. Mulder and A. Stemerding, "Threat, Attraction to Group, and Need for Strong Leadership," *Human Relations*, 16 (1963), 317–334.

[20] M. M. Berkun, H. M. Bialek, R. P. Kern, and K. Yagi, "Experimental Studies of Psychological Stress in Man," *Psychological Monographs*, vol. 76, no. 15 (Whole No. 534) (1962).

[21] For an excellent discussion, see Herbert C. Kelman, "Human Use of Human Subjects: The Problem of Deception in Social Psychological Experiments," *Psychological Bulletin*, 67 (1967), 1–11.

he or she be dismissed from the experiment? Also, in many settings, the investigator uses a confederate (someone posing as a subject) to introduce an experimental treatment (e.g., creating hostility or anxiety or whatever the investigator is interested in). The experimenter must be sure that this confederate behaves the same way toward the different treatment groups as well as protecting his identity. More specifically, the experimenter must be sure that differences in the experimental and control groups are not due to differential behavior on the part of the confederate.

Finally, the professions that do work in the behavioral area stand to suffer from this type of research. In a time when many people are looking to behavioral scientists to help in the understanding of some of the social ills facing the country it is far from fortuitous to be branded as deceivers and persons of slight credibility.

Suggestions.   Most universities and certain funding agencies now require a review of all research using human subjects. A copy of some of the questions asked is presented in Figure 19–1. This procedure permits professionals to judge the justification of research presented by their colleagues. The attempt to balance the value of an experiment against its potentially harmful effects is at least left up to a group of relatively impartial judges. These review procedures, although probably viewed by some as an intrusion of "academic freedom" are necessary checks against poor judgment.

But more is needed. Many experiments are still conducted which incorporate minor deceptions or discomforts. Every effort should be made to develop new techniques or strategies for studying the phenomenon in ways that do not use these techniques (e.g., role playing, simulations). It may be more expensive or require somewhat more ingenuity on the part of the investigator but all avenues should be explored.

One final rule of thumb should be suggested: Subjects should not leave an experiment more upset than when they arrived. Every effort should be taken to exclude people who might be more vulnerable than others. Clear and honest debriefing procedures should always be included. If subjects are still upset, the investigator should seriously consider discontinuing the investigation.

Testing

Criticism of psychological tests used for personality assessment or selection procedures has mounted steadily over the past 20 years. In

FIGURE 19–1

Department of Psychology
Review Form:
Use of Human Subjects

1. Date submitted: _____.
2. Period of proposed research: _____.
3. Name and academic title of principal investigator: _____
_____.
4. Name of other investigators: _____
_____.
5. Title of experiment: _____.

Please answer the questions listed below by encircling the applicable reply.

Yes	No	6.	Will anyone other than the individuals named above interact with the subject?
Yes	No	7.	Will any apparatus be attached to the subjects?
Yes	No	8.	Will any drugs be administered to the subjects?
Yes	No	9.	Will the subjects be exposed to any potentially harmful stimuli?
Yes	No	10.	Is the experiment likely to cause the subjects any stress or discomfort?
Yes	No	11.	Are there any other potential hazards to the subject?
Yes	No	12.	Will subjects under college age be used?
No	Yes	13.	Will paid subjects or subjects satisfying a course requirement receive appropriate compensation?
No	Yes	14.	Will subjects be permitted to withdraw from the experiment at any time?
Yes	No	15.	Will any deception be practiced upon the subjects?
Yes	No	16.	Will subjects be asked to reveal any embarrassing, sensitive, or confidential information about themselves or others?
No	Yes	17.	Will the subjects be fully informed of the procedure to be followed during the experiment?
Yes	No	18.	If this research is grant-supported, is review at the university level required by the grantor?

Approved by: _____.
Date of approval: _____.   File Number: _____.

1965 these attacks resulted in congressional investigations by members of both the Senate and the House of Representatives. These investigations prompted directives from the executive side of the government which restricted the use of certain psychological tests.

The types of tests which produced this outcry were numerous. There were objections to "quickie" tests which could supposedly assess meaningful personality characteristics and took only 10 minutes to administer. There were cries of discrimination about tests used to allocate students into "tracks" in the District of Columbia school system. Questions of privacy about personal matters were raised. One of the most frequently used personality inventories asks true-false questions such as "I am a special agent of God" or "Peculiar odors come to me at times." Other people objected to the labels assigned to them by tests. The basic issue to be evaluated is the subjects' right to privacy versus society's right to information it conceives as necessary to promote the general welfare. The problem is to specify what sorts of procedures are available to facilitate a judgment on whose rights take precedence.

Test Content. In many cases it is the content of a test which causes objections. People are offended by the questions and either refuse to answer or falsify their responses. There are a number of simple checks which an investigator can make before reaching this point.[22] Are there any legal restrictions on the information? Is it self-incriminating? Does it dwell on abnormal or immoral behavior? Will it have an adverse effect on anyone? What justifications exist to use a sensitive question rather than a less personal one?

Situational Issues. Even when tests are free of obnoxious content there are objections to their use. These objections are based upon the fact that most tests are used for either clinical or selection purposes. In the former setting the major issues are ones of confidentiality. The subject should have complete confidence that the test scores will remain confidential. Since both the person tested as well as the tester have the tested individual's best interests in mind, this should not present major problems. The American Psychological Association states that "information received in confidence is revealed only after most careful deliberation and when there is clear and imminent danger to an individual or to society, and then only to appropriate professional workers or public authorities."[23]

The situation which is most conducive to conflict, however, is where the investigator does not have the tested person's best interests at heart. Almost all job selection or education selection tests build in a conflict of interest. The person taking the test stands to lose something very important if he doesn't "do well" on the test; he'll fail to get a job or fail to be admitted to some institution in which he desires membership. The response to this setting is often faked answers.

Two possible suggestions can be made. First, it seems appropriate to argue that personality tests should be used in these types of settings only when necessary. Tests of personality characteristics or traits have

---

[22] Herbert S. Conrad, "Clearance of Questionnaires with Respect to 'Invasion of Privacy' Public Sensitivities, Ethical Standards, etc.," *American Psychologist,* 22 (1967), 356–59.

[23] *Casebook on Ethical Standards of Psychologists* (Washington, D.C.: American Psychological Association, 1967), p. 66.

typically not been good predictors of job performance.[24] Their reliabilities and validities are low when compared to tests of skills or behavior. In some situations it may be deemed necessary to use personality tests (choosing men for submarine duty, for example) but in most cases tests of intellectual or physical skills coupled with background characteristics serve as better predictors.[25] This standard would prevent situations where an individual failed to get a job because he was not sociable enough, or achievement-oriented enough on some personality test. Because these traits have questionable relationships with job performance, these kinds of judgments may well be discriminatory and perhaps illegal.

A second suggestion is that no matter what the test situation, the subject must be informed of his rights. He should be informed of how the test scores will be used and allowed some flexibility on questions of a private nature. He should have the option of not responding or of leaving, hopefully without penalty, if he refuses to answer questions deemed to be highly sensitive.

Restricted use of tests of character and explicit test contracts for the job selection setting would still not eliminate judgments about what is personal or sensitive and what is not. Nor would it help in the decision involving a real conflict between the public good and the individual's privacy. These judgments must be made by impartial professionals believed to be competent in the area involved. However, used correctly these standards would minimize the possibility of the individual's rights being abused or his privacy violated.

Financial Support

About the same time that the United States was involved in the fuss over the Dominican Republic (June 1965), we were accused of spying and espionage by the U.S. ambassador to Chile. Moreover, he claimed that the United States was using a social science project as a front.

The target of the criticism was called Project Camelot,[26] and it was

---

[24]John P. Campbell, Marvin D. Dunnette, Edward E. Lawler III, and Karl E. Weick, Jr., *Managerial Behavior, Performance, and Effectiveness* (New York: McGraw-Hill Book Company, 1970), chapters 6–9.

[25] Marvin D. Dunnette, *Personnel Selection and Placement* (Belmont, Calif.: Wadsworth Publishing Co. Inc., 1966).

[26] The May 1966 edition of the *American Psychologist* has three articles on this topic: John Walsh, "Foreign Affairs Research: Review Process Rises on Ruins of Camelot," pp. 438–40, Theodore R. Vallance, "Project Camelot: An Interim Postlude," pp. 441–44, and Irving L. Horowitz, "The Life and Death of Project Camelot," pp. 445–54.

described as "a project for measuring and forecasting the causes of revolutions and insurgency in underdeveloped areas of the world."[27] It also attempted to discover ways to cope with or eliminate these insurgencies or revolutions.

Camelot was sponsored by the U.S. Army through the Special Operations Research Organization in the amount of a $4 to $6 million contract for a three- to four-year period. Research was to be conducted in 12 Latin American countries, 3 in the Middle East, 4 in the Far East and France, Greece, and Nigeria.

After a number of discussions on the issue, the project was discontinued by the Department of Defense in July of the same year. The reactions of the academic as well as other interested communities of people was mixed. The U.S. government initiated tighter control on cross-cultural research, which was viewed by some as bordering on censorship. On the other hand, most people felt that Camelot was ill-advised.

Since that time, numerous groups have complained about government-supported or military-supported research projects. The question of who sponsors research, however, appears to be misguided; that is, sponsorship is neither inherently good nor bad. Certainly, a more important dimension is how the information generated will be used. Since one of the purposes of this project was to influence, politically, certain aspects of social change in other countries the work was probably unjustified. Social scientists do not have a right to meddle in the internal affairs of other countries.

The ramifications of the whole issue are twofold. First, when projects that are unethical in some way are publicized, control of some sort is sure to follow. Sometimes this control is within the profession. For example, the right to use any deception in experiments with student volunteers is reviewed by a committee of colleagues at most universities. In some cases, however, this control comes from outside as is now the case for certain cross-cultural projects. The State Department can screen *all cross-cultural* research done in foreign countries on government funds and many of the decisions about this research may rest on political problems of the moment. This is too bad.

Second, social scientists should be more aware of just how their research will be used. Will tests be discriminatory? Will test scores be divulged or used incorrectly by others? The ultimate aim of social science is to be able to predict behavior. The logical consequence of that

---

[27] Horowitz, "Life and Death of Project Camelot," p. 145.

aim is that behavior could also be controlled. That control could be a powerful thing. One must consider, therefore, how the research findings might be used, and hopefully, this consideration takes place before the project is undertaken.

Professional Behavior

Besides the issues related to the potential harm that can be done to others by research (deception, testing, and disclosure of findings), there are also some general ethical issues related to the behavior of the investigator.

Publications. Although the guidelines for publication credit are not altogether clear some work has been done. A survey of psychologists showed that in general "publication credit should be given only to persons who are very actively involved in contributing to a project and that authorships should never be given out of gratitude or deference to persons of higher status. They should only be given when considerable important work has been done, and authorship should reflect the relative significance of the contributions made."[28]

Conflicts of Interest. For many professionals working within organizations there are frequently questions of allegiance. Research conducted often produces results that may be embarrassing to the organization involved. A number of examples come to mind. We are only presented with the experiments that "successfully" show that a given product compares favorably with its competitors. What is the responsibility of an investigator who conducts investigations that fail to support the organization's product? The "Pentagon Papers" are an example of a situation where an individual felt that the results of an investigation were more important to the public at large than to the organization that conducted the study.

The dilemma is one where the professional feels responsibility to both the employer and profession, country, or some other "reference group." There are no principles that seem to be applicable to all situations. The individual must consult his conscience and should solicit the opinions of others both inside and outside his profession to gain perspective. The final decision is an individual one.

Application of Principles. Social scientists have occasionally been placed in the embarrassing situation of advocating something based on

---

[28] Don Spiegel and Patricia Keith-Spiegel, "Assignment of Publication Credits: Ethics and Practices of Psychologists," *American Psychologist,* 25 (1970), 747.

minimal evidence. In advertising a few years ago it was believed that flashing messages on a TV or movie screen at high speeds (so fast that people were not "aware" of seeing them) could influence their behavior. Current fads suggest that T groups are the panacea of management training. Inconclusive research on both of these topics calls for caution in the broad application of these ideas.[29] Social scientists are being asked to solve social problems and to do so requires the applications of our knowledge to "real life" settings. However, this application is a two-edged sword. On the other side lies the whole issue of ethics: What happens when something is tried and it does not work? Who gets hurt? The answer must be both the public and the profession. This is not a call for ivory towerism but simply what we believe to be an accurate reflection of reality. Both sides of the issue have to be considered when one is dealing with the lives of others.

---

[29] Campbell and Dunnette, "Effectiveness of T-Group Experiences," pp. 73–104.

part VI
Conclusion

chapter 20

Organizational Governance

Although they are not often treated as such, organizations are political systems, as much as they are social systems, decision systems, or communication systems. Organizations attend to the basic political fact of life—*the authoritative allocation of resources.* Their decision makers constantly work the allocation problem of who gets what, when, where, and why. This is the fundamental problem of all political systems. It encompasses the processes of legitimacy, authority, and power.

That governance is a major issue in organization theory hardly conveys its true significance. We could argue that governance is *the* issue. However, by so doing we would include too much. Let it be enough to say that by introducing the governmental dimension to organization theory we hope to see in perspective certain concepts like those found in influence theory, leadership theory, and theories of organizational modification. Additionally we also want to point out several directions that may attract theorists and practitioners alike in the future.

ORGANIZATIONS AS A SUBJECT OF POLITICAL INQUIRY

The political philosophy of Plato was shaped by his admiration for the Athenian *polis,* which was an organizational entity smaller and less intricate than a modern, medium-sized business corporation. Yet, small as they were, these ancient Greek political systems provided the themes for political discourse that have transcended time and place. Of remarkable durability, the themes of community, of political virtue, and of the resolution of tension in the polity have survived through the ages. We use them as anchoring-points for our discussion of organizational governance issues in this chapter.

Community

Plato was critical of a number of Greek city-states that were overly small, and could not enjoy the advantages of larger political organizations. He clearly understood the significance of efficiencies of scale, but he also put a limit on what he considered to be a manageable size. His ideal *polis* would have counted no more than 5,000 citizens.[1] Aristotle agreed with his mentor believing that everyone in the *polis* should at least be able to recognize everyone else. Thus the basic question emerged, of how the advantages of size could be maximized without depersonalizing the political process with the subsequent loss of the sense of community by the citizens of the *polis*. The problem has not gone away with the massification of modern society, if anything it has become more intense.

A dominant characteristic of contemporary American society is the large size, complexity, and impersonality of the organizations that compose it. This situation has become commonplace, and generally accepted, because of the great material benefits large organizations have brought with them. However, such benefits have not come without cost, which Wolin identifies as the loss of community.

> The rapid technological changes and high social mobility of industrial societies have left in their trial uprooted populations with a deep sense of loneliness and bewilderment. The symptoms of personal demoralization have preoccupied the psychologist, as the symptoms of social disorganization have, the sociologist. These sciences have agreed that modern man is desperately in need of 'integration.' His need to 'belong' and to experience satisfying relations with others can be fulfilled if he is able to 'identify' himself with an adequate group, one which will provide him with membership; that is, a defined role and assured expectations.[2]

All organizations are susceptible to giantism. Therefore, they are equally afflicted by the same human problems we often ascribe to gov-

---

[1] Of course, there were more "people" in some of these states, but slaves, women, and children were considered subhuman and, therefore, not thought of as citizens.

[2] Sheldon S. Wolin, *Politics and Vision* (Boston: Little, Brown and Company, 1960), p. 357.

ernment bureaucracies. Therefore, praise for the material advantages created by the business and industrial system must be tempered by blame for its contribution to human dislocation and disintegration. In earlier, and simpler, times the disruption of community and the alienation of the polity could often be traced directly to impersonal and insensitive governments. Presently, other large organizations, such as business, labor, and education add to the social malaise. Individual employees, union members, and students are frequently deprived of a sense of identity, and they despair that justice will ever be theirs as a matter of organizational right.

Many years ago, Woodrow Wilson wrote that, "A modern corporation is an economic society, a little economic state—and not always little, even as compared to states." Presently many corporations have larger populations, more resources, and infinitely more advanced administrative systems than the early nation-states that provided the models from which political science emerged. But the old struggle between efficiency and community persists, although large-scale rational organizations seem to be prevailing. The "citizens" of such organizations have acquired affluence, education, and some measure of material security through gains in efficiency. However, the price has been paid in alienation and loss of community.

As a system of government, the bureaucratized organization is the grossest despotism. Sometimes it is benevolent, sometimes it is malevolent, but at all times it is despotic. The elite, the management core of the organization, controls the power of government to legislate, to execute, and to adjudicate without corporate "citizens" having even the minimum protection from tyranny such as those afforded them as citizens of the United States by the checks and balances of the Constitution. One of the ironies of American society is that these islands of organizational despotism exist within a sea of relative political freedom nationally.

In some ways, the organization has become a substitute for the classical policy of early political theory. Wolin in his book, *Politics and Vision*,[3] laments this transference of alliance, because the organization while deflecting people from the traditional political commitments has not been capable of providing an adequate substitute for community. The abandonment of conventional politics means to Wolin the abandonment of participation by individuals as full-scale citizens in the affairs of the

---

[3] Ibid., chapter 10.

nation as well as in the subordinate organizations that make it up. The reason for this dreary assessment is the subject of the next theme.

Political Virtue

Wolin's discontent lies in the perversion of the exaulted purpose of politics. In classical form, politics was believed to be the most lofty human endeavor. It required the individual to introspect, to reflect on goals and values, and to engage in discourse with others. In short, politics demanded that the citizen be a philosopher. Through philosophy, man was led closer to a greater understanding of the ideal forms, which Plato said was tantamount to truth. From this understanding the ideal state could be constructed, but more importantly, man himself was purified and ennobled. Therefore, politics surpassed art, science, literature, and all else. The highest aspiration a citizen could hold was to be a "philosopher king" in his own right, since the enlightenment that came from politics was ultimately the source of virtue.

While this has been a battered ideal from the time of the ancient Greeks onward, the most profound assault on it has come just recently from the modern organization. It has, as we discussed, destroyed community, estranged citizens, deflected allegiances, and subverted participation in political processes regardless of level and institution. As Hart observes, the rise of modern organization has been accompanied by a parallel decline in politics. The reputation of the individual citizen to contribute significantly to political activity regardless of place or circumstances has been immeasurably diminished.[4] Not surprisingly, as the political role of the individual is forfeited, the function is filled by an elite exercising autocratic power. This consequence is clearly present in the despotism of organizations. In a few words, the modern organization is not a place where a person can find virtue.

The displacement of politics by organization creates problems, and the main one is that employees become alienated. Alienation has not gone unnoticed by management, if for no other reason than that it was assumed alienation has an inverse relationship to productivity. The less alienated are more productive!

It is impossible to list, much less elaborate upon, the many fancies that management has inflicted upon people in the interest of "more effective human-resource utilization." But it is fair to say that most of

---

[4] See David K. Hart, "Theories of Government Related to Decentralization and Citizen Participation," *Public Administration Review*, Special Issue, October 1972, p. 611.

these experiments arose out of management's realization that something was not right about the way people worked and the environment in which they worked. Further, management also understood, imperfectly, that human dislocations detracted from the accomplishment of organizational goals.

Consequently, management in the last 50 years, embarked upon a multitude of quasi-sociological and psychological programs that were supposed to substitute the basic satisfactions people lost through the decline of politics. Coupled with this went the almost pathetic yearning of executives that if somehow their subordinates could see their interests connected inextricably with management's everything would be just fine.

Of course, management has not been altogether soft-headed in its attempts to accomplish organizational reform. Many incentive programs, personnel techniques, task reorganization, and training and development programs have been straightforward efforts to satisfy fundamental work motivations. However, these attempts have been feeble in confrontation with the rational imperative of industrialization and bureaucratization. From the human standpoint this means that the application of labor and intelligence to tasks must be stripped as far as possible of the individualizing characteristics of the doer.

Individuality of the worker has no place in making automobile pistons. One reason why the machine is interposed between the worker and work is to protect against deviation from specifications by aberrent individuals. The analogue of the machine in the factory is the rule in the office.

Rules like machines separate humans from work. They evoke standard and predictable performance so that the imprint of the individual will not disrupt the smooth and uniform flow of paper through the organization. In the modern organization, the rules of bureaucracy have invaded the factory and the office has become mechanized. Rule and machines, in nearly every function of the large organization, have united to remove from people the opportunity for individual discretion in the performance of their work.

Generally speaking the logic of organization and management has held for many years that if personal work bears too much of the individual imprint, it disrupts the carefully calculated, interlocked efforts of others, thus impeding the efficiency of the entire organization. The interposition of rules and machines between people and work has had much to do with the alleviation of this concern. It has also thwarted individual self-expression and the sense of individual worth.

This line of reasoning is far from unknown in management and the literature of organization theory. Argyris and Maslow created the initial clap of thunder in the middle 1950s, and the subsequent rumbles about the estrangement of individuals from the organization have not ceased. The issue of alienation remains but it is assuming a different perspective as a result of changing contingencies in the environment of management during the last 15 years.

On the one hand, management is heir to past imperatives. They include a commitment to technological progress, mass production and mass distribution, standardization, the marshaling of enormous quantities of financial, material, and human resources, the exploitation of economies of scale, and most important of all, a bureaucratic system of organization dedicated to the rational arrangement of tasks under the centralized direction and control of a small administrative elite. Thus the size, impersonality, and repressiveness which attend mature bureaucracies are part of the past's legacies with which management must contend.

On the other hand, many organizations are being struck by different imperatives unique to the present and the future. They array themselves into two broad interacting forces. One is the acceleration of technological change. The other is the constantly improving quality of the work force. Its changing character has resulted from growing demand for technical expertise and higher levels of skill. It has also resulted from a broadening base of education more or less democratically available to all members of society.

The political climate of organization has changed somewhat in response to these contingencies. Emphasis on participation and involvement of employees in decision making and job design is seen by some as the way of the future. But as Hart asks, "Why should people participate?"[5] One answer that comes through in the literature is that, "it's good for them." Carole Pateman argues that some form of true industrial democracy at the grass-roots level of worker councils is an essential preliminary to the reinculcation of democratic values into society at large.[6] Thus, the participation movement in organizations is, in a larger sense, a modernized version of the classical ideal of human ennoblement through politics.

Another answer to Hart's question is perhaps more poignant. "People should participate because it is good for the organization." If, indeed,

---

[5] Ibid., p. 617.

[6] Carole Pateman, *Participation and Democratic Theory* (London: Cambridge University Press, 1970).

organizations are a substitute for the ancient Greek polis, then it follows that some process that satisfies a basic human need for political behavior must also be substituted if alienation is ever to be overcome. Participation in this context is a rational management practice that should be encouraged in order to make better use of human resources. There are strong findings in the research literature of the behavioral sciences that support this justification.

However, it is difficult to suppose that management would use participation for human ennoblement; it is much easier to believe they would use it for organizational efficiency. While these applications are not mutually exclusive the latter contaminates the former. The space demanded by organizational rationality fills the space required by politics in the sense imagined by the early political theorists. There is no room in organizations for philosophers.

Resolution of Tension

The third persisting theme of political inquiry is the resolution of tension between the moral nature of man and the need for order in society.[7] Every political theorist of consequence has held assumptions about man's moral nature. For example, Hobbes thought that man was essentially evil, while Rousseau believed man was essentially good. Quite obviously, these assumptions could not be "proven" in an empirical sense. They are a priori starting points which are *absolutely necessary* to postulate since systems of order are based upon them.

If, for instance, man is assumed to be basically evil, then it follows that governance systems should be designed to contain him so that he will not inflict damage on himself or his fellowmen. But if man is considered to be fundamentally compassionate, then governance systems should permit greater freedom because man can be relied upon to do good for himself and his community. However as much one believes in man's goodness, order, or the means for achieving order, is central to political theory. Order, society, and polity are generically similar concepts.

A chief concern in political science is how to make the means used for achieving order correspond to the nature of man. In politics such means are often described as forms of governance. As the mechanism for the "authoritative allocation of resources" governance systems can

---

[7] This subject is discussed more fully in William G. Scott and David K. Hart, "The Moral Nature of Man in Organizations," *Academy of Management Journal,* June 1971, pp. 241–55.

either promote or retard relative degrees of freedom in society. Governance is a form of control. To the extent that the type of control exercised (or the sort of order imposed) corresponds to man's nature in the polity, then tension between the citizens and the means used to achieve order in that policy is reduced. If the opposite is the case, then tension is increased.

Students of management theory also ask, what happens when a form of organizational governance does not correspond to the "nature of man"? They turned to research in psychology for answers and were told that employee alienation is caused by imposing on them a system of organization foreign to their nature. Chris Argyris, in particular, defends this conclusion in his book *Personality and Organization*.[8]

Alienation is a very important subject in management since it is responsible for reducing organizational consensus and heightening organizational conflict. Alienation is a critical organizational disease. It has been examined in management circles by virtually every behavioral science with the belief that whatever might be done to cure this disease ought to be given due consideration. Thus sociology, psychology, and social-psychology, to name the most influential of these sciences in management, take their turn at diagnosing organizational malaise.

However, alienation and conflict are symptoms of the disease; the disease itself is ironically caused by problems that the empirically oriented behavioral scientist is poorly equipped to analyze. The moral nature of man in confrontation with systems of order is a metaphysical issue that requires seeking answers to philosophical rather than empirical questions. Unfortunately management, given its present point of view does not engage in the basic exercises of political philosophy. They require management to move in an unaccustomed direction—moral speculation about fundamental human values.

Presently philosophical discourse in management has barely begun, and its level is no more than one might expect from a field dedicated to pragmatism, empiricism, and technical rationality. It is hardly any wonder that systems of organizational governance alienate some of their employee "citizens,"[9] and that the applied behavioral sciences are used mainly to patch up holes in management's rational organization designs.

---

[8] Chris Argyris, *Personality and Organization* (New York: Harper & Bros., 1957).

[9] Although apparently not to the extent that some humanist writers in the management field would have us believe. Recent surveys indicate a large proportion of workers are satisfied with their lot. This seems to indicate some reasonable success in the resolution of tension between "systems of order" and the "moral nature" of the people in them. See *Job Satisfaction: Is There a Trend?* Manpower Research Monograph No. 30 (U.S. Department of Labor, 1974).

In summary, the basic themes of political inquiry—community, political virtue, and resolution of tension—are applicable to organization governance. The difficulty is that management has not examined these themes from any perspective other than the one dictated by the paradigm of the field. Hence, community is sacrificed for efficiency, but if things get too bad the behavioral sciences are consulted about establishing synthetic "communities" within the organization by using such devices as sensitivity training or job enlargement work teams. The theme of virtue is not overlooked, but in management, organizational virtue is expressed as job performance. The virtuous individual contributes his mightiest to his specialized function in the interest of organizational welfare. Finally, the resolution of tension is paramount in management's concerns. But it is dealt with symptomatically and pragmatically. The causes of tension are not matters for philosophical speculation. Given these boundaries, we next need to consider the purpose and the nature of organizational governance.

THE PURPOSE AND NATURE OF ORGANIZATIONAL GOVERNANCE

The threefold *purpose* of organizational governance is to establish a community of interest among all organizational participants, to promote organizational rationality, and to resolve conflict. Examples of these governance goals abound in management thought and practice. As we observed in Chapter 1, mutuality or integration of interests has been a continuous managerial objective, assuming different forms over the years, but remaining fundamentally unchanged. Higher levels of rationality have also been striven for to enable people to improve their performance on their jobs—to behave virtuously. Reward systems are designed so that employees are encouraged to be virtuous by anticipation of tangible payoffs. Consensus, which is the obverse of conflict, is another managerial goal of long tradition. It is closely connected with community of interest and rationality, because it has been held from the time of Frederick W. Taylor that equity in the distribution of rewards for performance positively influences the way employees see their interests as inextricably connected to the organization.

Of the three purposes of governance, the resolution of conflict seems to be the most critical. The forms of organization governance that order behavior, define the nature of equity, and determine the means used for controlling arbitrariness in the administration of justice arise from it. They are expressed tangibly as organizational policy. Such policies reflect two basic processes that are essential to the governance of every organization. These processes sometimes are called distributive and corrective justice,[10] but we refer to them here as substantive and procedural due process in order to emphasize their quasi-legalistic function in organizations.[11] *The nature of organizational governance depends on the way these processes are implemented.*

Substantive Due Process

Decisions have to be made allocating organizational resources to various individuals, interest groups, and economic sectors falling within an organization's domain. These decisions are *legislative* because they set the terms and establish the standards for who gets power to use in varying amounts. The substantive "due process issue" in organization governance is how such decisions are made, and the consequences that result from particular legislative decision-making forms. Allocation decisions can be legislated democratically, autocratically, constitutionally, and a number of other ways with various degrees of shading and overlapping. One of the chief outcomes of a legislative system, whatever its form might be, is the way in which employees perceive *equity or fairness* in their treatment.[12]

It is a common observation that management has to balance the distribution of the wealth created by an organization's productive power among a number of interest groups, of which the "employees" have received the most attention in management literature. Some of the basic issues in substantive due process are obscured by the blanket term "employees." Clearly, within organizations *differential* rewards are distributed to employees depending on a number of factors, such as type of work performed, level in the hierarchy, the degree of bargaining power, and pure managerial whim. In any event, allocation decisions are institutionalized eventually into quasi-legalistic forms such as wage and salary administration programs.

---

[10] Wendell French, *The Personnel Management Process*, 3d ed. (Boston: Houghton Mifflin Company, 1974), chapter 8.

[11] While the term "quasi-legalistic" is an imperfect expression, it does convey an important idea. The forms of organizational governance represent a body of "law," regardless of how it is arrived at formally or informally, and regardless of whether it is written or merely generally "understood." Such laws regulate the behavioral transactions that occur within organizations.

[12] One empirical treatment of the consequences of inequity perception may be found in Charles S. Telly, Wendell L. French, and William G. Scott, "The Relationship of Inequity to Turnover among Hourly Workers," *Administrative Science Quarterly*, June, 1971, pp. 164–72.

Underlying distribution decisions are two important considerations. One is equity and the other concerns participation in the legislation of distribution policies. Research pertaining to both of these considerations has been discussed previously in Chapters 6 and 16 on "Motivation" and on "Organizational Change Techniques," respectively. Therefore, it is not necessary to document extensively here that these subjects have been given serious thought and are important to management theory and practice. What needs to be done is to place them in the perspective of governance.

Equity is perceptual and relative. A person "feels" justly or unjustly treated only in relation to how he or she perceives other people are being treated in the same situation. If a woman is paid less for doing the same work as a man, then it is appropriate that she feels that she has been done an injustice. However, most cases of inequitable treatment are not as clear as in this example. People may feel unjustly treated, even if no objective discrimination exists. The point is that a sense of equity exists in an individual's mind and it is arrived through his perceptual apparatus regardless of how imperfectly or accurately it feeds data to him.

The argument often made in the participation literature is that when allocation decisions are unilaterally legislated by management, it is easy for a real or imagined perception of injustice to creep into an individual's assessment of his reward status relative to others. This explains, in part at least, why participation in organization governance has had such strong appeal for some. It permits people, that is, employee "citizens," to have a voice in the legislative process that establishes the policies for the distribution of rewards.

Regardless of the extent of employee participation, the implementation of distributive justice is a fact of organizational life. In autocratic management situations, where there is little participation, the implied rule is that management alone is best qualified to allocate resources justly. In the best of circumstances it will do so benevolently. Alternatively in democratic management situations, employees are heavily relied on to contribute to allocation decisions. Most of the time participation in the legislative process varies considerably depending on the nature of the organizational situation. But it is important to note that many decisions about economic rewards, working conditions, and hours of work have been highly institutionalized by collective bargaining between labor and management. The collective bargaining agreement has been referred to as the constitution of industrial government.

Even so, such agreements relate only to the segment of the work force that is organized, and then only to a part of the conditions of employment. Employees have little to say about who supervises them, what the level of output will be, what standards of quality are maintained, what is produced, and what services are rendered. These are all management decisions that are made unilaterally.

According to the participation theorists, the "citizens" of the organization should have a say in them too, if the participative ideal is to be achieved. A widespread sense of equity will not be felt among organization citizens short of full-scale, grass-roots participation in legislative processes.

This is not the place to criticize the participation movement, but it is important to summarize some of its effects on organizational governance. First, writers like Carole Pateman see full participation widening the role played by employees in allocation decision making. This role is clearly within the substantive due process or distributive justice domain. Consequently, all employees are supposed to participate in the legislative processes of the organization. Second, not only is such participation ennobling, as previously discussed, it is also expected to heighten the perception of equity among organizational members. Third, full participation will revolutionize the way in which substantive due process presently proceeds in organizational governance. Instead of being a prerogative of management, it becomes a right that is extended to a broader decision base in the organization. Fourth, the power of organizational governance is thus transferred from a managerial elite to the masses of organizational citizens Fifth, the outcome of such a change in the nature of substantive due process administration is the *politicization* of the organization In other words the organization will cease having economic or efficiency goals as its primary aims, and become instead an arena for political activity. This extreme outcome requires some heavy tradeoffs between political and productivity goals, which society at present is unready to make. The implementation of partial participation programs is more likely. However, they will fall short of the revolutionary ideals of the radical participation movement.

Procedural Due Process

Given the fact that every organization develops quasi-legal codes for the distribution of resources, then it follows that if people think they are dealt with unjustly under the terms of these codes they should have the right to appeal. The purpose of procedural due process is to provide avenues for obtaining corrective justice. It is the judicial function in organizational governance.

As part of an organization's judicial system, formal due process procedures are designed to limit arbitrariness and unfairness in the administration of legislated policies. There are many examples of such systems.[13] Some of them may originate in the "benevolence" of management; that is, they may be granted to employees as a unilateral act of management. Some others may be traced to a popular movement on the part of employees, as unionization, to force management to give them channels for securing justice. Virtually every contract that management and unions sign contains a clause having a written grievance procedure. Still other appeal programs begin with public law. Most federal civil service employees have numerous avenues for appealing complaints of injustices guaranteed to them by civil service law and agency regulations. Thus, judicial procedures for implementing corrective justice in organizations are widespread.

Two principles underlie these procedures. The first principle is that appeal mechanisms must be available to all employee "citizens" without prejudice. This is to say that people ought to be able to appeal for justice within the organization without fear of reprisal. For example, some employees' complaints are against their immediate superiors. Regardless of which way appeal decisions go, employees should not have to risk discrimination if they return to the same work situation with the same boss. The second principle is the separation of governance power, which simply means that those who make and implement the "laws" of the organization should not interpret these laws in the process of rendering judgments on disputes that arise from them. An atmosphere of judicial objectivity is difficult to maintain when the "judge" also occupies legislative and executive roles in the organization.

While these two principles are the minimum requirements necessary to assure that the adjudication of disputes is done fairly and dispassionately, they are frequently "honored in the breech rather than in the observance" of organizational governance. Since the separation of power is virtually unheard of in bureaucracy, and since many employees do not have the benefit of protection by "third parties" outside the organization, the administration of corrective justice is left to managerial goodwill. The situation is much like one described in the previous section

---

[13] See William G. Scott, *The Management of Conflict* (Homewood, Ill.: Irwin-Dorsey Press, 1965), where *formal* appeal systems in organizations are discussed.

on "Substantive Due process." As management is relied upon to make benevolent decisions unlaterally in the distribution of resources, so also in procedural due process, the aggrieved employee must rely upon management's judicial widsom to right wrongs.

More often than not the level of corrective justice in organizations has not progressed beyond the feudal practice which allowed aggrieved people to approach the lord or the king with the cry of "haro" that signified they were seeking redress of a injustice.[14] Likewise, in modern organizations, the "cry of haro" frequently is directed *informally* to a key executive who acts in the role of a judge in resolving conflicts and correcting injustices. Evan has shown that ". . . a very high proportion of the respondents in the industrial laboratory—which does not have a formal appeal system—perceives a due process norm to be institutionalized and have internalized such a norm."[15] This aspect of organizational governance, which is judicial, has not been emphasized as much as the legislative (policy making) or the executive (implementation) aspects of governance in management theory and practice.

Nevertheless, the procedural due process function must be performed. As with substantive due process, *how* it is performed determines the nature of the governance activity. Present practices of corrective justice do not contribute to the democratization of organizations except indirectly, because the institutionalization of corrective justice norms is a restraint on the absolute authority of management. Just how much of a restraint it is depends entirely upon the particular organization in question—its structure of authority, style of management, relationship with other organizations, and so on.

The informal approach to corrective justice has the advantage of flexibility, but it does little to protect the employees *right* to appeal and to prevent unfairness in the administration of justice. The formal approach, that depends upon written guarantees and specified legalistic procedures, gives the assurance that appeal privileges are available, but they have the danger that employee appeals will become bogged down in elaborate judicial machinery.

Another difficulty in procedural due process is that the "laws" of the organization are seldom codified. Consequently, who knows what

---

[14] See A. A. Berle, Jr., *The 20th Century Capitalist Revolution* (New York: Harcourt, Brace and Company, 1954), chapter 3.

[15] William M. Evan, "Due Process of Law in a Government and an Industrial Research Laboratory," *Proceedings of the Academy of Management*, 1965, p. 115.

is appealable and what is not?[16] The lack of codification results in clogging the judicial activity with gripes and complaints. While these minor expressions of discontent are often important barometers of morale, they tend to create a lot of noise in the system that prevents major incidents of individual injustice from being heard and resolved. However, the problems posed by legislative codification in organizations are many and large. We will deal with them more fully in the following section on the mode of the constitutional organization.

MODELS OF ORGANIZATION GOVERNANCE

We have looked into the purpose and nature of organization governance, and we have investigated two activities pertaining to the essential governance processes of distributive and corrective justice. Now we must carry the inquiry further in an effort to find other guiding principles behind the ways that management governs organizations. Five models of governance are reviewed—the constitutional, autocratic, democratic, federal, and totalitarian. Each model represents an "ideal type" in the sense that it is seldom found in a pure state in practice. However, these models do have distinctive characteristics, that represent major currents in both practical and theoretical applications of governance ideas.

The Constitutional Model

The constitutional model is the most general of the five. It grows out of the bargaining model of exchange relationships, the role of equity in organization, and the process of organizational politicization. Constitutionalization emphasizes the role of law in the relationships that emerge among various interest groups and power centers in organization. However, it does not make normative qualifications about the nature of these laws. Strictly speaking, there are no good or bad constitutional processes, although there may be good or bad organizational governance designs which promote or discourage the achievement of organizational objectives In this sense, the contingency approach and constitutionalization parallel one another. The constitutional model also directs attention to certain questions that pertain to codification of organization law. We cannot

---

[16] With the exception of collective bargaining agreements, where that which is appealable to the grievance procedure is limited to alleged violations of the contract itself and nothing else.

go far in understanding governance activity without giving consideration to these problems.

The constitution of an organization is not a single document. Rather, it is a body of agreements (some externally imposed, some internally generated, some formally explicit, some merely understood) which arise to govern administrative practices with respect to the rights of organizational participants. Certain of the forces which have created these laws are outside the organization, others stem from dynamics within. Of the former we are familiar with, for example, the impact of unionism on management and the effect of public policy on the affairs of business organizations. These external determinants of organizational law are enormously important in understanding the body of individual rights which covers matters ranging from employment security to fair employment practices. Of similar significance are the various arrangements by which individual appeals may be heard through grievance procedures in union contracts or hearing boards in regulating government agencies.

Lesser known, but of equal importance, is the system of rights, duties, and obligations of individuals that emerges from the processes of organizational life itself. These intraorganizational laws, and provisions for appeal under them, have received little formal treatment in the past. We restrict our discussion to these latter developments, fully appreciating the role played by extraorganizational forces in molding the character of organizational law.

Assumptions of the Constitutional Organization. A priori assumptions about the inherent goodness or defectiveness of man, and the desirability of a dominant hierarchy are not essential to this discussion. Rather, the operational assumption with which we start is that man is a political animal and that the collective entities in which he seeks collaborative goals are governmental systems. In this light, power, in the words of Merriam, is ". . . a phenomenon of group cohesion and aggregation, a child of group necessity or utility, a function of the social relations of men."[17] Thus power in interpersonal relations does not have to be swept under the rug or wished away. The justification for its use is in the interest of the aggregate governed, but with due regard for individual rights determined by extra and internal organizational influences. These influences may take many forms; that is, the law may be formulated in many ways—by unilateral formulation of bureaucratic rules, by win-lose struggles between contending parties at interest, by bargain-

---

[17] Charles E. Merrim, *Political Power* (Glencoe, Ill.: The Free Press, 1950), p. 16.

ing and compromise, or by rational problem solving. But regardless of how the law comes to be, it is the basis governing interpersonal relationships.

The Process of Constitutionalization. The constitution is the place where the plural interests of organizational participants come together. This is not to say that any participant interests are forsaken necessarily or that something like true power equalizaton is achieved in an organization. Rather, the constitution is the manifestation of an agreement where organizational participants have established the terms of their relationships.

Concretely the constitution may cover formalistically organizationwide rules of tenure. Or informally within an organizational unit special rules could regulate a coffee break. However, whether or not the terms of the constitution are stated formally or informally, these terms represent *points of tangency* among people and groups with potentially conflicting interests.

Of course, these tangency points emerge in many ways. They may appear as the result of trading and bargaining transactions.[18] They may arise from rational problem solving.[19] They may be forced out of the very structure of organizations that emphasize lateral relationships and project forms. They may result from stress reduction behavior in conflict situations.[20] Or they may be the product of the bureaucratic process of formalization.[21] Any one or a combination of these forces can supply the dynamics that end in the "writing of the laws of organizations." These processes may be thought of as leading to a convergence of interests in the organization as a whole or localized (departmentalized) segments within it.

There are three realms of interest—those converging, those diverging, and those emerging. Convergent interests represent the sphere of relationships which have been constitutionalized. That is, the law has been established and the parties live under it. This does not mean that these relationships will not change or that they have been removed from the subject of further negotiation. They are less a source of ongoing tension and conflict as the other areas.

---

[18] Leonard Sayles, *Managerial Behavior* (New York: McGraw-Hill Book Company, 1964).

[19] Robert R. Blake, Herbert A. Shepard, and Jane S. Mouton, *Managing Intergroup Conflict in Industry* (Houston: Gulf Publishing Co., 1964).

[20] Robert L. Kahn et al., *Organizational Stress* (New York: John Wiley & Sons, Inc., 1964).

[21] Scott, *The Management of Conflict,* chapter 4.

The areas of divergent interests are those where the issues are clear but the conflicts unresolved. However, the *protocols are established for reconciliation but the terms of the constitutions are not decided.*

Finally, the emerging areas of interest are undefined. Thus their nature and dimensions are ambiguous. But, what is more important, the protocols for resolving conflicts of interest here have not been established. It is in these emerging regions that the most dramatic changes in organizational relationships happen.

Questions and Issues in the Constitutional Organization. Some administrators are flirting with certain aspects of the constitutional concept in their organizations. They are, for instance, writing employee "bills of rights," setting up appeal systems, legitimizing informal exchanges and trading activities, all of which are passed off as constitutionalization. Partly the reason for this flurry of interest is that the "rule of law" in organizations is a deceptively attractive idea, which ignores the fact that constitutionalization is an amoral process.

As citizens of a nation in which such a rule prevails we are used to participating in government through the voting mechanism, and we expect just treatment within the structure of our legal system. Further, we believe that the checks and balances of the Constitution will support pluralism in our society through which the rights and interests of a diverse people are respected. However, enormous problems appear when it comes to the transference of some of the principles of governance to which we are accustomed as citizens of the United States to the organizations in which we spend the bulk of our lives.

1. Who are the citizens of an organization? This is perhaps the most basic issue of all, since the determination of citizenship specifies the rights, duties, and obligations of some and excludes other. For example, in a business organization the employees certainly are citizens. But what about the stockholders of a corporation, or its customers, or its suppliers? Are they citizens also? Consider the university. Who are its citizens—the faculty, the administrators, the staff, the students?

One problem which has plagued universities is the role of students in policy making. Activists argue that students are full-fledged citizens and should have equal rights of participation in legislative activities. Others say that students are transient, and therefore do not have to live with the decisions they make. Much organizational malaise in universities has been caused by the failure to face the question of citizenship. This raises the unpopular issue that for administrative systems it may not make sense to consider all their citizens as equals. It could be that the constitutional process in organizations is workable only when different classes of citizens are identified with different rights, duties, and obligations pertaining to each class.

2. *What are the rights of citizens in the legislative (policy-making) process of organization?* This question is easily as difficult as the first, since it pertains to the nature of citizen *participation* in the governance of organizations. Three alternative forms of participation are implied by this question: (*a*) direct participation in the policy-making activities of the organization, (*b*) citizen election of representatives to the policy-making process, (*c*) direct electoral control over decision makers.

a. Direct participation in policy councils probably would not be very satisfactory, especially if the organization relies heavily on the expertise of technical specialists and management. Imagine, for example, direct stockholders participation in the policy decisions of General Electric! Either the unfortunate stockholders would be confounded by the experts or they would reduce General Electric to chaos.

b. The elected representative alternative seems to work fairly well in some kinds of organizations as labor unions or university senates, where delegates can express the interests of their constituency to the officialdom of the organization. The problem, however, is to make the officials of the organization responsive to the interests of the membership, which increases in difficulty with the progressive entrenchment of bureaucracy.

c. One way to assure responsiveness is to have the executives of organizations subject to periodic election, reelection, or votes of confidence by their constituency. However, when such recommendations are made even in a "free" environment as that of a university, the reaction of administrators is less than enthusiastic, in fact it is downright hostile.

3. *What are the rights of citizens in the judicial system of an organization by which they obtain redress of wrongs?* This question concerns organization formal system of corrective justice that exist outside the conventional machinery of union grievance procedures. Since many organizational citizens are not union members, the availability of appeal systems is an important judicial device that buttresses the constitution of the organization. After all, what good is there in simply having organizational laws, if the citizens have no way of achieving justice when their rights under the law have been violated?

Two approaches to judicial systems have been tried in a limited number of organizations: (*a*) unilaterally established appeal systems, (*b*) the ombudsman.

a. The administrators of some organizations have set up unilaterally, appeal systems available to all organization members. These systems have in common a step-by-step method of settling complaints. That is, if an appellant does not get satisfaction (or settlement) at one level in the appeal machinery, he can carry his case to a higher level. The obvious fact unilaterally established programs is that they are creatures of the management elite of the organization. People who are not in this elite would fear reprisals if they lodged complaints against the organization or some members of it. Thus, appeal programs have not been terribly successful means to achieve justice or resolve conflict.

b. The use of an ombudsman is an approach that attempts to reduce the fear of reprisal. The ombudsman is a kind of arbitrator who hears cases brought before him by aggrieved members of an organization. His decisions in such cases are final and binding on all parties. The ombudsman technique was used first in the Scandinavian countries, offering a means by which unhappy citizens could get redress of grievances against agencies of the government.

This technique has achieved some popularity in this country recently at the level of local government, in some corporations, and in universities.[22] However, establishing a function of ombudsman is not a sweeping trend. In certain instances, where it has been tried, universities for example, it has not been a startling success. In the case of one university, the administration persisted in appointing as ombudsman a member of administration. This violates one of the principal tenets of ombudsmanship—the person filling the role should not be connected in any way with the organization he is serving. He must be, in the interest of impartiality, a detached, outside observer, above reproach, having had no previous affiliation with the organization.

4. In the final analysis does constitutionalization solve the difficult problems of justice and equity in organizations? The answer regrettably must be no, since as we have emphasized, constitutionalization does not address normative issues. It concerns ways by which the power of governance is distributed and institutionalized in organizations. When the process is worked through, then mechanisms of governance appear to formalize the relationships among various interest segments of the organization. These mechanism are but the minimum requirements for justice, and even with them there is no assurance that management will be equitable.

---

[22] See Isidore Silver, "The Corporate Ombudsman," *Harvard Business Review,* June 1967, p. 77–87.

Therefore, we must always look beyond the constitutional process for justice and equity.[23] Some say we should rely ultimately on the "spirit" of leadership. Whereas, others who are not so optimistic about the benevolence of leadership, prefer that justice is obtained through good legalistic and procedural means. Actually equity depends on both spirit and procedures with one reenforcing the other, but neither ignoring the normative dimensions of governance. This is precisely what the remaining models of organization governance attempt to do.

The Autocratic Model

Almost from the beginning of management theory there were hints about the "best" way for executives to govern organizations. The classical theorist felt that such structural imperatives as coordination, control, and the integration of specialized tasks could be achieved only by the centralization of authority in a management core that exercised unilateral decision-making power through a rigid chain of command. This view of organization led to a system of governance that was unequivocally autocratic because it was based upon the dominance of organizational hierarchy.

But even more fundamental than this view of organization was the vision of the nature of man held by the classicists. The argument has been advanced that the classicists' image of man was pessimistic in the extreme.[24] Their opinion was that man, being weak and corrupt, would act in ways that thwart organizational rationality. These acts, even though they work against economic self-interest, would be committed anyway because people are ignorant, arbitrary, and evil.

Given such a view, it is easy enough to understand why the classists preferred a governance system constructed so that an enlightened elite of managers could control effectively a mass of unenlightened workers. The autocratic, elitist structure of formal organization is the system of governance that gives administrators maximum control leverage to beat back predatory man when he threatens the rational processes of organizations.

From these views of man and organization emerged a system of governance that we have discussed at length in this book. Bureaucracy, or

---

[23] See William G. Scott, "Organization Government: The Prospects for a Truly Participative System," *Public Administration Review,* January–February 1969, p. 43–52.

[24] Scott and Hart, "Moral Nature of Man," pp. 241–45.

classical theory, has evolved means of governance that permit managers to exercise great repressive power. It is precisely against this power, and against the system of governance permitting it, that the organizational humanists reacted. In their quest for organizational modification, the humanists pick democracy (or participation) as an alternative form of governance.

The Democratic Model

Democratic theory is the polar extreme of autocracy. Its ideological difference is caught by Schlesinger's statement that, "The reform of institutions becomes an indispensable part of the enterprise of democracy. But the reform of institutions can never be a substitute for the reform of man."[25]

According to the assumptions of democratic theory, for man to realize his dignity, goodness, and freedom requires the minimization of personal dependence. Put another way, equality is the indispensable component for individual happiness and social harmony. Essentially, then, man is by nature antiautocratic, antihierarchy, antitotalitarian. That man is "ungood," that he quarrels, and often does violent, antisocial things, results from faulty institutions which have kept him subjugated by hierarchy in an unfulfilled state. This, as democratic theory goes, is opposed to his instincts and his nature.

So, we may ask, if man is democratically inclined why does he not assert himself and cast off autocratic influences? The answer is that man has been kept ignorant and has been misled so long he has neither the moral fortitude nor the material means to do so. The dominant elites want to maintain the ignorance of their subjects for selfish reasons, rather than to promote the development of virtuous, enlightened subjects.

Therefore, the reconstitution of man, who has been corrupted by evil institutions, has top priority in democratic theory. Reformed man is to be made aware of his dignity and freedom so that he will be able to participate in the democratic heritage of which he has been so long deprived. Thus the remaking of man is a process of democratization using education as a catalyst.

If we could say nothing else about organizational humanism, we could at least say with certainty that it is democratic to the core of its spirit.

---

[25] Arthur S. Schlesinger, Jr., *The Vital Center* (Boston: Houghton Mifflin Company, 1949), p. 250.

It clearly calls for molding people to accept the ideals of democratic liberalism. Warren Bennis, more than any other writer has caught the thrust of this movement and has stated its premises well in his book. Summarizing the impact on management of democratic theory supported by the behavioral sciences he says that it has forced.

1. Reconceptualization of man (along the lines which we have already elaborated);
2. A new concept of power based on collaboration and reason;
3. A reformulation of organizational values reflecting a humanistic bias.

Warning, however, that utopia is not yet at hand Bennis goes on to say

> The last thing I want to do is overstate the case, trapping us all in a false dream. I do not mean that these transformations of man, power, and organizational values are fully accepted, or even understood, to say nothing of implemented in day-to-day organizational affairs. These changes may be light-years away from actual adoption. I do mean that they have gained wide intellectual acceptance in enlightened management quarters, that they have caused a terrific amount of rethinking and search behavior on the part of many organizational planners, and that they have been used as a basis for policy formulation by certain large organizations, mainly industrial leviathans, but also by many other nonindustrial institutions.[26]

Bennis rightly emphasizes intellectual acceptance of democratic principles. The ideological posture is in fact a logical necessity to the requisites of industrial humanism. A few examples show why:

1. The democratic man is an aware man. One conclusion we must underscore in the work of Maslow[27] and Argyris[28] is that the self-actualization process includes the development of democratic consciousness. As Maslow rhapsodizes: "We must ultimately assume at the highest theoretical levels of eupsychian theory, a preference or tendency to identify with more and more of the world, moving toward the ultimate of mysticism, a fusion with the world, or peak experience, cosmic consciousness, etc."[29]

Somewhat more mundanely, as man becomes aware of himself and

---

[26] Warren G. Bennis, *Changing Organizations* (New York: McGraw-Hill Book Company, 1966), p. 188.

[27] Abraham H. Maslow, *Eupsychian Management* (Homewood, Ill.: Richard D. Irwin, Inc., 1965).

[28] Chris Argyris, *Personality and Organization* (New York: Harper & Bros., 1957).

[29] Maslow, *Eupsychian Management,* p. 33.

begins to realize his potential, he, at the same time, is sensitized to the feelings of others. But beyond this he learns the content of their interpersonal relations. Such consciousness, such awareness, is the blood and bone of finding consensus, which, in turn, is the essence of the democratic process.

2. *The democratic man is able to solve problems rationally and creatively through groups.* Blake, Shepard, and Mouton tell us that conflicts are not resolved effectively because of relational inadequacies between groups, or their representatives, at points of tangency in organizations.[30] Blake, and his coauthors see creative problem solving as the rational approach to conflict resolution between groups. By unrestrained communication between people who are skilled in effective social behavior, differences between groups may be settled and the grounds for conflict eliminated. But what is most important is that authentic interactions produce innovative solutions to conflicts. Because these solutions are the product of joint group efforts, they become the vehicles for securing intergroup cooperation. All this provides the climate for an individual's commitment to wider intergroup goals, rather than to the narrow interests of the group with which he immediately identifies. This approach reflects the long-run gains of collaboration through reason. It contrasts with problem solving by win-lose conflict or raw coercion.

3. *Man's democratic inclinations are reinforced, rather than opposed, by organizational values.* Bennis comes through with clarity on this requisite. It boils down to the crucial matter of organizational health. Bennis observes the parallel between the criteria of organizational health and mental health: "to perceive reality, both internal and external, and to examine unflinchingly the positions of these realities in order to act intelligently."[31] These criteria hold equally for individuals and organizations.

From this general observation, Bennis draws three norms of organization health.

a. Adaptability. The ability of an organization to learn and to change programs of action.
b. Identity. The ability of an organization to know what it is and what it stands for.
c. Reality testing. The ability of an organization to know its field of relationships, and to appraise its role in it realistically.

---

[30] Blake, Shepard, and Mouton, *Managing Intergroup Conflict.*
[31] Bennis, *Changing Organizations,* p. 51.

It is evident that no organization which is healthy would embrace values and practices which were contrary to the nature and well-being of its participants. Reality testing helps find paths of action. But the problem of when reality testing is real and not merely a case of organizational self-delusion remains. Besides, there are many "realities" that might be tested; the choice is not limited to democratic or autocratic extremes. This is exactly what the contingency approach tells us.

In light of the foregoing discussion we turn to Bennis's "democracy is inevitable" proposition. Bennis attributes shifting organizational values to both ideological and occupational determinants. He sees the organization of the future governed by values which reflect:

1. Full and free communication, regardless of rank and power.
2. A reliance on consensus, rather than on the more customary forms of coercion or compromise, to manage conflict.
3. The idea that influence is based on technical competence and knowledge rather than on the vagaries of personal whims or prerogatives of power.
4. An atmosphere that permits and even encourages emotional expression as well as task-oriented acts.
5. A basically human bias, one which accepts the inevitability of conflict between the organization and the individual but which is willing to cope with and mediate this conflict on rational grounds.[32]

Whether these are democratic or psychoanalytic values is a matter of interpretation. However, Bennis chooses to call them democratic, so we cannot argue because democracy is a term with a variety of definitions. The question is will the democratic departure attempt to extract from the organizational condition more than there is in it in the first place? Can the will to dominate, the instinct of hierarchy, and the desire for personal power be supplanted in organizational life by free dialogue, rationality in conflict resolution, and consensus in decision making to the extent that people will have in the organization a vehicle for emotive and rational expression?

The organization humanist will answer, yes—to a degree unknown in organizations in the past. But somehow it is hard for us to believe that the emerging governance forms will fit the simplistic democratic-participative model the humanists propose any more than they fit the autocratic model. How is it possible for example to account governmentally for such complex phenomenon, of which we spoke in previous chap-

---

[32] Ibid., p. 19.

ters, as: technological-structural relationships, structural politization, authority-power-influence, and balance and conflict? It appears to us that the democratizing of organizational governance is just too pat a solution.

A further objection to the "democracy is inevitable" proposition hinges on its exclusiveness. It tends to close the door to other alternatives for organizational government except the one directly opposed to it—autocracy. One gets the impression from the literature that the lines have been drawn. Choice is crystallized in two ideological alternatives between which there is very little chance for reconciliation. However, is it so clearly the case of either autocracy or democracy? Or is there evolving in organizational government "other ways" which have gone largely unnoticed?

The Federal and Totalitarian Models

Federalism and totalitarianism are the modern counterparts of democracy and autocracy. Federalism has many features in common with democracy, as totalitarianism has with autocracy, although there are several noteworthy exceptions. First, *both federalism and totalitarianism are governance alternatives made possible, indeed made necessary, by technology and organizational complexity.* Second, these emerging governance models have not been examined as minutely as their forerunners. Therefore, third, they do not have cults of true believers broadcasting their merits; and similarly they do not have critics. In short, little is being said of them, one way or the other, as governance alternatives.

Nevertheless, as organizational complexity increases, and as technology advances, the old battles between autocratic and democratic management grow more and more irrelevant. The contingency approach to the constitutionalization process in organizational governance is ascending in management thought. While this approach has merit, as we have said, it is much too ambiguous to suit the long-range planning needs of pragmatic managers. They need something "definite" around which to plan organizational designs and governance strategies. So while it is acknowledged that as constitutionalization works its way along as a *process*, it must *end up* with something concrete in the form of a governmental system. Thus, we conclude that in many instances, although not all certainly, the future of governance forms of organizations may be federal or totalitarian in nature.

The federalist alternative is an analogue of the democratic model of organizational government. Its presuppositions about the nature of man and the ideals of organizational justice are similar to democratic theory. However, it differs from democratic theory in several important ways.

First, the federalist alternative recognizes the complexity of organizations, and the need to structure tasks into team efforts.

Second, it takes into account the organization of work into modules of expertise (teams or work groups). These modules are in a sense tightly bound communities, centering on the effective performance of tasks by highly qualified professionals.

Third, the federalist alternative recognizes that the separate community modules are related to each other, some intimately, some loosely. As a consequence of these relationships coordination is needed. But the kind of coordination is more self-coordination among professionals, than it is coordination directed by hierarchy.

Fourth, hierarchy is not eliminated in the federalist model, although the nature of its function is changed. Hierarchy becomes more facilitative in nature, establishing the climate to permit effective interaction and coordination among quasi-independent task modules. Of course, hierarchy must retain the responsibility for goal setting and top policy initiation, but its conventional role of command would diminish as self-coordination among professionals in the task modules improves.

What we have described as the federalist alternative is in reality a collegial organization of the sort found sometimes in major universities. Some believe that such a model will be extended to other types of organizations as professionalization and advanced technology make greater inroads into business concerns, nonprofit service organizations, and public agencies. Further, emerging organizational structures as the matrix system open the way for a federalist approach to be implemented in governance.

In summary the federalist alternative incorporates many of the forces already at work in organizations. It can embrace:

a. The need for community.
b. The growing intensity of political relationships.
c. The rising expectations both emotional and professional of organization citizens.
d. The processes of power and influence.
e. The achievement of organizational balance through the self-discipline of professionals.

f. The need for flexibility and adaptability to change.

g. The accelerating trends toward organizational development programs.

h. The growing use of matrix organizations.

i. The need to retain, but also the need to redefine the role of hierarchy in many organizations.

j. A system of governance which may be more compatible with the mechanisms of constitutionalization than existing forms.

k. The tendency of certain organizations to adopt professional norms, rather than bureaucratic norms, of evaluation to measure the performance of many of its citizens.

Briefly, the federalist alternative is not only emotionally appealing, but because it is task oriented, also seems to suit the rational and technological imperatives that are rendering old models of governance obsolete.

However, federalism is not the only way to go, totalitarianism is a grim, but logically possible, alternative. Through the totalitarian model the governance norms of organizations are imposed and enforced by managerial elites in hierarchies not unlike those prescribed by the autocratic model. But there is an essential difference. Hannah Arendt called totalitarianism the only modern form of governance. It is modern, in her estimation, because it uses advanced technology to achieve total control of organizational behavior and processes.

While the old autocracies strove for such pervasive controls, their leaders were ultimately frustrated because they had crude means for achieving them. The reason why totalitarianism is modern is because it uses modern engineering and behavioral technology to create organizational controls unthought of by conventional autocracies. Less and less is left to chance.

The totalitarian governance model does not need an image of man as evil to be beaten back, or an image of man possessing unfulfilled goodness waiting to be released. All it requires is that man is thought of, and thinks of himself, as malleable. When this metaphysical hurdle is surmounted, then science can be freed to shape behavior into those forms that are useful in serving the rational necessities of organization without moral obstacles.

Human inputs are dealt with obliquely in management. Man has been accounted for in management systems as an essentially inaccessible variable. However, it is inconvenient to the dedicated practioner to have his most crucial variable—man—lie outside of his system designs. But because of the primitive state of behavioral science, human inputs have remained sticky, confounding variables within otherwise elegantly constructed systems. In short, management has always felt the need "to do something about man" but did not know where to turn.

Management has been presented with economic man, organization man, and self-fulfilling man, each with his own peculiar moral attributes that seemed to satisfy managerial needs for a time. Now management is confronted with the urgency of having a "man for all systems." In this instance too an innate image will emerge—a *technical* image of man.

Such an image is required by modern management through its quest for organizational flexibility and adaptability. This image is beginning to form, although its outlines lack definition. The fact that images of man do not come from the mainstream of management thought should not detain us. William H. Whyte, Jr's. book, *The Organization Man,* was not a management book per se, but it is now part of the body of management literature. We believe that much the same will happen to the chief works of B. F. Skinner, especially his book *Beyond Freedom and Dignity.* This book contains the requisite management image for man in our times—a bundle of chemical and electrical processes that can be shaped and reshaped by manipulating reenforcement schedules in order to change behavior reliably to suit environmental contingencies. This image reduces man to a technical puzzle to be solved through behaviorism.

Skinner's assumptions about human behavior are subtle and profound, which make his contributions to management have landmark significance. However, his importance is *not* based upon the scientific feasibility of operant conditioning. Rather, his significance lies in what he says about the nature of man. Further, this philosophical position provides the optimal image of man for a society dominated by organizations whose primary object is to survive in turbulent conditions by rapid and successful adaptation to change. What is clear beyond question is that people must be adaptable before the organizations they occupy can adjust effectively. Thus, the attempt to reduce all human behavior to technical puzzle solving has obvious appeal for management contingency planning and controlling.

Not surprisingly, the technical image of man is accompanied by a model of organization which we have discussed earlier as the contingency approach. We noted how dependent some contemporary management authors are upon Skinner for basic contingency concepts. It is not a very large step from the organization model of contingency to the constitutional model of organization government. But as we have said the process of constitutionalization ends with a system of organization government. The concern is that the process will end with totalitarianism.

Such a concern is real enough, since if nothing else is to be learned from management history it is that management is not organically inclined toward democratic practices, that technology results in greater, not lesser, degrees of centralization, and that organization is hierarchial so that dominence in one form or another is a likely and expected outcome. Consequently the line of least resistance organizationally is for management to apply technology to achieve higher levels of control. This is totalitarian behavior in its purest form, and it is helped along by the amoral pragmatism of the contingency approach, by Skinner's technical image of man, by the process orientation of the constitutional model of governance, and most of all, by people themselves succumbing to the moral imperatives placed on them in the interest of organizational survival.

Thus, we end with the possibility of managerial "saviors" arriving with the philosophical definitions necessary to justify changes in organizational structure and processes. More important, however, is the image of humanity that they will bring with them, for it is likely to be designed with the technically rational imperatives of organization at interest. We concur with the familiar injunction, "Save us from our saviors!"

Indexes

Name Index

Subject Index

This book has been set in 10 and 9 point Caledonia, leaded 3 points. Part numbers are in 24 point and 36 point Scotch Roman italic, and part titles are in 24 point Scotch Roman. Chapter numbers are in 24 point Scotch Roman and 30 point Scotch Roman italic, and chapter titles are in 24 point Scotch Roman italic. The size of the type page is 27 by 45 picas.

LIBRARY
BRYAN COLLEGE
DAYTON, TN. 37321

56349

DATE DUE